"IF I COULD BE REINCARNATED AS ANYONE, WHO WOULD I BE" PART 2: A PROFESSIONAL BASEBALL PLAYER. I AM TOTALLY UNKNOWN DURING MY DAYS PLAYING AS AN AMATEUR. I AM THE SIXTH PERSON TO BE ASKED BY THE HANSHIN TIGERS IN THE DRAFT PICK, AND GO PRO AT THE AGE OF 20. DESPITE OPPOSITION FROM THE COACHES, I KEEP MY OWN UNIQUE STYLE OF BATTING BY PROVING THAT IT CAN WORK ON THE FIELD. BY MY THIRD YEAR, I WILL HAVE BECOME THE BATTING LEADER, AND THEN I GAIN THE TITLE OF "TRIPLE CROWN" FIVE TIMES. I RETIRE EVEN THOUGH MY TALENT HAS NOT BEEN COMPLETELY TAPPED. AS A STRATEGIST FOR HEAD COACH KAWATOU, THE TIGERS ARE LED TO LAST PLACE IN THE LEAGUE FOR STRAIGHT YEARS. MY LIFETIME BATTING AVERAGE IS .385. TOTAL HOME RUNS, 575.
—YOSHIHIRO TOGASHI, 1991

Yoshihiro Togashi's manga career began in 1986 when, at the age of 20, he won the coveted Tezuka Award for new manga artists. He debuted in the Japanese **Weekly Shonen Jump** magazine in 1988 with the romantic comedy **Tende Shôwaru Cupid.** From 1990 to 1994 he wrote and drew the smash hit fighting manga **YuYu Hakusho,** which was followed by the darkly humorous science-fiction series **Level E** and the adventure story **Hunter x Hunter.** In 1999 he married the manga artist Naoko Takeu

YUYU HAKUSHO VOL. 2
The SHONEN JUMP Graphic Novel Edition

This graphic novel contains material that was originally published in
English in **SHONEN JUMP** #5-8.

STORY AND ART BY
YOSHIHIRO TOGASHI

English Adaptation/Gary Leach
Translation/Lillian Olsen
Touch-Up Art & Lettering/Cynthia Dobson
Graphics & Cover Design/Sean Lee
Senior Editor/Jason Thompson

Associate Managing Editor/Albert Totten
Managing Editor/Annette Roman
Editor in Chief/Hyoe Narita
Production Manager/Noboru Watanabe
Sr. Director of Licensing & Acquisitions/Rika Inouye
V.P. of Marketing/Liza Coppola
V.P. of Strategic Development/Yumi Hoashi
Publisher/Seiji Horibuchi

PARENTAL ADVISORY
YuYu Hakusho is rated "T" for teens. It may contain violence, lan-
guage, alcohol or tobacco usage, or suggestive situations. It is recommended for ages 13 and up.

Printed in Canada.

Published by VIZ, LLC
P.O. Box 77010 • San Francisco, CA 94107

SHONEN JUMP Graphic Novel Edition
10 9 8 7 6 5 4 3 2 1
First printing, October 2003

www.viz.com

THE WORLD'S
MOST POPULAR MANGA

GRAPHIC NOVEL
www.shonenjump.com

SHONEN JUMP GRAPHIC NOVEL

YuYu HAKUSHO ™

Vol.2
LONESOME GHOSTS

STORY AND ART BY
YOSHIHIRO TOGASHI

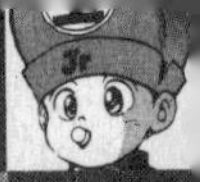

THE STORY SO FAR...

Yusuke Urameshi was a teen delinquent until one selfless act changed his life...by ending it. When he died saving a little kid from a speeding car, the afterlife didn't know what to do with him, so they decided to give him a test to come back to life. But until the test is over, Yusuke's spirit can only inhabit his comatose body one day every month, and the laws of the afterlife strictly forbid him from talking to anyone he knows. And on the same day that Yusuke was in his body, his friend Keiko was kidnapped by gang members! How can he save her without blowing his chance for resurrection?

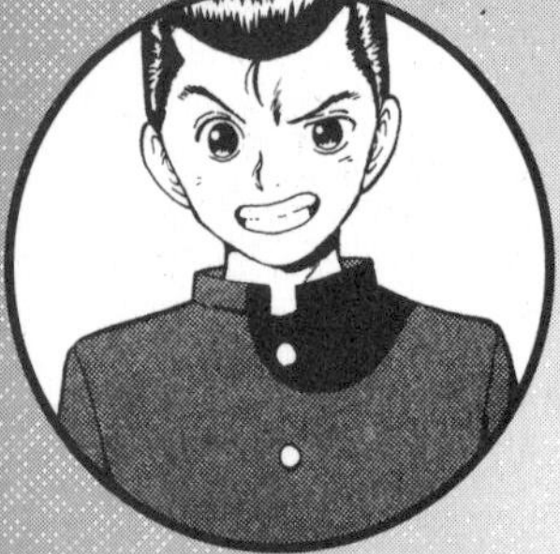

YUSUKE URAMESHI 浦飯幽助

The toughest 8th grader at Sarayashiki Junior High, and now the toughest ghost in Tokyo.

ぼたん BOTAN

Often seen riding an oar, Botan is the ferrywoman of the Sanzu River, known as the River Styx in Western mythology. She keeps track of Yusuke's spiritual progress, helping him do good deeds while he's a ghost.

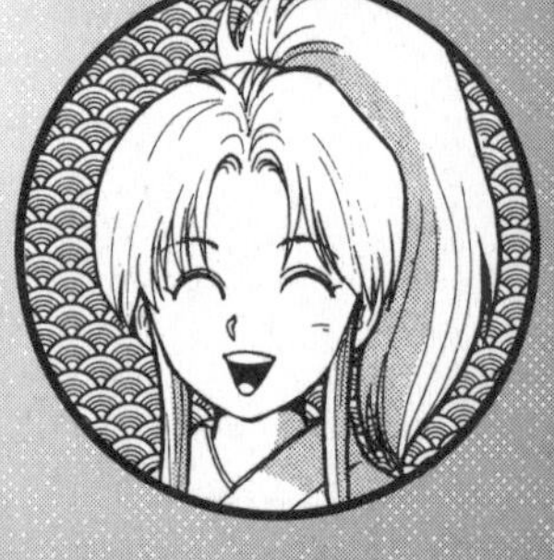

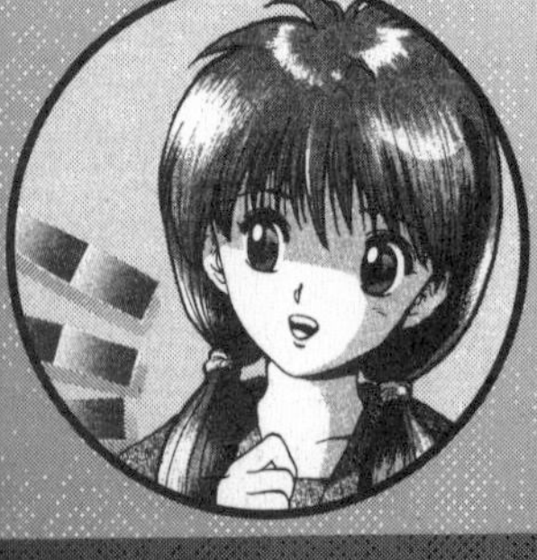

KEIKO YUKIMURA 雪村螢子

Yusuke's childhood friend, and maybe more than that. She's the only one who knows for sure that Yusuke is a ghost, and she helps take care of his comatose body.

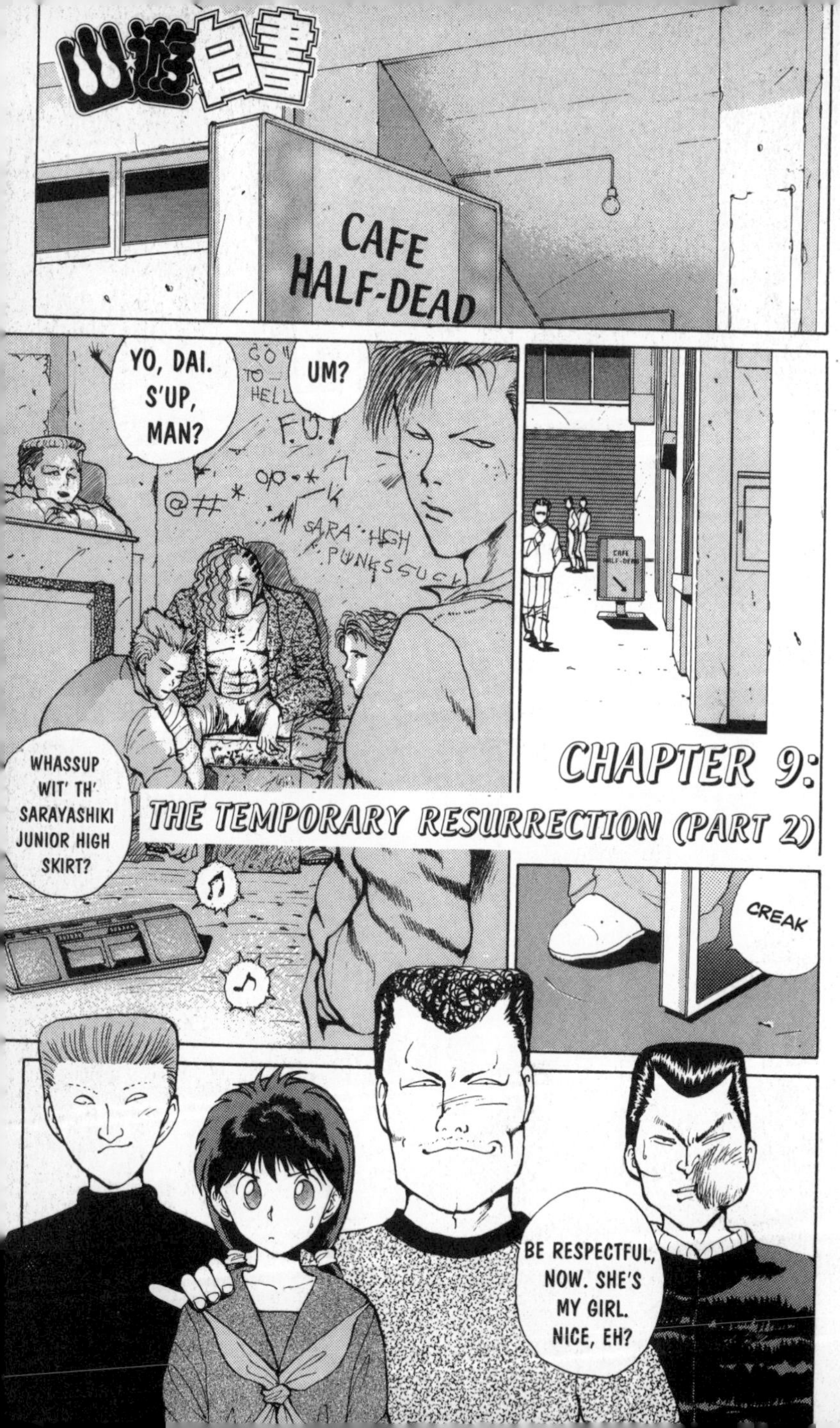
CAFE HALF-DEAD
CAFE HALF-DEAD
CHAPTER 9:
THE TEMPORARY RESURRECTION (PART 2)
YO, DAI. S'UP, MAN?
UM?
GO TO HELL
F.U.!
SARA HIGH PUNKS SUCK
WHASSUP WIT' TH' SARAYASHIKI JUNIOR HIGH SKIRT?
CREAK
BE RESPECTFUL, NOW. SHE'S MY GIRL. NICE, EH?

READ THIS WAY

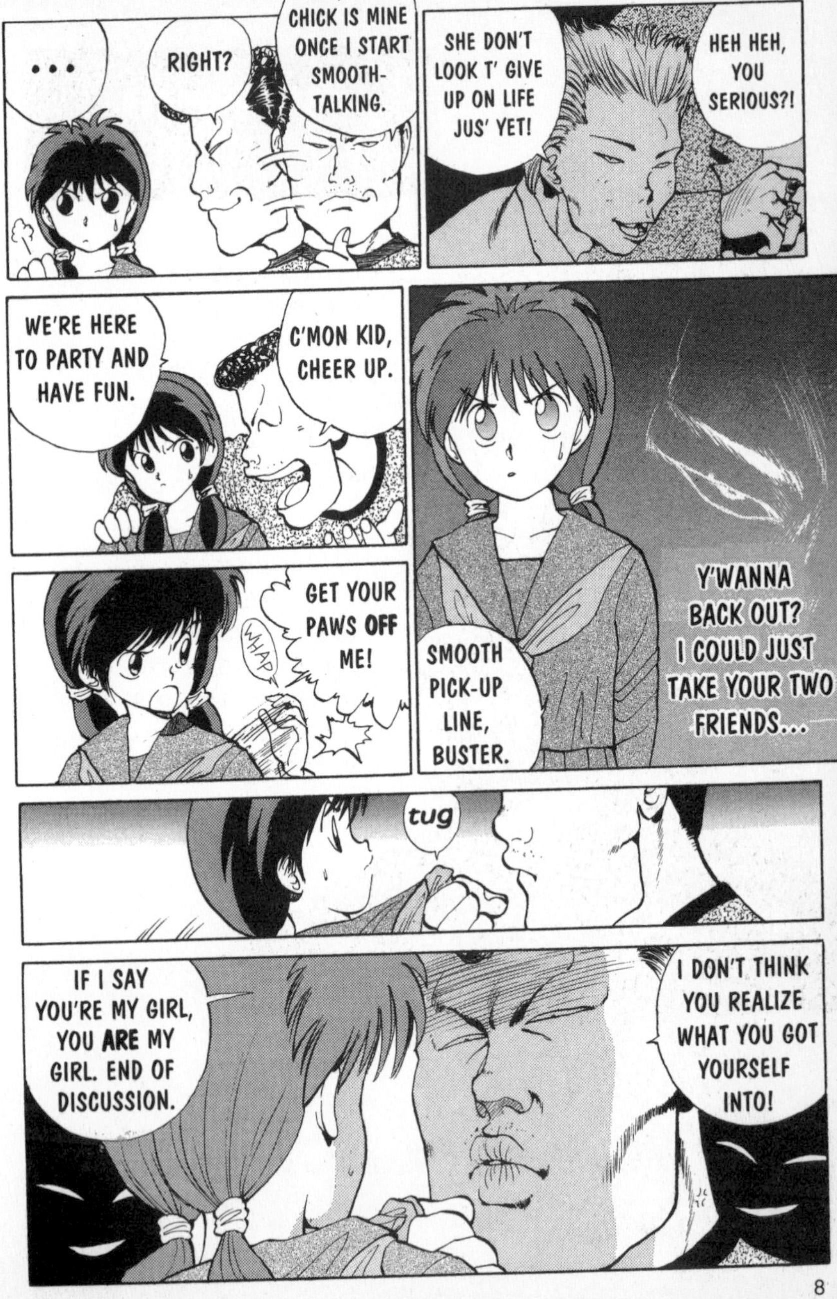
HEH HEH, YOU SERIOUS?!
SHE DON'T LOOK T' GIVE UP ON LIFE JUS' YET!
HEY, ANY CHICK IS MINE ONCE I START SMOOTH-TALKING.
RIGHT?
...
Y'WANNA BACK OUT? I COULD JUST TAKE YOUR TWO FRIENDS...
SMOOTH PICK-UP LINE, BUSTER.
C'MON KID, CHEER UP.
WE'RE HERE TO PARTY AND HAVE FUN.
GET YOUR PAWS **OFF** ME!
WHAP
tug
I DON'T THINK YOU REALIZE WHAT YOU GOT YOURSELF INTO!
IF I SAY YOU'RE MY GIRL, YOU **ARE** MY GIRL. END OF DISCUSSION.

WHAT HAPPENED IN THE LAST EPISODE

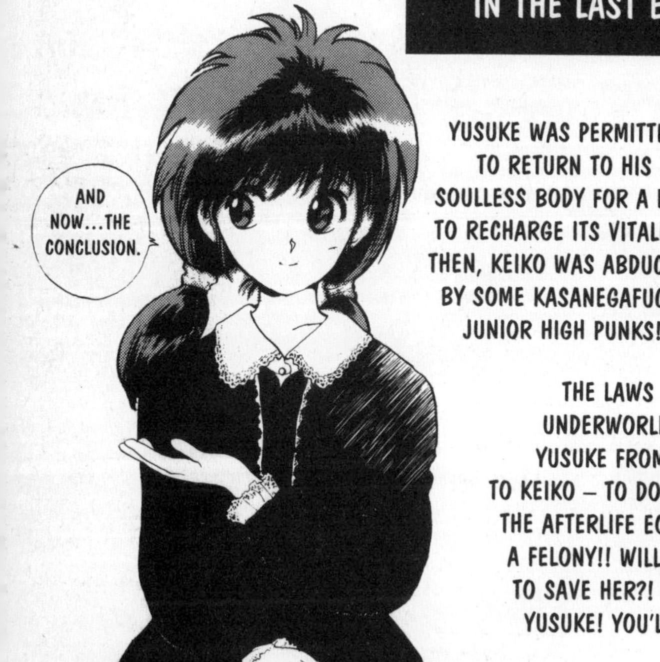
AND NOW...THE CONCLUSION.

YUSUKE WAS PERMITTED TO RETURN TO HIS SOULLESS BODY FOR A DAY TO RECHARGE ITS VITALITY. THEN, KEIKO WAS ABDUCTED BY SOME KASANEGAFUCHI JUNIOR HIGH PUNKS!!

THE LAWS OF THE UNDERWORLD FORBID YUSUKE FROM TALKING TO KEIKO – TO DO SO WOULD BE THE AFTERLIFE EQUIVALENT OF A FELONY!! WILL HE BE ABLE TO SAVE HER?! GOOD LUCK, YUSUKE! YOU'LL NEED IT!!

CHAPTER 9:

THE TEMPORARY RESURRECTION (PART 2)

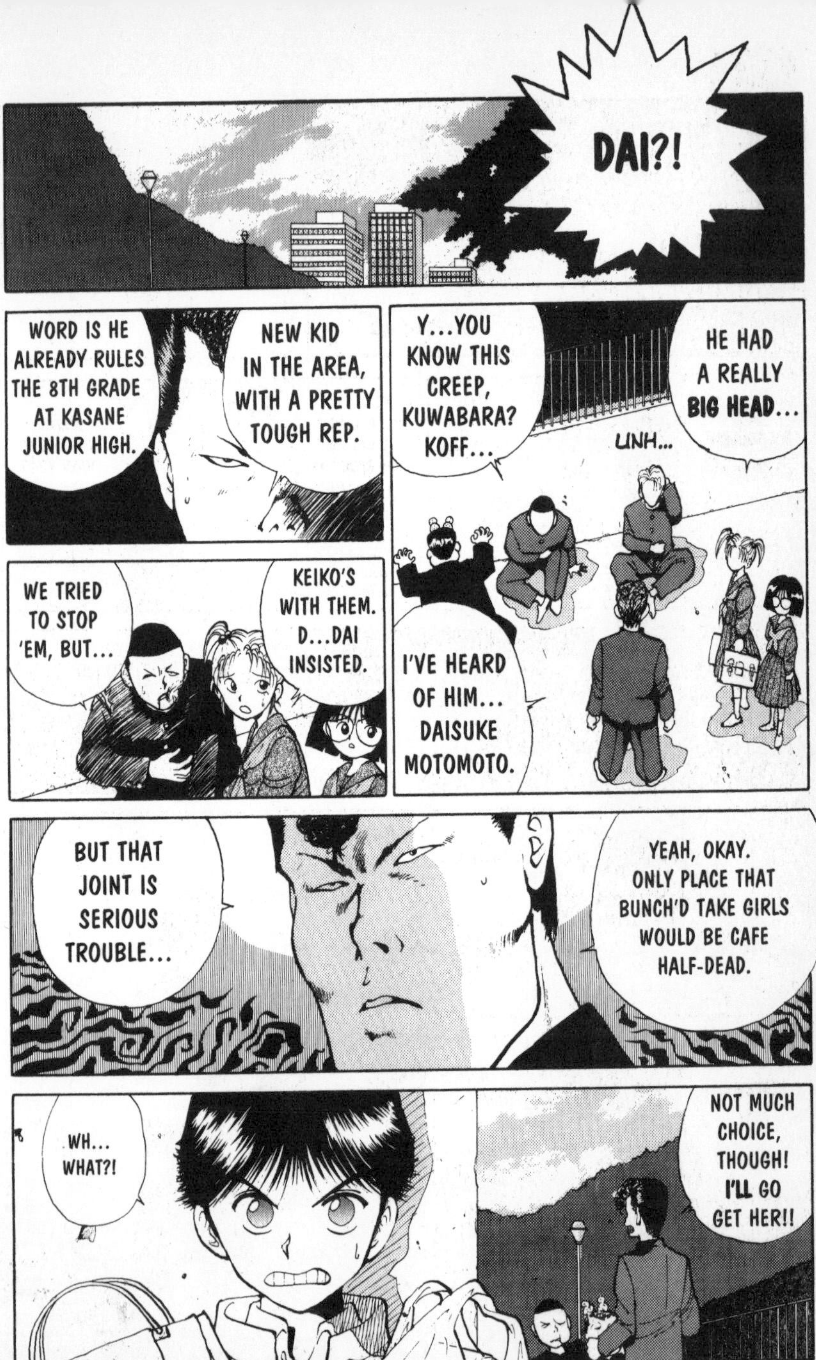
DAI?!
HE HAD A REALLY BIG HEAD...
UNH...
Y...YOU KNOW THIS CREEP, KUWABARA? KOFF...
I'VE HEARD OF HIM... DAISUKE MOTOMOTO.
NEW KID IN THE AREA, WITH A PRETTY TOUGH REP.
WORD IS HE ALREADY RULES THE 8TH GRADE AT KASANE JUNIOR HIGH.
KEIKO'S WITH THEM. D...DAI INSISTED.
WE TRIED TO STOP 'EM, BUT...
YEAH, OKAY. ONLY PLACE THAT BUNCH'D TAKE GIRLS WOULD BE CAFE HALF-DEAD.
BUT THAT JOINT IS SERIOUS TROUBLE...
NOT MUCH CHOICE, THOUGH! I'LL GO GET HER!!
WH... WHAT?!

READ THIS WAY

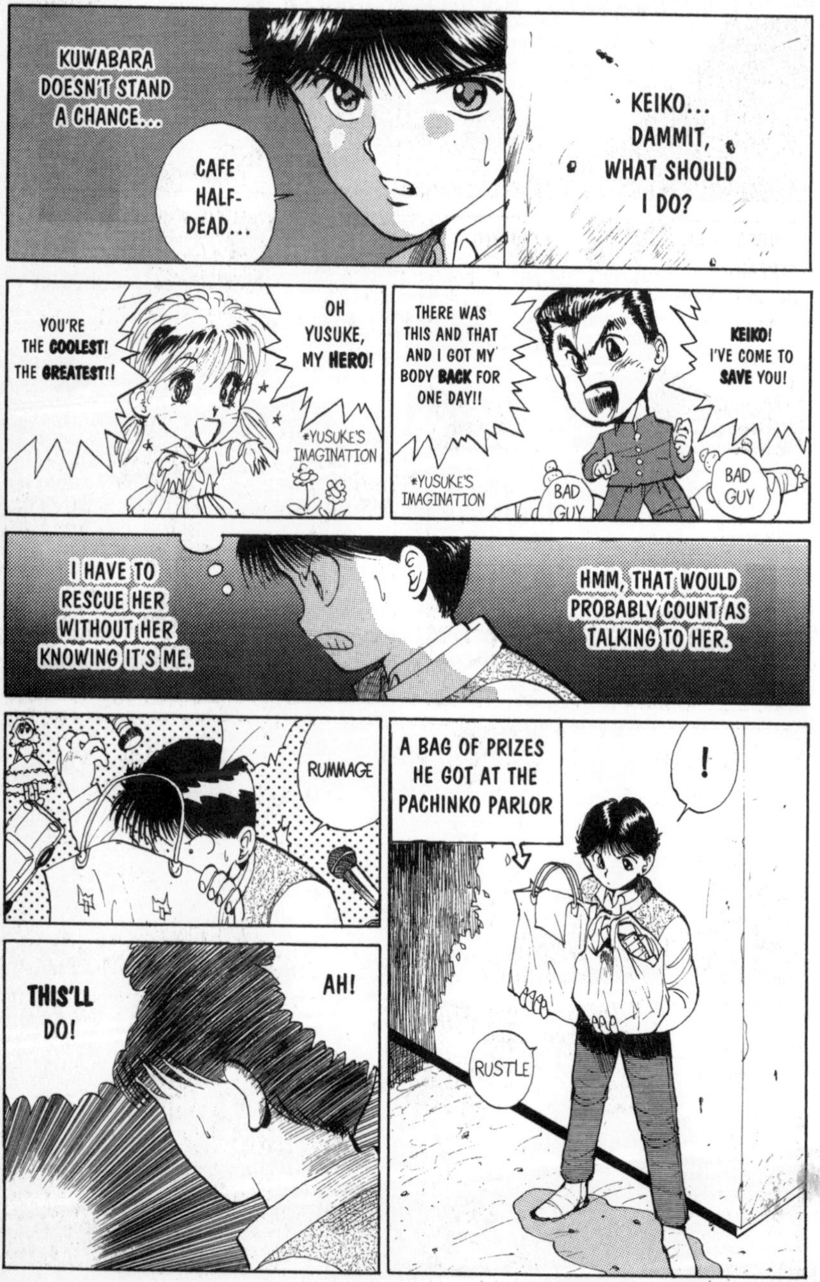
KEIKO... DAMMIT, WHAT SHOULD I DO?
KUWABARA DOESN'T STAND A CHANCE...
CAFE HALF-DEAD...
KEIKO! I'VE COME TO SAVE YOU!
THERE WAS THIS AND THAT AND I GOT MY BODY BACK FOR ONE DAY!!
BAD GUY
BAD GUY
*YUSUKE'S IMAGINATION
OH YUSUKE, MY HERO!
YOU'RE THE COOLEST! THE GREATEST!!
*YUSUKE'S IMAGINATION
HMM, THAT WOULD PROBABLY COUNT AS TALKING TO HER.
I HAVE TO RESCUE HER WITHOUT HER KNOWING IT'S ME.
!
A BAG OF PRIZES HE GOT AT THE PACHINKO PARLOR
RUSTLE
RUMMAGE
AH!
THIS'LL DO!

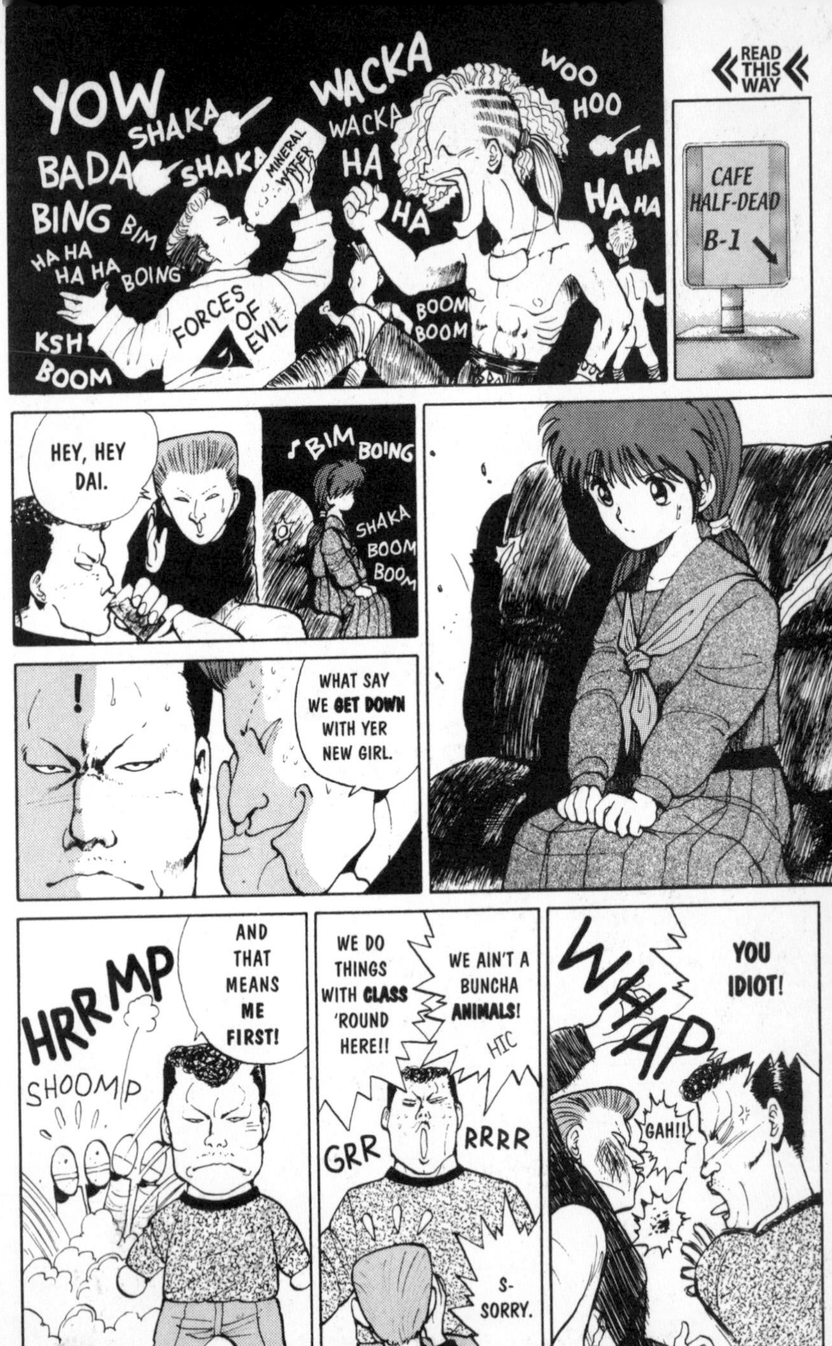
READ THIS WAY
CAFE HALF-DEAD
B-1
WOO HOO
HA
HA HA
WACKA
WACKA
HA
HA
MINERAL WATER
SHAKA
SHAKA
YOW
BADA
BING BIM
HA HA HA HA
BOING
BOOM BOOM
FORCES OF EVIL
KSH BOOM
BIM BOING
SHAKA BOOM BOOM
HEY, HEY DAI.
WHAT SAY WE GET DOWN WITH YER NEW GIRL.
!
YOU IDIOT!
WHAP
GAH!!
S-SORRY.
WE AIN'T A BUNCHA ANIMALS!
HIC
WE DO THINGS WITH CLASS 'ROUND HERE!!
GRR
RRRR
AND THAT MEANS ME FIRST!
HRRMP
SHOOMP

READ THIS WAY

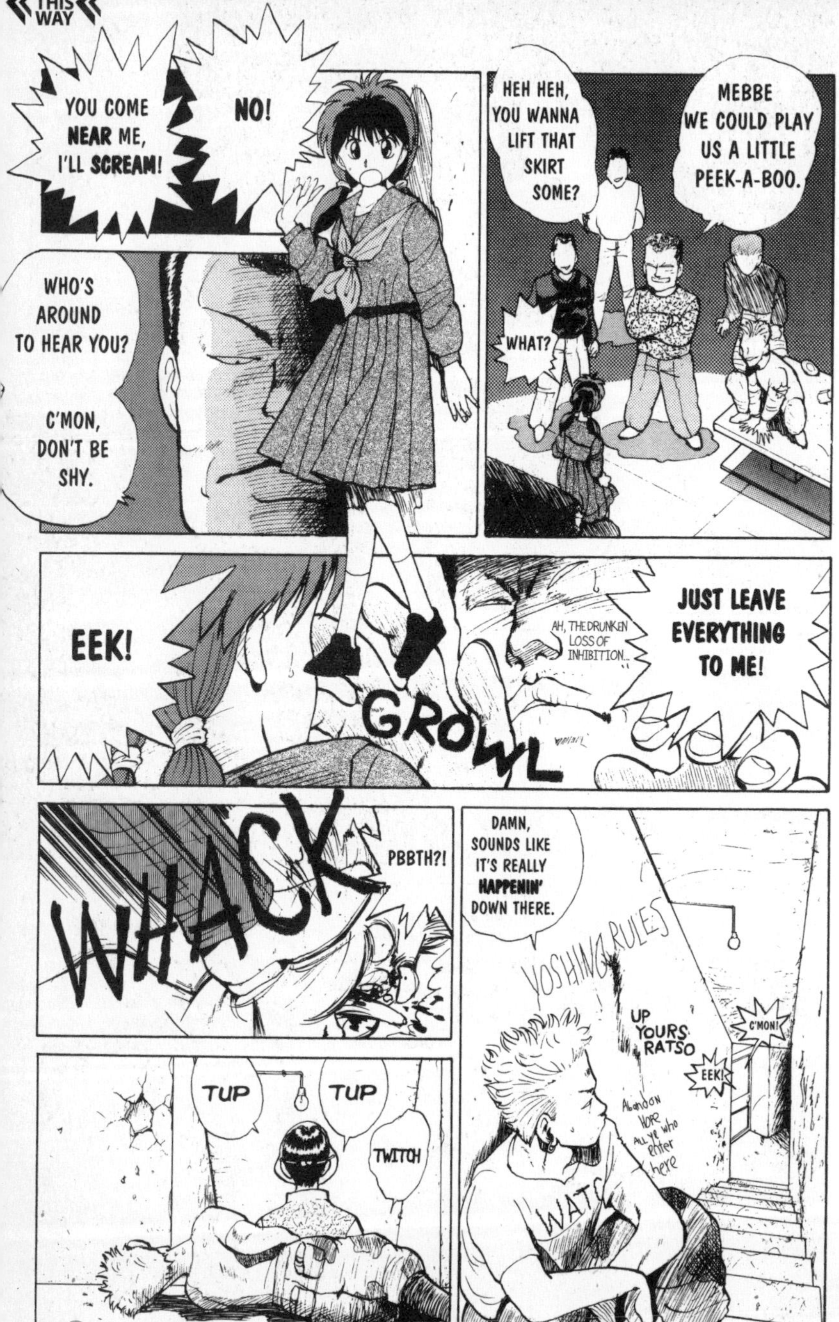
MEBBE WE COULD PLAY US A LITTLE PEEK-A-BOO.
HEH HEH, YOU WANNA LIFT THAT SKIRT SOME?
WHAT?
NO!
YOU COME NEAR ME, I'LL SCREAM!
WHO'S AROUND TO HEAR YOU?
C'MON, DON'T BE SHY.
JUST LEAVE EVERYTHING TO ME!
AH, THE DRUNKEN LOSS OF INHIBITION...
GROWL
EEK!
DAMN, SOUNDS LIKE IT'S REALLY HAPPENIN' DOWN THERE.
YOSHINO RULES
C'MON!
UP YOURS RATSO
EEK!
Abandon Hope All ye who Enter here
WATC
PBBTH?!
WHACK
TUP
TUP
TWITCH

...
AW, GREAT.
LI'L WILDCAT! DIDN'T MEAN TO HIT THAT HARD!
SHE'S DOWN FOR THE COUNT NOW, THOUGH.
THAT'LL MAKE IT EASIER TO HAVE OUR FUN.
HUFFA HUFFA
WHAT?! TAKE ADVANTAGE OF AN UNCONSCIOUS GIRL?!
GOOD THINKING.
SHH
WHAM
HAH? WHO'S THAT?!
OOH, HE'S NERVOUS
JUST SOMEONE PASSING THROUGH.
HA HA HA, Y'GOTTA BE KIDDIN'!
WHAT A DOPE!

A MASK FOUND AMONG THE PRIZES.

READ THIS WAY

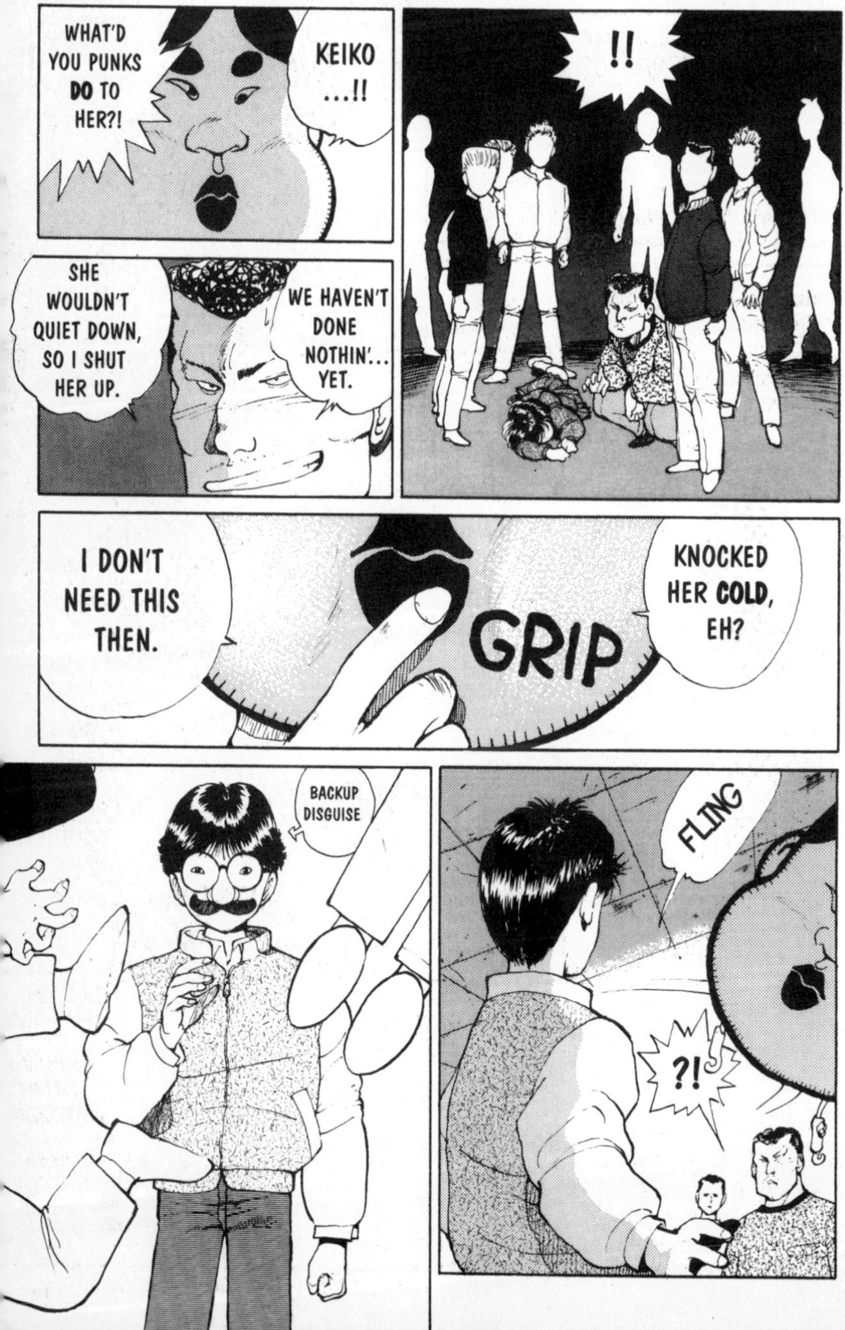

!!
KEIKO ...!!
WHAT'D YOU PUNKS DO TO HER?!
WE HAVEN'T DONE NOTHIN'... YET.
SHE WOULDN'T QUIET DOWN, SO I SHUT HER UP.
KNOCKED HER COLD, EH?
GRIP
I DON'T NEED THIS THEN.
FLING
?!
BACKUP DISGUISE

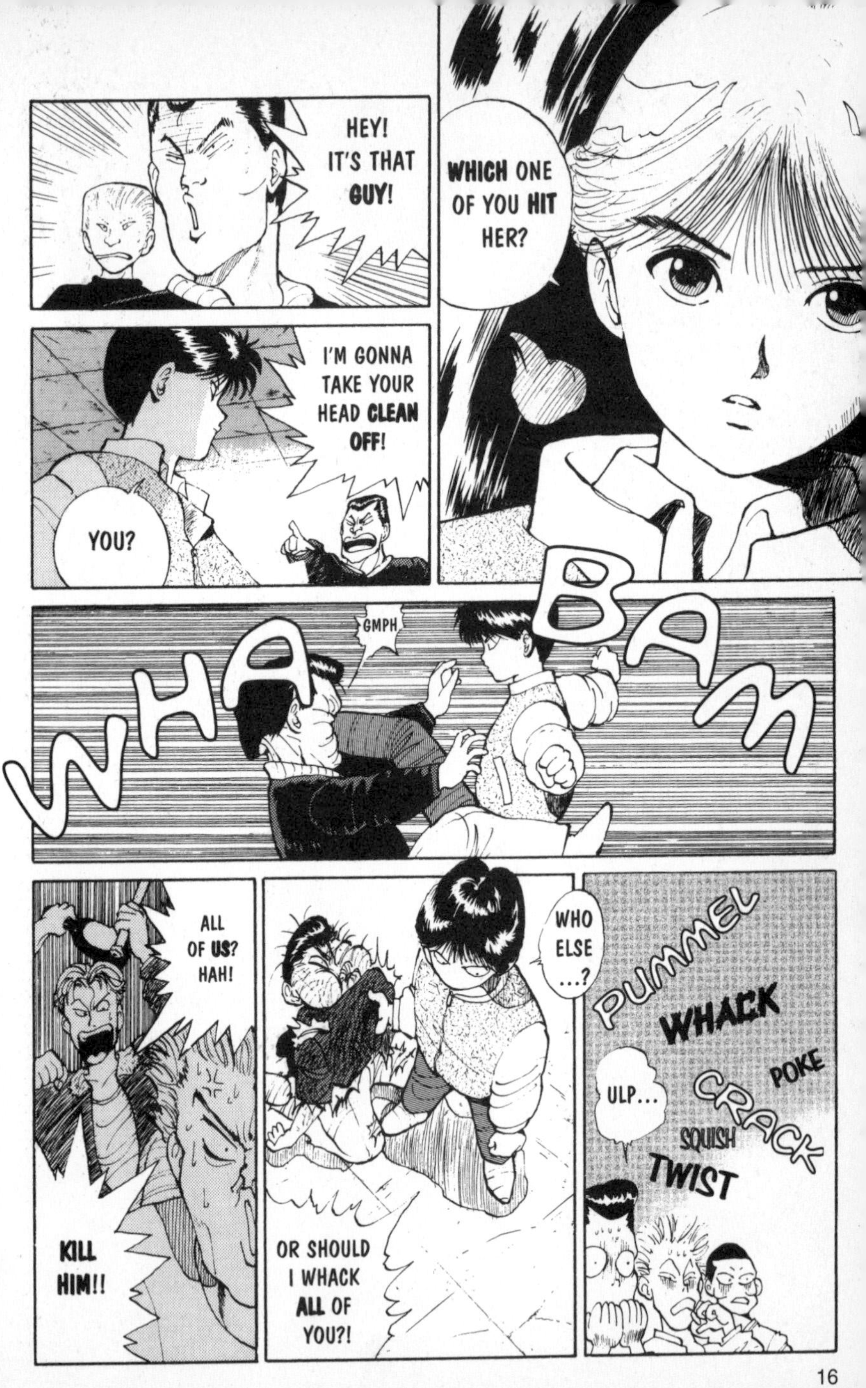
WHICH ONE OF YOU HIT HER?
HEY! IT'S THAT GUY!
I'M GONNA TAKE YOUR HEAD CLEAN OFF!
YOU?
BAM
GMPH
WHA
PUMMEL
WHACK
POKE
CRACK
ULP...
SQUISH
TWIST
WHO ELSE ...?
OR SHOULD I WHACK ALL OF YOU?!
ALL OF US? HAH!
KILL HIM!!

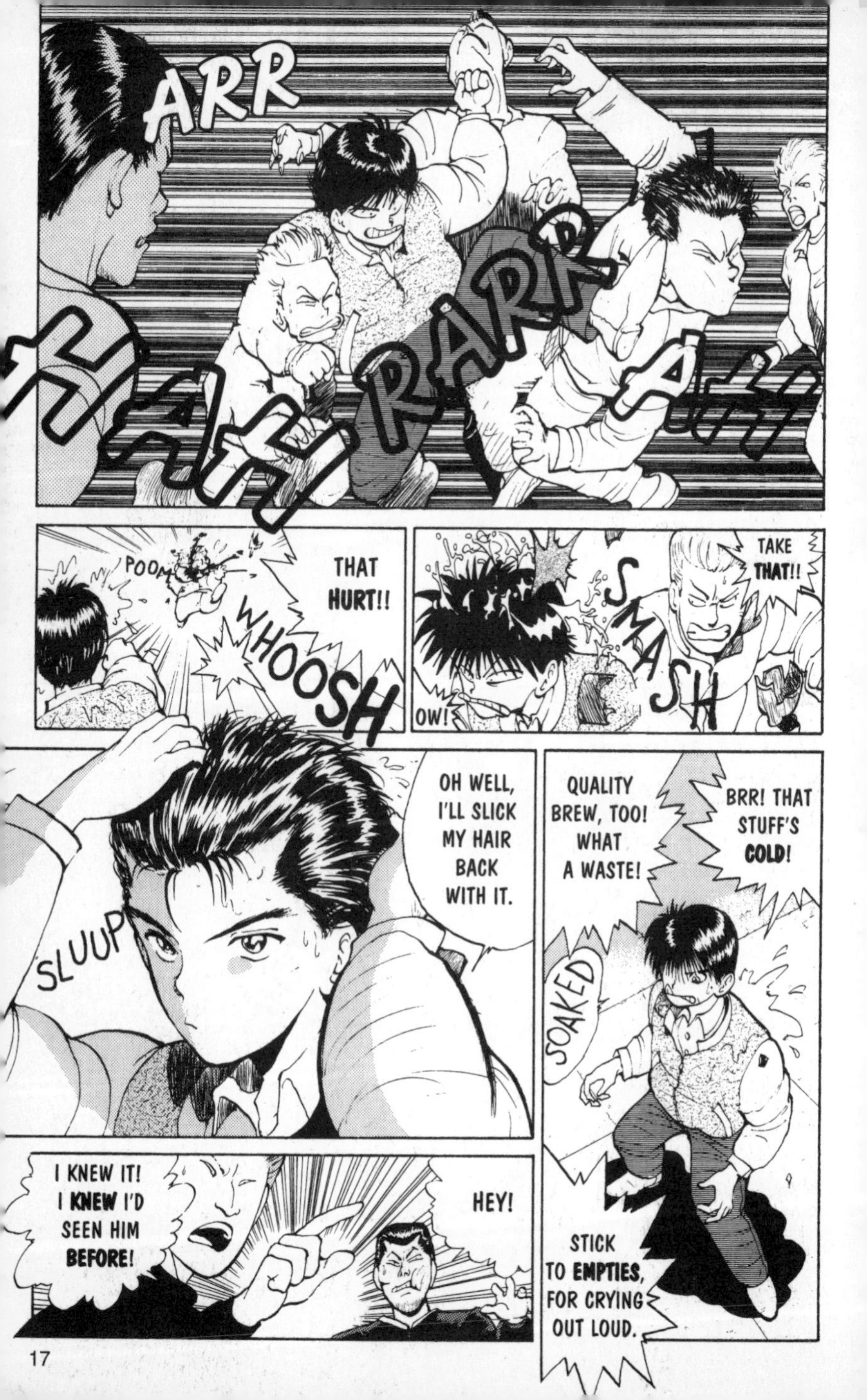
ARR
HAAH
RARR
AHH
TAKE THAT!!
SMASH
OW!
THAT HURT!!
WHOOSH
POOM
BRR! THAT STUFF'S COLD!
QUALITY BREW, TOO! WHAT A WASTE!
SOAKED
STICK TO EMPTIES, FOR CRYING OUT LOUD.
OH WELL, I'LL SLICK MY HAIR BACK WITH IT.
SLUUP
HEY!
I KNEW IT! I KNEW I'D SEEN HIM BEFORE!

READ THIS WAY

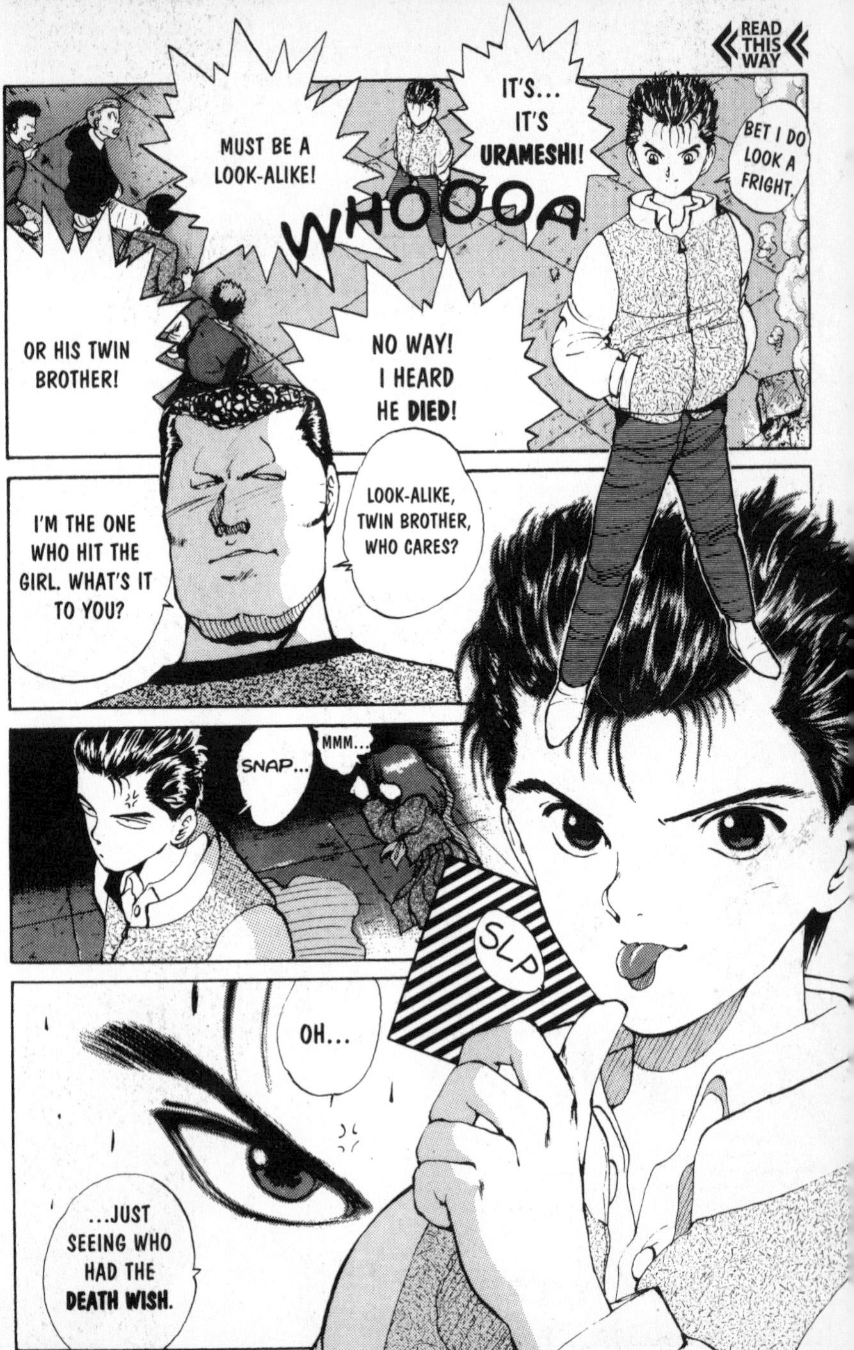
BET I DO LOOK A FRIGHT.
IT'S... IT'S URAMESHI!
MUST BE A LOOK-ALIKE!
WHOOOA
NO WAY! I HEARD HE DIED!
OR HIS TWIN BROTHER!
SLP
LOOK-ALIKE, TWIN BROTHER, WHO CARES?
I'M THE ONE WHO HIT THE GIRL. WHAT'S IT TO YOU?
MMM...
SNAP...
OH...
...JUST SEEING WHO HAD THE DEATH WISH.

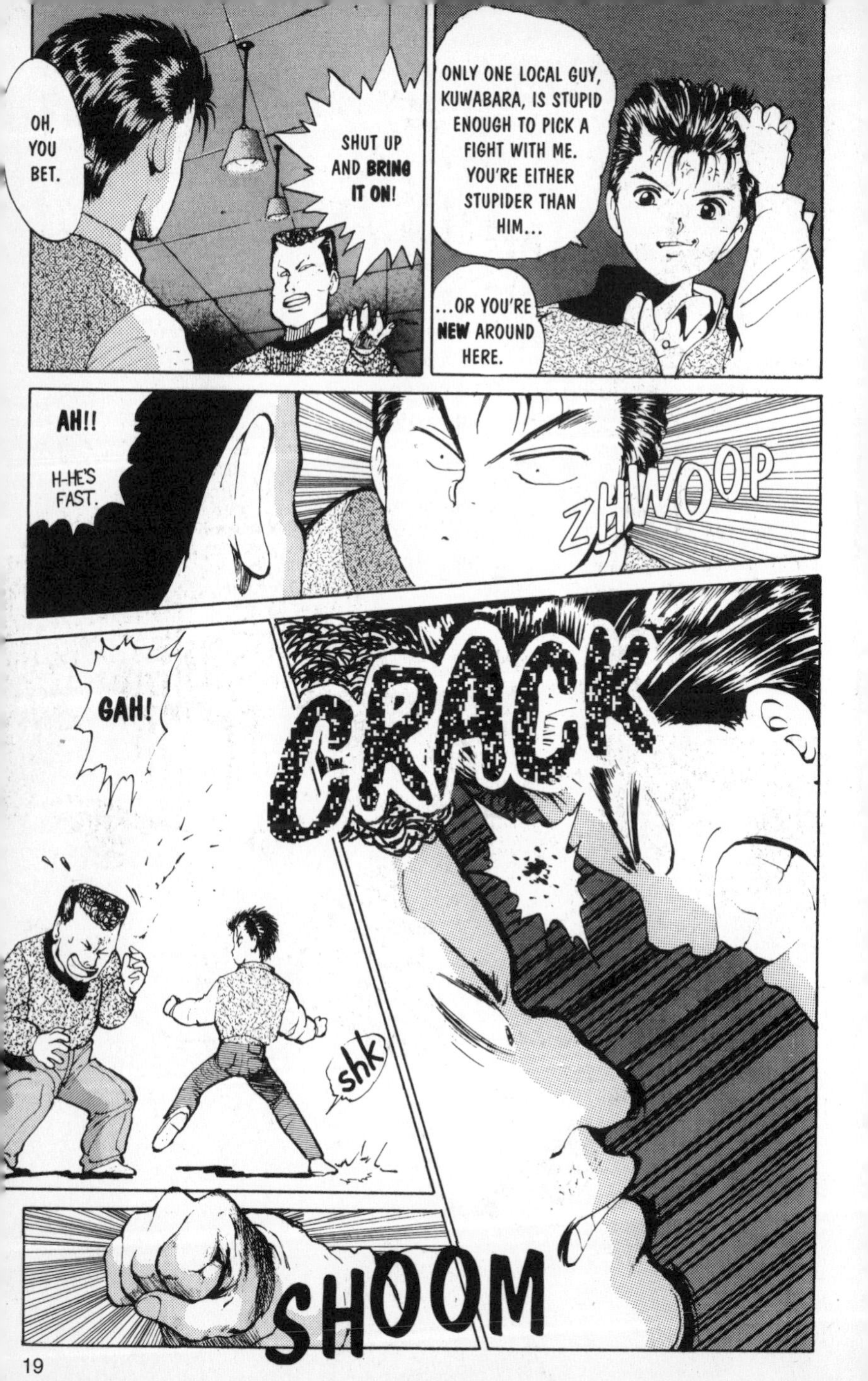
ONLY ONE LOCAL GUY, KUWABARA, IS STUPID ENOUGH TO PICK A FIGHT WITH ME. YOU'RE EITHER STUPIDER THAN HIM...
...OR YOU'RE NEW AROUND HERE.
SHUT UP AND BRING IT ON!
OH, YOU BET.
ZHWOOP
AH!!
H-HE'S FAST.
CRACK
GAH!
shk
SHOOM

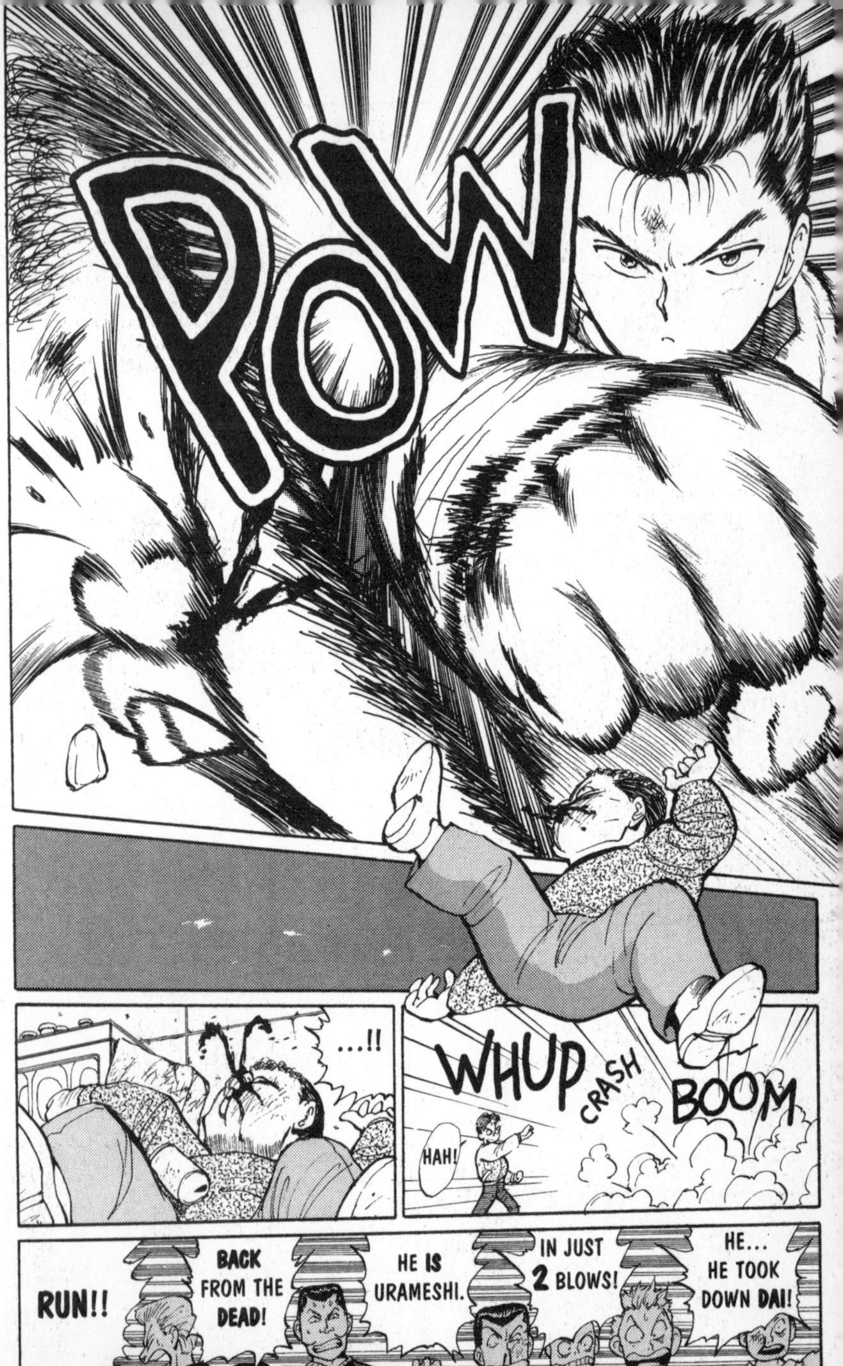
POW
BOOM
CRASH
WHUP
HAH!
...!!
HE... HE TOOK DOWN DAI!
IN JUST 2 BLOWS!
HE IS URAMESHI.
BACK FROM THE DEAD!
RUN!!

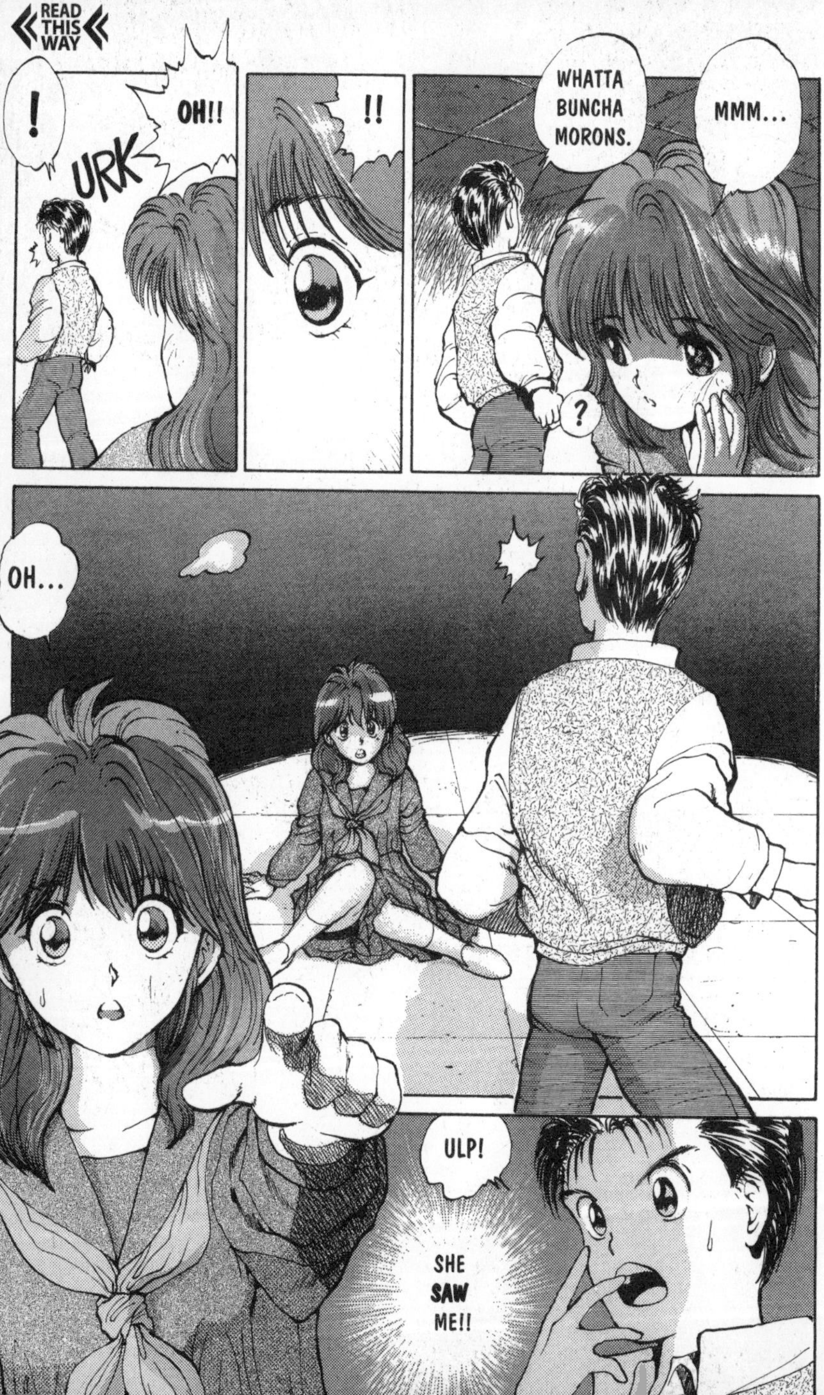
READ THIS WAY
MMM...
WHATTA BUNCHA MORONS.
?
!!
OH!!
!
URK
OH...
ULP!
SHE SAW ME!!

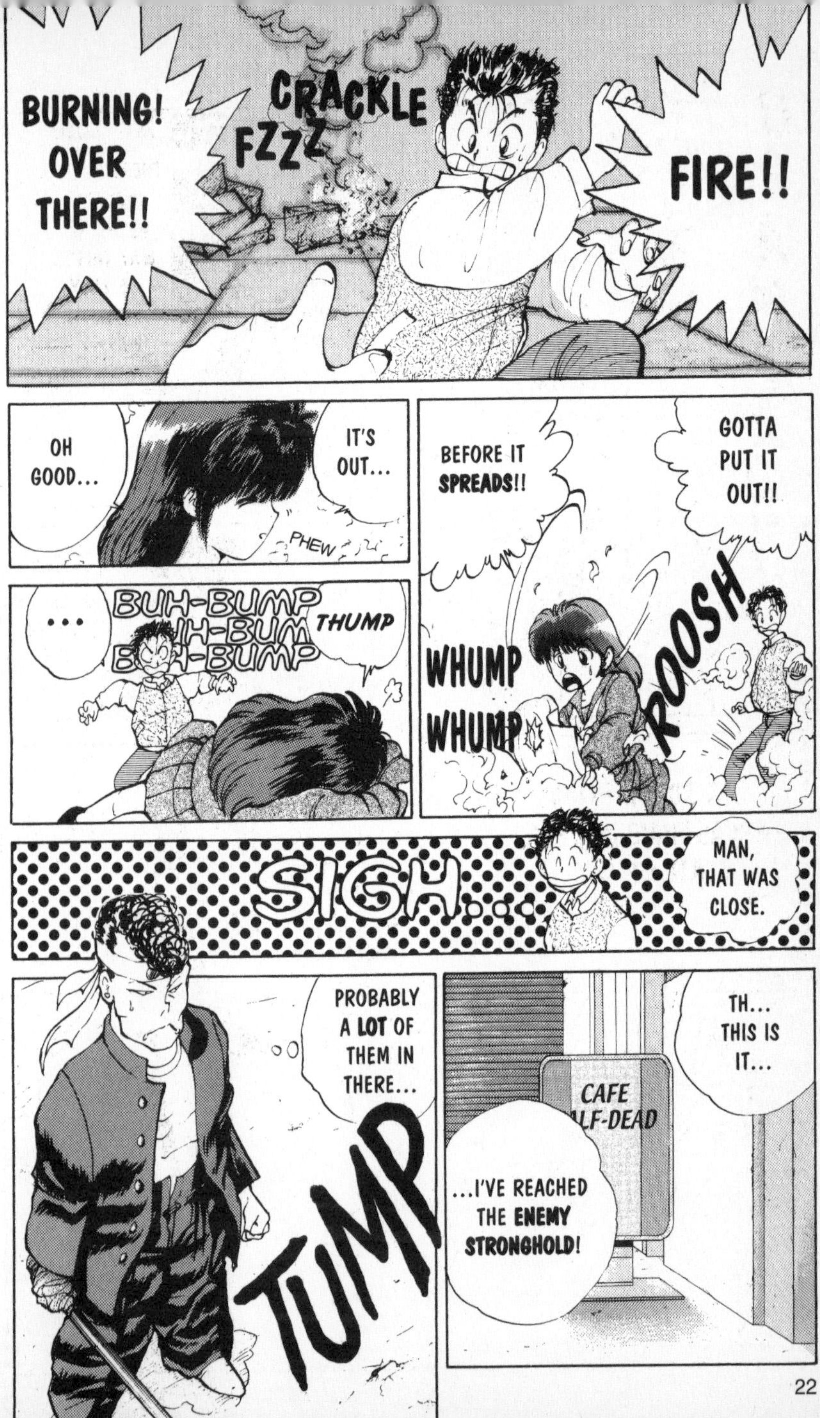
FIRE!!
CRACKLE
FZZZ
BURNING! OVER THERE!!
GOTTA PUT IT OUT!!
BEFORE IT SPREADS!!
ROOSH
WHUMP WHUMP
IT'S OUT...
OH GOOD...
PHEW
...
THUMP
BUH-BUMP
MAN, THAT WAS CLOSE.
SIGH...
TH... THIS IS IT...
CAFE
...I'VE REACHED THE ENEMY STRONGHOLD!
PROBABLY A LOT OF THEM IN THERE...
TUMP

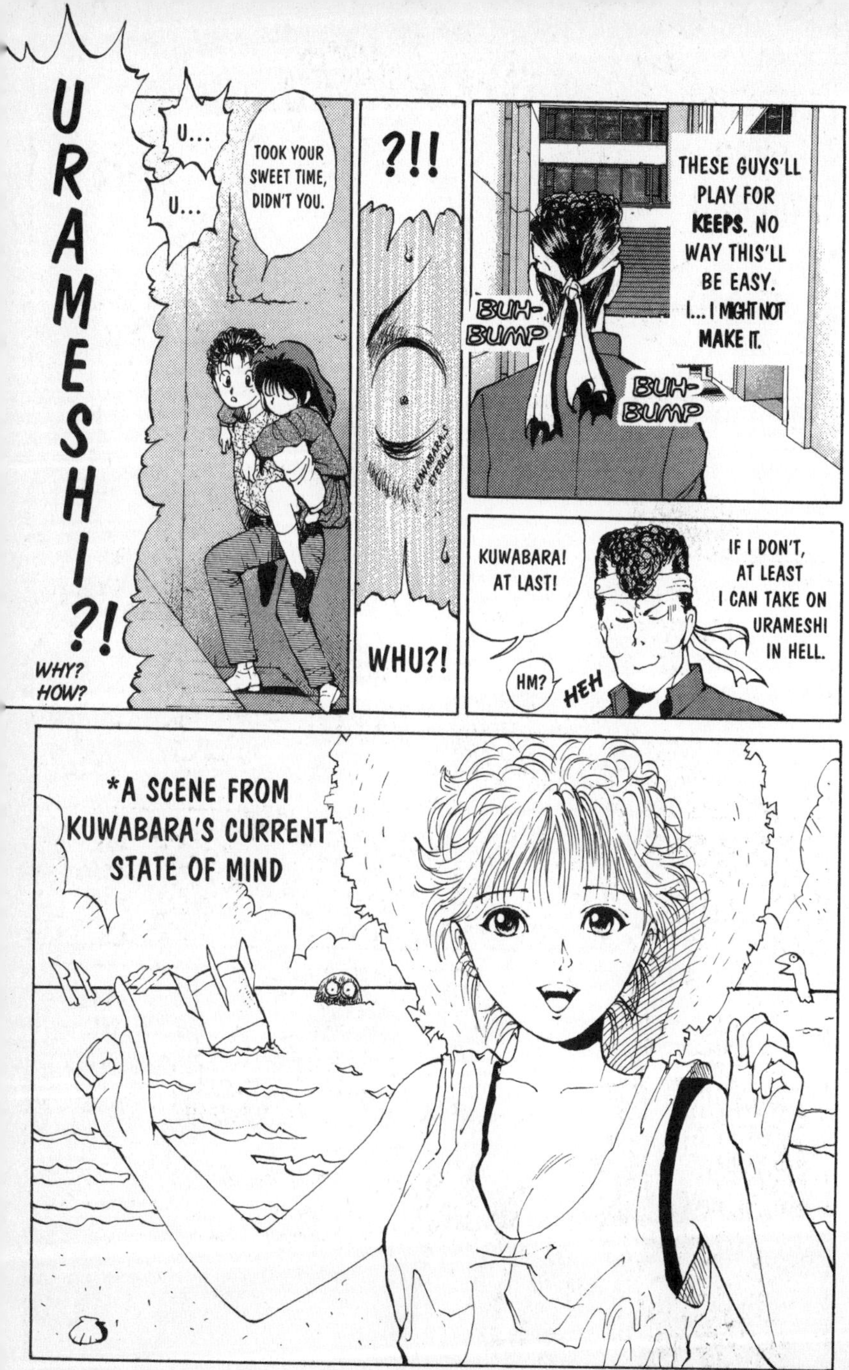
THESE GUYS'LL PLAY FOR KEEPS. NO WAY THIS'LL BE EASY. I... I MIGHT NOT MAKE IT.
BUH-BUMP
BUH-BUMP
IF I DON'T, AT LEAST I CAN TAKE ON URAMESHI IN HELL.
HEH
KUWABARA! AT LAST!
HM?
?!!
KUWABARA'S EYEBALL
WHU?!
TOOK YOUR SWEET TIME, DIDN'T YOU.
U...
U...
URAMESHI?!
WHY? HOW?
*A SCENE FROM KUWABARA'S CURRENT STATE OF MIND

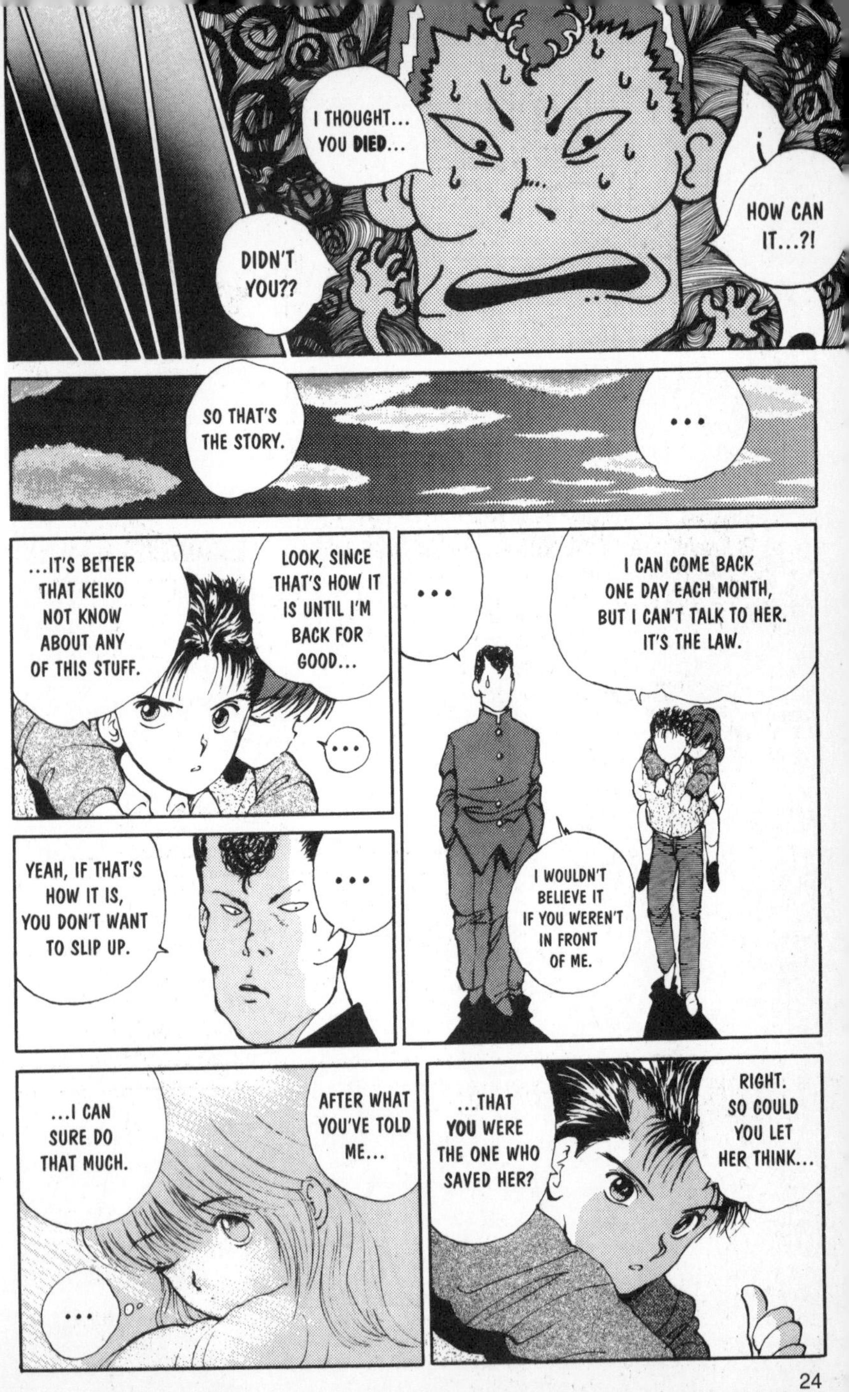
HOW CAN IT...?!
I THOUGHT... YOU DIED...
DIDN'T YOU??
...
SO THAT'S THE STORY.
I CAN COME BACK ONE DAY EACH MONTH, BUT I CAN'T TALK TO HER. IT'S THE LAW.
...
I WOULDN'T BELIEVE IT IF YOU WEREN'T IN FRONT OF ME.
LOOK, SINCE THAT'S HOW IT IS UNTIL I'M BACK FOR GOOD...
...IT'S BETTER THAT KEIKO NOT KNOW ABOUT ANY OF THIS STUFF.
...
...
YEAH, IF THAT'S HOW IT IS, YOU DON'T WANT TO SLIP UP.
RIGHT. SO COULD YOU LET HER THINK...
...THAT YOU WERE THE ONE WHO SAVED HER?
AFTER WHAT YOU'VE TOLD ME...
...I CAN SURE DO THAT MUCH.
...

READ THIS WAY

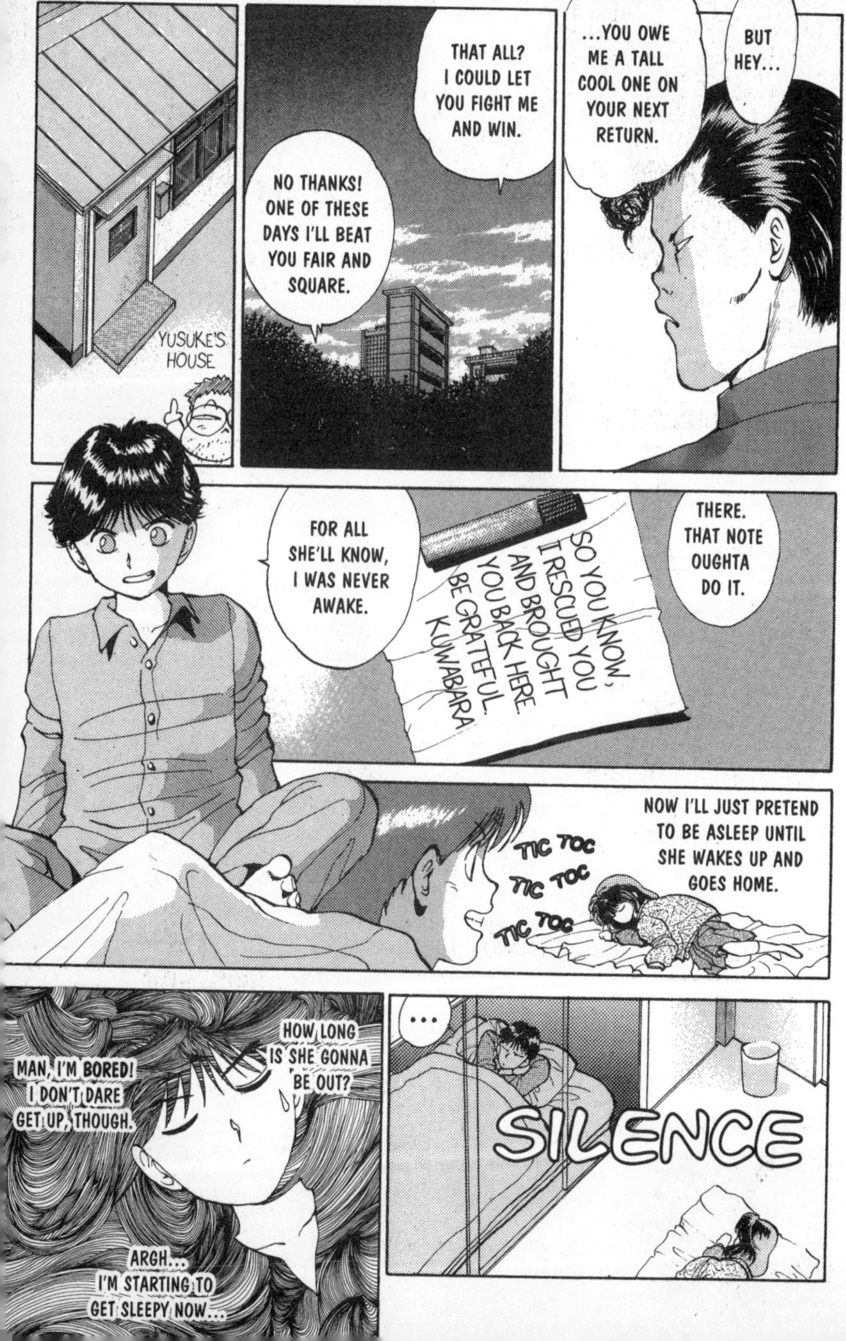

BUT HEY...
...YOU OWE ME A TALL COOL ONE ON YOUR NEXT RETURN.
THAT ALL? I COULD LET YOU FIGHT ME AND WIN.
NO THANKS! ONE OF THESE DAYS I'LL BEAT YOU FAIR AND SQUARE.
YUSUKE'S HOUSE
THERE. THAT NOTE OUGHTA DO IT.
SO YOU KNOW, I RESCUED YOU AND BROUGHT YOU BACK HERE. BE GRATEFUL. KUWABARA
FOR ALL SHE'LL KNOW, I WAS NEVER AWAKE.
NOW I'LL JUST PRETEND TO BE ASLEEP UNTIL SHE WAKES UP AND GOES HOME.
TIC TOC
TIC TOC
TIC TOC
...
SILENCE
HOW LONG IS SHE GONNA BE OUT?
MAN, I'M BORED! I DON'T DARE GET UP, THOUGH.
ARGH... I'M STARTING TO GET SLEEPY NOW...

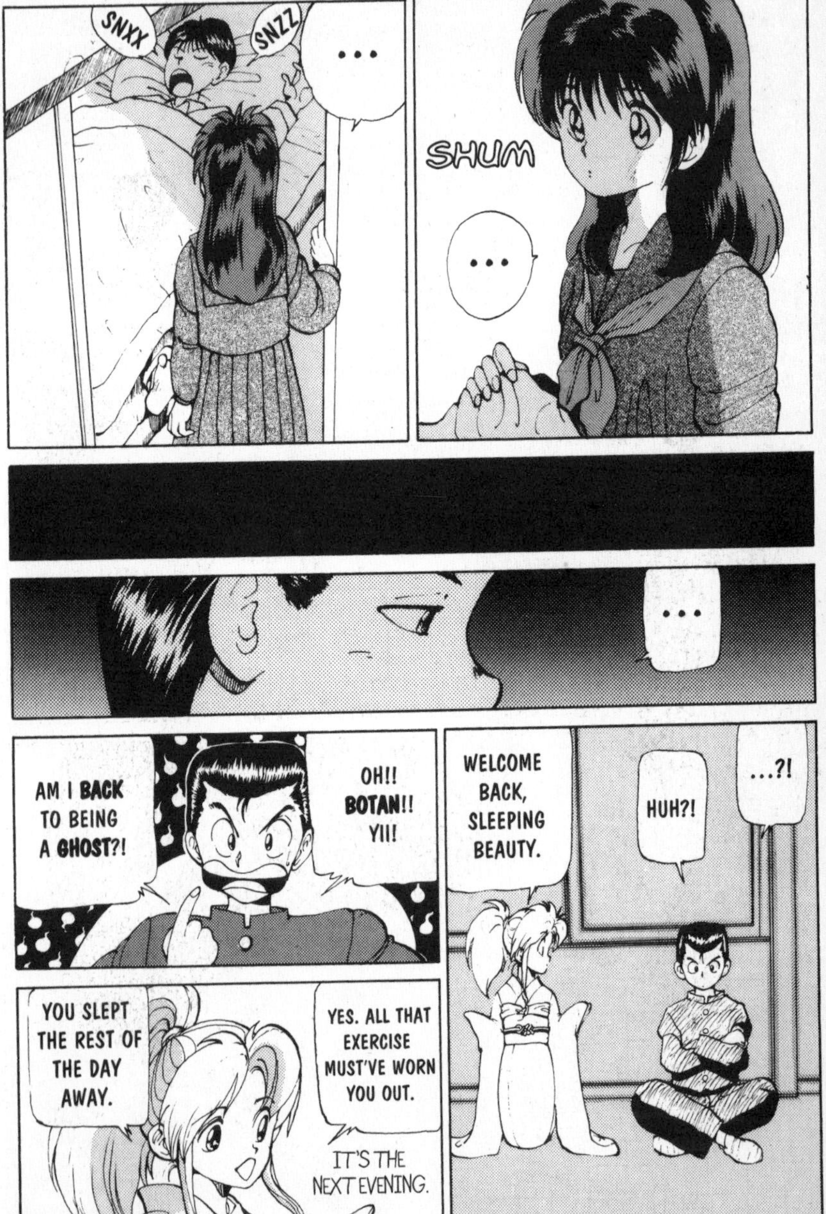
SHUM
...
...
SNZZ
SNXX
...
...?!
HUH?!
WELCOME BACK, SLEEPING BEAUTY.
OH!! BOTAN!! YII!
AM I BACK TO BEING A GHOST?!
YES. ALL THAT EXERCISE MUST'VE WORN YOU OUT.
IT'S THE NEXT EVENING.
YOU SLEPT THE REST OF THE DAY AWAY.

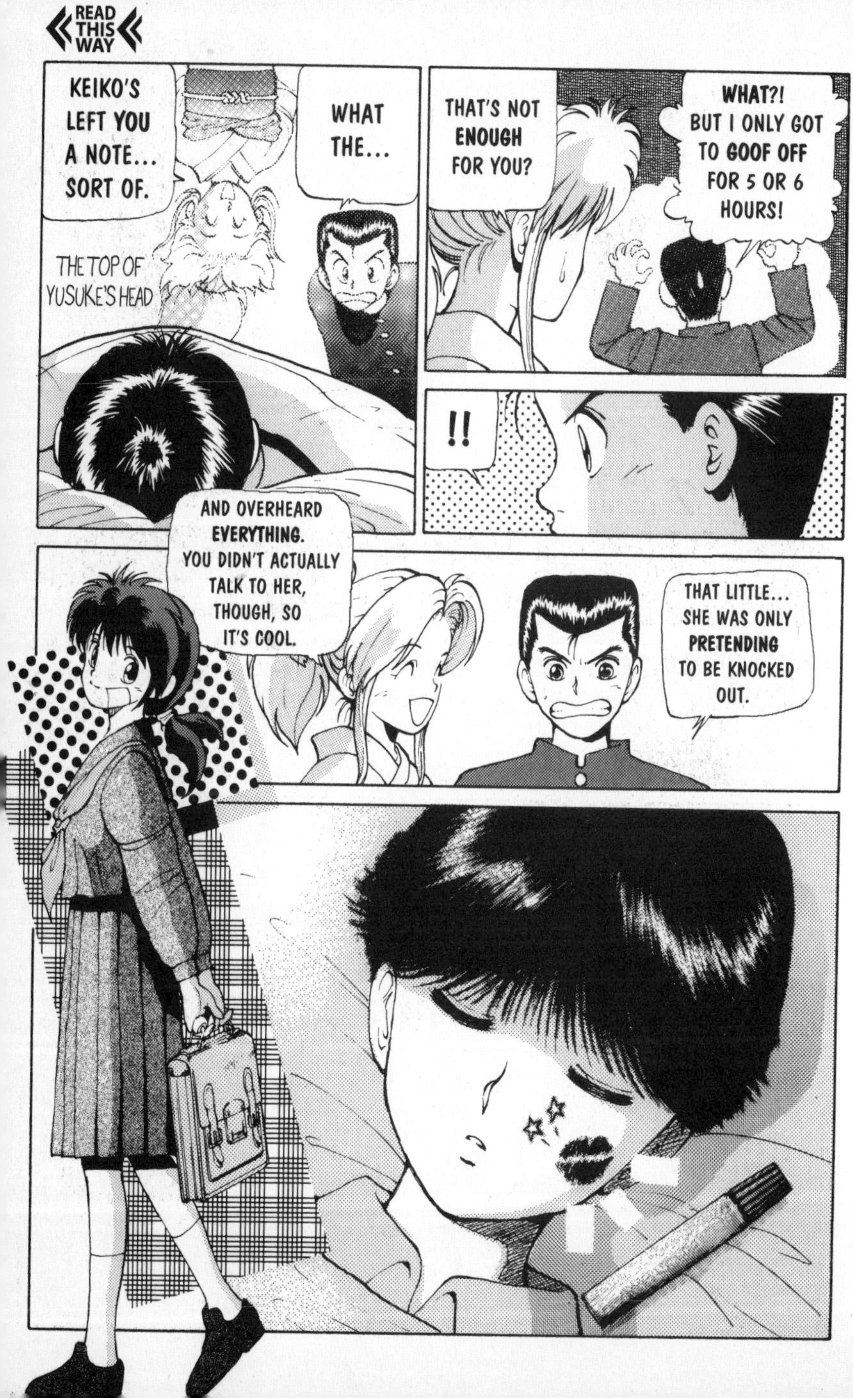
READ THIS WAY
WHAT?! BUT I ONLY GOT TO GOOF OFF FOR 5 OR 6 HOURS!
THAT'S NOT ENOUGH FOR YOU?
!!
WHAT THE...
KEIKO'S LEFT YOU A NOTE... SORT OF.
THE TOP OF YUSUKE'S HEAD
THAT LITTLE... SHE WAS ONLY PRETENDING TO BE KNOCKED OUT.
AND OVERHEARD EVERYTHING. YOU DIDN'T ACTUALLY TALK TO HER, THOUGH, SO IT'S COOL.

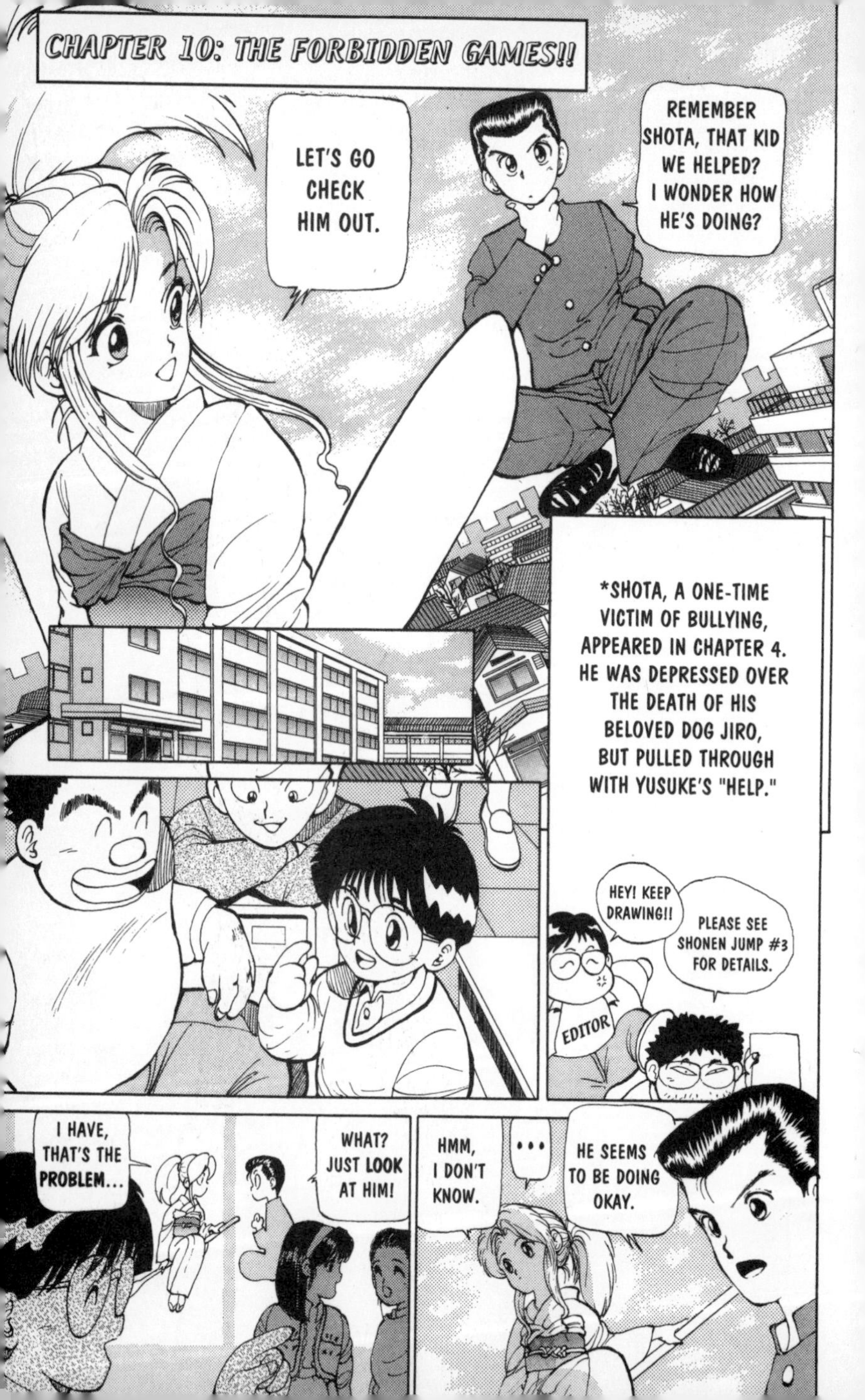
CHAPTER 10: THE FORBIDDEN GAMES!!
REMEMBER SHOTA, THAT KID WE HELPED? I WONDER HOW HE'S DOING?
LET'S GO CHECK HIM OUT.
*SHOTA, A ONE-TIME VICTIM OF BULLYING, APPEARED IN CHAPTER 4. HE WAS DEPRESSED OVER THE DEATH OF HIS BELOVED DOG JIRO, BUT PULLED THROUGH WITH YUSUKE'S "HELP."
HEY! KEEP DRAWING!!
PLEASE SEE SHONEN JUMP #3 FOR DETAILS.
EDITOR
HE SEEMS TO BE DOING OKAY.
...
HMM, I DON'T KNOW.
WHAT? JUST LOOK AT HIM!
I HAVE, THAT'S THE PROBLEM...

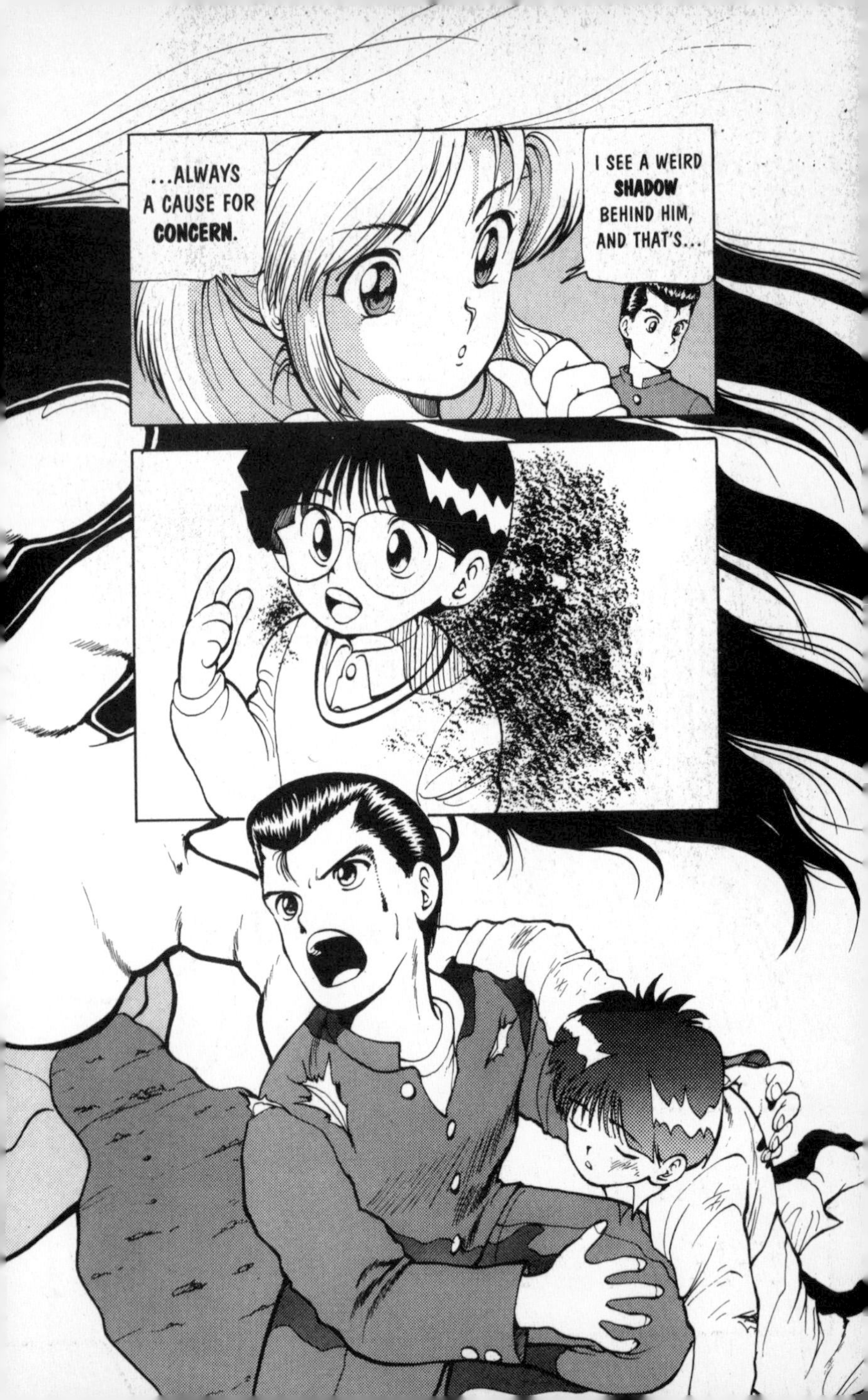
I SEE A WEIRD SHADOW BEHIND HIM, AND THAT'S...
...ALWAYS A CAUSE FOR CONCERN.

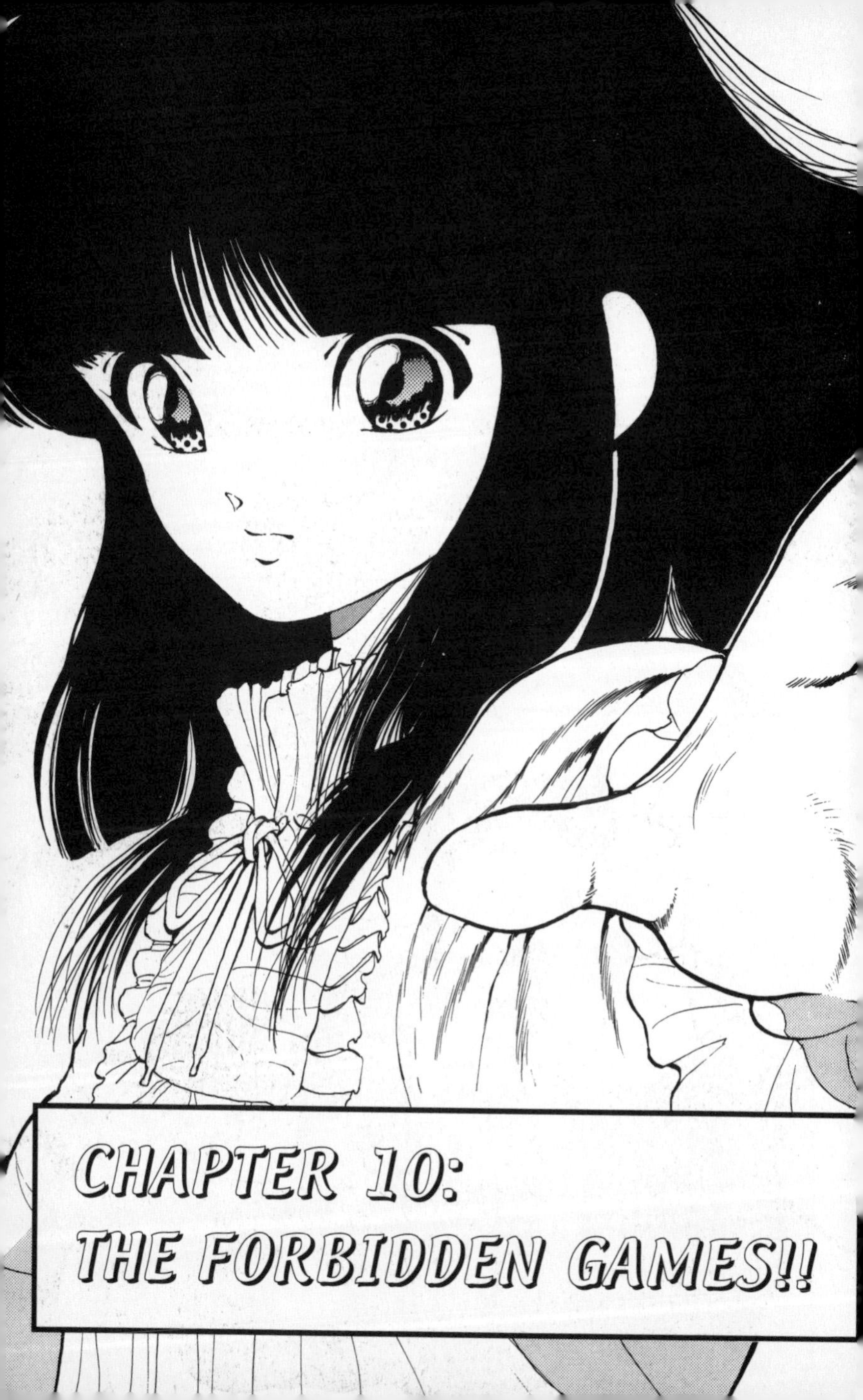
CHAPTER 10:
THE FORBIDDEN GAMES!!

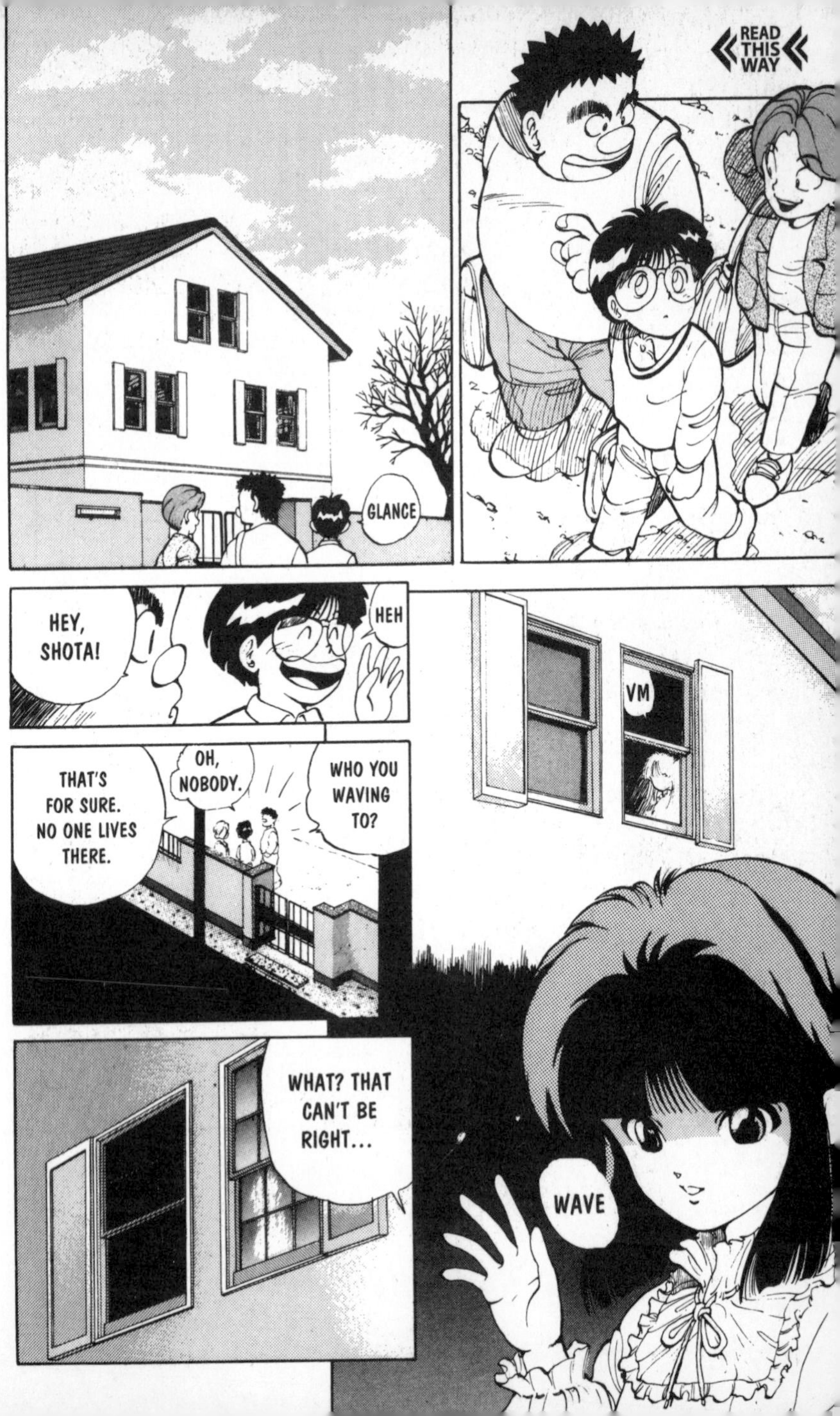
READ THIS WAY
GLANCE
VM
WAVE
HEH
HEY, SHOTA!
WHO YOU WAVING TO?
OH, NOBODY.
THAT'S FOR SURE. NO ONE LIVES THERE.
WHAT? THAT CAN'T BE RIGHT...

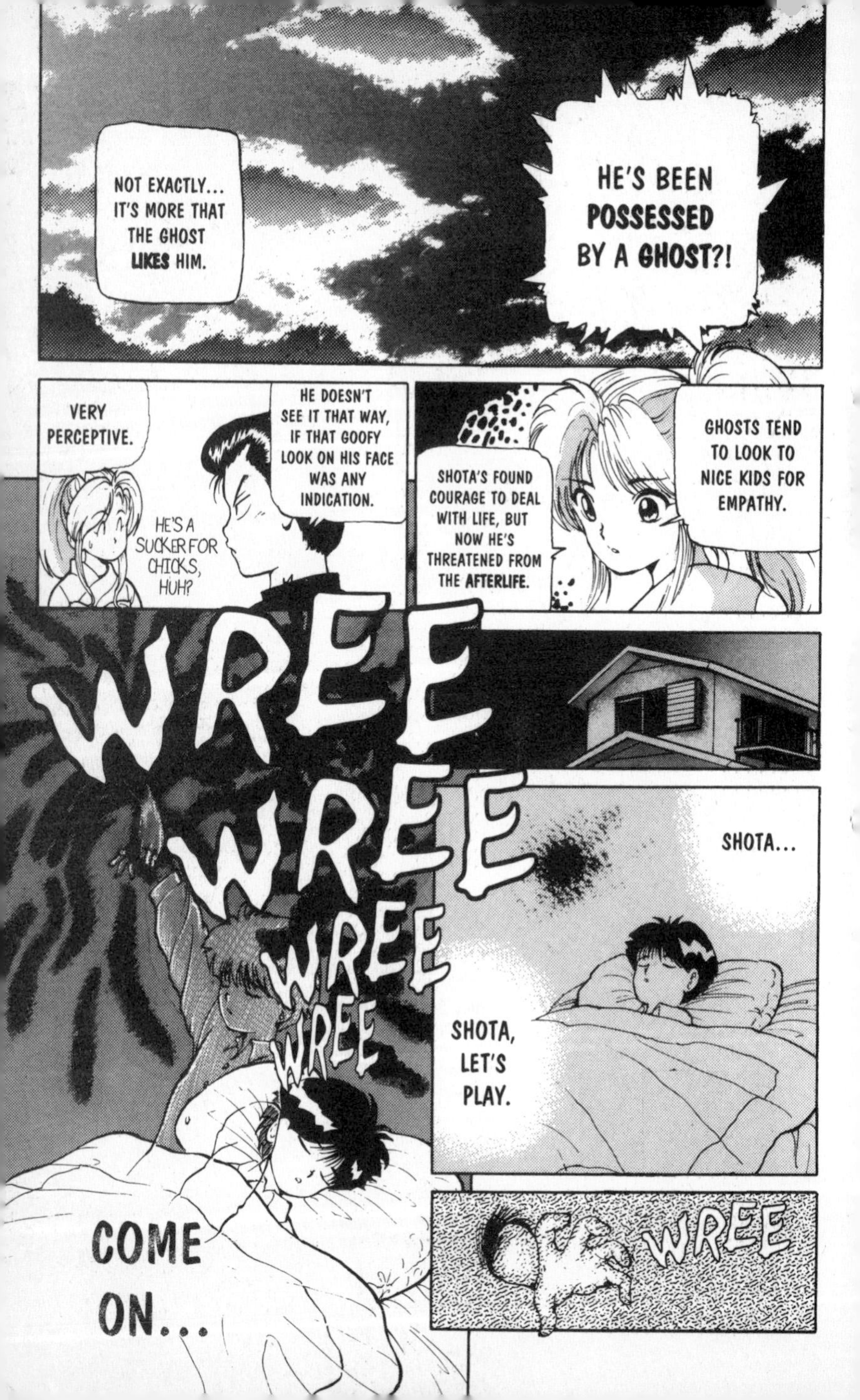
HE'S BEEN POSSESSED BY A GHOST?!
NOT EXACTLY... IT'S MORE THAT THE GHOST LIKES HIM.
GHOSTS TEND TO LOOK TO NICE KIDS FOR EMPATHY.
SHOTA'S FOUND COURAGE TO DEAL WITH LIFE, BUT NOW HE'S THREATENED FROM THE AFTERLIFE.
HE DOESN'T SEE IT THAT WAY, IF THAT GOOFY LOOK ON HIS FACE WAS ANY INDICATION.
VERY PERCEPTIVE.
HE'S A SUCKER FOR CHICKS, HUH?
SHOTA...
SHOTA, LET'S PLAY.
WREE
WREE
WREE
WREE
WREE
COME ON...

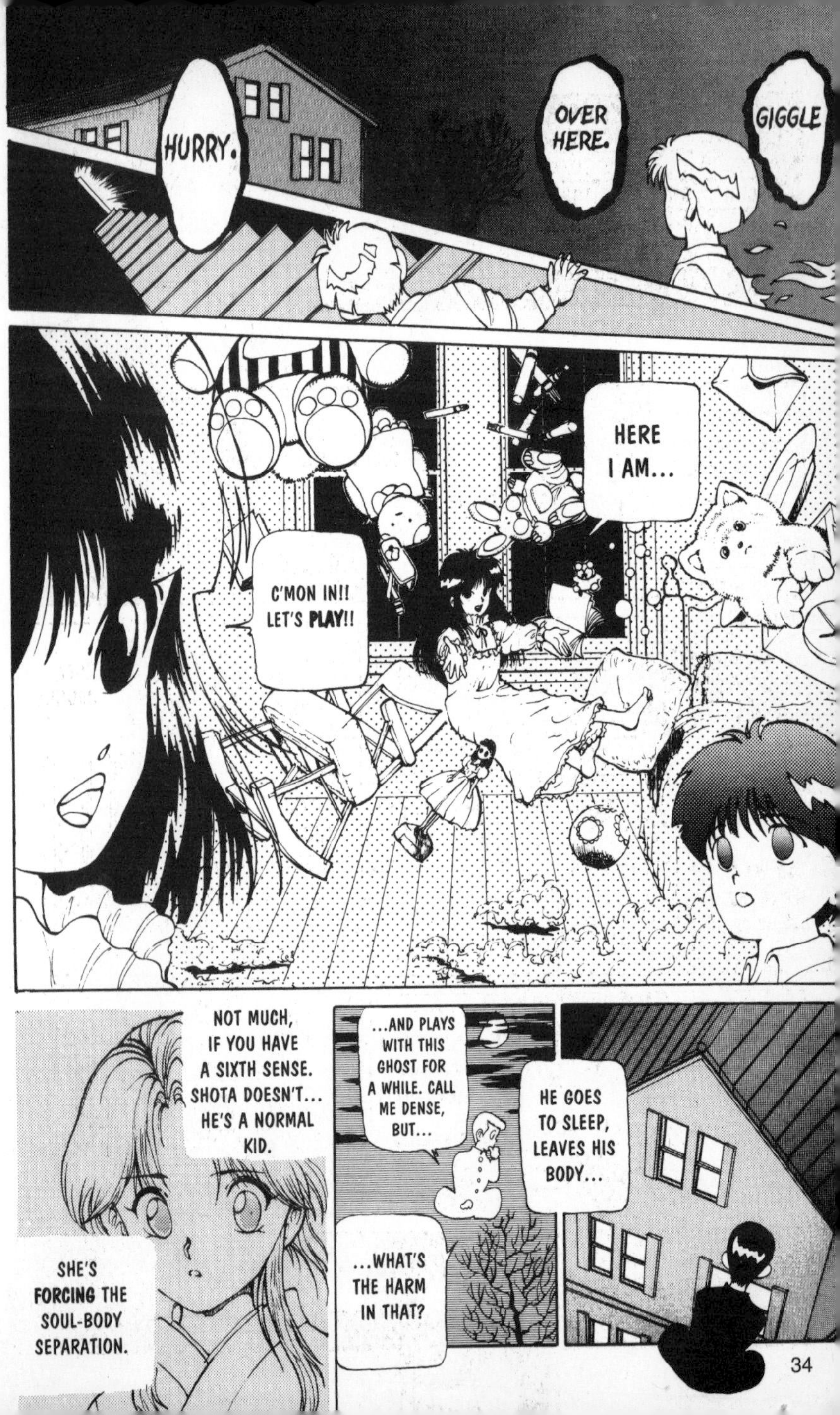
GIGGLE
OVER HERE.
HURRY.
HERE I AM...
C'MON IN!! LET'S **PLAY**!!
HE GOES TO SLEEP, LEAVES HIS BODY...
...AND PLAYS WITH THIS GHOST FOR A WHILE. CALL ME DENSE, BUT...
...WHAT'S THE HARM IN THAT?
NOT MUCH, IF YOU HAVE A SIXTH SENSE. SHOTA DOESN'T... HE'S A NORMAL KID.
SHE'S **FORCING** THE SOUL-BODY SEPARATION.

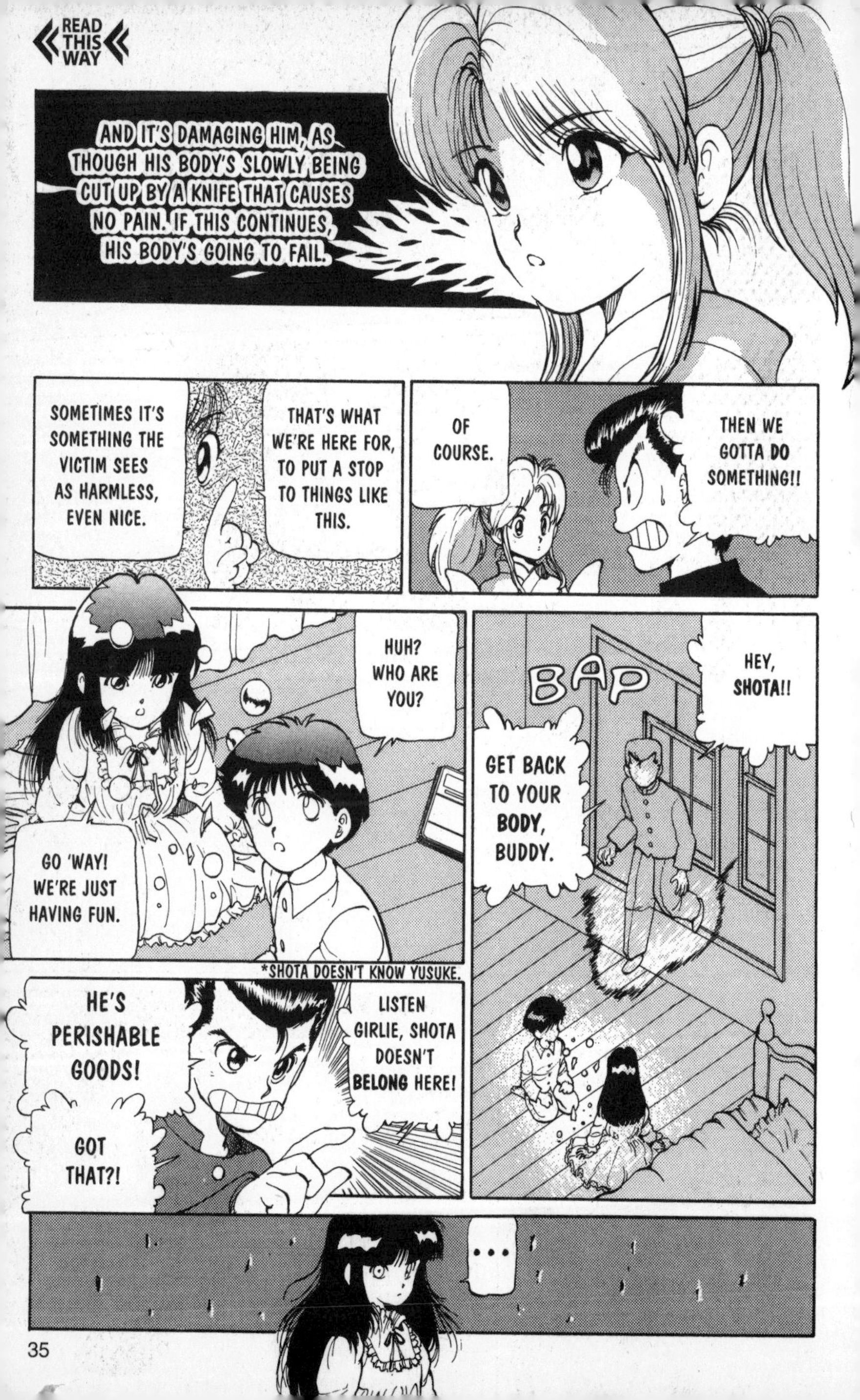
READ THIS WAY
AND IT'S DAMAGING HIM, AS THOUGH HIS BODY'S SLOWLY BEING CUT UP BY A KNIFE THAT CAUSES NO PAIN. IF THIS CONTINUES, HIS BODY'S GOING TO FAIL.
THEN WE GOTTA DO SOMETHING!!
OF COURSE.
THAT'S WHAT WE'RE HERE FOR, TO PUT A STOP TO THINGS LIKE THIS.
SOMETIMES IT'S SOMETHING THE VICTIM SEES AS HARMLESS, EVEN NICE.
HEY, SHOTA!!
BAP
GET BACK TO YOUR BODY, BUDDY.
HUH? WHO ARE YOU?
GO 'WAY! WE'RE JUST HAVING FUN.
*SHOTA DOESN'T KNOW YUSUKE.
LISTEN GIRLIE, SHOTA DOESN'T BELONG HERE!
HE'S PERISHABLE GOODS!
GOT THAT?!
...

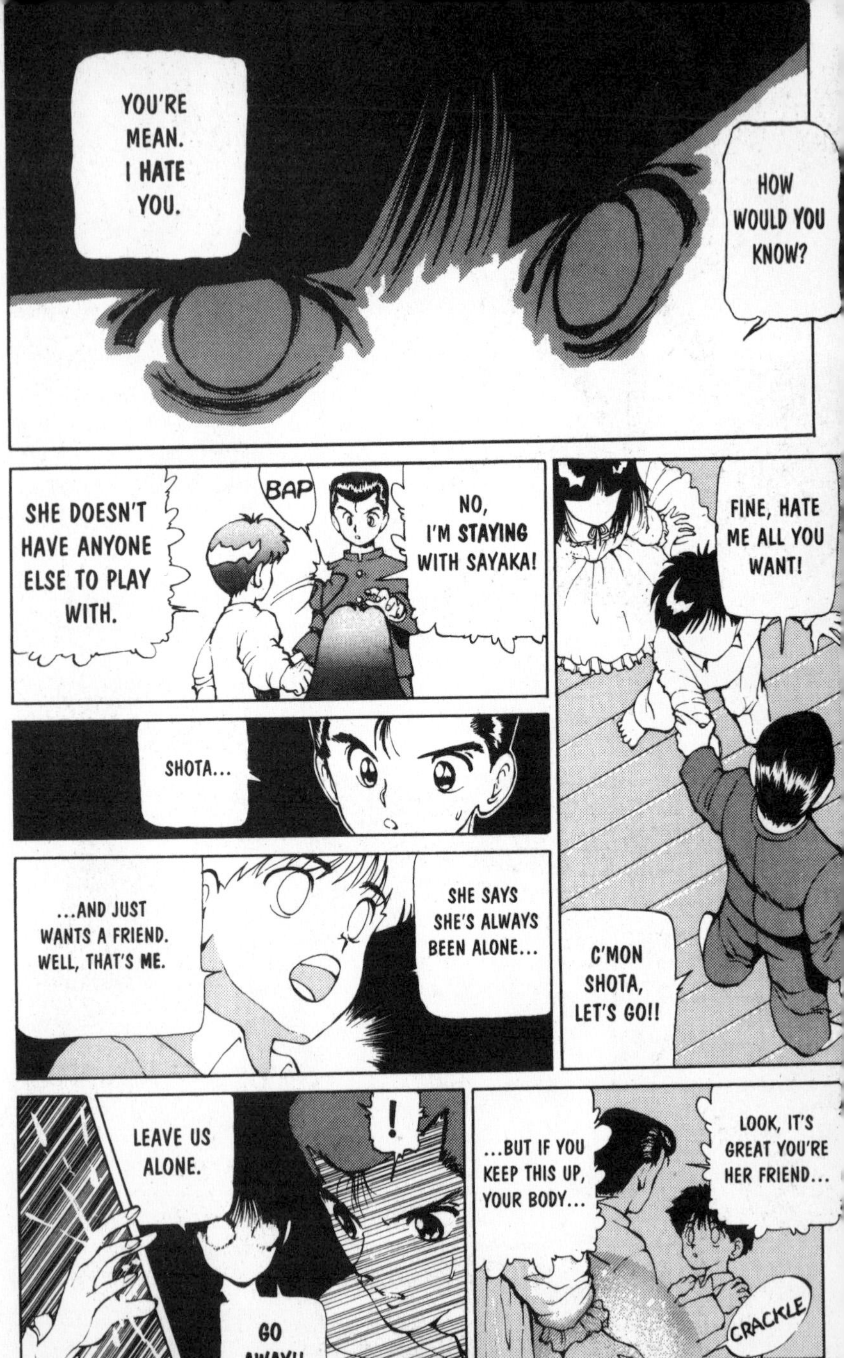
HOW WOULD YOU KNOW?
YOU'RE MEAN. I HATE YOU.
FINE, HATE ME ALL YOU WANT!
C'MON SHOTA, LET'S GO!!
NO, I'M STAYING WITH SAYAKA!
BAP
SHE DOESN'T HAVE ANYONE ELSE TO PLAY WITH.
SHOTA...
SHE SAYS SHE'S ALWAYS BEEN ALONE...
...AND JUST WANTS A FRIEND. WELL, THAT'S ME.
LOOK, IT'S GREAT YOU'RE HER FRIEND...
...BUT IF YOU KEEP THIS UP, YOUR BODY...
CRACKLE
!
LEAVE US ALONE.
GO AWAY!!

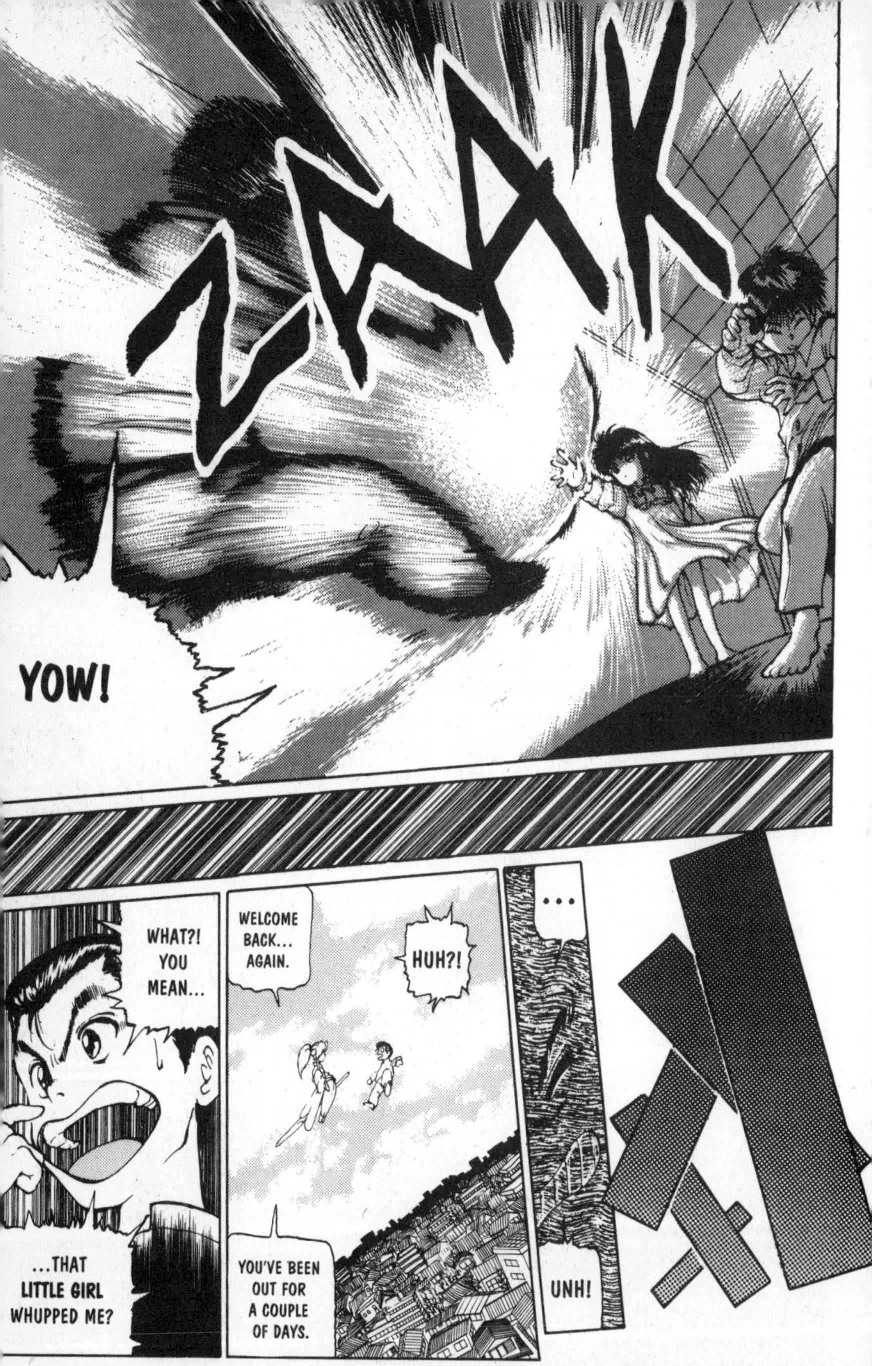
ZAAK
YOW!
...
UNH!
WELCOME BACK... AGAIN.
HUH?!
YOU'VE BEEN OUT FOR A COUPLE OF DAYS.
WHAT?! YOU MEAN...
...THAT LITTLE GIRL WHUPPED ME?

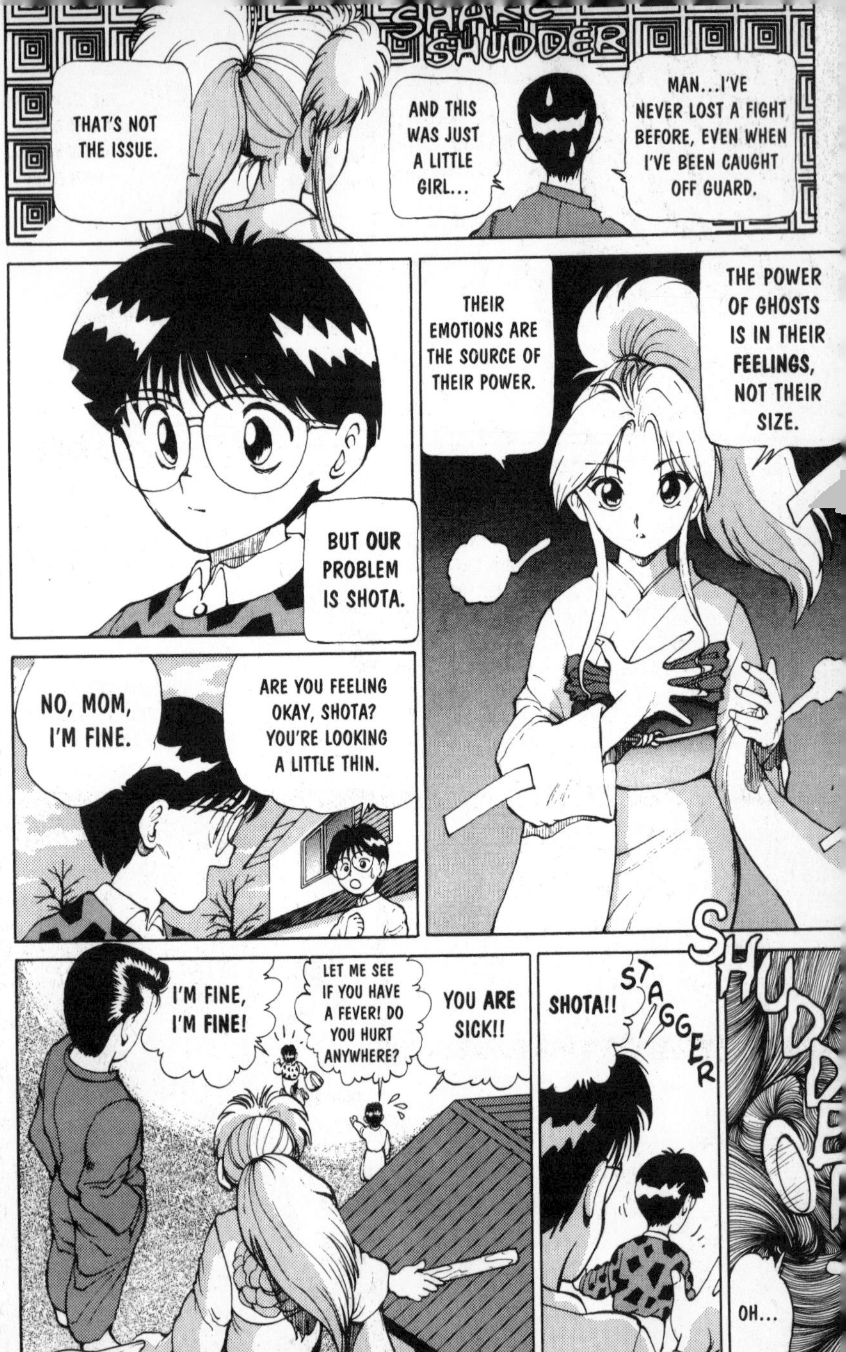
SHUDDER
MAN...I'VE NEVER LOST A FIGHT BEFORE, EVEN WHEN I'VE BEEN CAUGHT OFF GUARD.
AND THIS WAS JUST A LITTLE GIRL...
THAT'S NOT THE ISSUE.
THE POWER OF GHOSTS IS IN THEIR **FEELINGS**, NOT THEIR SIZE.
THEIR EMOTIONS ARE THE SOURCE OF THEIR POWER.
BUT **OUR** PROBLEM IS SHOTA.
ARE YOU FEELING OKAY, SHOTA? YOU'RE LOOKING A LITTLE THIN.
NO, MOM, I'M FINE.
SHUDDER
STAGGER
SHOTA!!
OH...
YOU **ARE** SICK!!
LET ME SEE IF YOU HAVE A FEVER! DO YOU HURT ANYWHERE?
I'M FINE, I'M **FINE**!

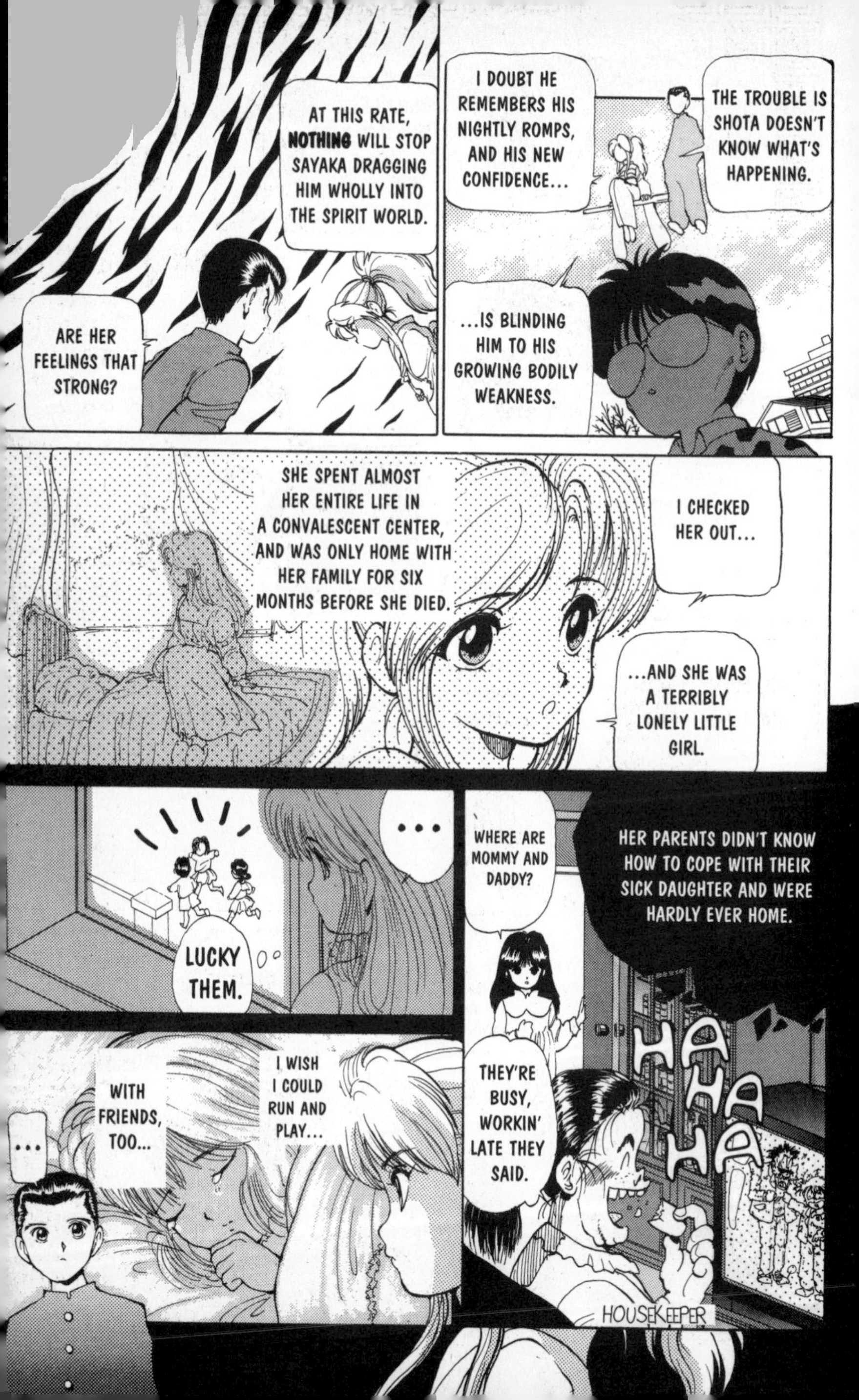
THE TROUBLE IS SHOTA DOESN'T KNOW WHAT'S HAPPENING.
I DOUBT HE REMEMBERS HIS NIGHTLY ROMPS, AND HIS NEW CONFIDENCE...
...IS BLINDING HIM TO HIS GROWING BODILY WEAKNESS.
AT THIS RATE, NOTHING WILL STOP SAYAKA DRAGGING HIM WHOLLY INTO THE SPIRIT WORLD.
ARE HER FEELINGS THAT STRONG?
I CHECKED HER OUT...
...AND SHE WAS A TERRIBLY LONELY LITTLE GIRL.
SHE SPENT ALMOST HER ENTIRE LIFE IN A CONVALESCENT CENTER, AND WAS ONLY HOME WITH HER FAMILY FOR SIX MONTHS BEFORE SHE DIED.
HER PARENTS DIDN'T KNOW HOW TO COPE WITH THEIR SICK DAUGHTER AND WERE HARDLY EVER HOME.
WHERE ARE MOMMY AND DADDY?
THEY'RE BUSY, WORKIN' LATE THEY SAID.
HA HA HA
HOUSEKEEPER
...
LUCKY THEM.
I WISH I COULD RUN AND PLAY...
WITH FRIENDS, TOO...
...

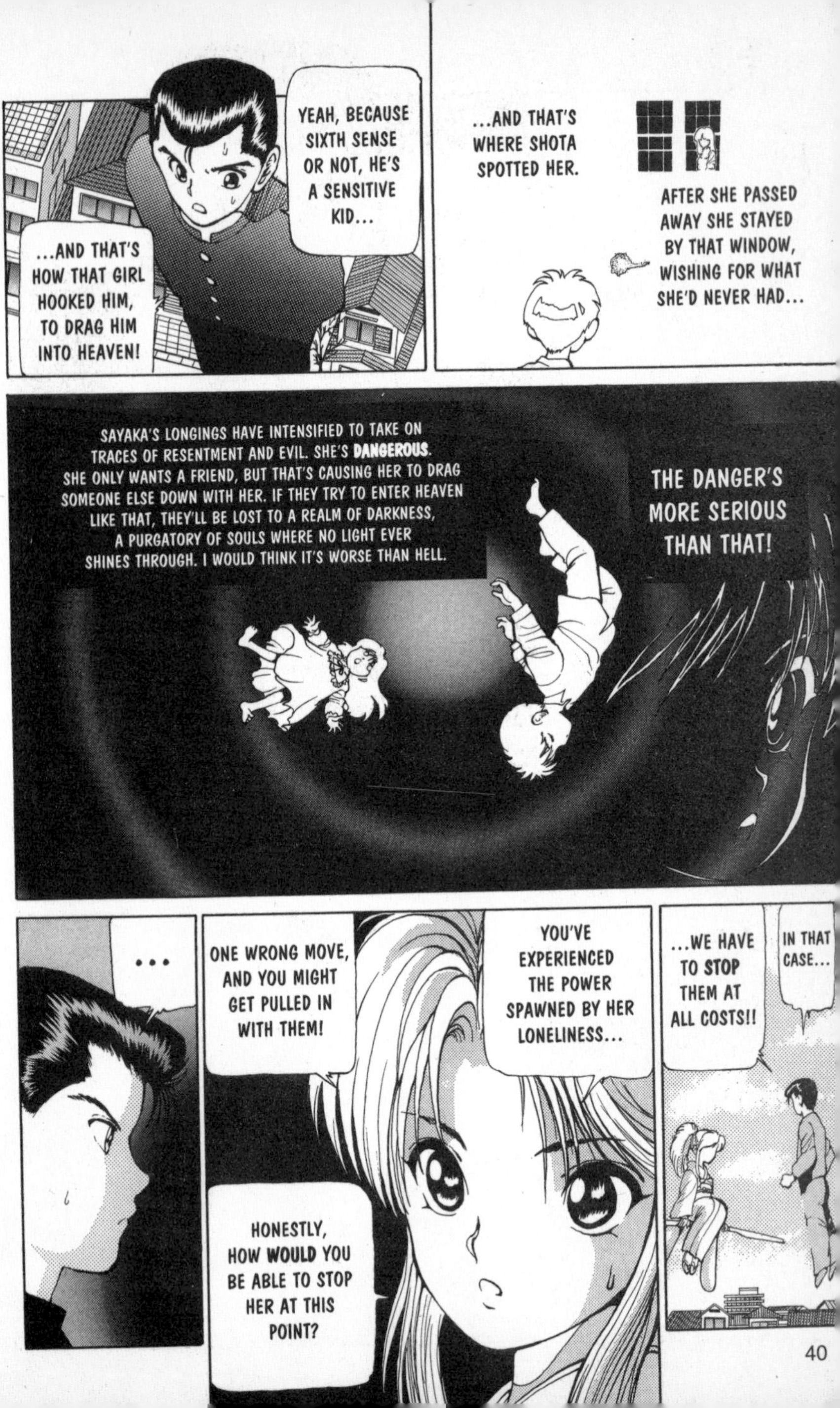
AFTER SHE PASSED AWAY SHE STAYED BY THAT WINDOW, WISHING FOR WHAT SHE'D NEVER HAD...
...AND THAT'S WHERE SHOTA SPOTTED HER.
YEAH, BECAUSE SIXTH SENSE OR NOT, HE'S A SENSITIVE KID...
...AND THAT'S HOW THAT GIRL HOOKED HIM, TO DRAG HIM INTO HEAVEN!
THE DANGER'S MORE SERIOUS THAN THAT!
SAYAKA'S LONGINGS HAVE INTENSIFIED TO TAKE ON TRACES OF RESENTMENT AND EVIL. SHE'S **DANGEROUS**. SHE ONLY WANTS A FRIEND, BUT THAT'S CAUSING HER TO DRAG SOMEONE ELSE DOWN WITH HER. IF THEY TRY TO ENTER HEAVEN LIKE THAT, THEY'LL BE LOST TO A REALM OF DARKNESS, A PURGATORY OF SOULS WHERE NO LIGHT EVER SHINES THROUGH. I WOULD THINK IT'S WORSE THAN HELL.
IN THAT CASE...
...WE HAVE TO **STOP** THEM AT ALL COSTS!!
YOU'VE EXPERIENCED THE POWER SPAWNED BY HER LONELINESS...
ONE WRONG MOVE, AND YOU MIGHT GET PULLED IN WITH THEM!
HONESTLY, HOW **WOULD** YOU BE ABLE TO STOP HER AT THIS POINT?
...

READ THIS WAY

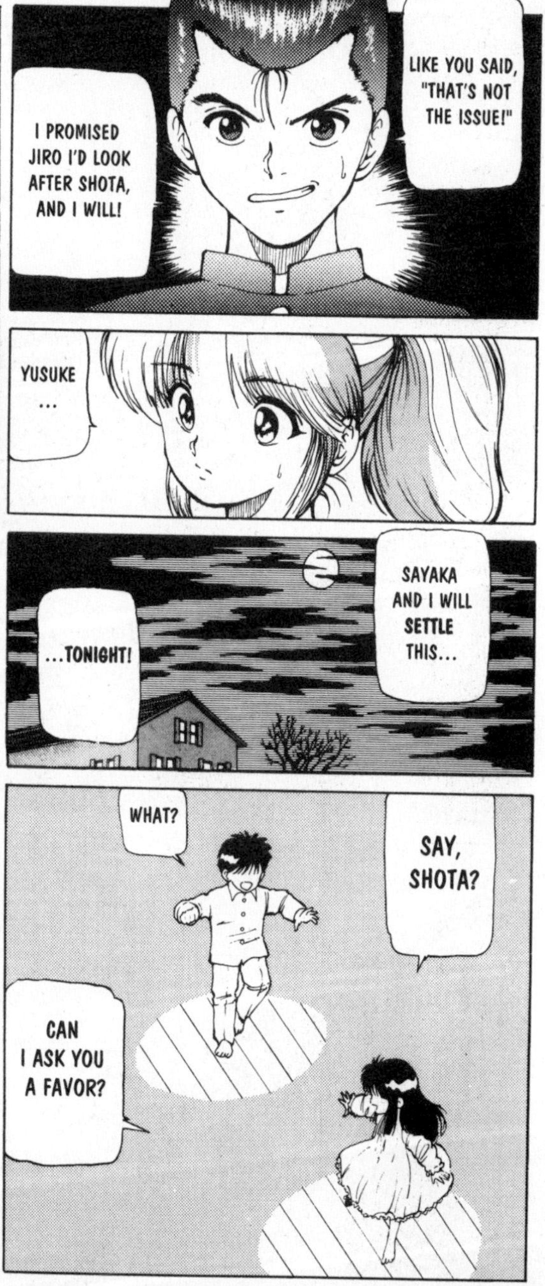
LIKE YOU SAID, "THAT'S NOT THE ISSUE!"
I PROMISED JIRO I'D LOOK AFTER SHOTA, AND I WILL!
YUSUKE ...
SAYAKA AND I WILL SETTLE THIS...
...TONIGHT!
SAY, SHOTA?
WHAT?
CAN I ASK YOU A FAVOR?

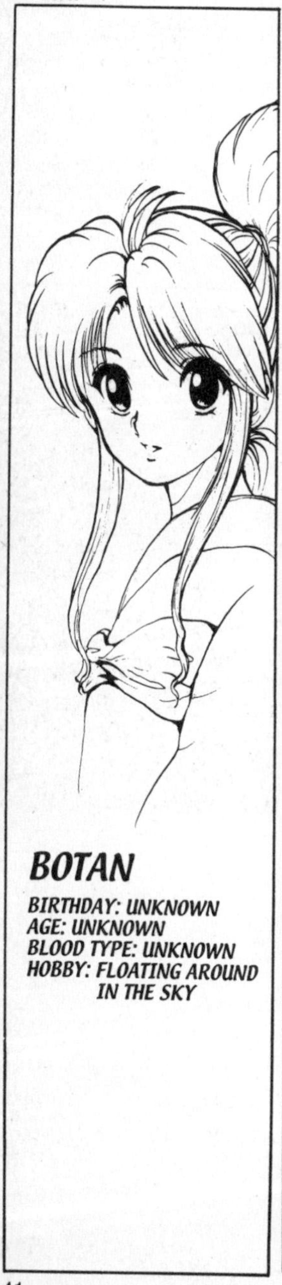
BOTAN
BIRTHDAY: UNKNOWN
AGE: UNKNOWN
BLOOD TYPE: UNKNOWN
HOBBY: FLOATING AROUND IN THE SKY

READ THIS WAY

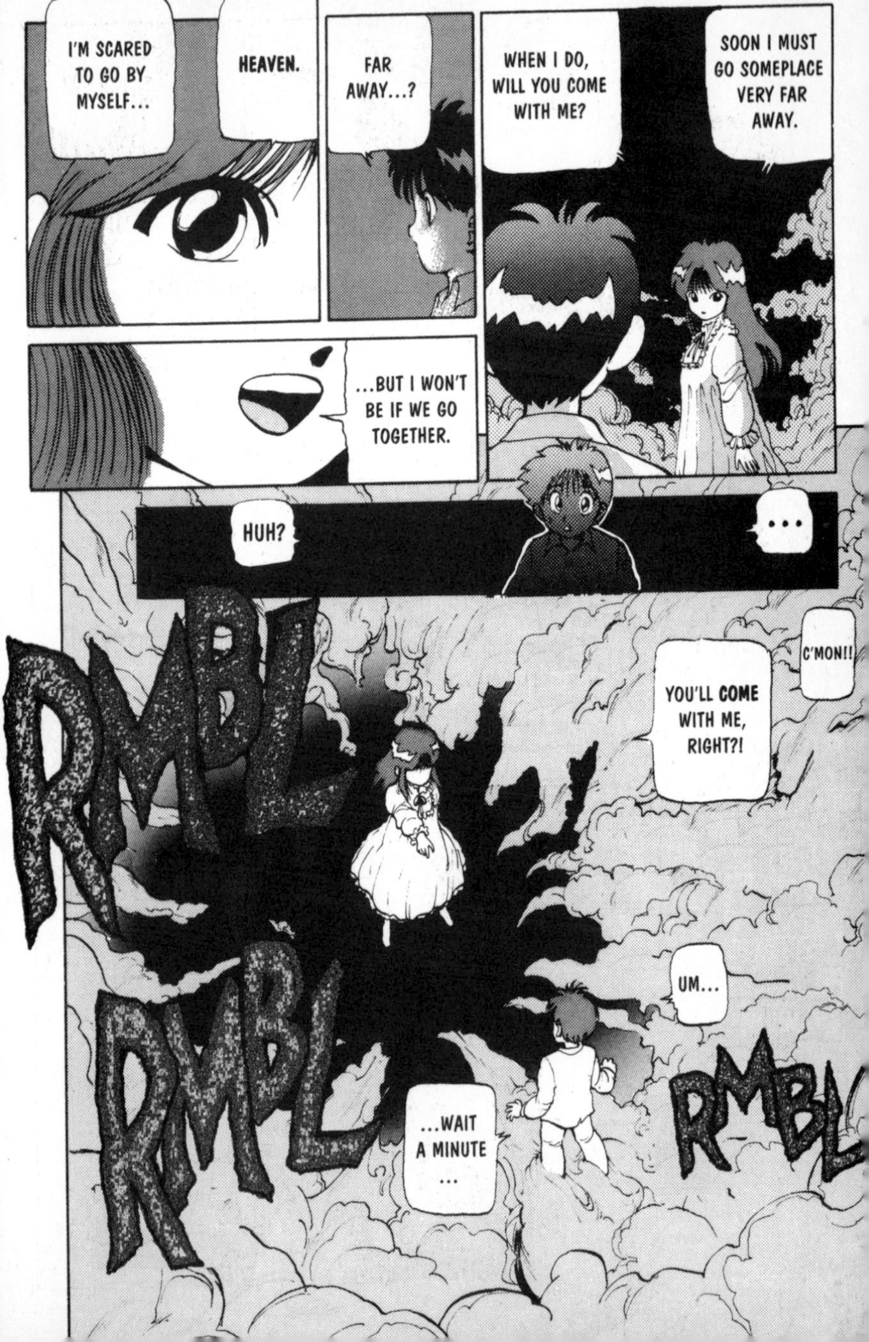
SOON I MUST GO SOMEPLACE VERY FAR AWAY.
WHEN I DO, WILL YOU COME WITH ME?
FAR AWAY...?
HEAVEN.
I'M SCARED TO GO BY MYSELF...
...BUT I WON'T BE IF WE GO TOGETHER.
...
HUH?
C'MON!!
YOU'LL COME WITH ME, RIGHT?!
RMBL
UM...
RMBL
...WAIT A MINUTE ...
RMBL

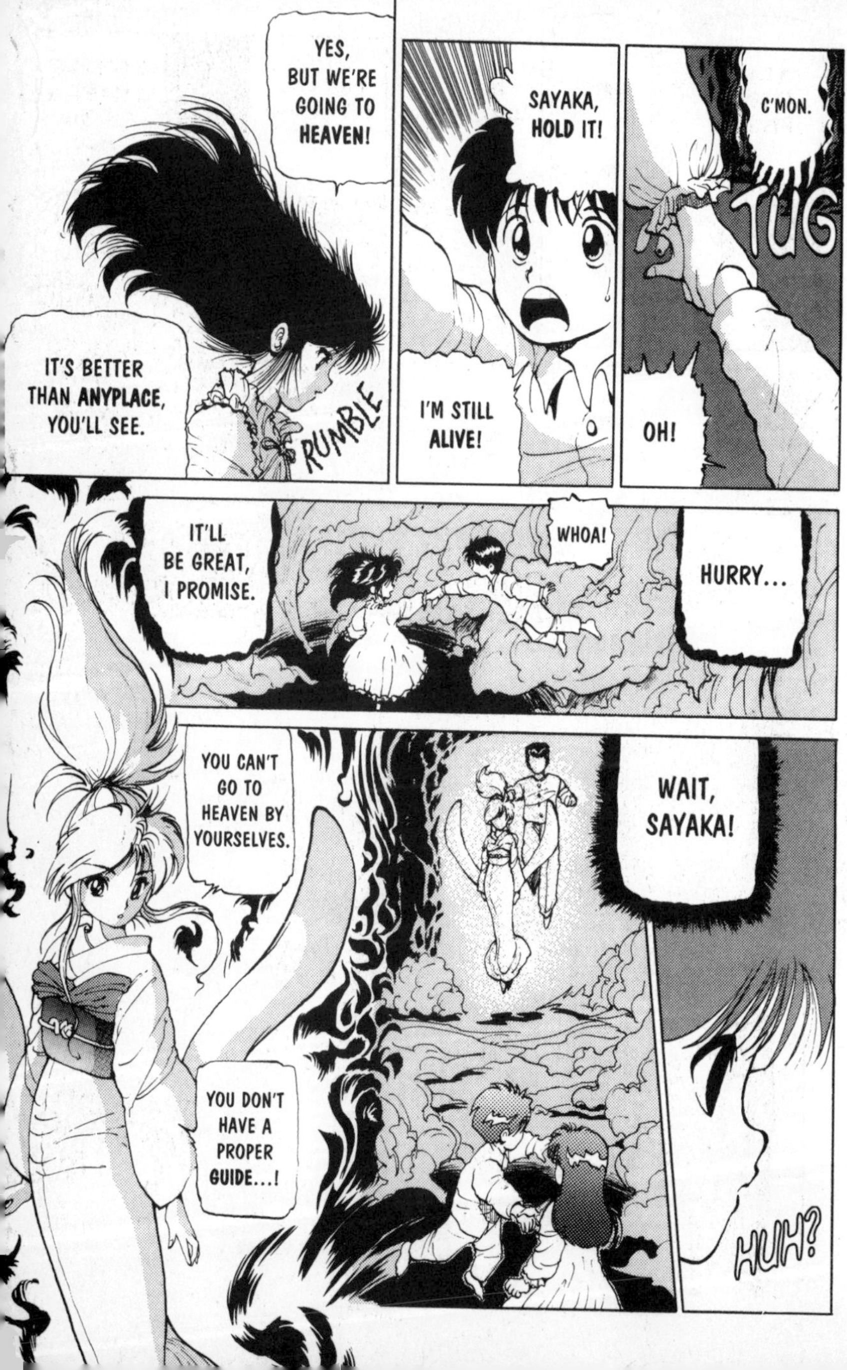
C'MON.
TUG
OH!
SAYAKA, HOLD IT!
I'M STILL ALIVE!
YES, BUT WE'RE GOING TO HEAVEN!
IT'S BETTER THAN ANYPLACE, YOU'LL SEE.
RUMBLE
HURRY...
WHOA!
IT'LL BE GREAT, I PROMISE.
WAIT, SAYAKA!
HUH?
YOU CAN'T GO TO HEAVEN BY YOURSELVES.
YOU DON'T HAVE A PROPER GUIDE...!

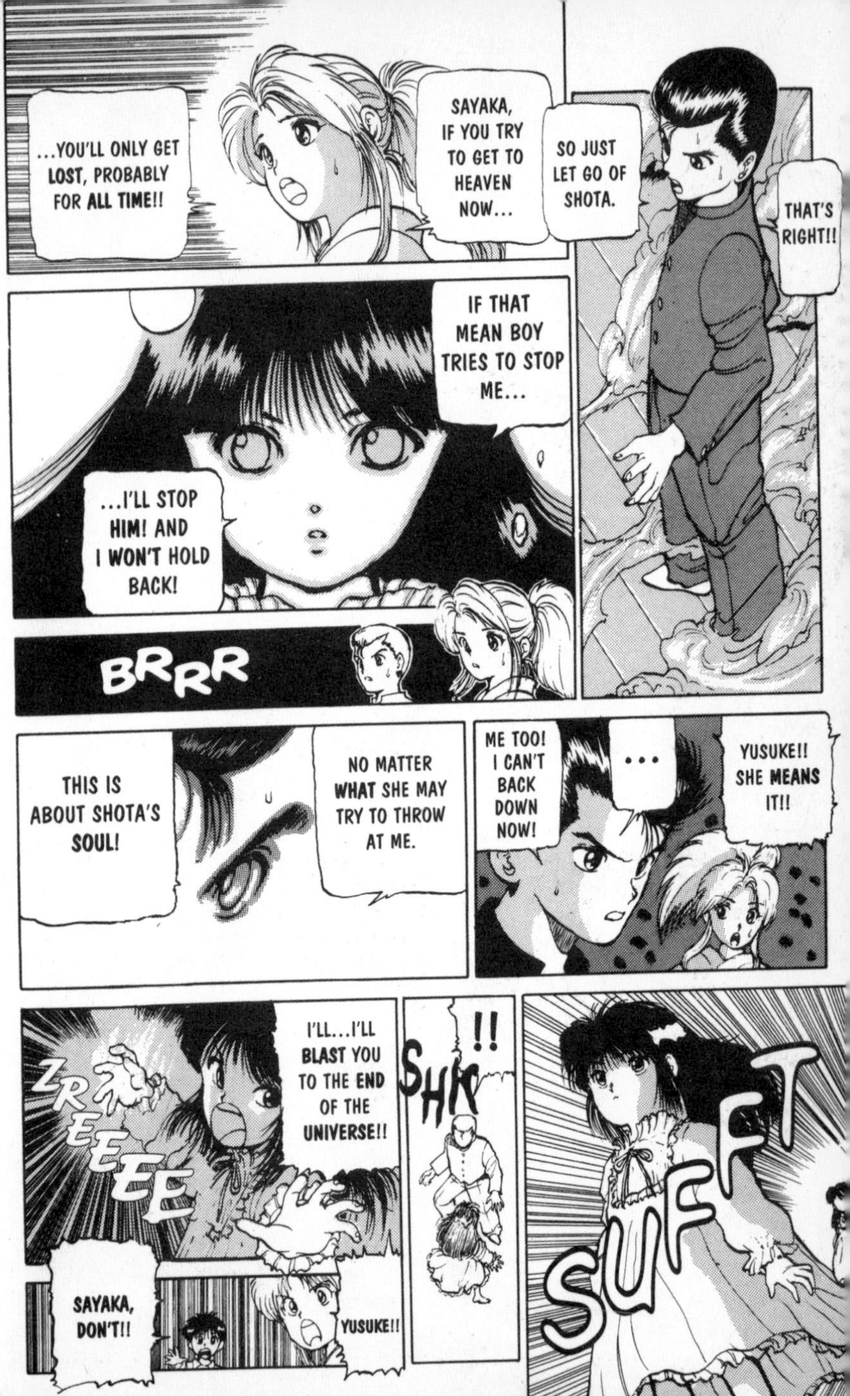
THAT'S RIGHT!!
SO JUST LET GO OF SHOTA.
SAYAKA, IF YOU TRY TO GET TO HEAVEN NOW...
...YOU'LL ONLY GET LOST, PROBABLY FOR ALL TIME!!
IF THAT MEAN BOY TRIES TO STOP ME...
...I'LL STOP HIM! AND I WON'T HOLD BACK!
BRRR
YUSUKE!! SHE MEANS IT!!
...
ME TOO! I CAN'T BACK DOWN NOW!
NO MATTER WHAT SHE MAY TRY TO THROW AT ME.
THIS IS ABOUT SHOTA'S SOUL!
SUFFT
!!
SHK
I'LL...I'LL BLAST YOU TO THE END OF THE UNIVERSE!!
ZREEEEEE
YUSUKE!!
SAYAKA, DON'T!!

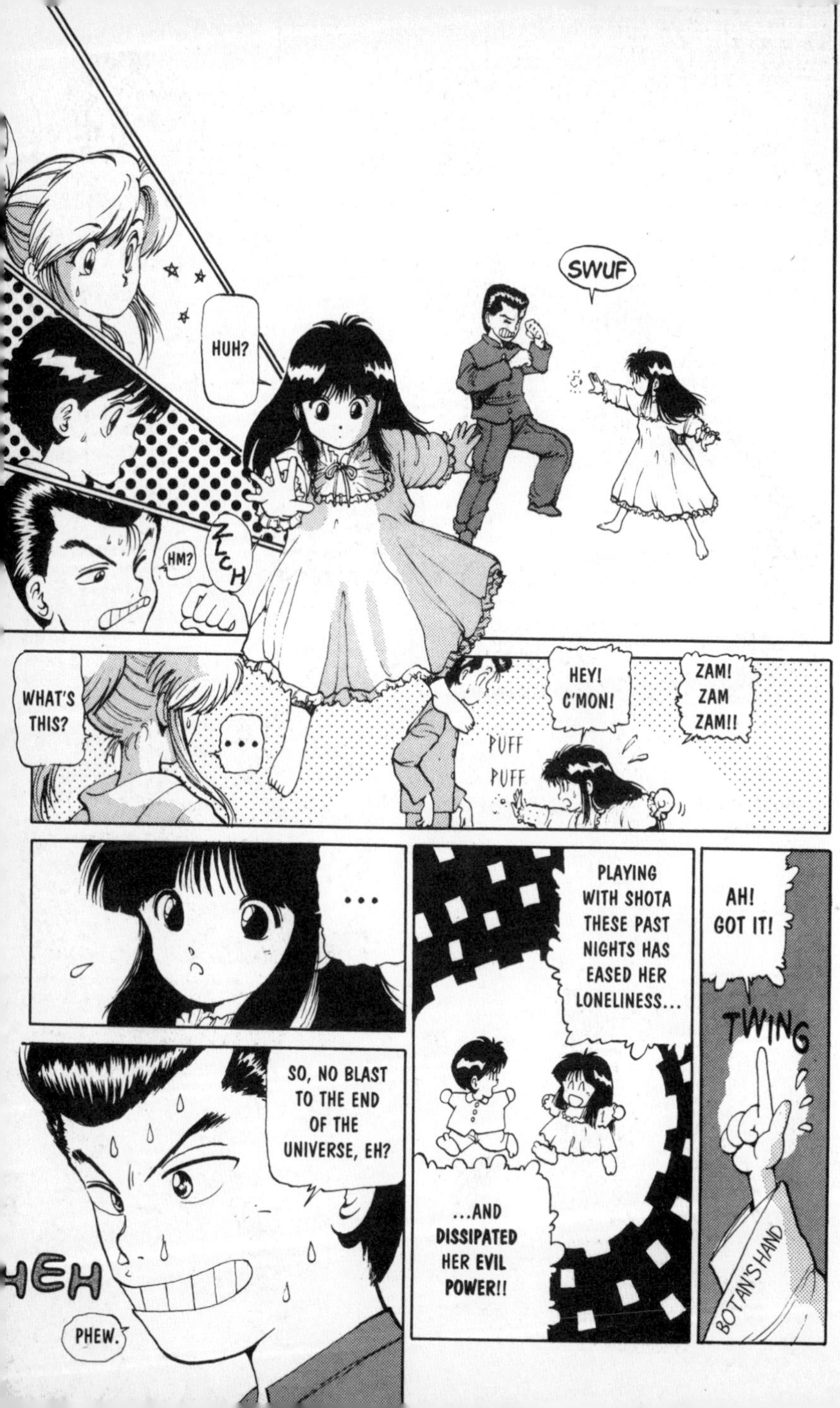
SWUF
HUH?
ZLCH
HM?
ZAM! ZAM ZAM!!
HEY! C'MON!
PUFF PUFF
WHAT'S THIS?
...
AH! GOT IT!
TWING
BOTAN'S HAND
PLAYING WITH SHOTA THESE PAST NIGHTS HAS EASED HER LONELINESS...
...AND DISSIPATED HER EVIL POWER!!
...
SO, NO BLAST TO THE END OF THE UNIVERSE, EH?
HEH
PHEW.

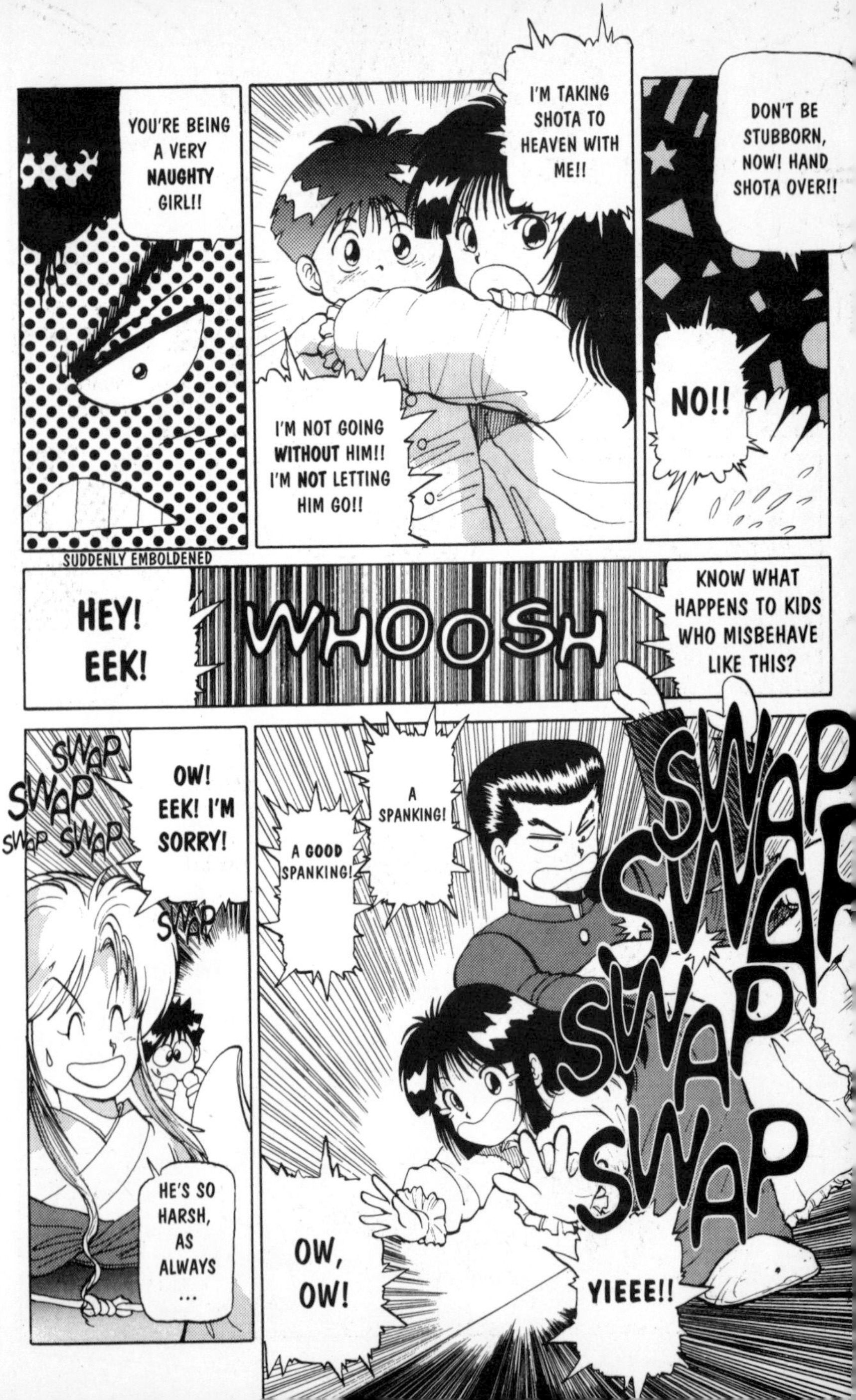
DON'T BE STUBBORN, NOW! HAND SHOTA OVER!!
NO!!
I'M TAKING SHOTA TO HEAVEN WITH ME!!
I'M NOT GOING WITHOUT HIM!! I'M NOT LETTING HIM GO!!
YOU'RE BEING A VERY NAUGHTY GIRL!!
SUDDENLY EMBOLDENED
KNOW WHAT HAPPENS TO KIDS WHO MISBEHAVE LIKE THIS?
WHOOSH
HEY! EEK!
A SPANKING!
A GOOD SPANKING!
SWAP SWAP SWAP SWAP
YIEEE!!
OW, OW!
SWAP SWAP SWAP SWAP
OW! EEK! I'M SORRY!
SWAP
HE'S SO HARSH, AS ALWAYS ...

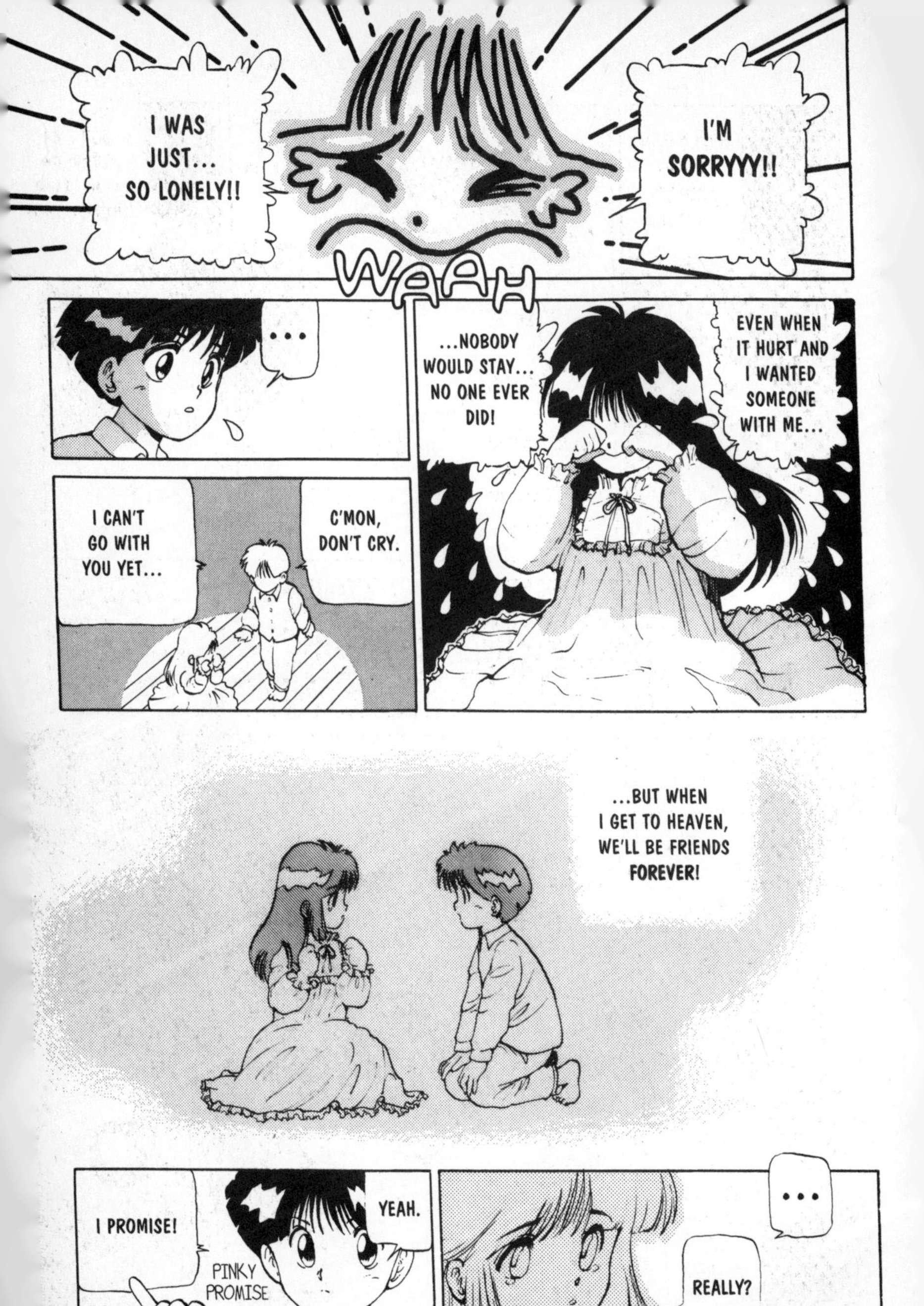
I'M SORRYYY!!
I WAS JUST... SO LONELY!!
WAAH
EVEN WHEN IT HURT AND I WANTED SOMEONE WITH ME...
...NOBODY WOULD STAY... NO ONE EVER DID!
...
C'MON, DON'T CRY.
I CAN'T GO WITH YOU YET...
...BUT WHEN I GET TO HEAVEN, WE'LL BE FRIENDS FOREVER!
...
REALLY?
YEAH.
I PROMISE!
PINKY PROMISE

READ THIS WAY

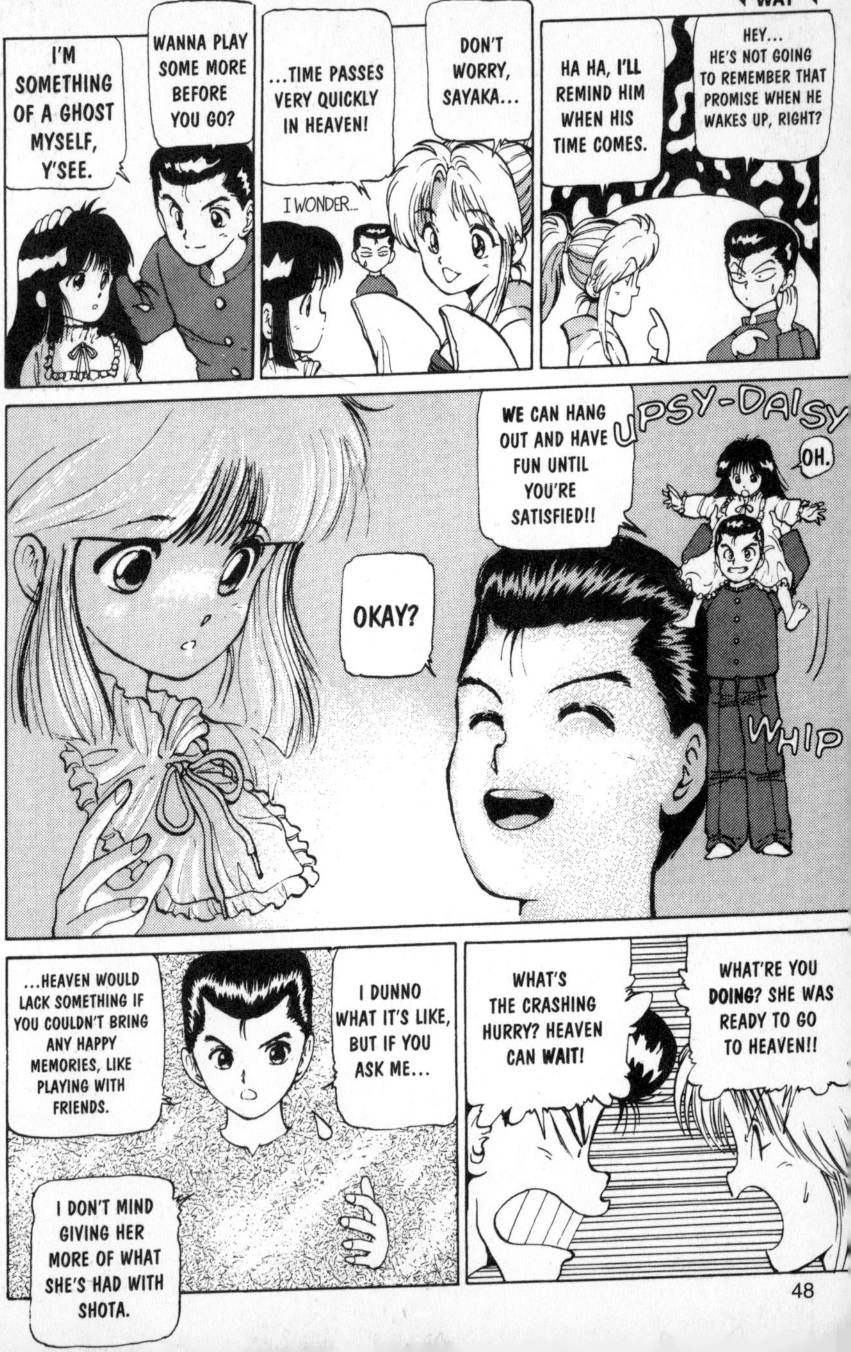

HEY... HE'S NOT GOING TO REMEMBER THAT PROMISE WHEN HE WAKES UP, RIGHT?
HA HA, I'LL REMIND HIM WHEN HIS TIME COMES.
DON'T WORRY, SAYAKA...
...TIME PASSES VERY QUICKLY IN HEAVEN!
I WONDER...
WANNA PLAY SOME MORE BEFORE YOU GO?
I'M SOMETHING OF A GHOST MYSELF, Y'SEE.
UPSY-DAISY
OH.
WE CAN HANG OUT AND HAVE FUN UNTIL YOU'RE SATISFIED!!
WHIP
OKAY?
WHAT'RE YOU DOING? SHE WAS READY TO GO TO HEAVEN!!
WHAT'S THE CRASHING HURRY? HEAVEN CAN WAIT!
I DUNNO WHAT IT'S LIKE, BUT IF YOU ASK ME...
...HEAVEN WOULD LACK SOMETHING IF YOU COULDN'T BRING ANY HAPPY MEMORIES, LIKE PLAYING WITH FRIENDS.
I DON'T MIND GIVING HER MORE OF WHAT SHE'S HAD WITH SHOTA.

READ THIS WAY

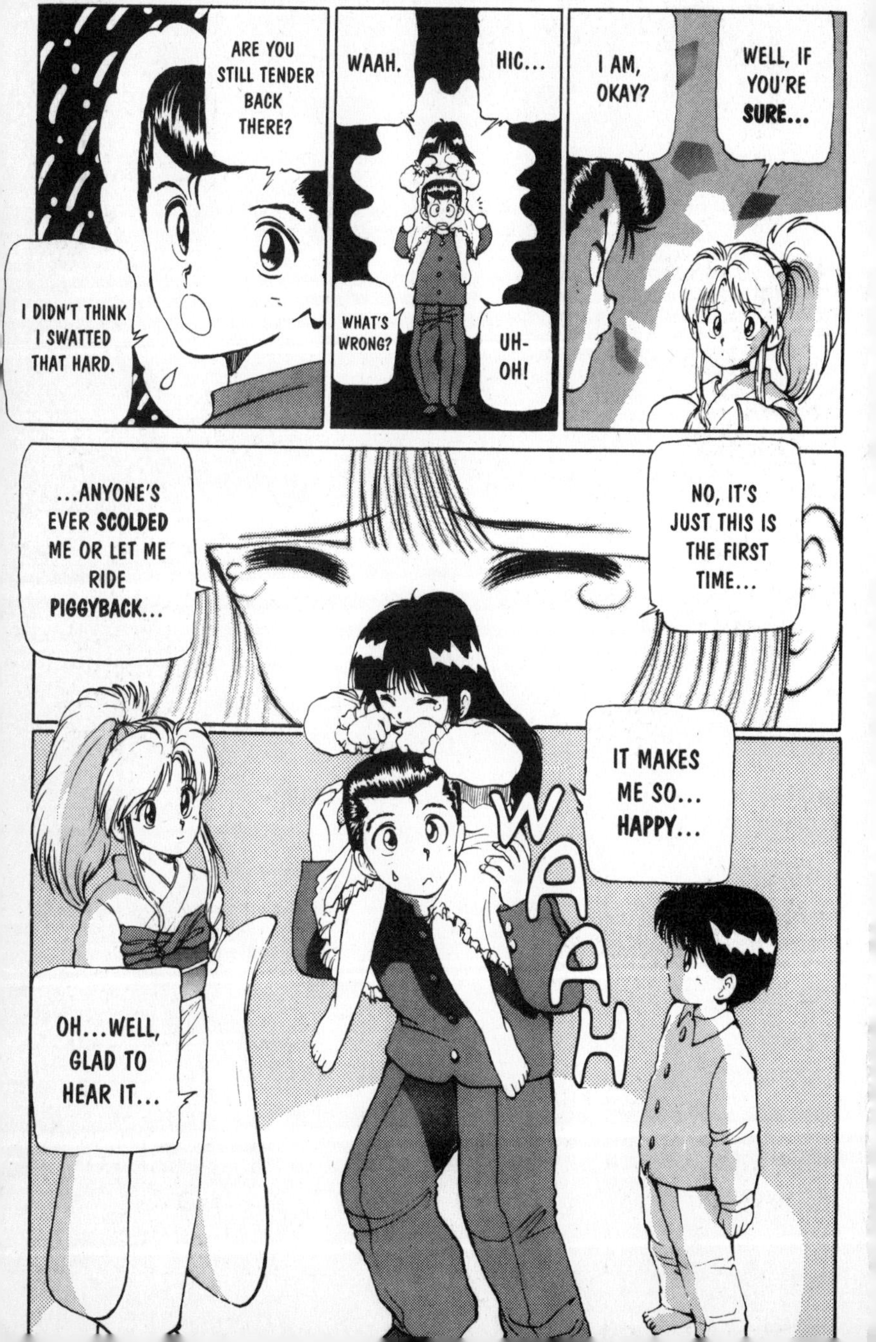
WELL, IF YOU'RE SURE...
I AM, OKAY?
HIC...
WAAH.
UH-OH!
WHAT'S WRONG?
ARE YOU STILL TENDER BACK THERE?
I DIDN'T THINK I SWATTED THAT HARD.
NO, IT'S JUST THIS IS THE FIRST TIME...
...ANYONE'S EVER SCOLDED ME OR LET ME RIDE PIGGYBACK...
IT MAKES ME SO... HAPPY...
WAAAH
OH...WELL, GLAD TO HEAR IT...

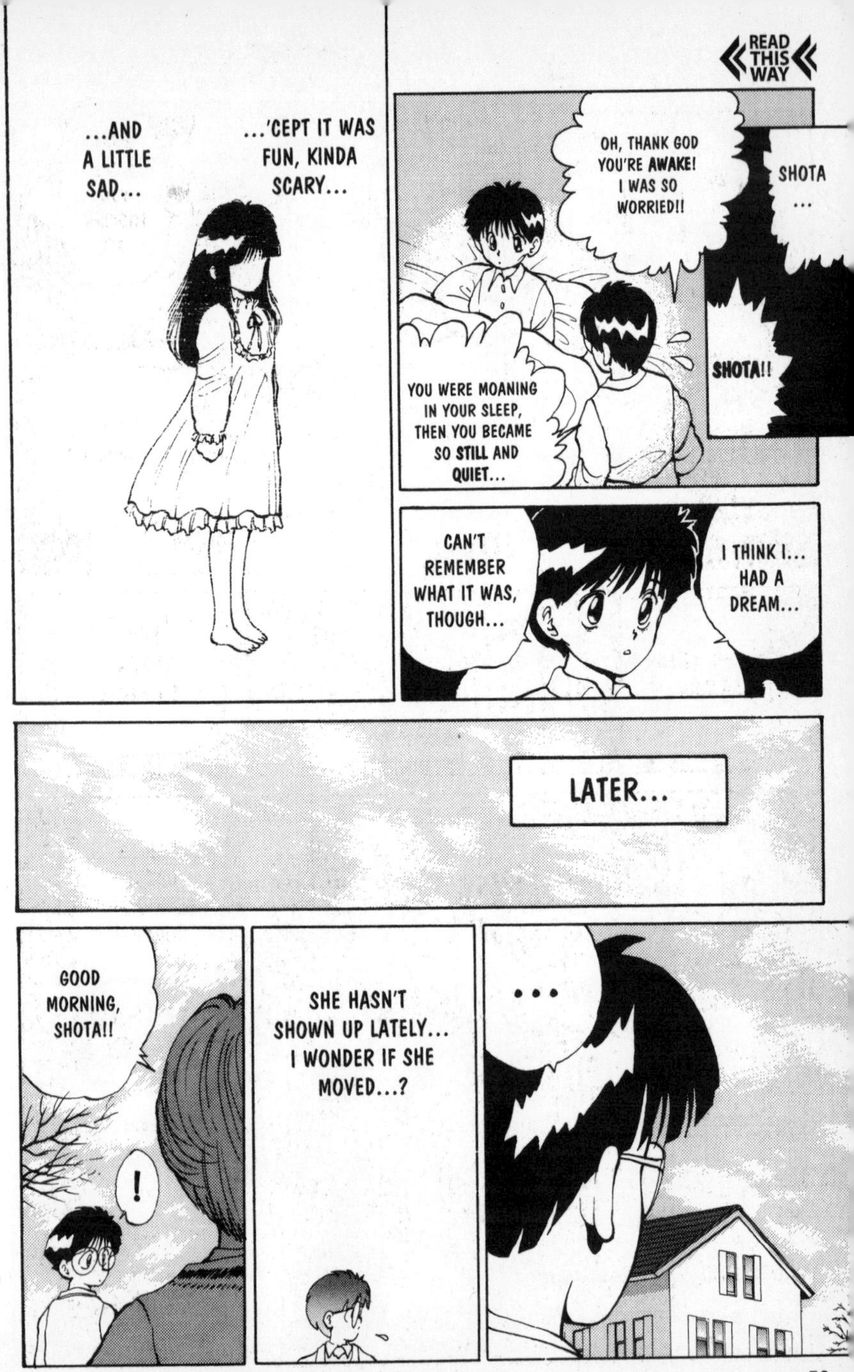

READ THIS WAY
SHOTA...
SHOTA!!
OH, THANK GOD YOU'RE AWAKE! I WAS SO WORRIED!!
YOU WERE MOANING IN YOUR SLEEP, THEN YOU BECAME SO STILL AND QUIET...
I THINK I... HAD A DREAM...
CAN'T REMEMBER WHAT IT WAS, THOUGH...
...'CEPT IT WAS FUN, KINDA SCARY...
...AND A LITTLE SAD...
LATER...
...
SHE HASN'T SHOWN UP LATELY... I WONDER IF SHE MOVED...?
GOOD MORNING, SHOTA!!
!

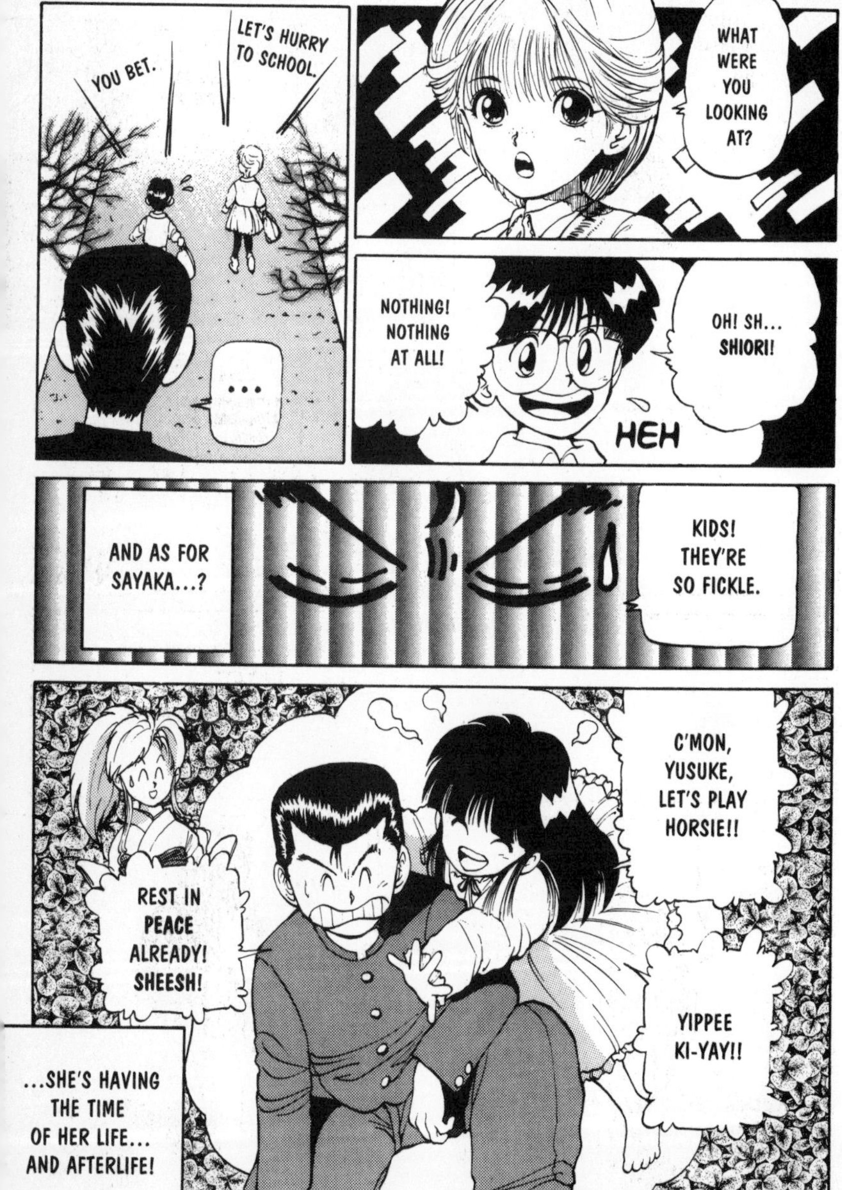
WHAT WERE YOU LOOKING AT?
OH! SH... SHIORI!
NOTHING! NOTHING AT ALL!
HEH
LET'S HURRY TO SCHOOL.
YOU BET.
...
KIDS! THEY'RE SO FICKLE.
AND AS FOR SAYAKA...?
C'MON, YUSUKE, LET'S PLAY HORSIE!!
YIPPEE KI-YAY!!
REST IN PEACE ALREADY! SHEESH!
...SHE'S HAVING THE TIME OF HER LIFE... AND AFTERLIFE!

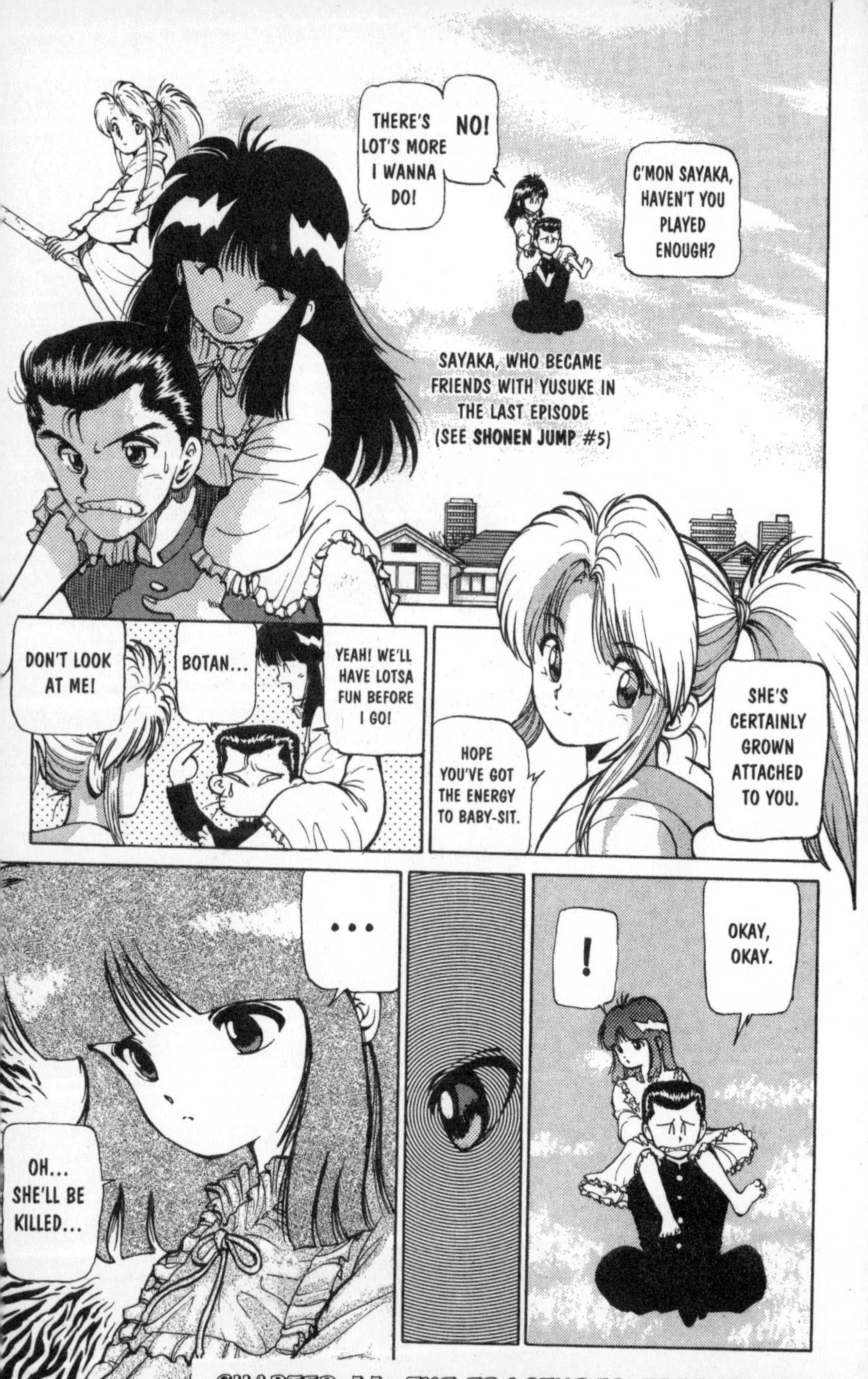
C'MON SAYAKA, HAVEN'T YOU PLAYED ENOUGH?
NO!
THERE'S LOT'S MORE I WANNA DO!
SAYAKA, WHO BECAME FRIENDS WITH YUSUKE IN THE LAST EPISODE (SEE SHONEN JUMP #5)
SHE'S CERTAINLY GROWN ATTACHED TO YOU.
HOPE YOU'VE GOT THE ENERGY TO BABY-SIT.
YEAH! WE'LL HAVE LOTSA FUN BEFORE I GO!
BOTAN...
DON'T LOOK AT ME!
OKAY, OKAY.
!
...
OH... SHE'LL BE KILLED...

CHAPTER 11: THE FRACTURED FRIENDSHIP

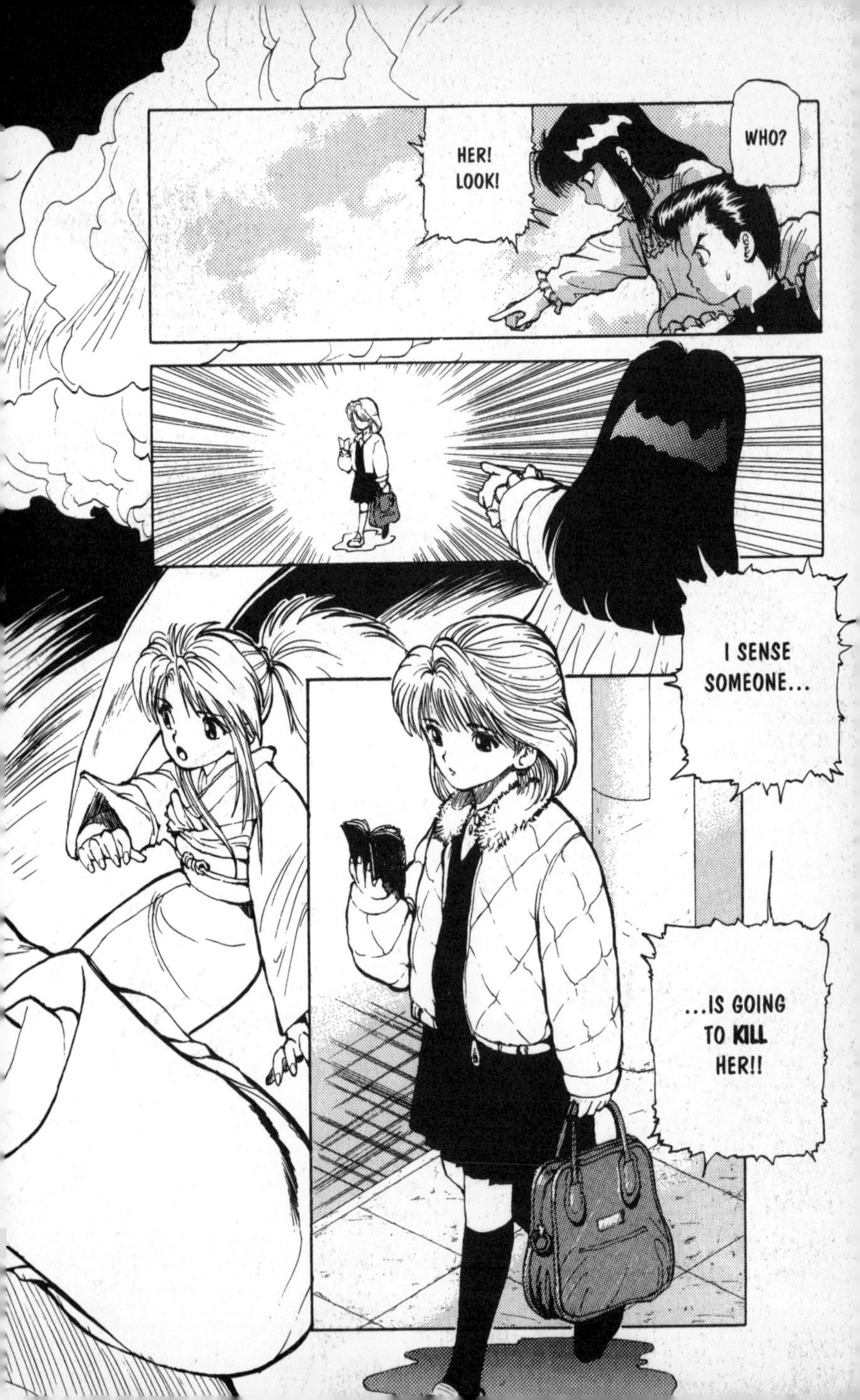
WHO?
HER! LOOK!
I SENSE SOMEONE...
...IS GOING TO KILL HER!!

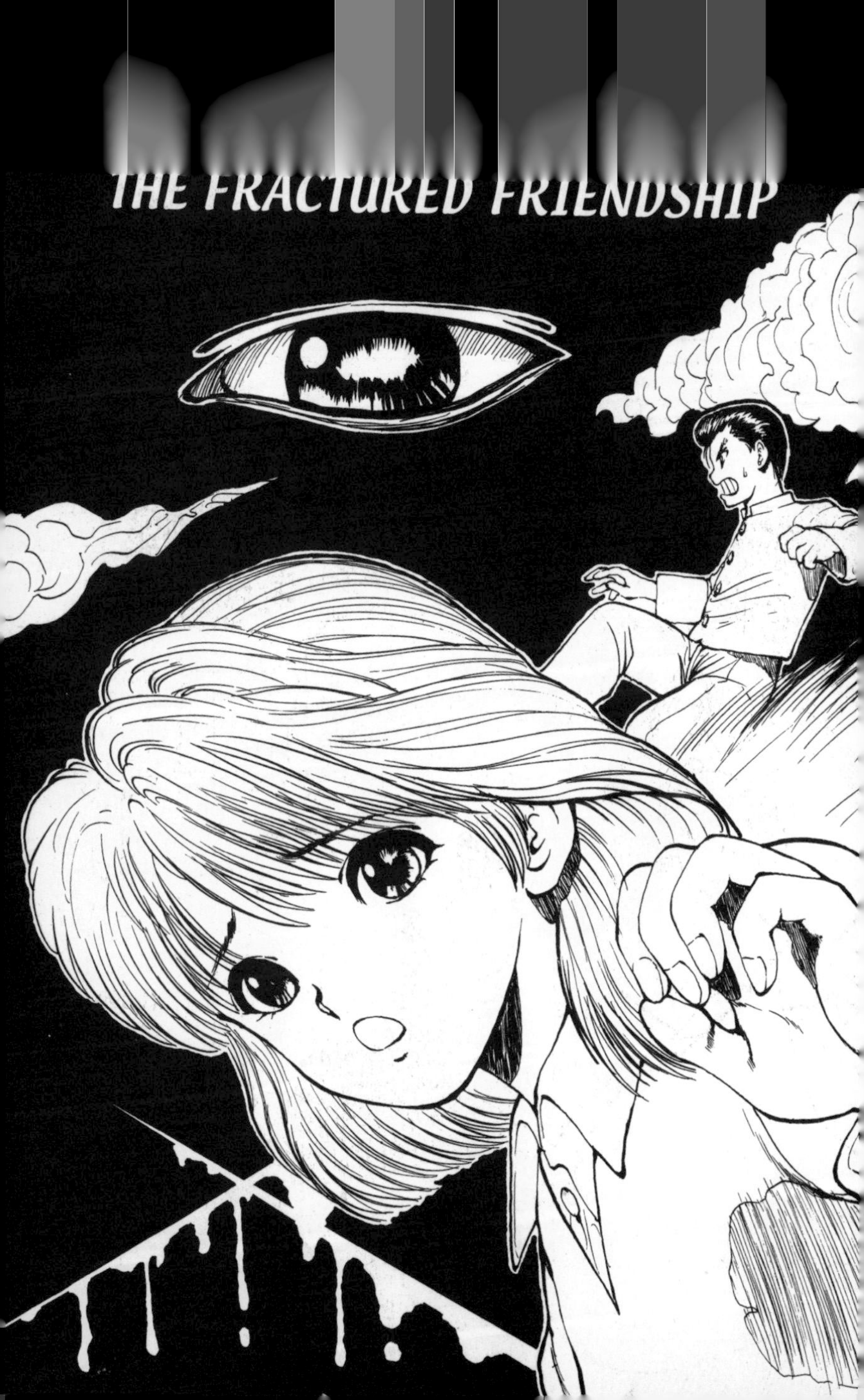
THE FRACTURED FRIENDSHIP

READ THIS WAY

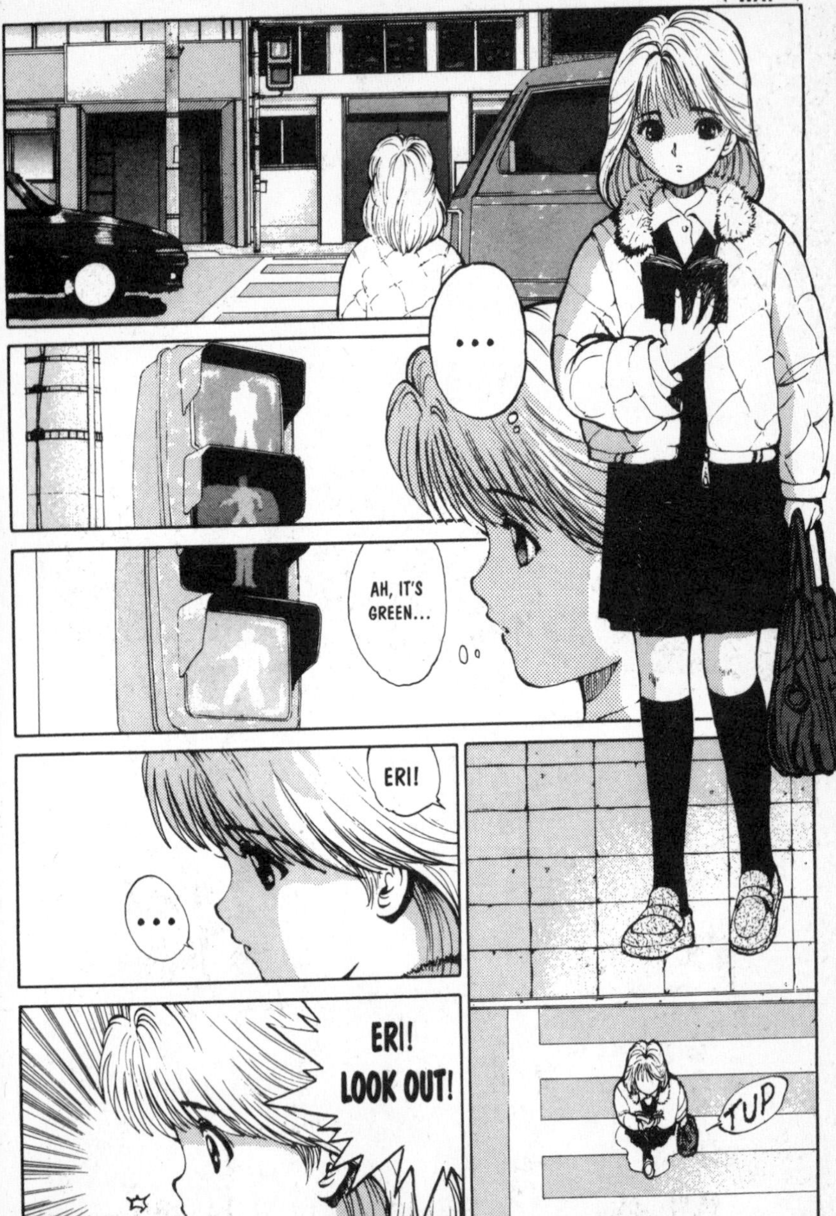
...
AH, IT'S GREEN...
ERI!
...
TUP
ERI! LOOK OUT!

READ THIS WAY

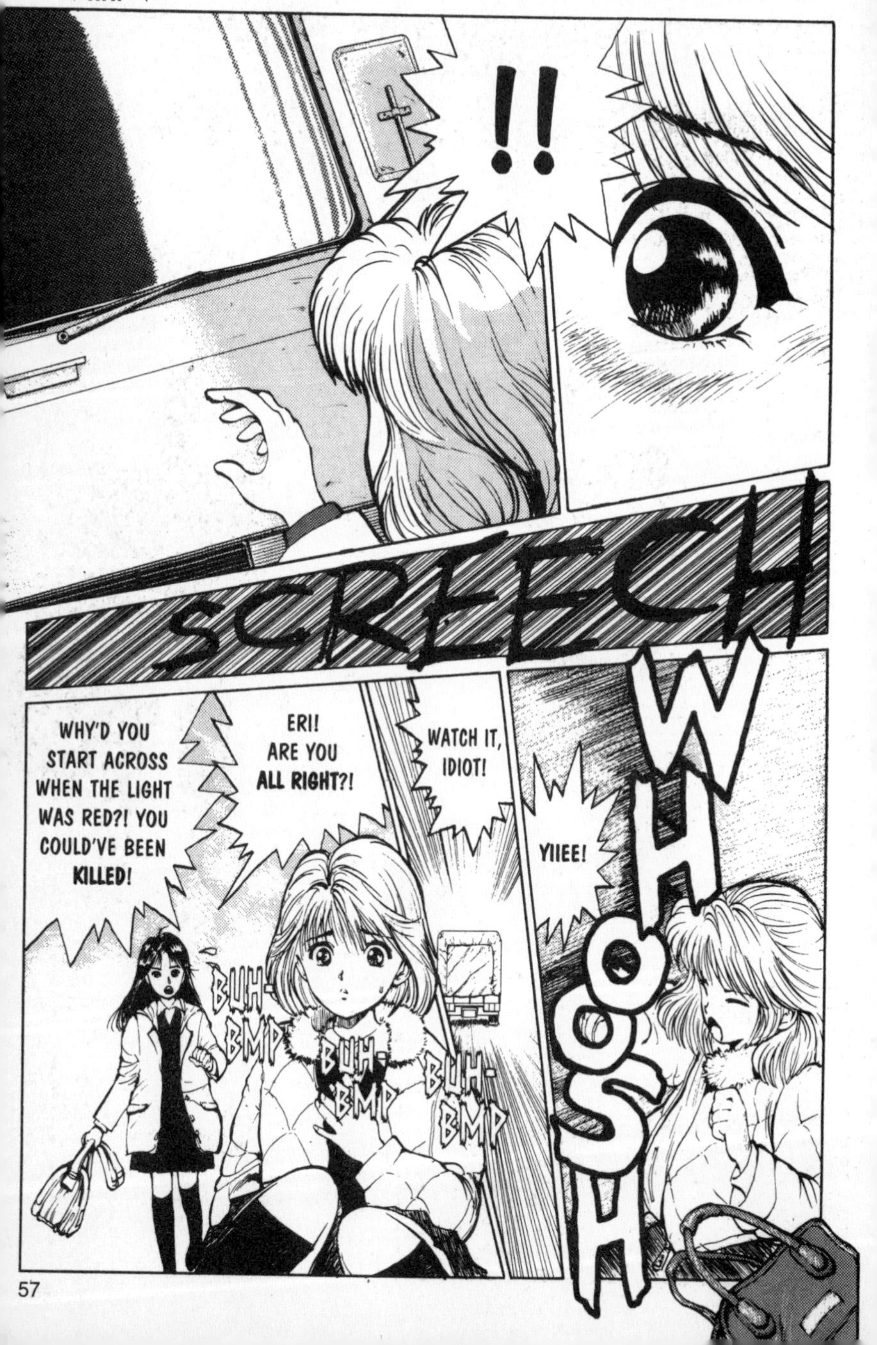
!!
SCREECH
WHOOSH
YIIEE!
WATCH IT, IDIOT!
ERI! ARE YOU ALL RIGHT?!
WHY'D YOU START ACROSS WHEN THE LIGHT WAS RED?! YOU COULD'VE BEEN KILLED!
BUH-BMP
BUH-BMP
BUH-BMP

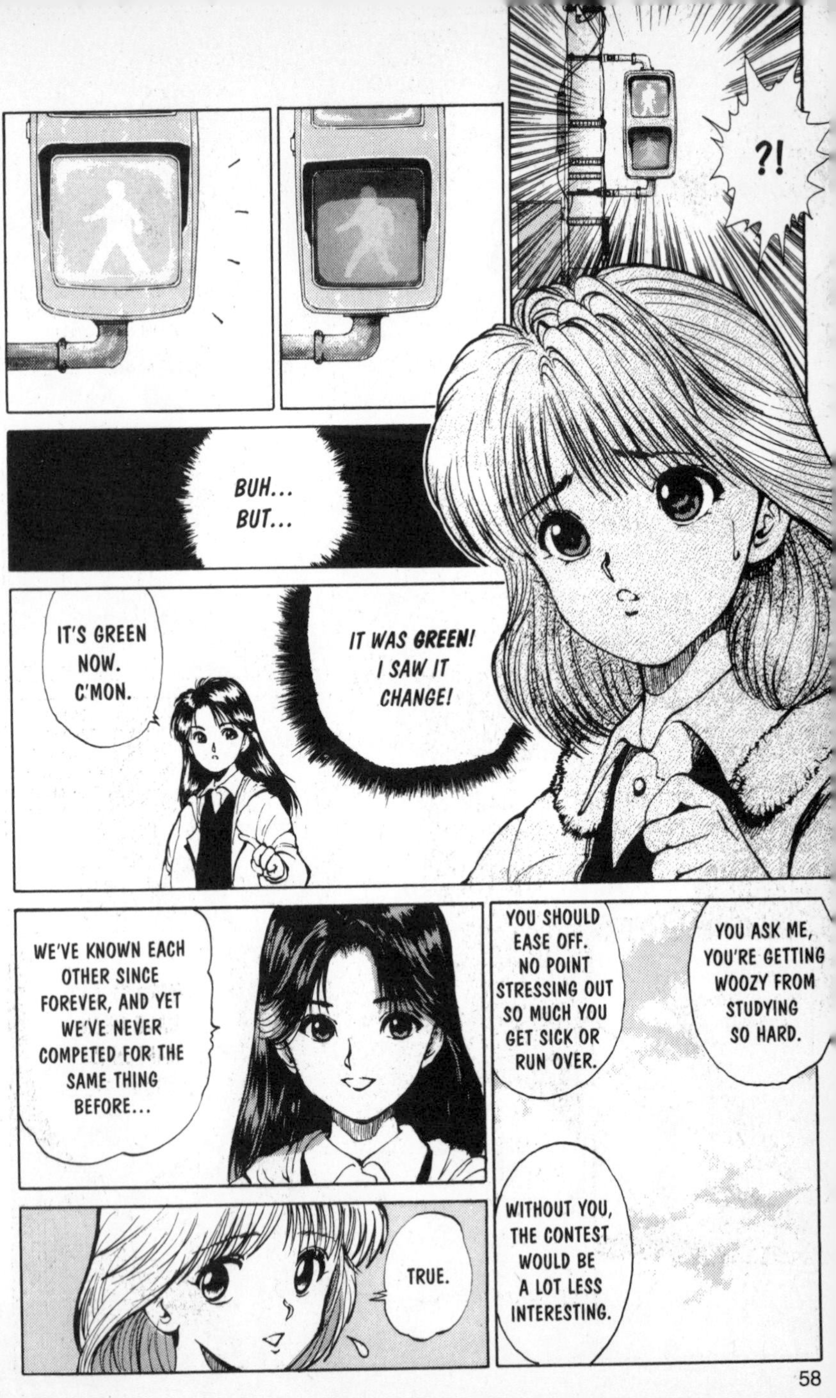
?!
BUH... BUT...
IT WAS GREEN! I SAW IT CHANGE!
IT'S GREEN NOW. C'MON.
YOU ASK ME, YOU'RE GETTING WOOZY FROM STUDYING SO HARD.
YOU SHOULD EASE OFF. NO POINT STRESSING OUT SO MUCH YOU GET SICK OR RUN OVER.
WITHOUT YOU, THE CONTEST WOULD BE A LOT LESS INTERESTING.
WE'VE KNOWN EACH OTHER SINCE FOREVER, AND YET WE'VE NEVER COMPETED FOR THE SAME THING BEFORE...
TRUE.

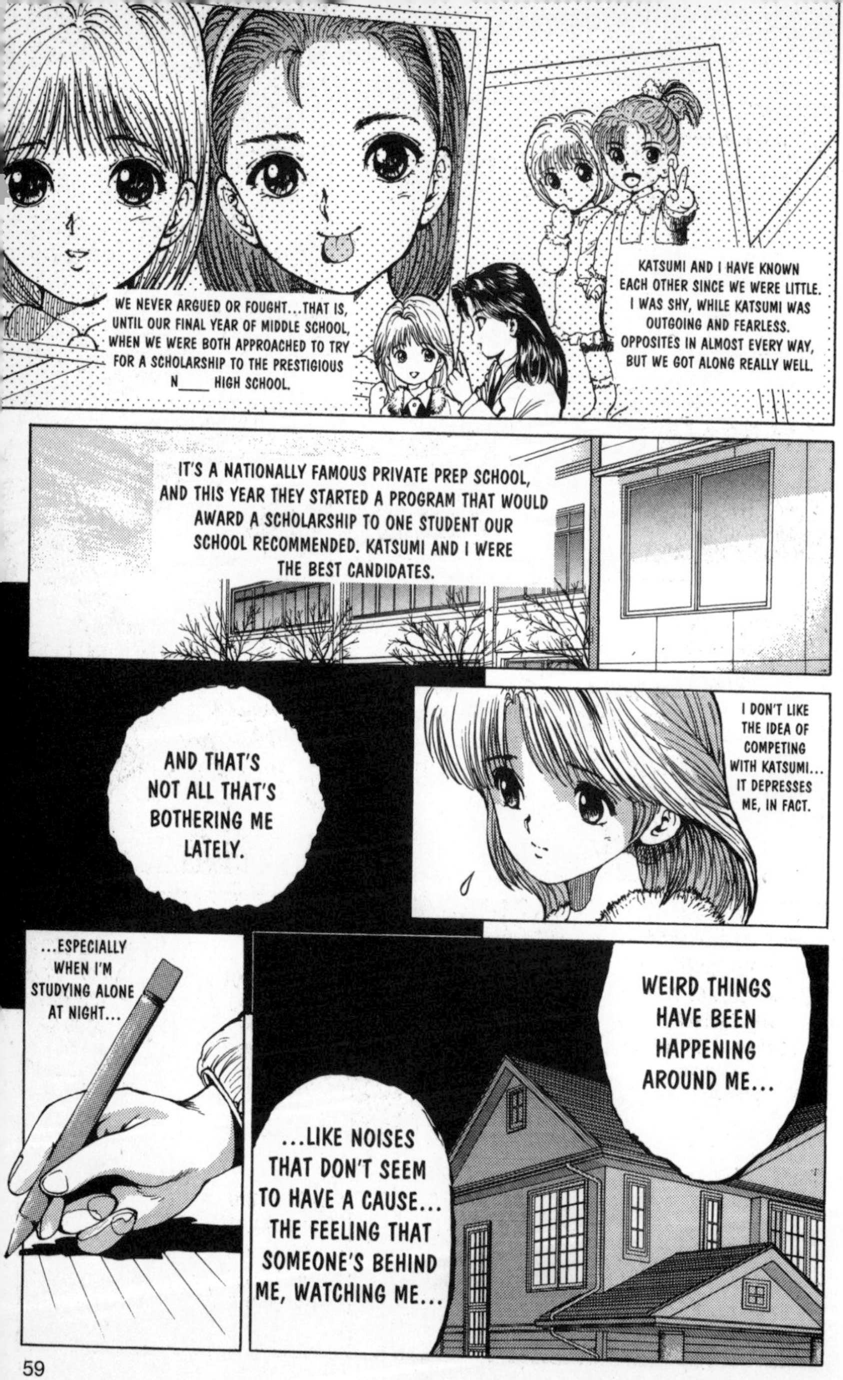
KATSUMI AND I HAVE KNOWN EACH OTHER SINCE WE WERE LITTLE. I WAS SHY, WHILE KATSUMI WAS OUTGOING AND FEARLESS. OPPOSITES IN ALMOST EVERY WAY, BUT WE GOT ALONG REALLY WELL.
WE NEVER ARGUED OR FOUGHT...THAT IS, UNTIL OUR FINAL YEAR OF MIDDLE SCHOOL, WHEN WE WERE BOTH APPROACHED TO TRY FOR A SCHOLARSHIP TO THE PRESTIGIOUS N____ HIGH SCHOOL.
IT'S A NATIONALLY FAMOUS PRIVATE PREP SCHOOL, AND THIS YEAR THEY STARTED A PROGRAM THAT WOULD AWARD A SCHOLARSHIP TO ONE STUDENT OUR SCHOOL RECOMMENDED. KATSUMI AND I WERE THE BEST CANDIDATES.
I DON'T LIKE THE IDEA OF COMPETING WITH KATSUMI... IT DEPRESSES ME, IN FACT.
AND THAT'S NOT ALL THAT'S BOTHERING ME LATELY.
WEIRD THINGS HAVE BEEN HAPPENING AROUND ME...
...LIKE NOISES THAT DON'T SEEM TO HAVE A CAUSE... THE FEELING THAT SOMEONE'S BEHIND ME, WATCHING ME...
...ESPECIALLY WHEN I'M STUDYING ALONE AT NIGHT...

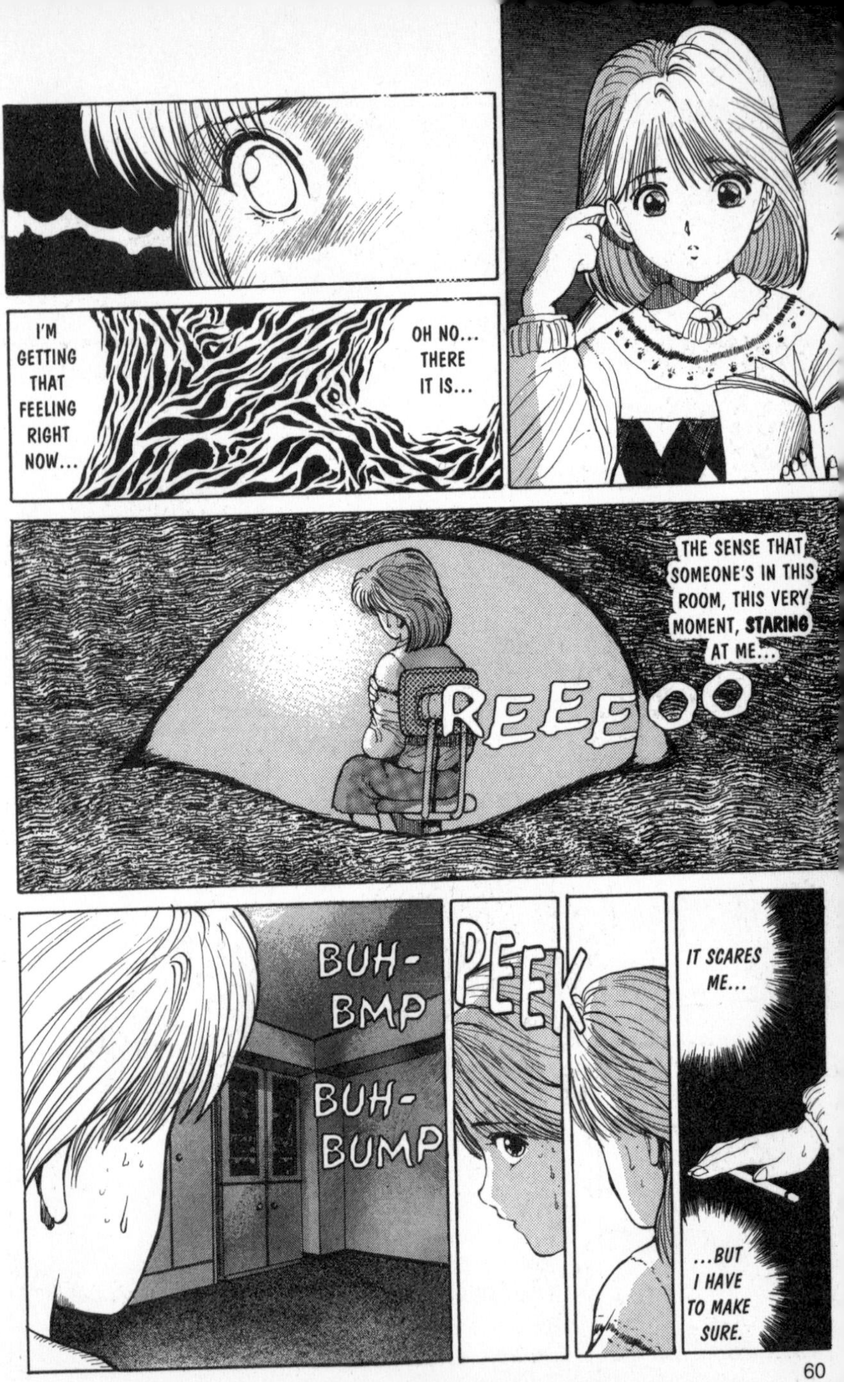
OH NO... THERE IT IS...
I'M GETTING THAT FEELING RIGHT NOW...
THE SENSE THAT SOMEONE'S IN THIS ROOM, THIS VERY MOMENT, STARING AT ME...
REEEOO
IT SCARES ME...
...BUT I HAVE TO MAKE SURE.
PEEK
BUH-BMP
BUH-BUMP

READ THIS WAY

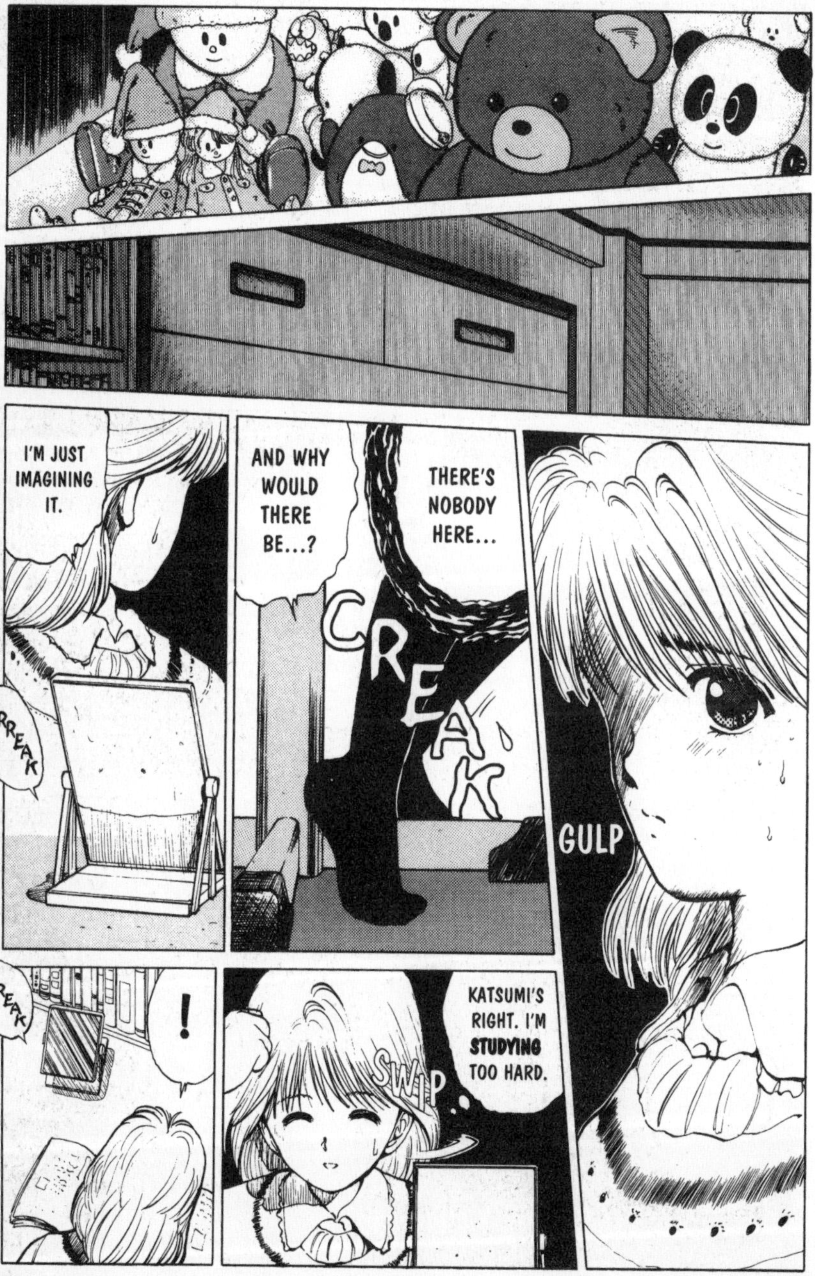
GULP
THERE'S NOBODY HERE...
AND WHY WOULD THERE BE...?
CREAK
I'M JUST IMAGINING IT.
CRREAK
KATSUMI'S RIGHT. I'M **STUDYING** TOO HARD.
SWIP
!
CRRREAK

CRREAK

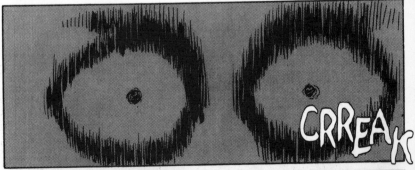

CRREAK

I CAME
TO THE NEXT
MORNING.

READ THIS WAY

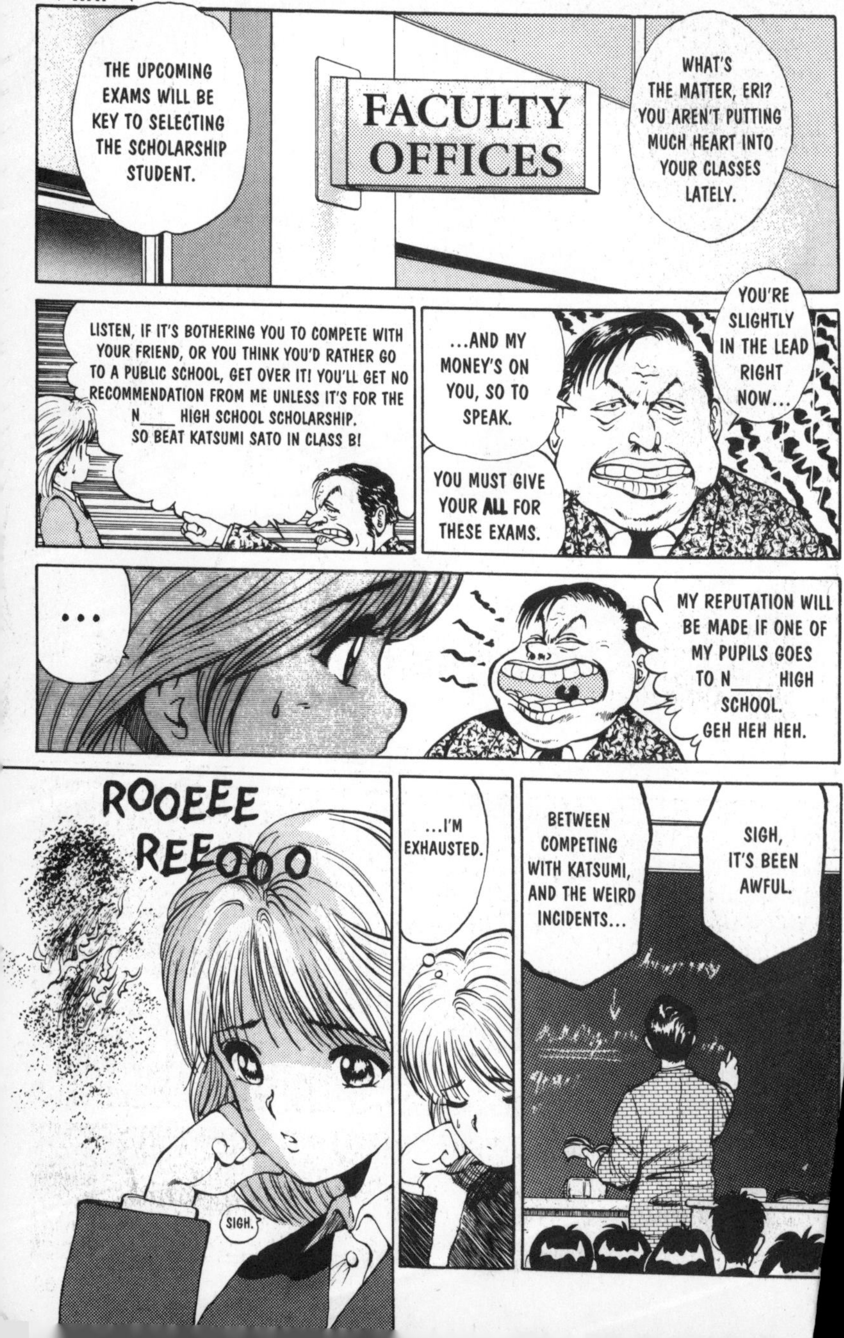
WHAT'S THE MATTER, ERI? YOU AREN'T PUTTING MUCH HEART INTO YOUR CLASSES LATELY.
FACULTY OFFICES
THE UPCOMING EXAMS WILL BE KEY TO SELECTING THE SCHOLARSHIP STUDENT.
YOU'RE SLIGHTLY IN THE LEAD RIGHT NOW...
...AND MY MONEY'S ON YOU, SO TO SPEAK.
YOU MUST GIVE YOUR ALL FOR THESE EXAMS.
LISTEN, IF IT'S BOTHERING YOU TO COMPETE WITH YOUR FRIEND, OR YOU THINK YOU'D RATHER GO TO A PUBLIC SCHOOL, GET OVER IT! YOU'LL GET NO RECOMMENDATION FROM ME UNLESS IT'S FOR THE N____ HIGH SCHOOL SCHOLARSHIP. SO BEAT KATSUMI SATO IN CLASS B!
MY REPUTATION WILL BE MADE IF ONE OF MY PUPILS GOES TO N____ HIGH SCHOOL. GEH HEH HEH.
...
SIGH, IT'S BEEN AWFUL.
BETWEEN COMPETING WITH KATSUMI, AND THE WEIRD INCIDENTS...
...I'M EXHAUSTED.
ROOEEE REEOOO
SIGH.

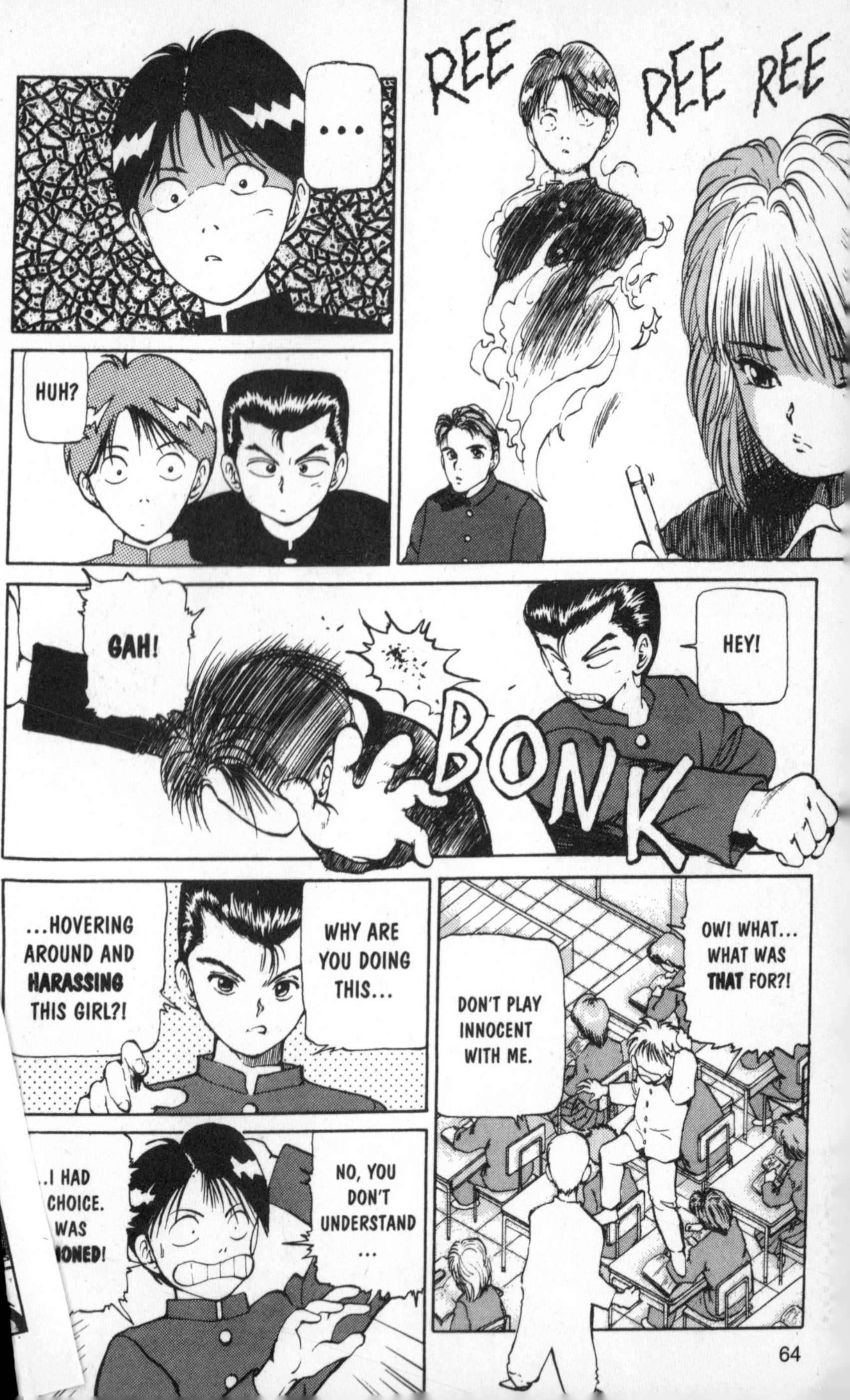
REE REE REE
...
HUH?
HEY!
BONK
GAH!
OW! WHAT... WHAT WAS THAT FOR?!
DON'T PLAY INNOCENT WITH ME.
WHY ARE YOU DOING THIS...
...HOVERING AROUND AND HARASSING THIS GIRL?!
NO, YOU DON'T UNDERSTAND ...
.I HAD CHOICE. WAS ONED!

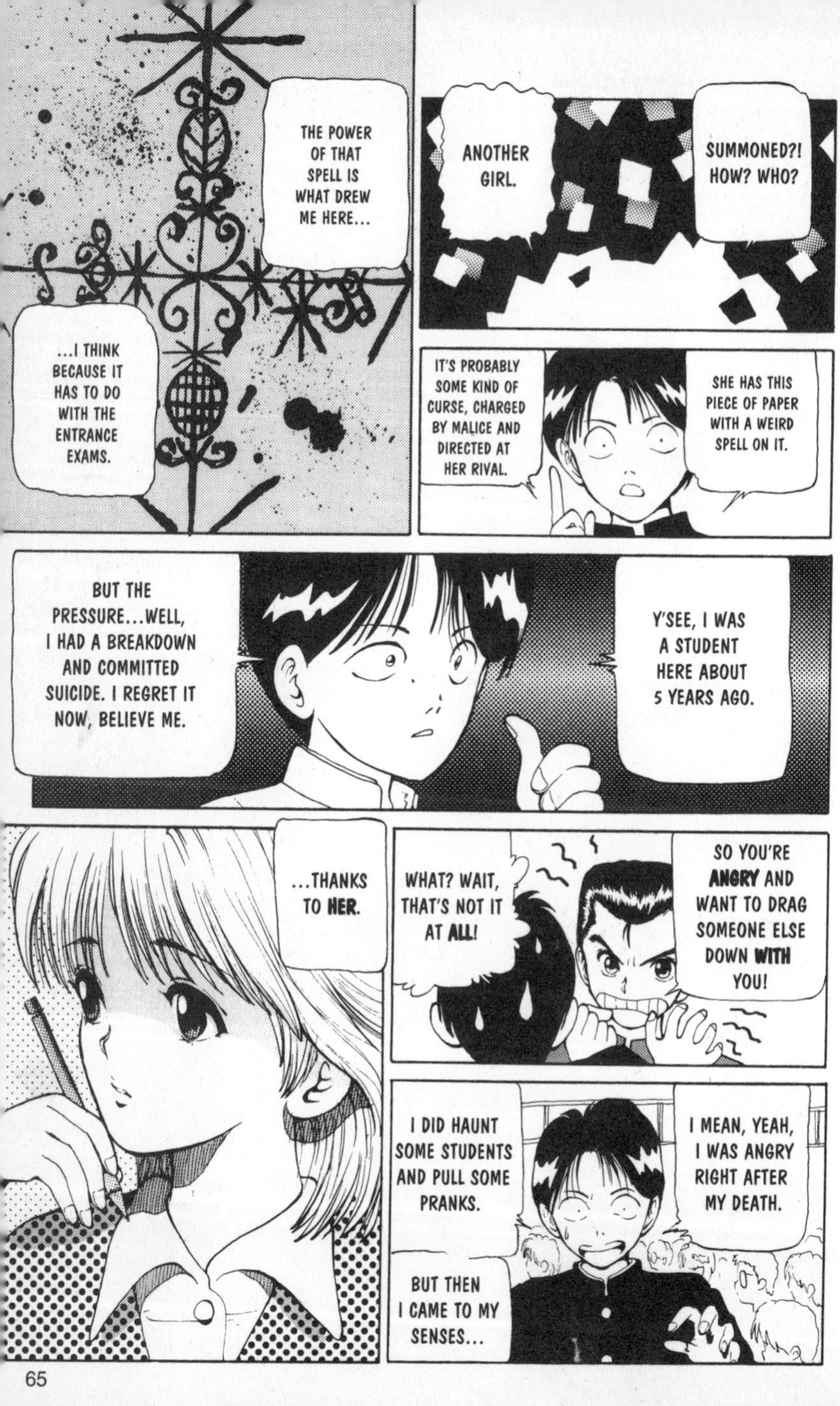
SUMMONED?! HOW? WHO?
ANOTHER GIRL.
SHE HAS THIS PIECE OF PAPER WITH A WEIRD SPELL ON IT.
IT'S PROBABLY SOME KIND OF CURSE, CHARGED BY MALICE AND DIRECTED AT HER RIVAL.
THE POWER OF THAT SPELL IS WHAT DREW ME HERE...
...I THINK BECAUSE IT HAS TO DO WITH THE ENTRANCE EXAMS.
Y'SEE, I WAS A STUDENT HERE ABOUT 5 YEARS AGO.
BUT THE PRESSURE...WELL, I HAD A BREAKDOWN AND COMMITTED SUICIDE. I REGRET IT NOW, BELIEVE ME.
SO YOU'RE ANGRY AND WANT TO DRAG SOMEONE ELSE DOWN WITH YOU!
WHAT? WAIT, THAT'S NOT IT AT ALL!
I MEAN, YEAH, I WAS ANGRY RIGHT AFTER MY DEATH.
I DID HAUNT SOME STUDENTS AND PULL SOME PRANKS.
BUT THEN I CAME TO MY SENSES...
...THANKS TO HER.

READ THIS WAY

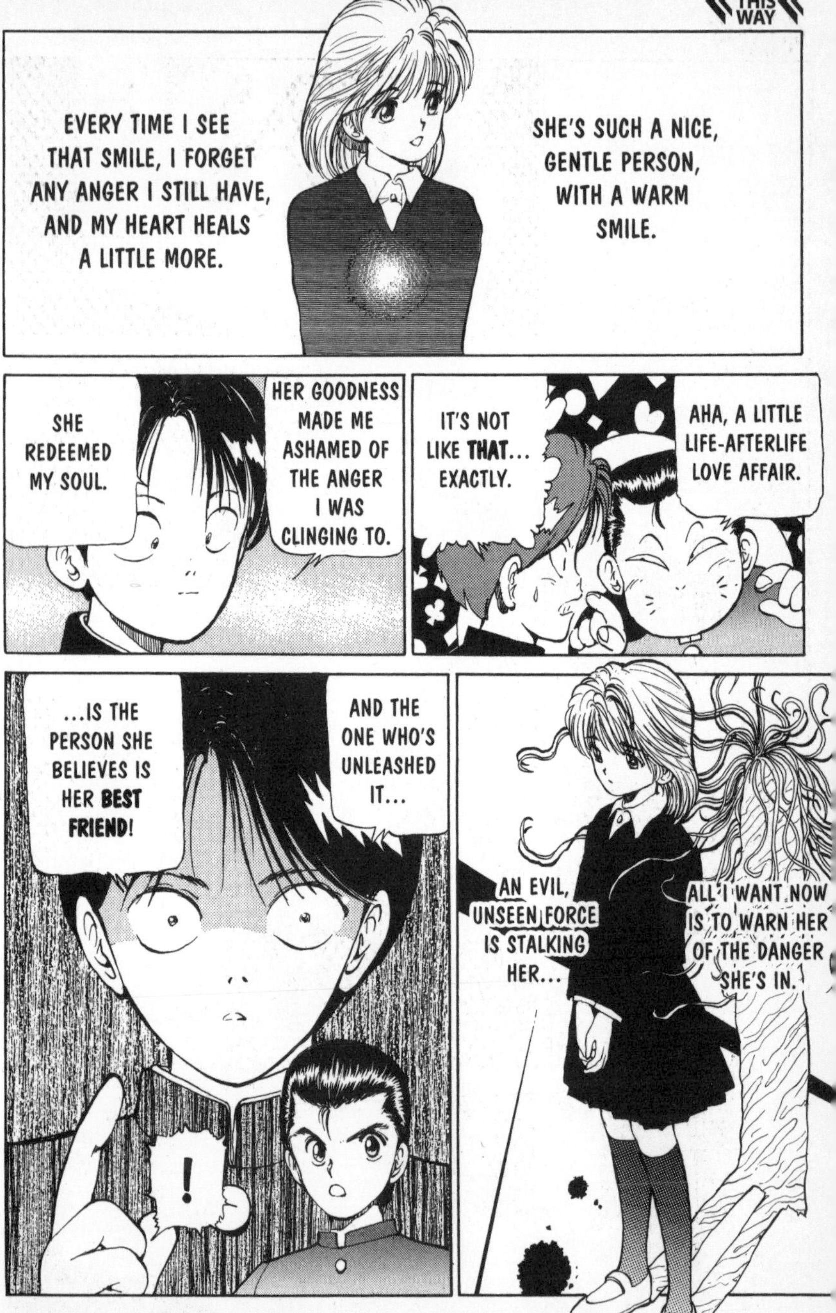
SHE'S SUCH A NICE, GENTLE PERSON, WITH A WARM SMILE.
EVERY TIME I SEE THAT SMILE, I FORGET ANY ANGER I STILL HAVE, AND MY HEART HEALS A LITTLE MORE.
AHA, A LITTLE LIFE-AFTERLIFE LOVE AFFAIR.
IT'S NOT LIKE **THAT**... EXACTLY.
HER GOODNESS MADE ME ASHAMED OF THE ANGER I WAS CLINGING TO.
SHE REDEEMED MY SOUL.
ALL I WANT NOW IS TO WARN HER OF THE DANGER SHE'S IN.
AN EVIL, UNSEEN FORCE IS STALKING HER...
AND THE ONE WHO'S UNLEASHED IT...
...IS THE PERSON SHE BELIEVES IS HER **BEST FRIEND**!
!

READ THIS WAY

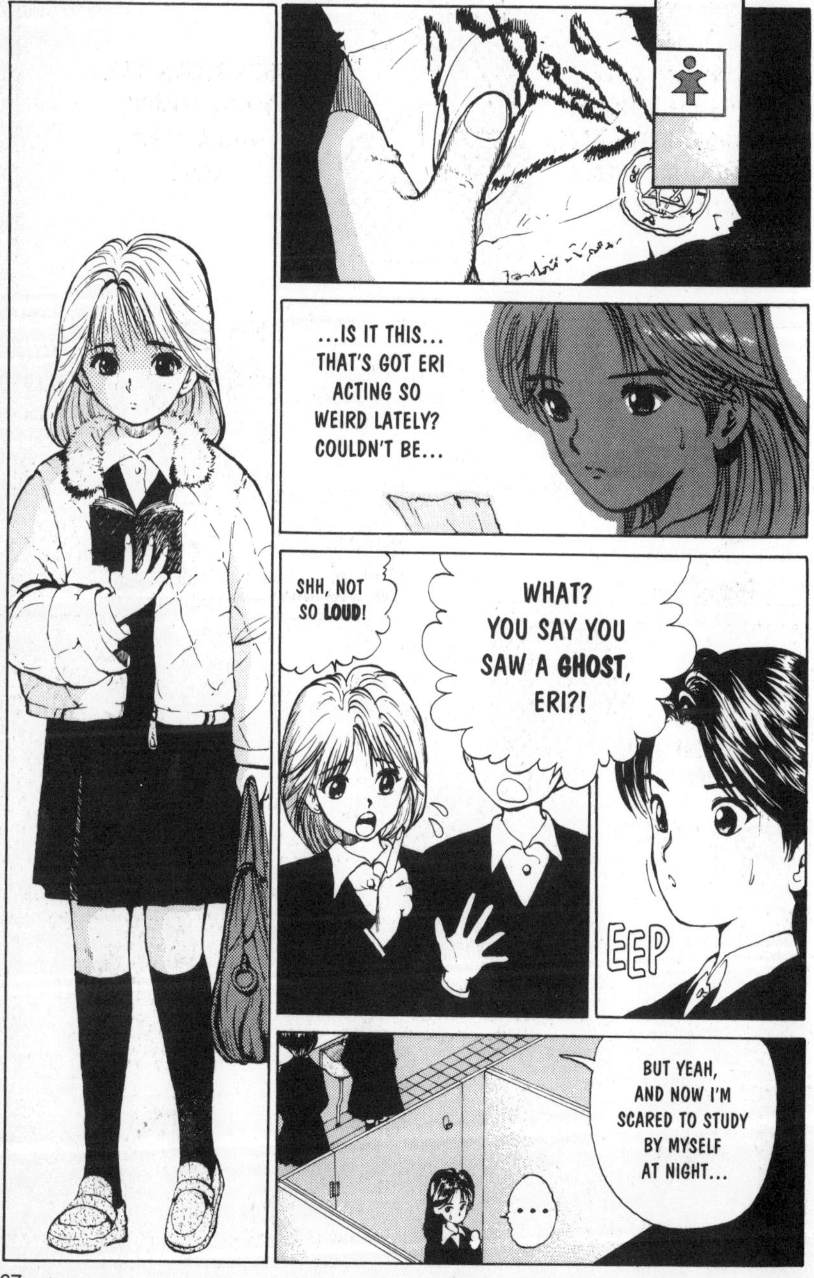
...IS IT THIS... THAT'S GOT ERI ACTING SO WEIRD LATELY? COULDN'T BE...
EEP
WHAT? YOU SAY YOU SAW A **GHOST**, ERI?!
SHH, NOT SO **LOUD**!
BUT YEAH, AND NOW I'M SCARED TO STUDY BY MYSELF AT NIGHT...
...

READ THIS WAY

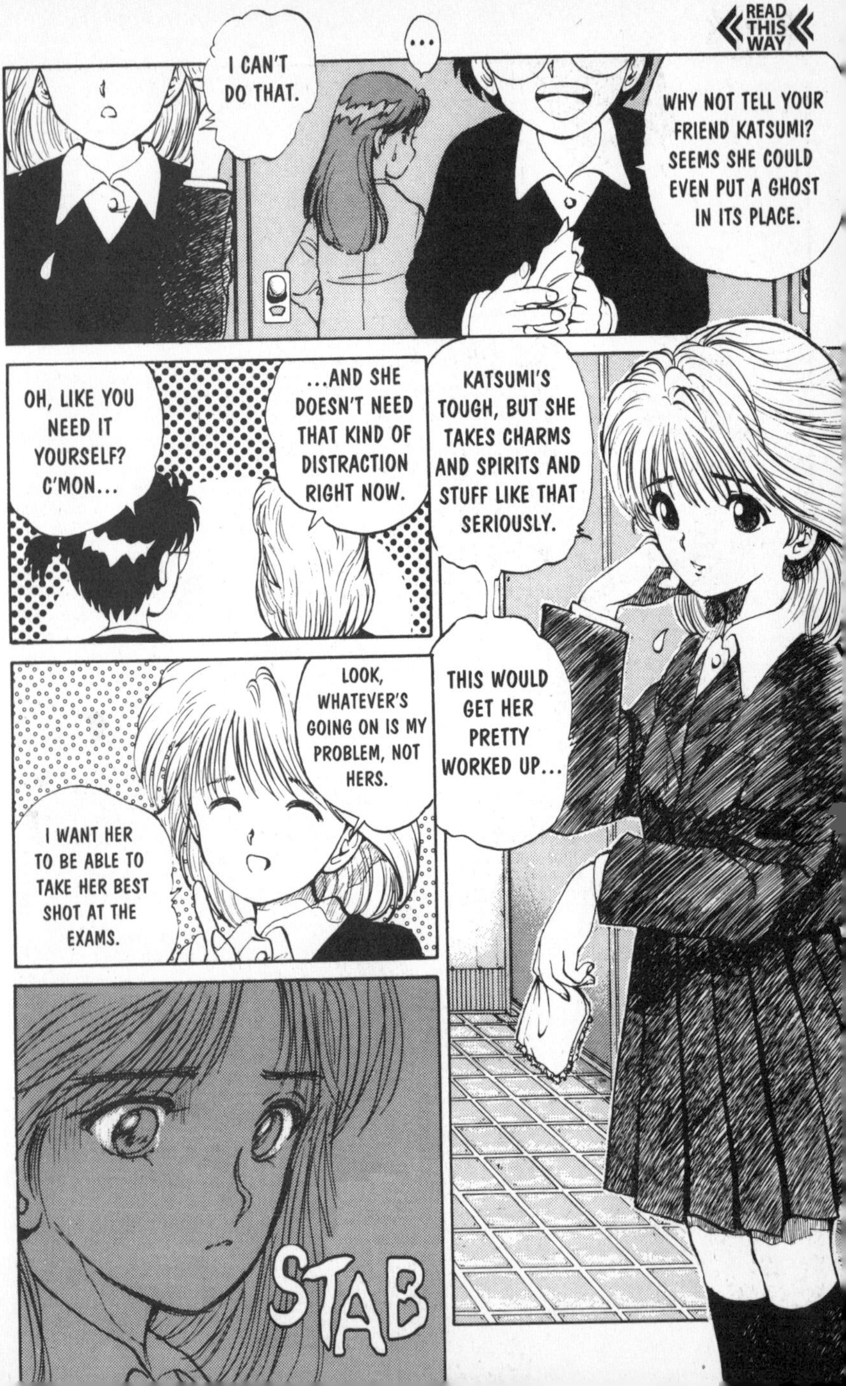

WHY NOT TELL YOUR FRIEND KATSUMI? SEEMS SHE COULD EVEN PUT A GHOST IN ITS PLACE.
...
I CAN'T DO THAT.
KATSUMI'S TOUGH, BUT SHE TAKES CHARMS AND SPIRITS AND STUFF LIKE THAT SERIOUSLY.
THIS WOULD GET HER PRETTY WORKED UP...
...AND SHE DOESN'T NEED THAT KIND OF DISTRACTION RIGHT NOW.
OH, LIKE YOU NEED IT YOURSELF? C'MON...
LOOK, WHATEVER'S GOING ON IS MY PROBLEM, NOT HERS.
I WANT HER TO BE ABLE TO TAKE HER BEST SHOT AT THE EXAMS.
STAB

READ THIS WAY

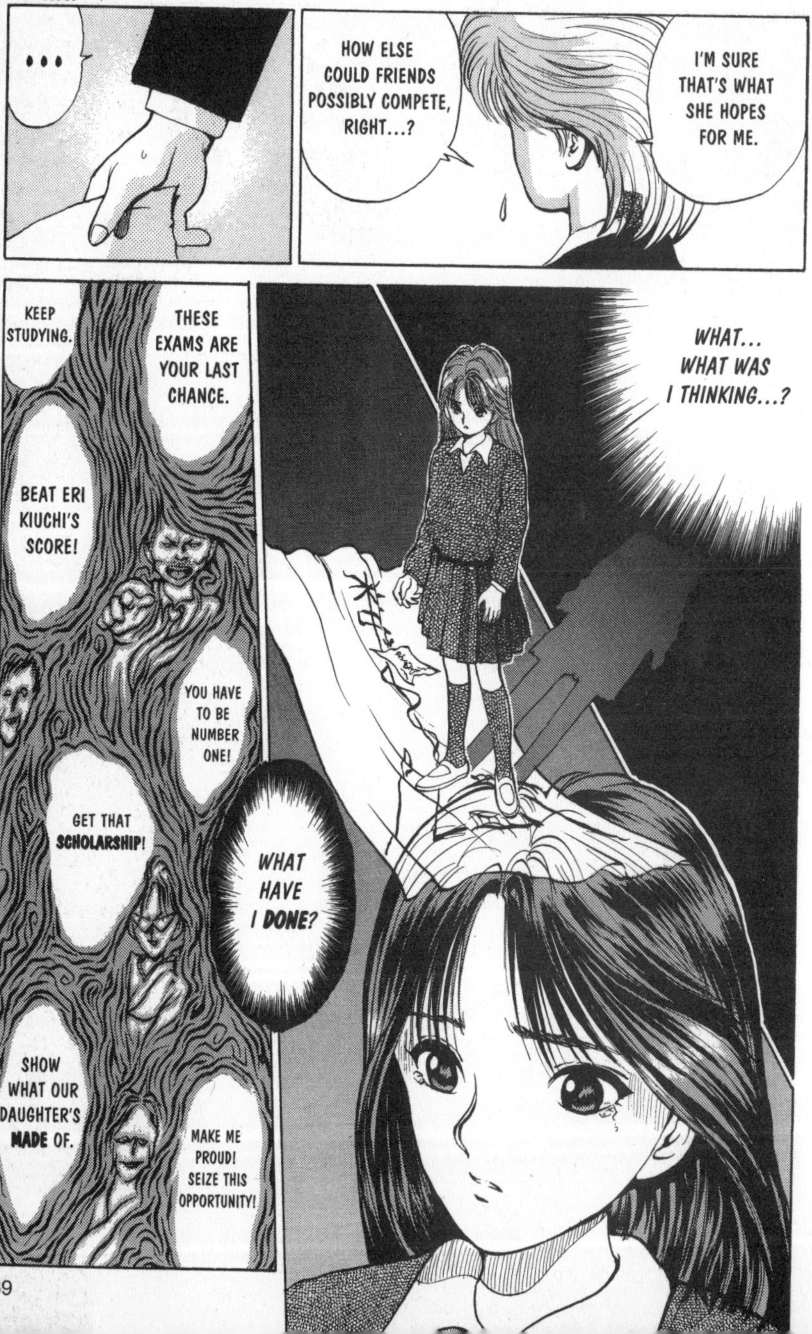
I'M SURE THAT'S WHAT SHE HOPES FOR ME.
HOW ELSE COULD FRIENDS POSSIBLY COMPETE, RIGHT...?
...
WHAT... WHAT WAS I THINKING...?
WHAT HAVE I DONE?
THESE EXAMS ARE YOUR LAST CHANCE.
KEEP STUDYING.
BEAT ERI KIUCHI'S SCORE!
YOU HAVE TO BE NUMBER ONE!
GET THAT SCHOLARSHIP!
MAKE ME PROUD! SEIZE THIS OPPORTUNITY!
SHOW WHAT OUR DAUGHTER'S MADE OF.

READ THIS WAY

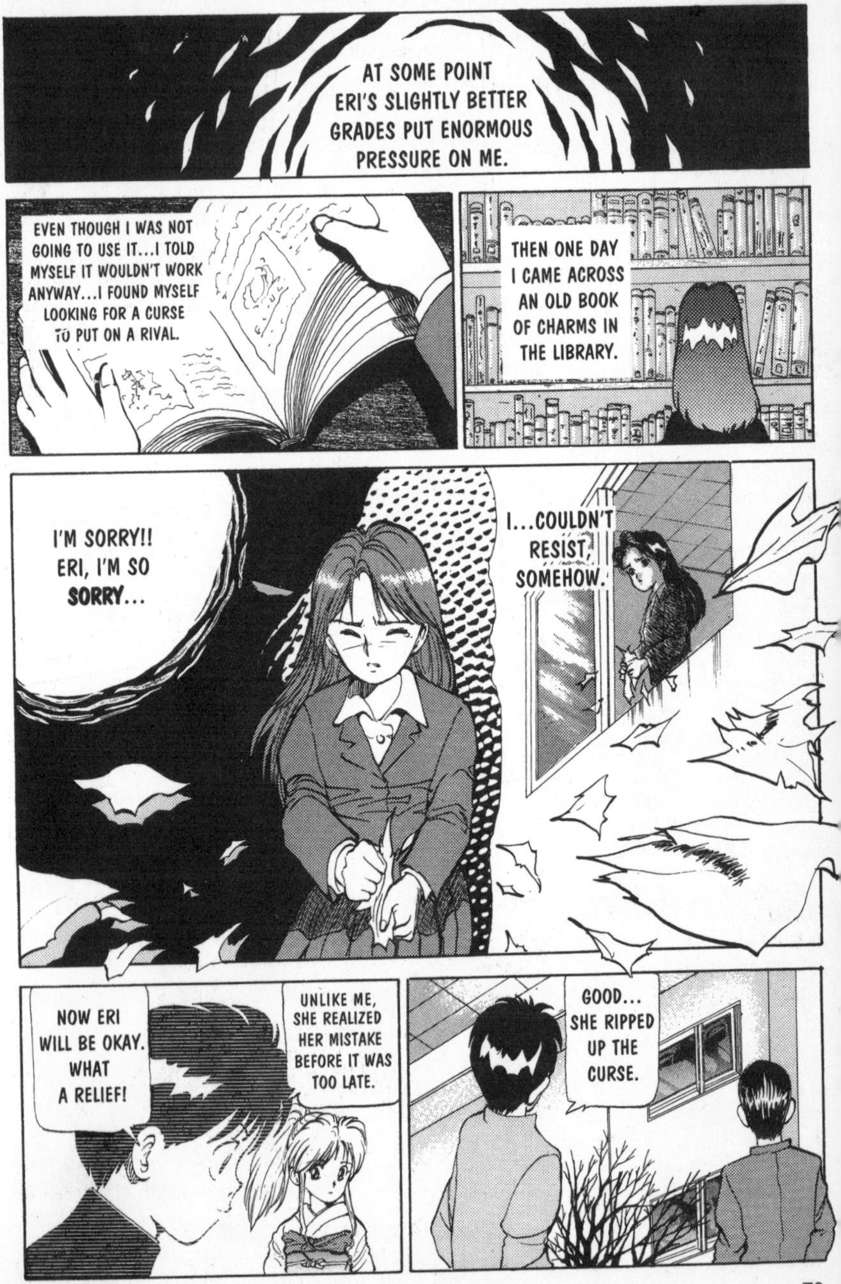
AT SOME POINT ERI'S SLIGHTLY BETTER GRADES PUT ENORMOUS PRESSURE ON ME.
THEN ONE DAY I CAME ACROSS AN OLD BOOK OF CHARMS IN THE LIBRARY.
EVEN THOUGH I WAS NOT GOING TO USE IT...I TOLD MYSELF IT WOULDN'T WORK ANYWAY...I FOUND MYSELF LOOKING FOR A CURSE TO PUT ON A RIVAL.
I...COULDN'T RESIST, SOMEHOW.
I'M SORRY!! ERI, I'M SO **SORRY**...
GOOD... SHE RIPPED UP THE CURSE.
UNLIKE ME, SHE REALIZED HER MISTAKE BEFORE IT WAS TOO LATE.
NOW ERI WILL BE OKAY. WHAT A RELIEF!

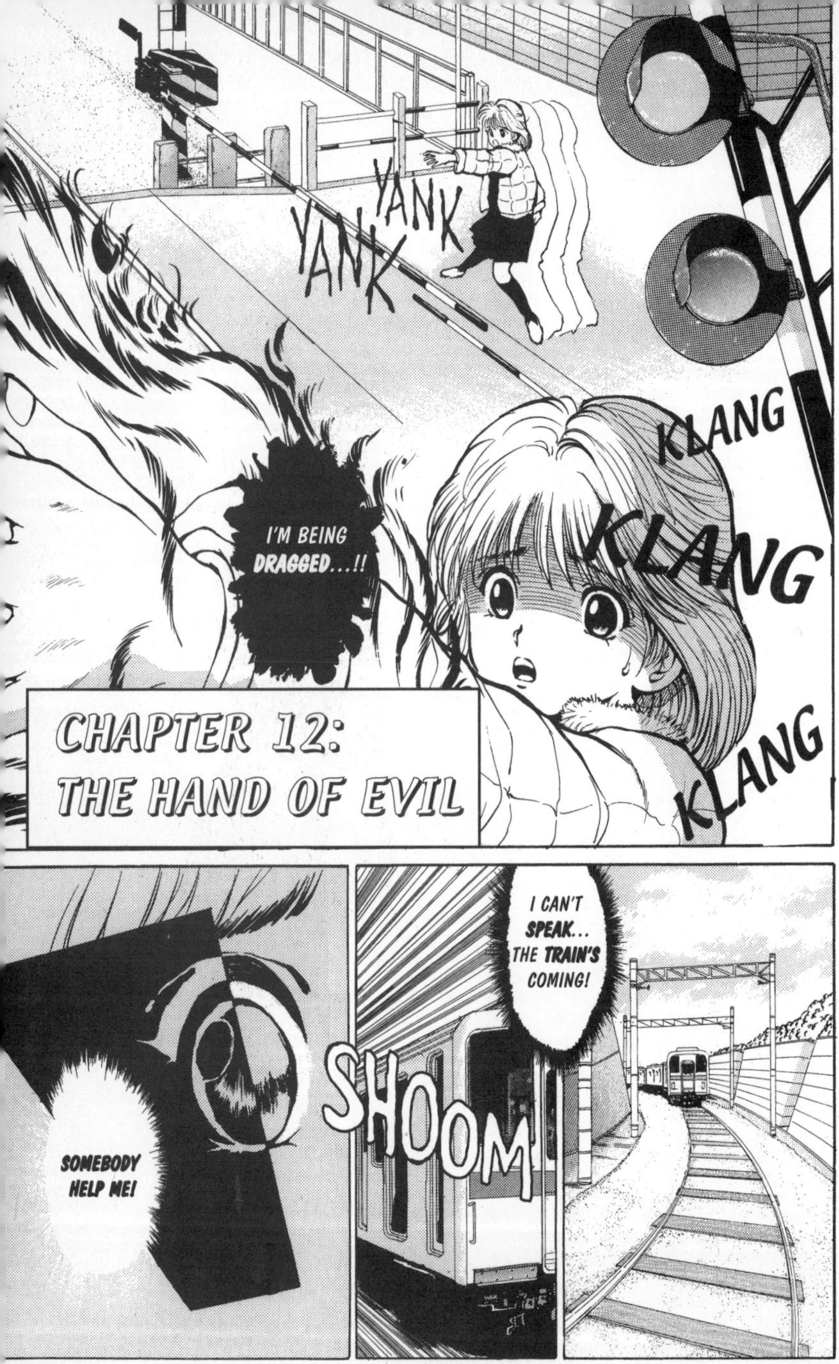
KLANG
KLANG
KLANG
YANK
YANK
I'M BEING DRAGGED...!!
CHAPTER 12:
THE HAND OF EVIL
I CAN'T SPEAK... THE TRAIN'S COMING!
SHOOM
SOMEBODY HELP ME!

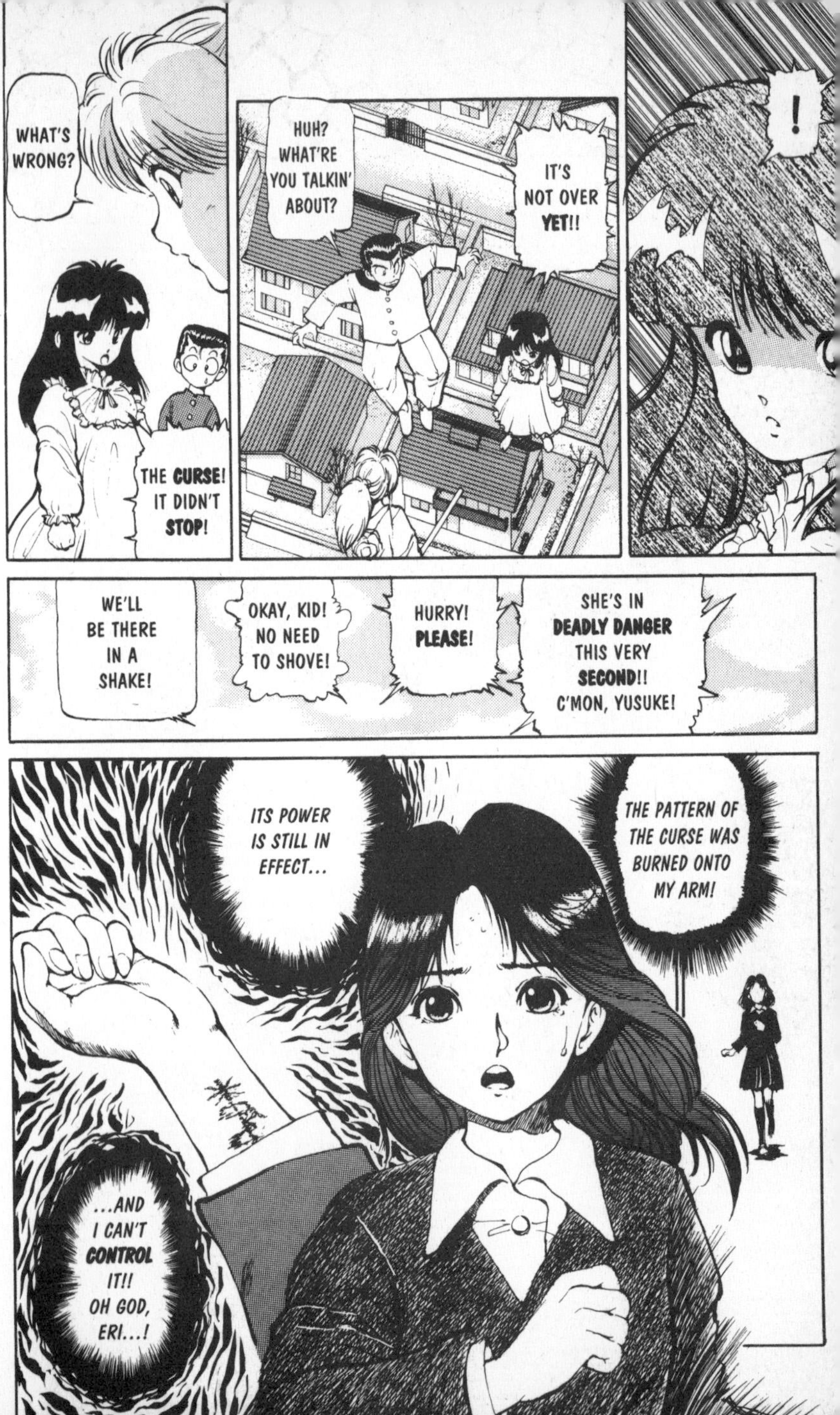
!
IT'S NOT OVER YET!!
HUH? WHAT'RE YOU TALKIN' ABOUT?
WHAT'S WRONG?
THE CURSE! IT DIDN'T STOP!
SHE'S IN DEADLY DANGER THIS VERY SECOND!! C'MON, YUSUKE!
HURRY! PLEASE!
OKAY, KID! NO NEED TO SHOVE!
WE'LL BE THERE IN A SHAKE!
THE PATTERN OF THE CURSE WAS BURNED ONTO MY ARM!
ITS POWER IS STILL IN EFFECT...
...AND I CAN'T CONTROL IT!! OH GOD, ERI...!

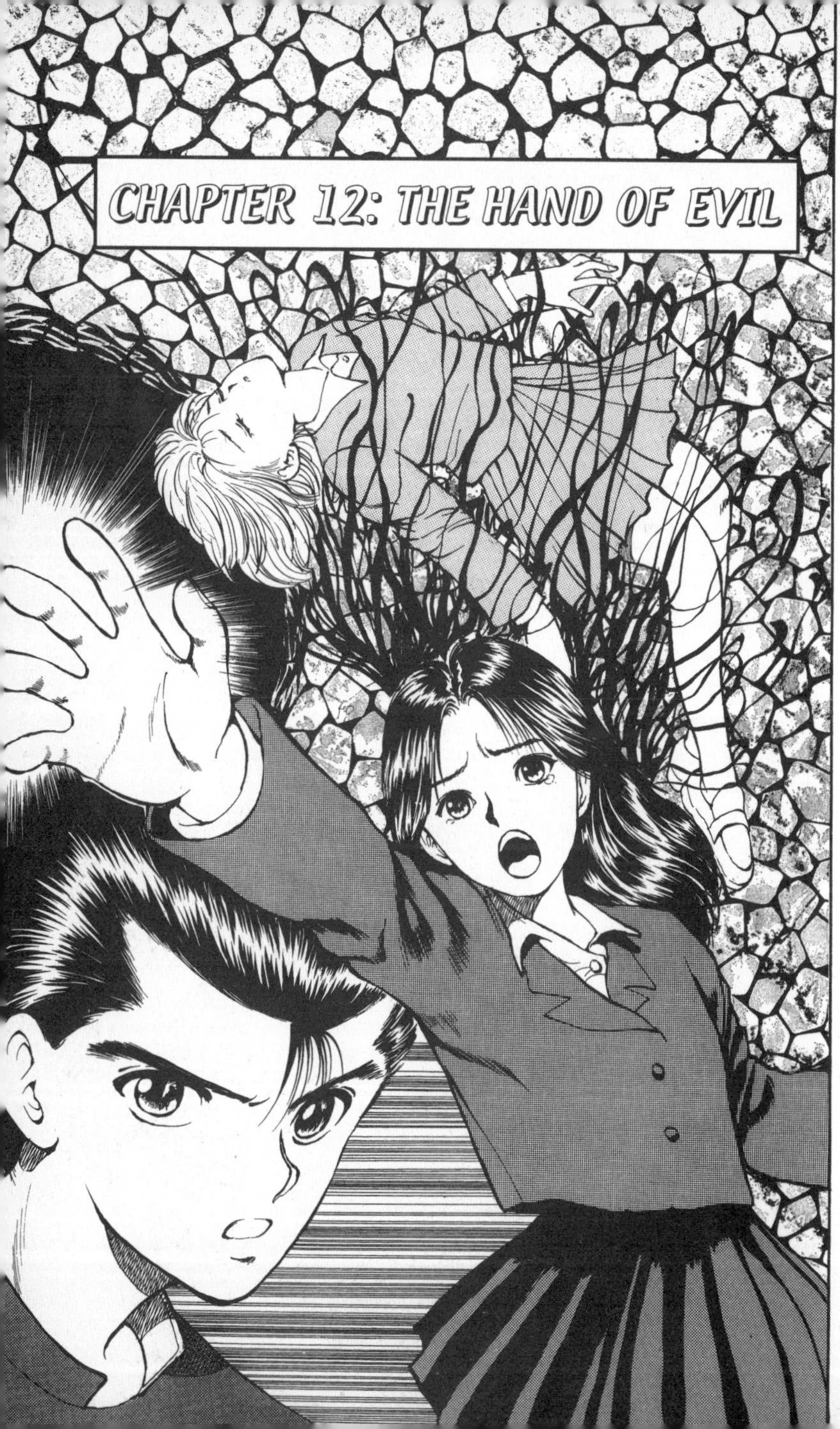
CHAPTER 12: THE HAND OF EVIL

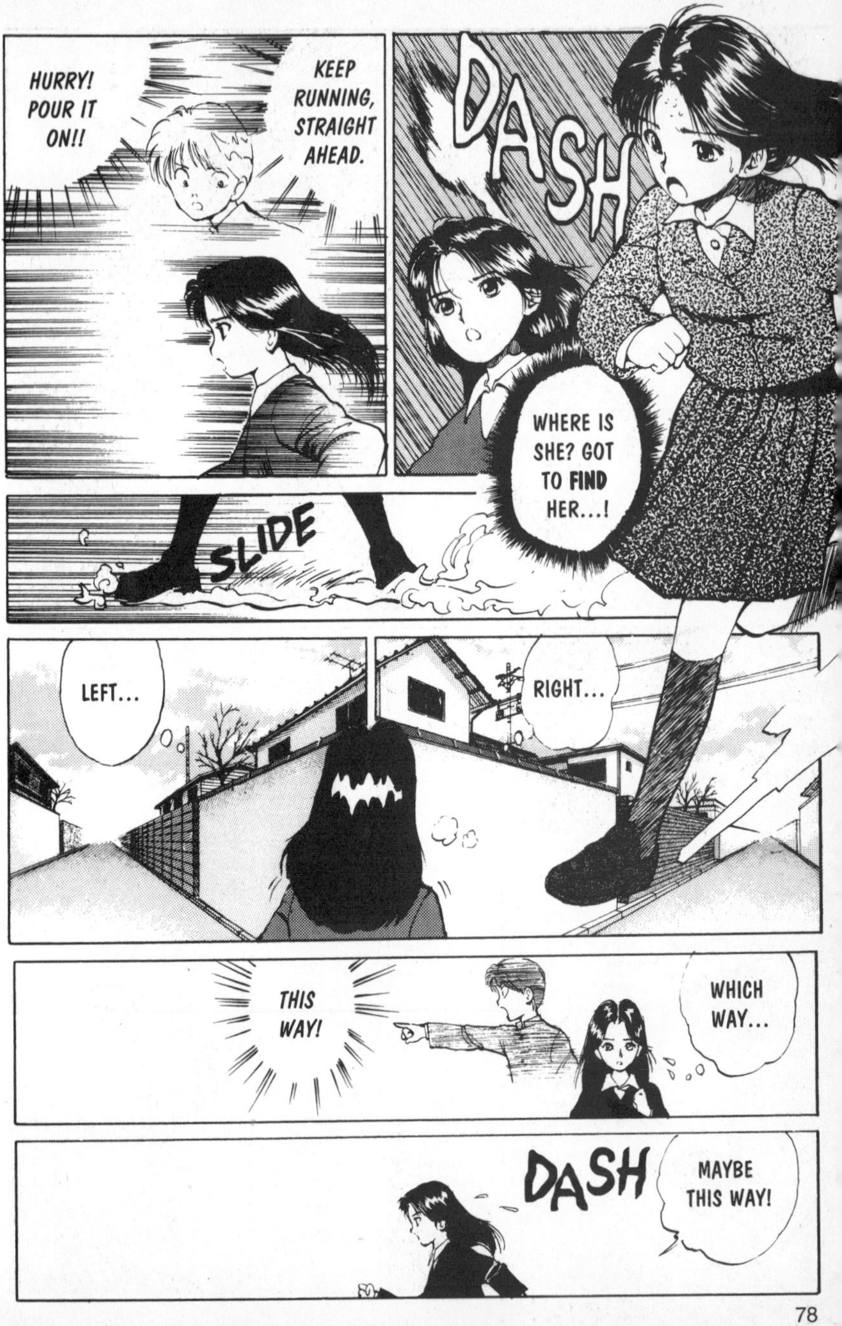
DASH
WHERE IS SHE? GOT TO FIND HER...!
KEEP RUNNING, STRAIGHT AHEAD.
HURRY! POUR IT ON!!
SLIDE
RIGHT...
LEFT...
WHICH WAY...
THIS WAY!
MAYBE THIS WAY!
DASH

READ THIS WAY

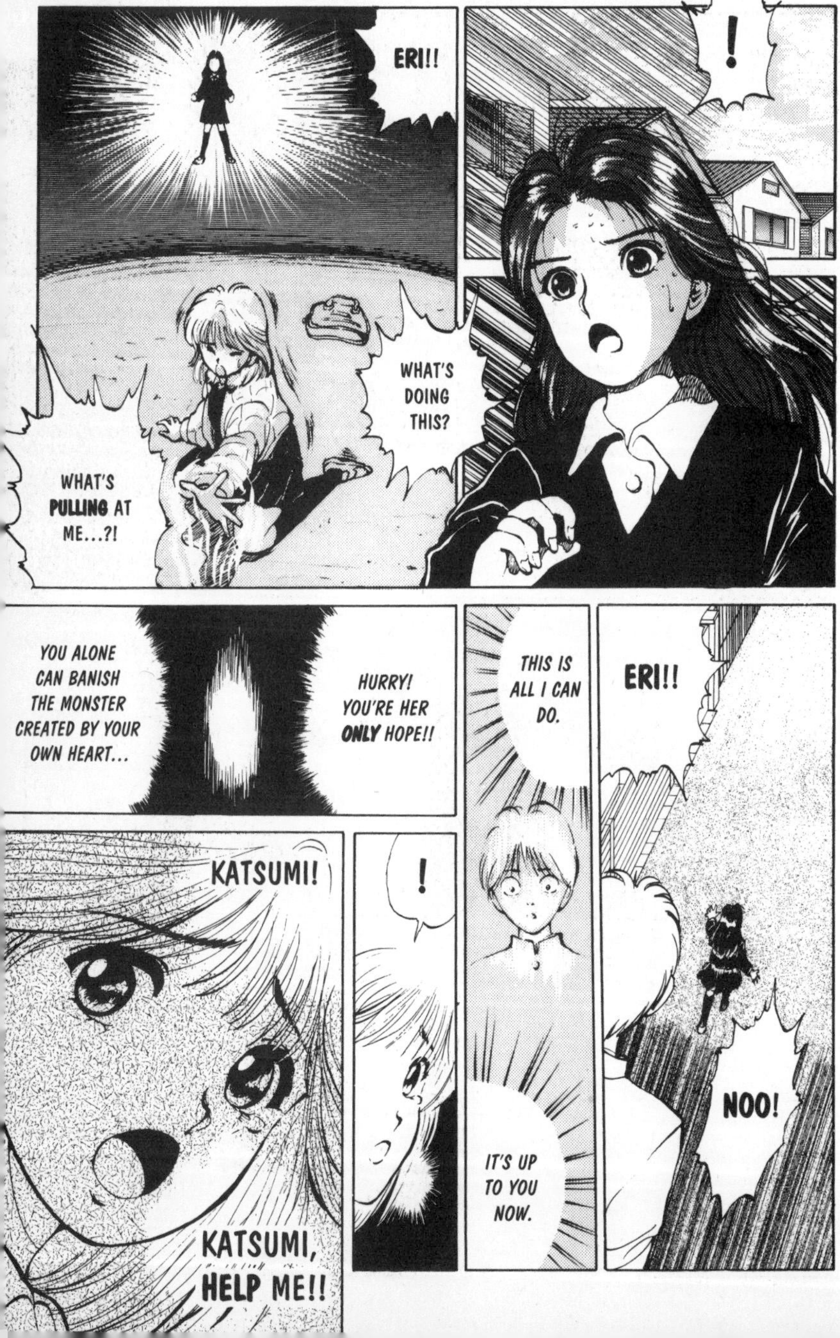

!
ERI!!
WHAT'S DOING THIS?
WHAT'S PULLING AT ME...?!
ERI!!
NOO!
THIS IS ALL I CAN DO.
IT'S UP TO YOU NOW.
HURRY! YOU'RE HER ONLY HOPE!!
YOU ALONE CAN BANISH THE MONSTER CREATED BY YOUR OWN HEART...
!
KATSUMI!
KATSUMI, HELP ME!!

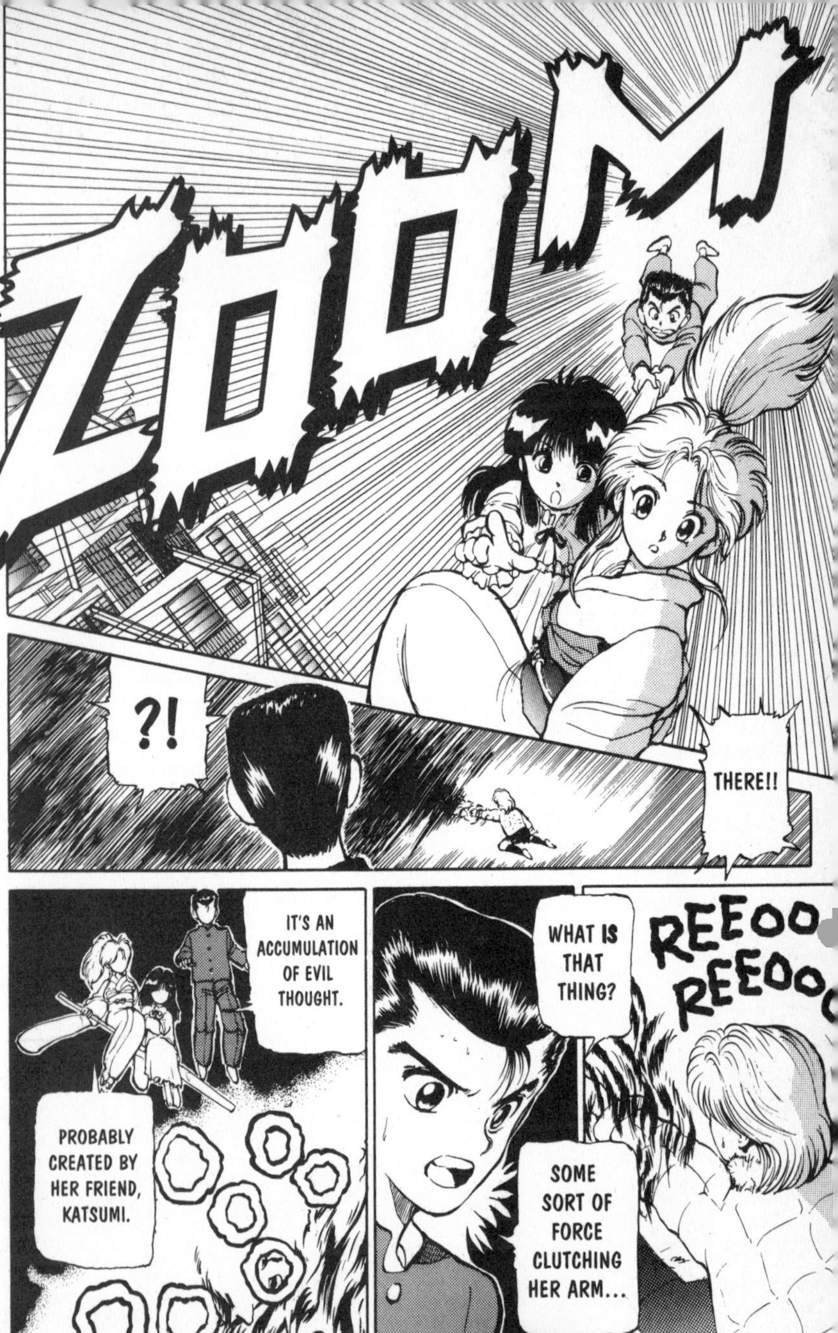
ZOOM
THERE!!
?!
REEOO
REEOO
WHAT IS THAT THING?
SOME SORT OF FORCE CLUTCHING HER ARM...
IT'S AN ACCUMULATION OF EVIL THOUGHT.
PROBABLY CREATED BY HER FRIEND, KATSUMI.

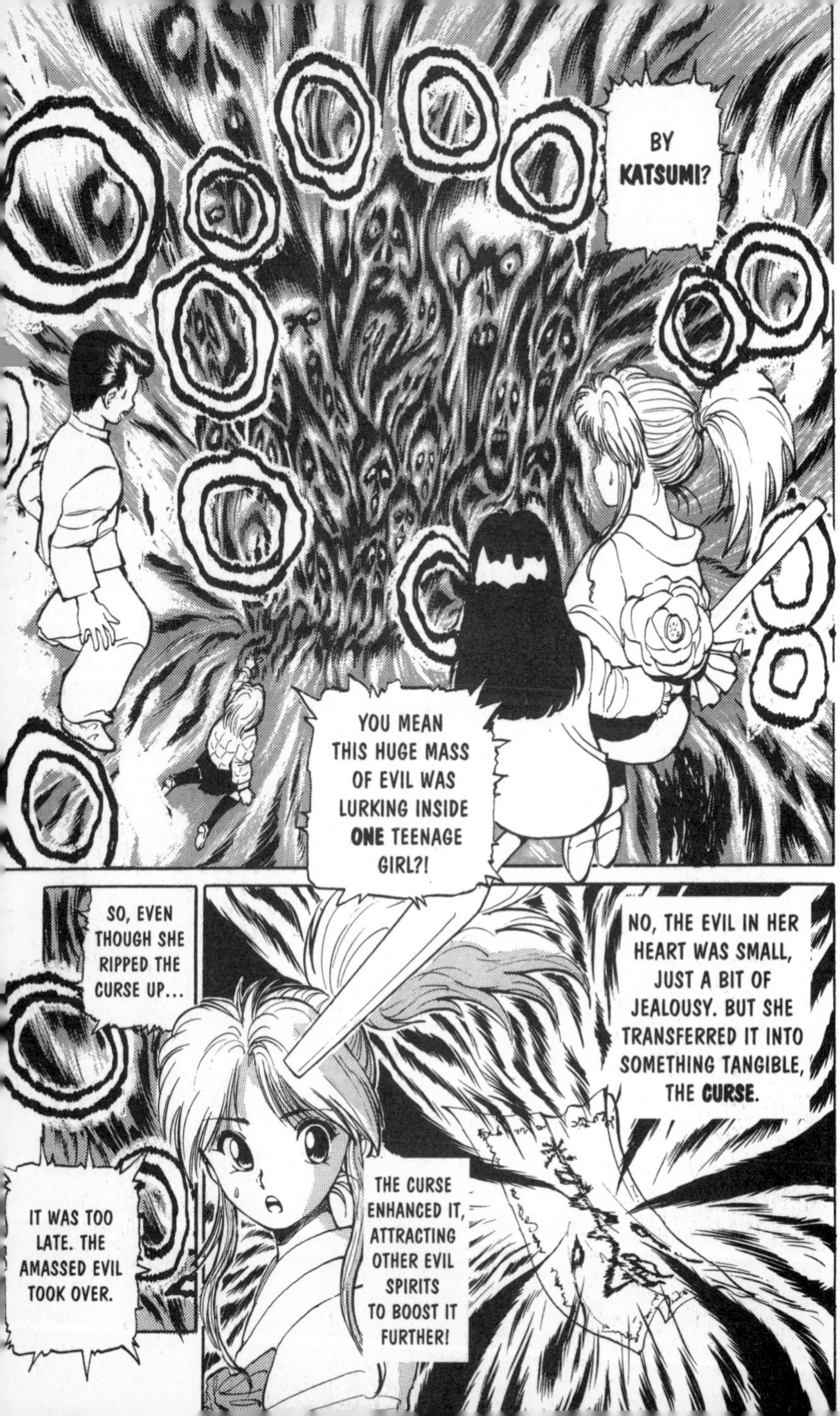
BY KATSUMI?
YOU MEAN THIS HUGE MASS OF EVIL WAS LURKING INSIDE ONE TEENAGE GIRL?!
NO, THE EVIL IN HER HEART WAS SMALL, JUST A BIT OF JEALOUSY. BUT SHE TRANSFERRED IT INTO SOMETHING TANGIBLE, THE CURSE.
THE CURSE ENHANCED IT, ATTRACTING OTHER EVIL SPIRITS TO BOOST IT FURTHER!
SO, EVEN THOUGH SHE RIPPED THE CURSE UP...
IT WAS TOO LATE. THE AMASSED EVIL TOOK OVER.

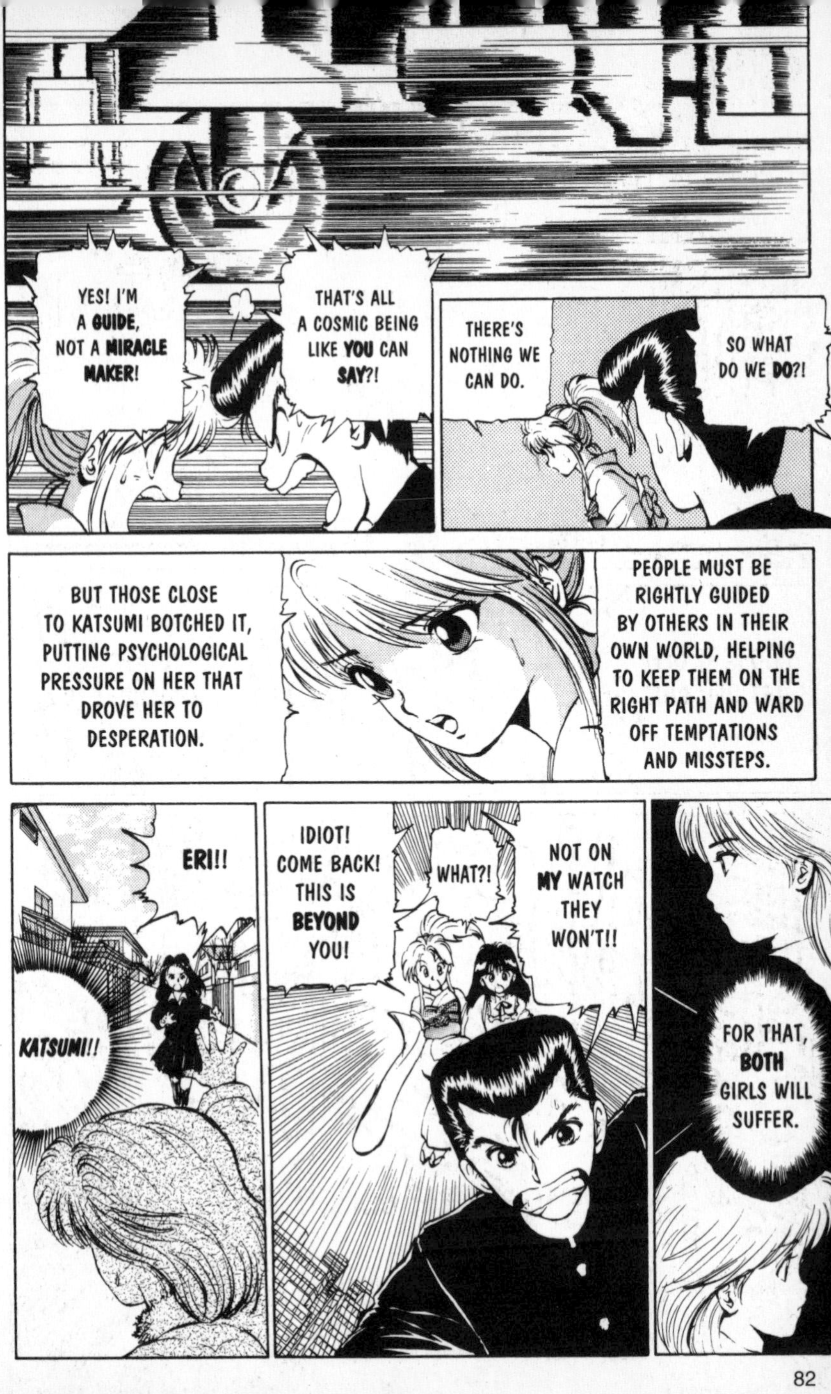
SO WHAT DO WE DO?!
THERE'S NOTHING WE CAN DO.
THAT'S ALL A COSMIC BEING LIKE YOU CAN SAY?!
YES! I'M A GUIDE, NOT A MIRACLE MAKER!
PEOPLE MUST BE RIGHTLY GUIDED BY OTHERS IN THEIR OWN WORLD, HELPING TO KEEP THEM ON THE RIGHT PATH AND WARD OFF TEMPTATIONS AND MISSTEPS.
BUT THOSE CLOSE TO KATSUMI BOTCHED IT, PUTTING PSYCHOLOGICAL PRESSURE ON HER THAT DROVE HER TO DESPERATION.
FOR THAT, BOTH GIRLS WILL SUFFER.
NOT ON MY WATCH THEY WON'T!!
WHAT?!
IDIOT! COME BACK! THIS IS BEYOND YOU!
ERI!!
KATSUMI!!

READ THIS WAY

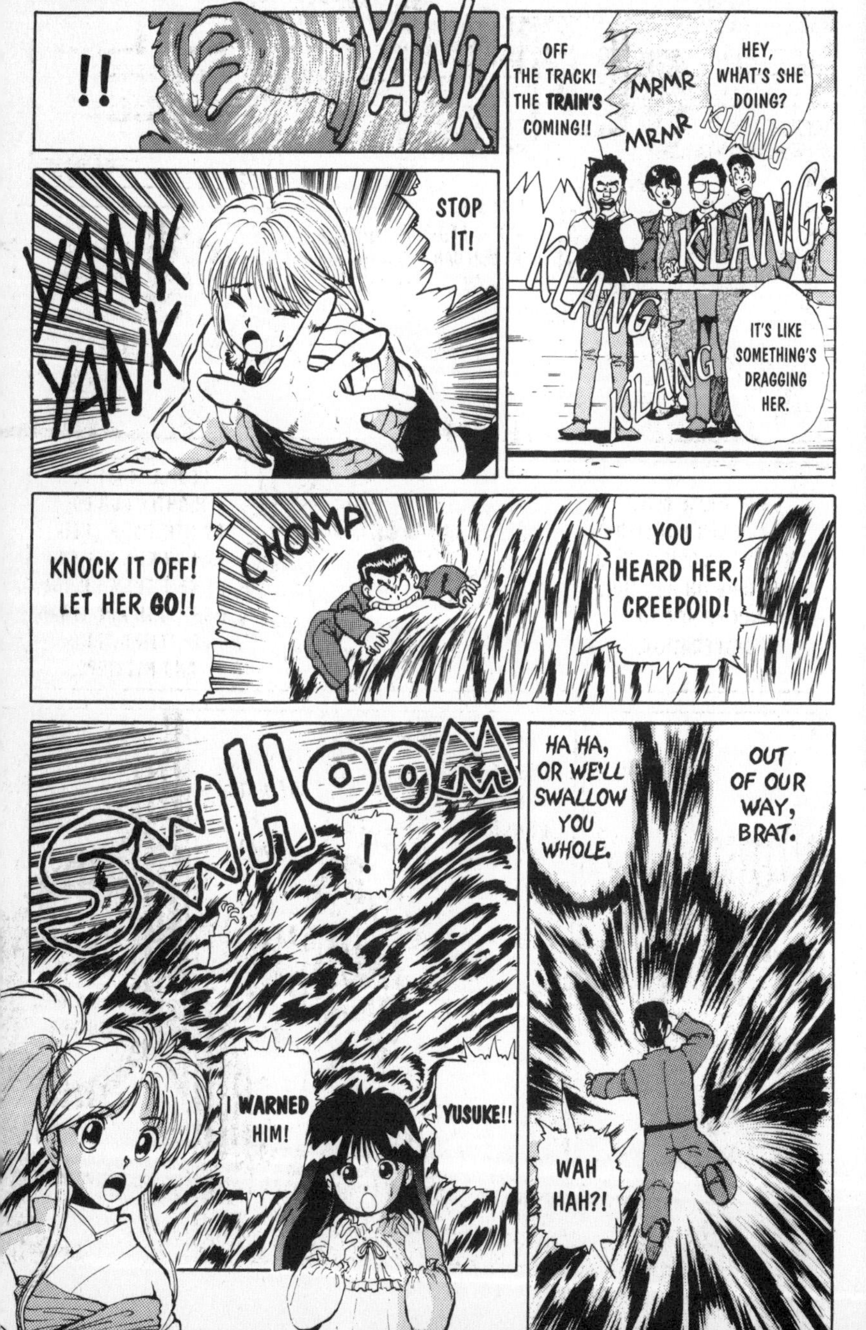
HEY, WHAT'S SHE DOING?
MRMR
OFF THE TRACK! THE **TRAIN'S** COMING!!
MRMR
KLANG
KLANG
KLANG
KLANG
IT'S LIKE SOMETHING'S DRAGGING HER.
YANK
!!
STOP IT!
YANK YANK
YOU HEARD HER, CREEPOID!
CHOMP
KNOCK IT OFF! LET HER **GO**!!
OUT OF OUR WAY, BRAT.
HA HA, OR WE'LL SWALLOW YOU WHOLE.
WAH HAH?!
SWHOOM
!
YUSUKE!!
I WARNED HIM!

READ THIS WAY

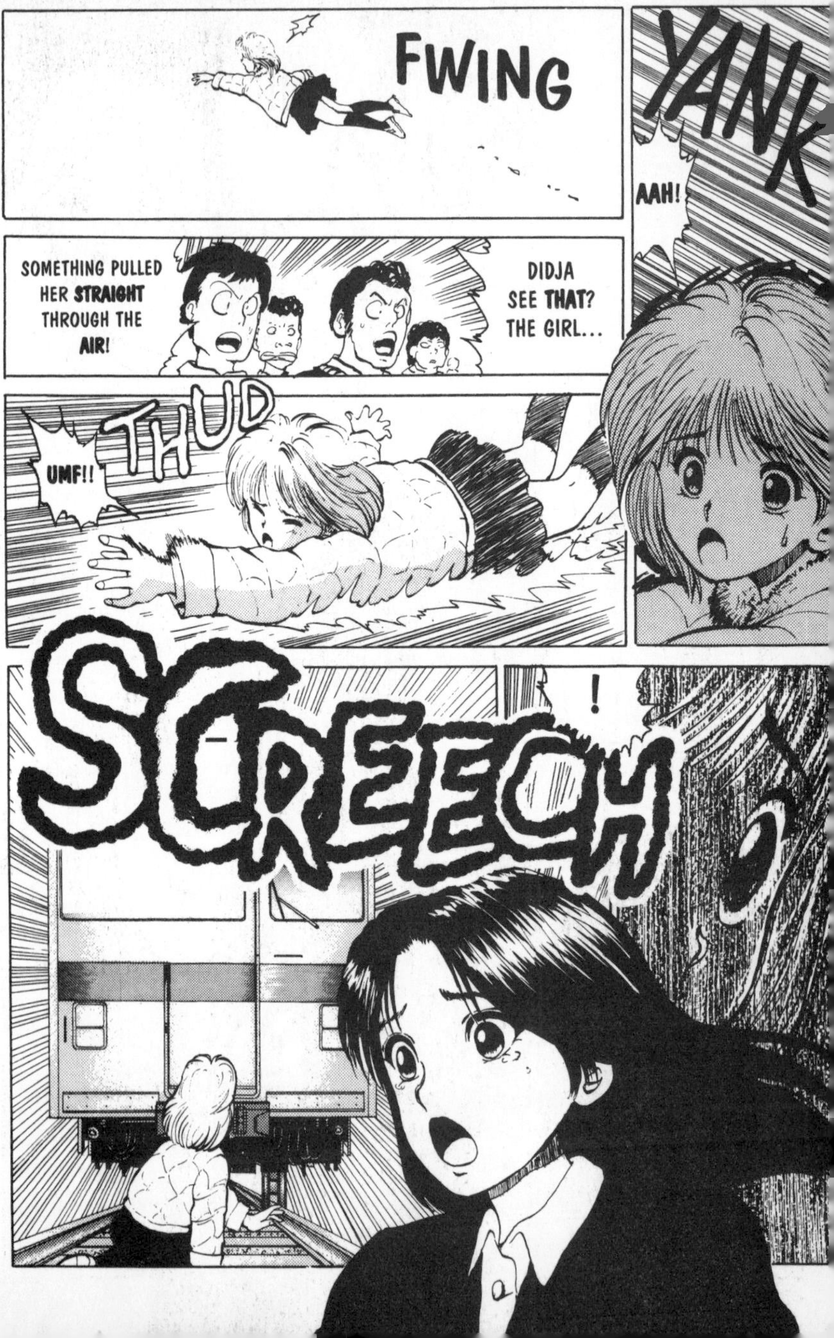
YANK
AAH!
FWING
DIDJA SEE THAT? THE GIRL...
SOMETHING PULLED HER STRAIGHT THROUGH THE AIR!
THUD
UMF!!
!
SCREECH

READ THIS WAY

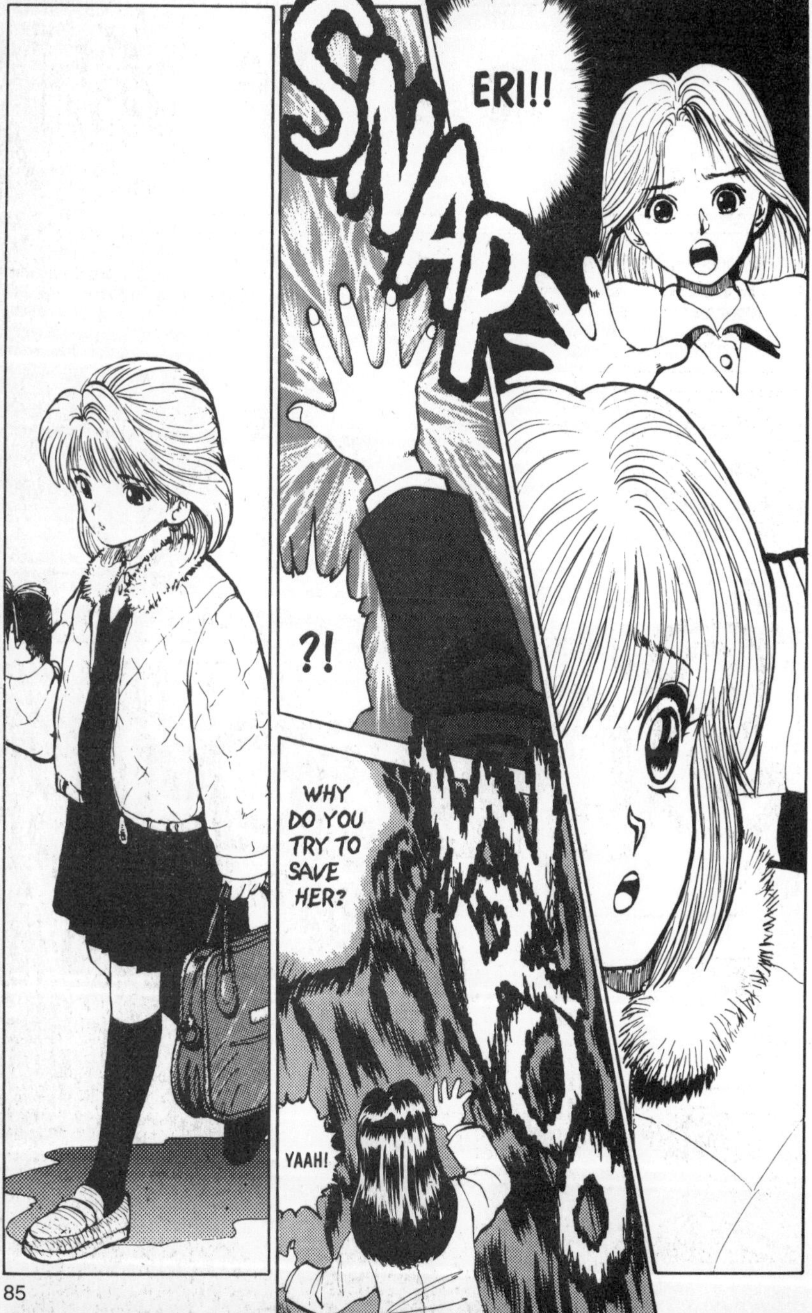
ERI!!
SNAP
?!
WHY DO YOU TRY TO SAVE HER?
YAAH!

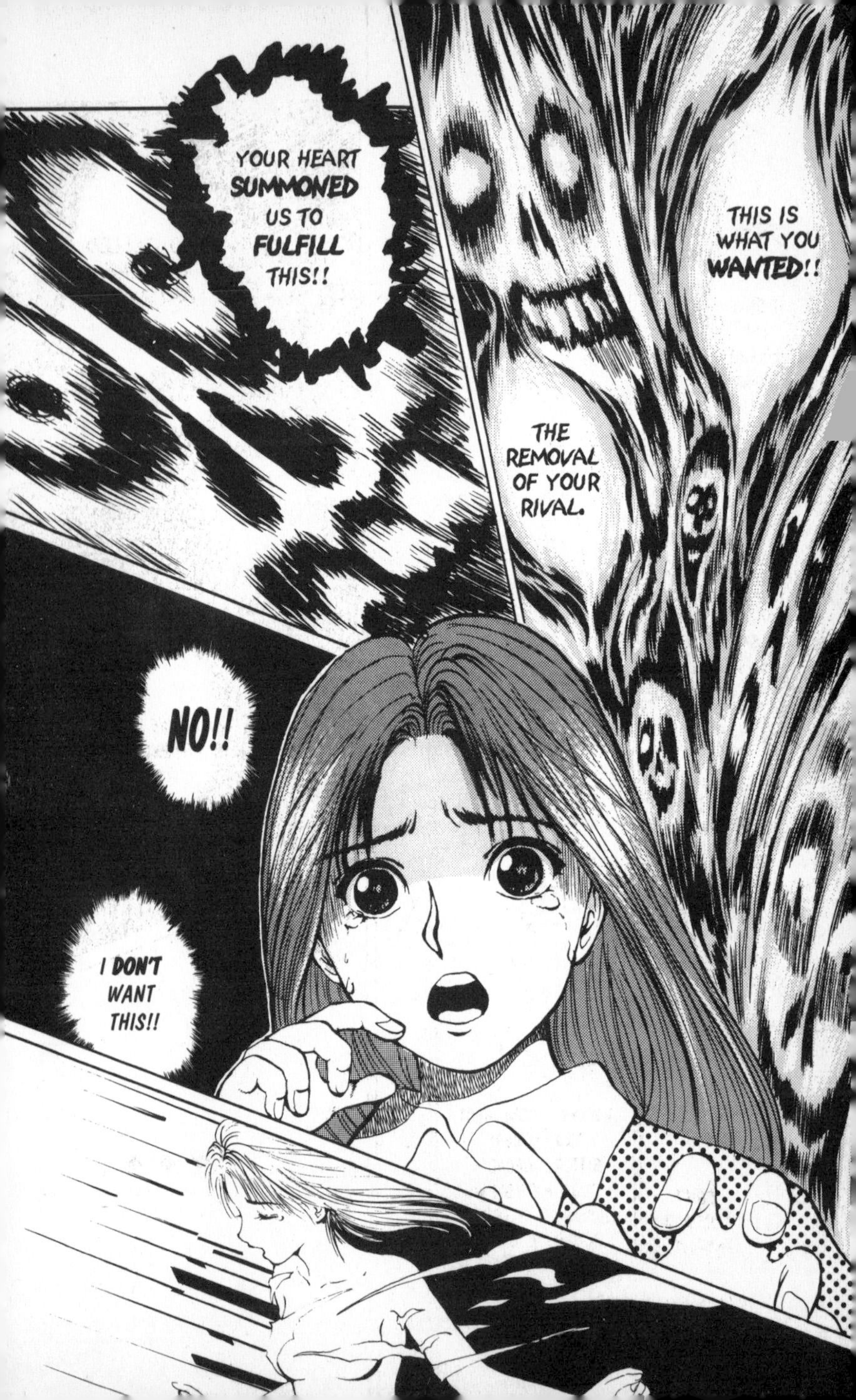
THIS IS WHAT YOU WANTED!!
THE REMOVAL OF YOUR RIVAL.
YOUR HEART SUMMONED US TO FULFILL THIS!!
NO!!
I DON'T WANT THIS!!

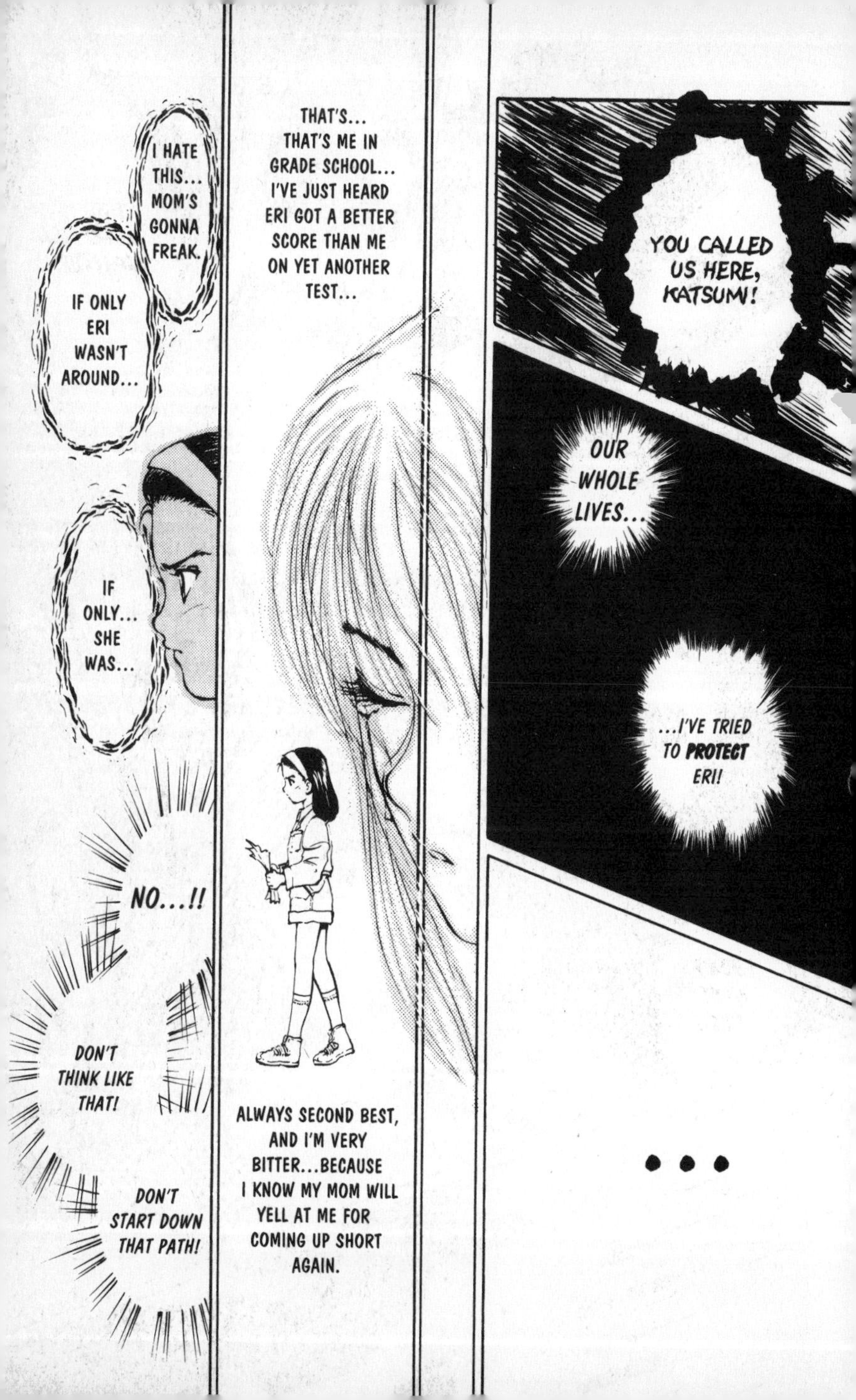
YOU CALLED US HERE, KATSUMI!
OUR WHOLE LIVES...
...I'VE TRIED TO PROTECT ERI!
• • •
THAT'S... THAT'S ME IN GRADE SCHOOL... I'VE JUST HEARD ERI GOT A BETTER SCORE THAN ME ON YET ANOTHER TEST...
ALWAYS SECOND BEST, AND I'M VERY BITTER...BECAUSE I KNOW MY MOM WILL YELL AT ME FOR COMING UP SHORT AGAIN.
I HATE THIS... MOM'S GONNA FREAK.
IF ONLY ERI WASN'T AROUND...
IF ONLY... SHE WAS...
NO...!!
DON'T THINK LIKE THAT!
DON'T START DOWN THAT PATH!

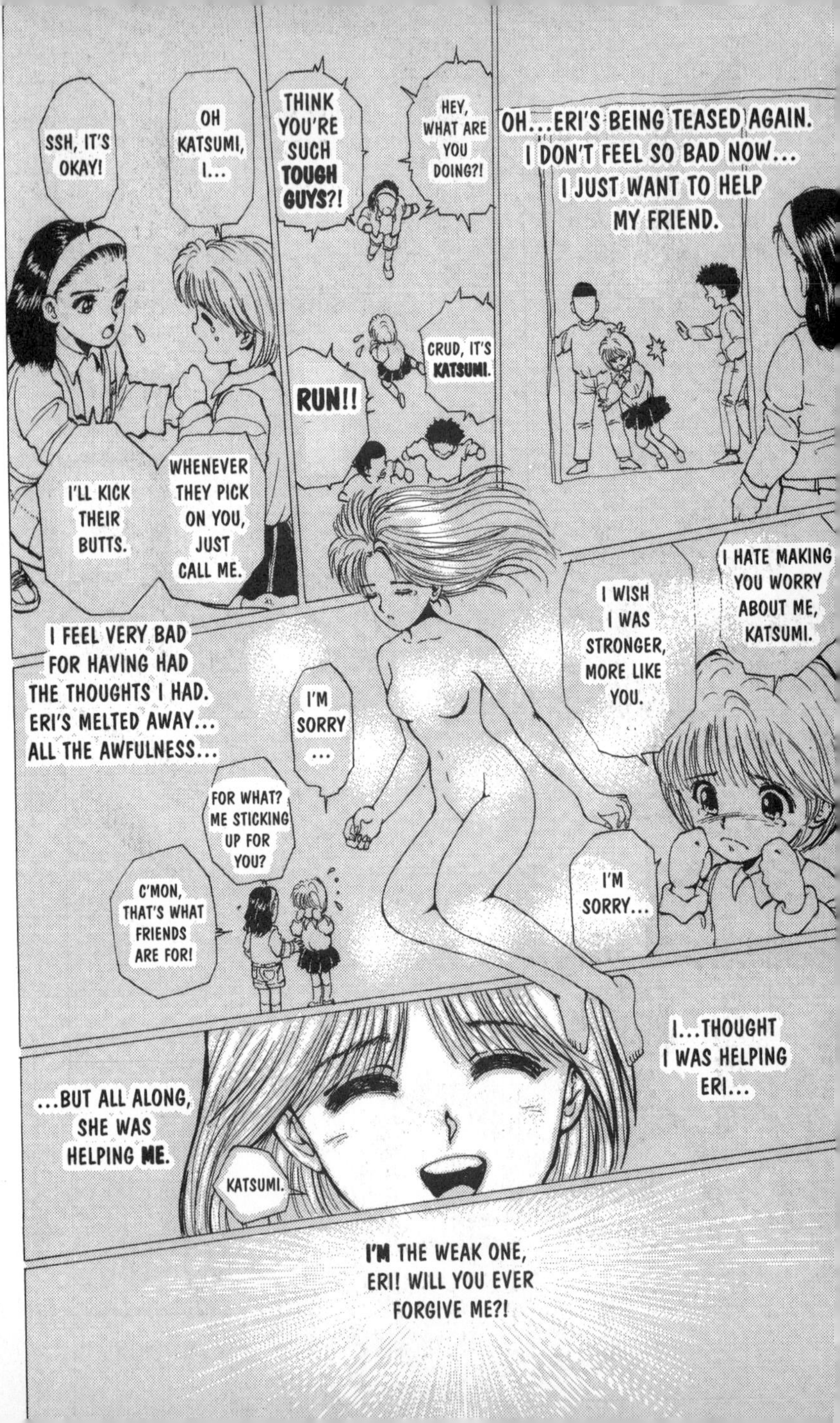
OH...ERI'S BEING TEASED AGAIN. I DON'T FEEL SO BAD NOW... I JUST WANT TO HELP MY FRIEND.
HEY, WHAT ARE YOU DOING?!
THINK YOU'RE SUCH TOUGH GUYS?!
CRUD, IT'S KATSUMI.
RUN!!
OH KATSUMI, I...
SSH, IT'S OKAY!
WHENEVER THEY PICK ON YOU, JUST CALL ME.
I'LL KICK THEIR BUTTS.
I HATE MAKING YOU WORRY ABOUT ME, KATSUMI.
I WISH I WAS STRONGER, MORE LIKE YOU.
I'M SORRY...
I FEEL VERY BAD FOR HAVING HAD THE THOUGHTS I HAD. ERI'S MELTED AWAY... ALL THE AWFULNESS...
I'M SORRY ...
FOR WHAT? ME STICKING UP FOR YOU?
C'MON, THAT'S WHAT FRIENDS ARE FOR!
I...THOUGHT I WAS HELPING ERI...
...BUT ALL ALONG, SHE WAS HELPING ME.
KATSUMI.
I'M THE WEAK ONE, ERI! WILL YOU EVER FORGIVE ME?!

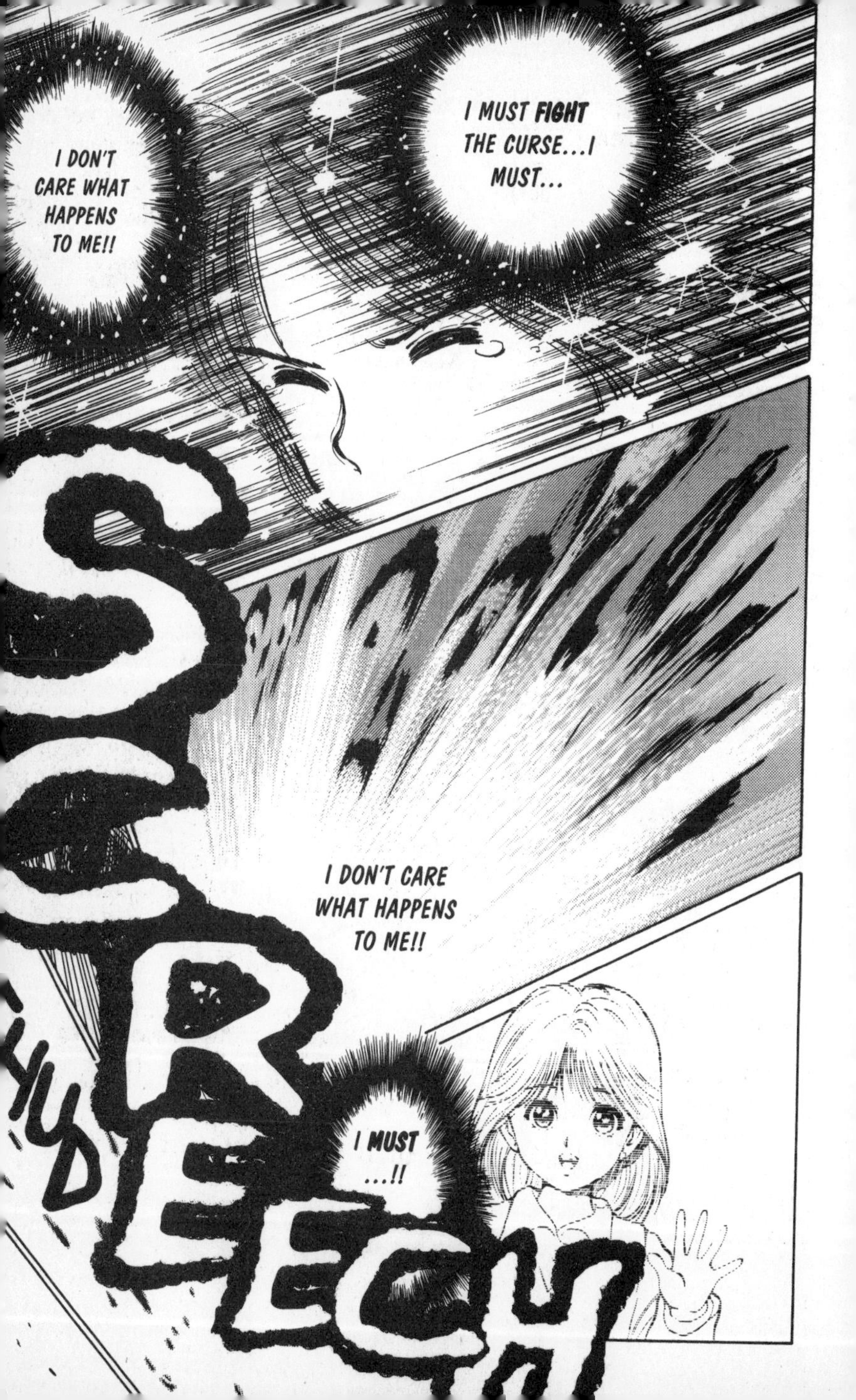
I MUST **FIGHT** THE CURSE...I MUST...
I DON'T CARE WHAT HAPPENS TO ME!!
I DON'T CARE WHAT HAPPENS TO ME!!
SCREECH
I **MUST** ...!!

READ THIS WAY

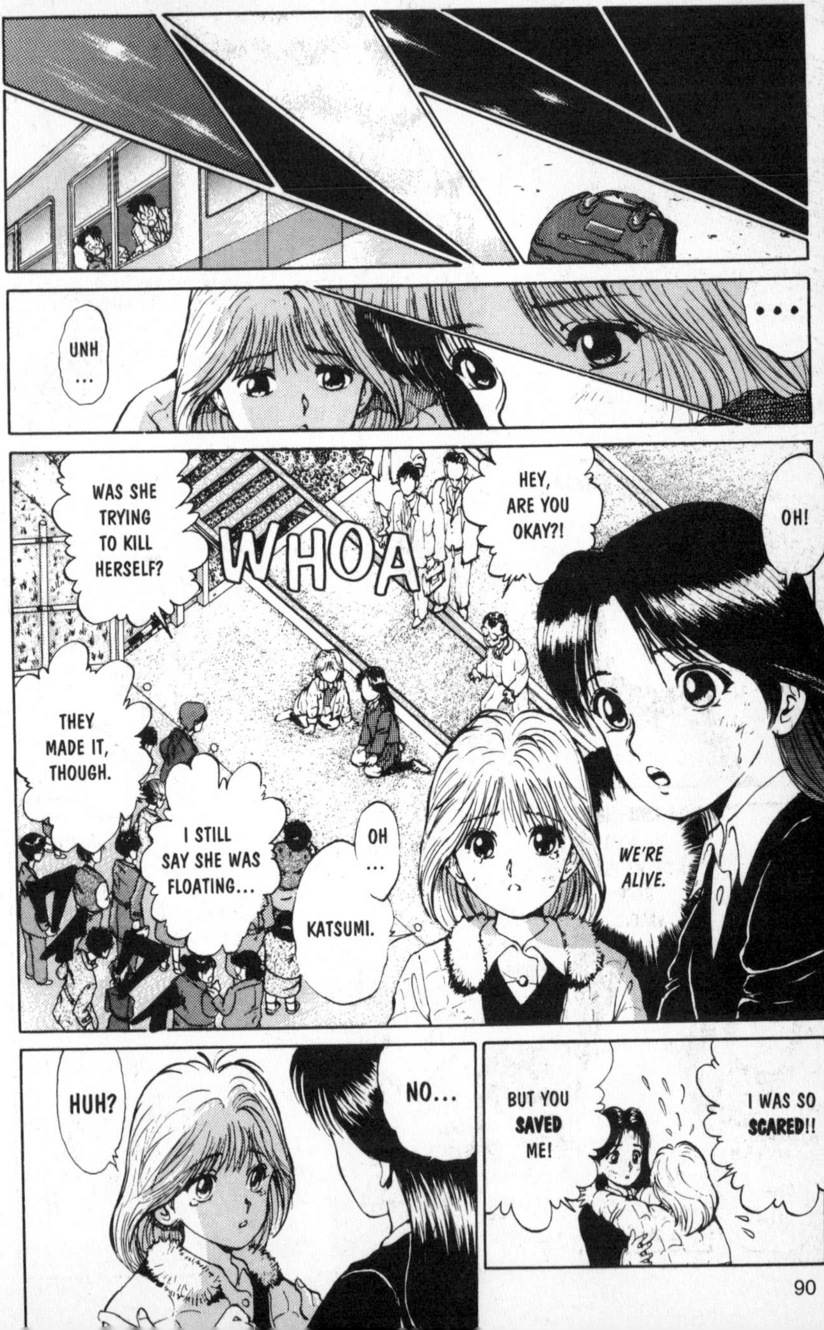

• • •
UNH ...
OH!
HEY, ARE YOU OKAY?!
WHOA
WAS SHE TRYING TO KILL HERSELF?
WE'RE ALIVE.
OH ...
KATSUMI.
THEY MADE IT, THOUGH.
I STILL SAY SHE WAS FLOATING...
I WAS SO SCARED!!
BUT YOU SAVED ME!
NO...
HUH?

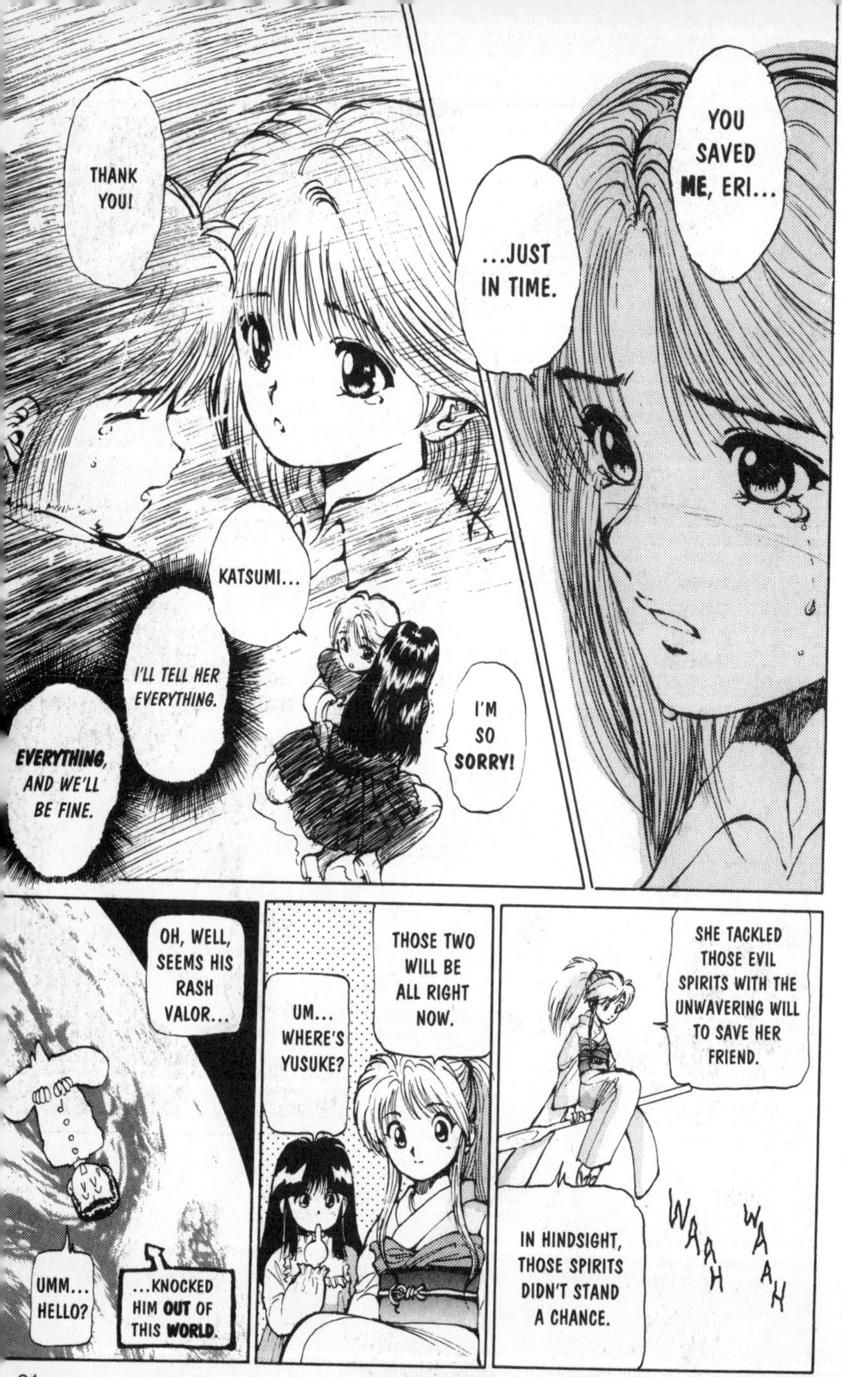
YOU SAVED ME, ERI...
...JUST IN TIME.
THANK YOU!
KATSUMI...
I'M SO SORRY!
I'LL TELL HER EVERYTHING.
EVERYTHING, AND WE'LL BE FINE.
SHE TACKLED THOSE EVIL SPIRITS WITH THE UNWAVERING WILL TO SAVE HER FRIEND.
IN HINDSIGHT, THOSE SPIRITS DIDN'T STAND A CHANCE.
WAAH WAAH
THOSE TWO WILL BE ALL RIGHT NOW.
UM... WHERE'S YUSUKE?
OH, WELL, SEEMS HIS RASH VALOR...
...KNOCKED HIM OUT OF THIS WORLD.
UMM... HELLO?

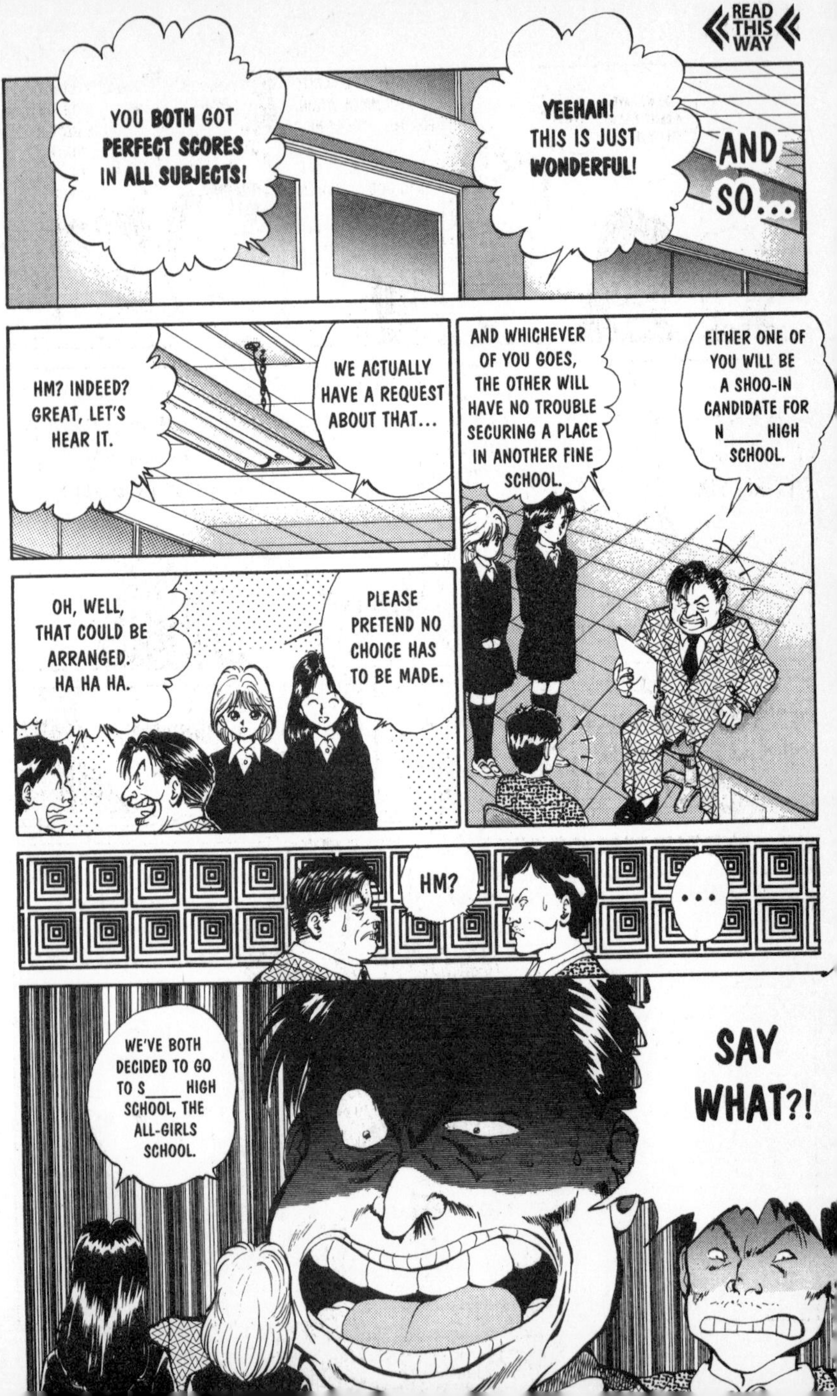
READ THIS WAY
AND SO...
YEEHAH! THIS IS JUST WONDERFUL!
YOU BOTH GOT PERFECT SCORES IN ALL SUBJECTS!
EITHER ONE OF YOU WILL BE A SHOO-IN CANDIDATE FOR N____ HIGH SCHOOL.
AND WHICHEVER OF YOU GOES, THE OTHER WILL HAVE NO TROUBLE SECURING A PLACE IN ANOTHER FINE SCHOOL.
WE ACTUALLY HAVE A REQUEST ABOUT THAT...
HM? INDEED? GREAT, LET'S HEAR IT.
PLEASE PRETEND NO CHOICE HAS TO BE MADE.
OH, WELL, THAT COULD BE ARRANGED. HA HA HA.
...
HM?
SAY WHAT?!
WE'VE BOTH DECIDED TO GO TO S____ HIGH SCHOOL, THE ALL-GIRLS SCHOOL.

THANK YOU!

YOU SAVED ME, ERI...

...JUST IN TIME.

KATSUMI...

I'LL TELL HER EVERYTHING.

EVERYTHING, AND WE'LL BE FINE.

I'M SO SORRY!

OH, WELL, SEEMS HIS RASH VALOR...

UMM... HELLO?

...KNOCKED HIM **OUT** OF THIS **WORLD**.

UM... WHERE'S YUSUKE?

THOSE TWO WILL BE ALL RIGHT NOW.

SHE TACKLED THOSE EVIL SPIRITS WITH THE UNWAVERING WILL TO SAVE HER FRIEND.

IN HINDSIGHT, THOSE SPIRITS DIDN'T STAND A CHANCE.

WAAH WAAH

YOU **BOTH** GOT **PERFECT SCORES** IN **ALL SUBJECTS!**

YEEHAH! THIS IS JUST **WONDERFUL!**

AND SO...

HM? INDEED? GREAT, LET'S HEAR IT.

WE ACTUALLY HAVE A REQUEST ABOUT THAT...

AND WHICHEVER OF YOU GOES, THE OTHER WILL HAVE NO TROUBLE SECURING A PLACE IN ANOTHER FINE SCHOOL.

EITHER ONE OF YOU WILL BE A SHOO-IN CANDIDATE FOR N____ HIGH SCHOOL.

OH, WELL, THAT COULD BE ARRANGED. HA HA HA.

PLEASE PRETEND NO CHOICE HAS TO BE MADE.

HM?

· · ·

WE'VE BOTH DECIDED TO GO TO S____ HIGH SCHOOL, THE ALL-GIRLS SCHOOL.

SAY WHAT?!

READ THIS WAY

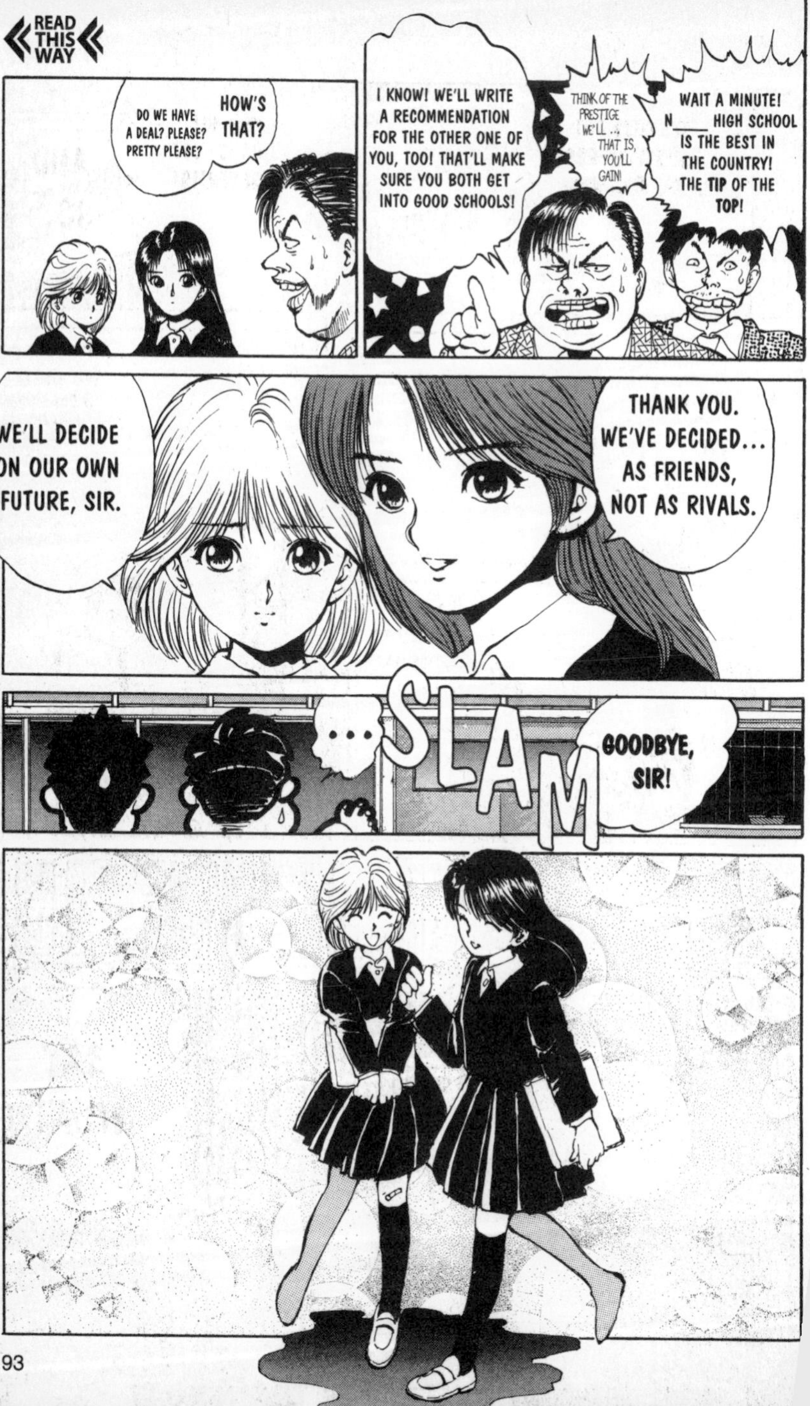
WAIT A MINUTE! N____ HIGH SCHOOL IS THE BEST IN THE COUNTRY! THE TIP OF THE TOP!
THINK OF THE PRESTIGE WE'LL ...! THAT IS, YOU'LL GAIN!
I KNOW! WE'LL WRITE A RECOMMENDATION FOR THE OTHER ONE OF YOU, TOO! THAT'LL MAKE SURE YOU BOTH GET INTO GOOD SCHOOLS!
HOW'S THAT?
DO WE HAVE A DEAL? PLEASE? PRETTY PLEASE?
THANK YOU. WE'VE DECIDED... AS FRIENDS, NOT AS RIVALS.
WE'LL DECIDE ON OUR OWN FUTURE, SIR.
GOODBYE, SIR!
SLAM
...

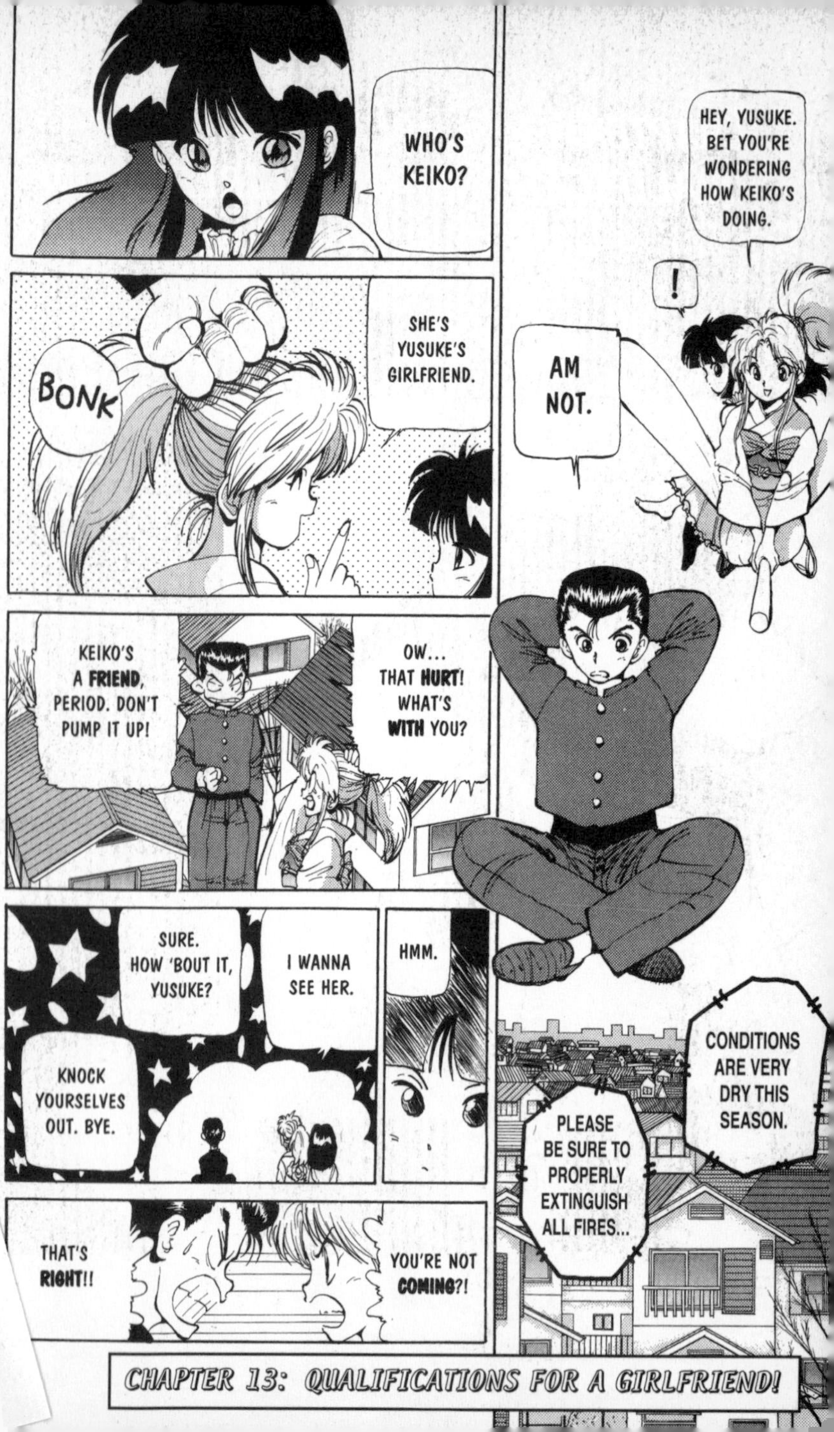

HEY, YUSUKE. BET YOU'RE WONDERING HOW KEIKO'S DOING.
!
AM NOT.
CONDITIONS ARE VERY DRY THIS SEASON.
PLEASE BE SURE TO PROPERLY EXTINGUISH ALL FIRES...
CHAPTER 13: QUALIFICATIONS FOR A GIRLFRIEND!
WHO'S KEIKO?
SHE'S YUSUKE'S GIRLFRIEND.
BONK
OW... THAT HURT! WHAT'S WITH YOU?
KEIKO'S A FRIEND, PERIOD. DON'T PUMP IT UP!
HMM.
I WANNA SEE HER.
SURE. HOW 'BOUT IT, YUSUKE?
KNOCK YOURSELVES OUT. BYE.
YOU'RE NOT COMING?!
THAT'S RIGHT!!

QUALIFICATIONS FOR A GIRLFRIEND!

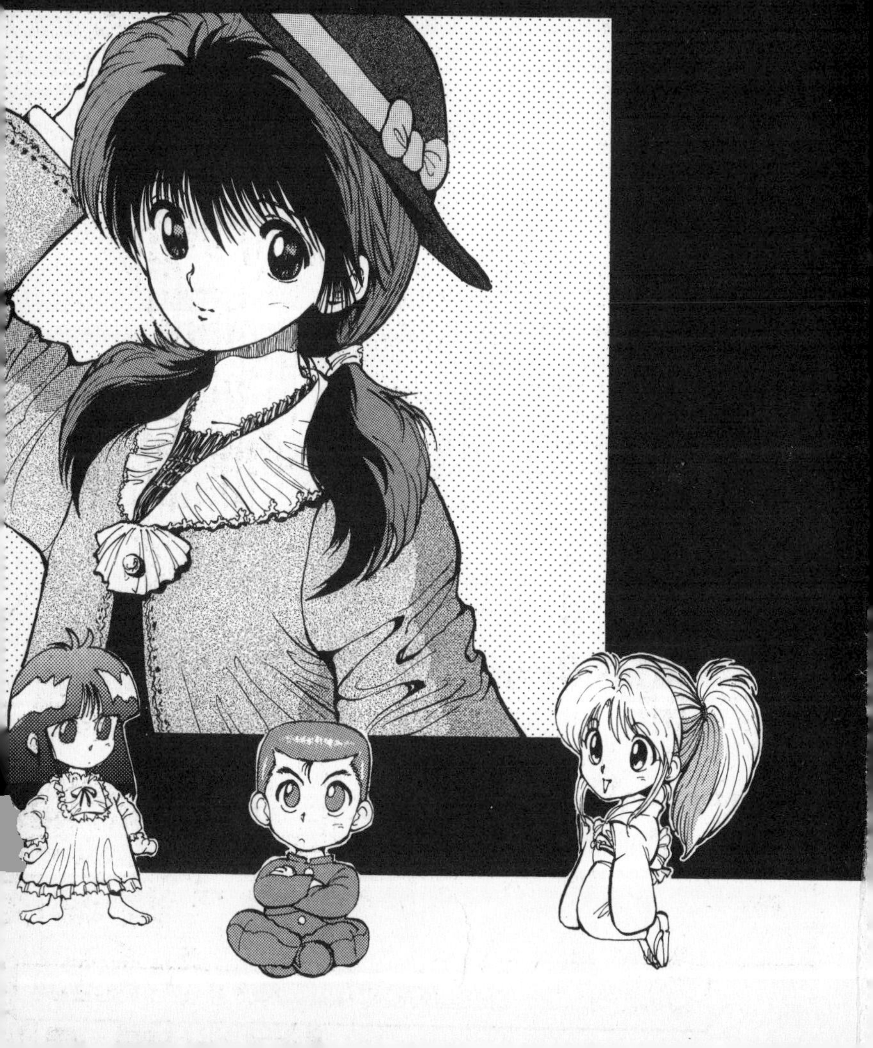

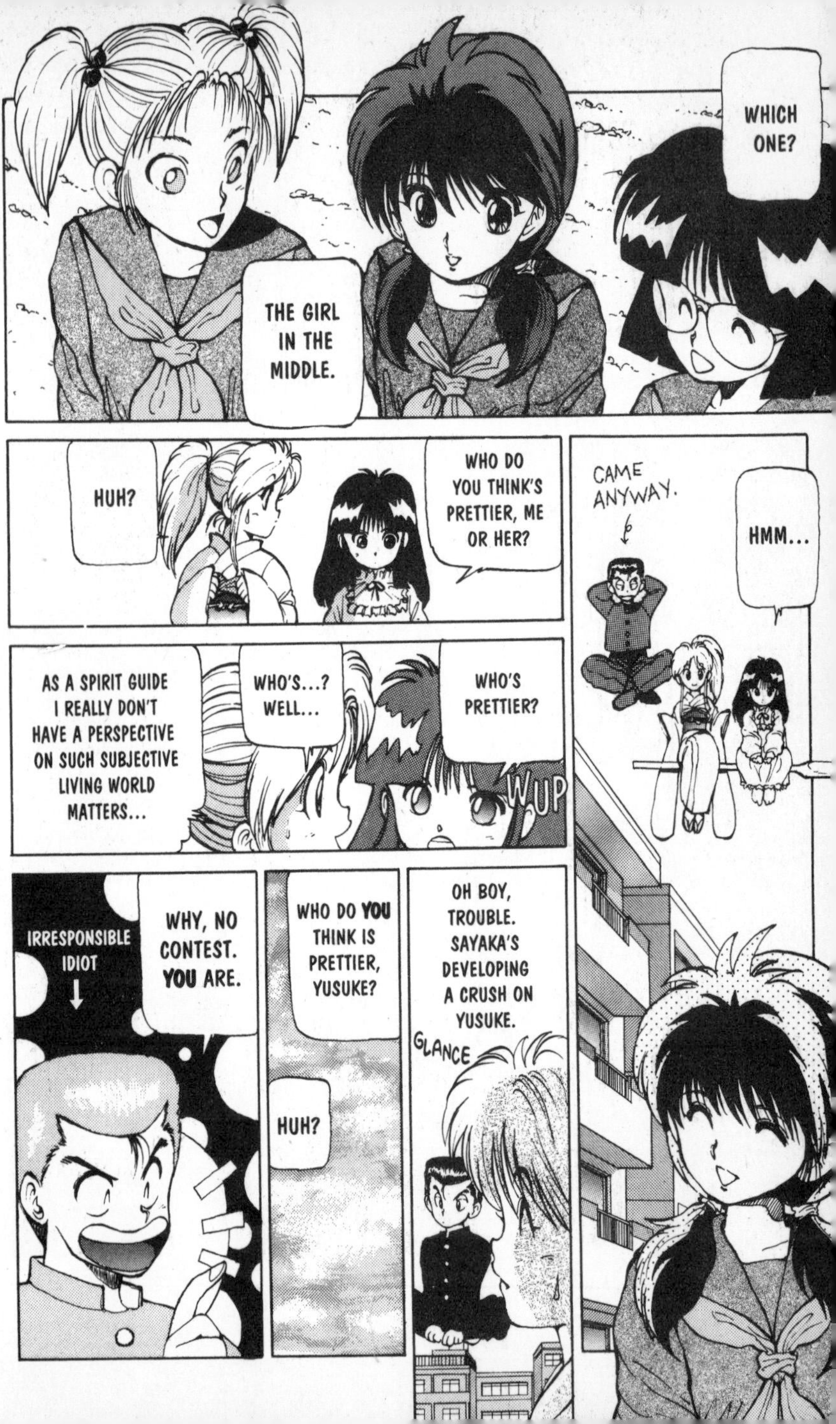
WHICH ONE?
THE GIRL IN THE MIDDLE.
HMM...
CAME ANYWAY.
WHO DO YOU THINK'S PRETTIER, ME OR HER?
HUH?
WHO'S PRETTIER?
WUP
WHO'S...? WELL...
AS A SPIRIT GUIDE I REALLY DON'T HAVE A PERSPECTIVE ON SUCH SUBJECTIVE LIVING WORLD MATTERS...
OH BOY, TROUBLE. SAYAKA'S DEVELOPING A CRUSH ON YUSUKE.
GLANCE
WHO DO YOU THINK IS PRETTIER, YUSUKE?
HUH?
WHY, NO CONTEST. YOU ARE.
IRRESPONSIBLE IDIOT

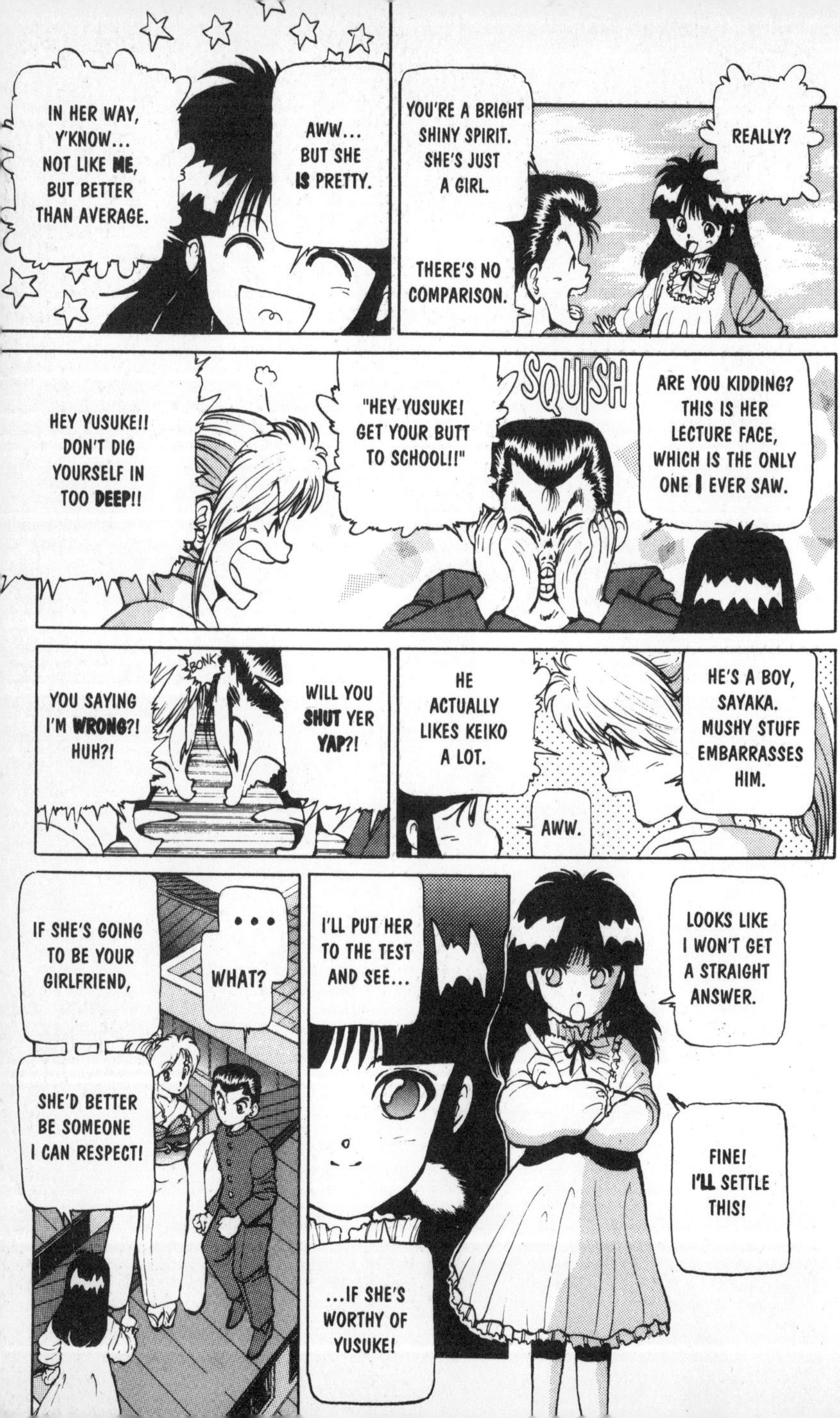
REALLY?
YOU'RE A BRIGHT SHINY SPIRIT. SHE'S JUST A GIRL.
THERE'S NO COMPARISON.
AWW... BUT SHE IS PRETTY.
IN HER WAY, Y'KNOW... NOT LIKE ME, BUT BETTER THAN AVERAGE.
ARE YOU KIDDING? THIS IS HER LECTURE FACE, WHICH IS THE ONLY ONE I EVER SAW.
SQUISH
"HEY YUSUKE! GET YOUR BUTT TO SCHOOL!!"
HEY YUSUKE!! DON'T DIG YOURSELF IN TOO DEEP!!
HE'S A BOY, SAYAKA. MUSHY STUFF EMBARRASSES HIM.
HE ACTUALLY LIKES KEIKO A LOT.
AWW.
WILL YOU SHUT YER YAP?!
BONK
YOU SAYING I'M WRONG?! HUH?!
LOOKS LIKE I WON'T GET A STRAIGHT ANSWER.
FINE! I'LL SETTLE THIS!
I'LL PUT HER TO THE TEST AND SEE...
...IF SHE'S WORTHY OF YUSUKE!
...
WHAT?
IF SHE'S GOING TO BE YOUR GIRLFRIEND,
SHE'D BETTER BE SOMEONE I CAN RESPECT!

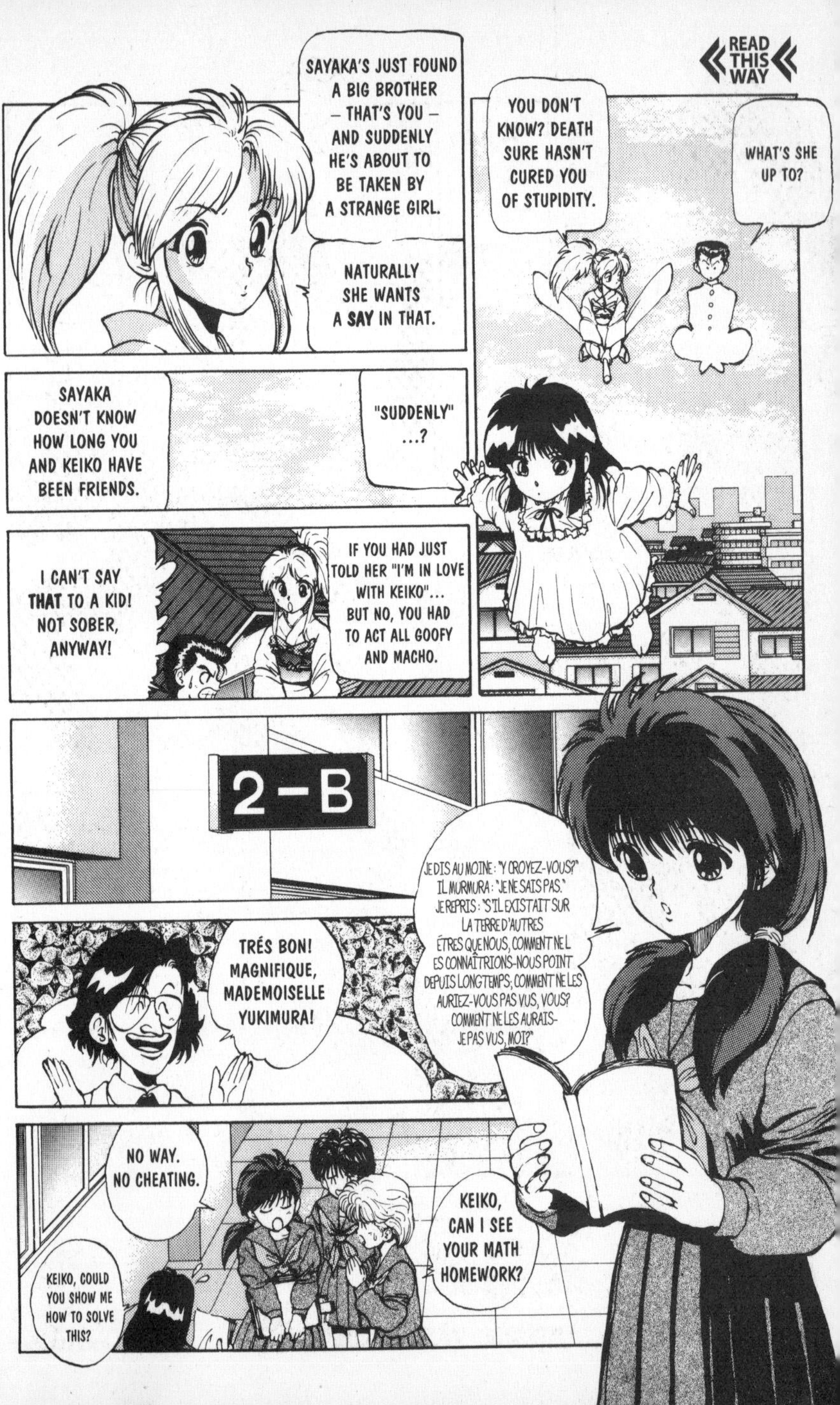
READ THIS WAY
WHAT'S SHE UP TO?
YOU DON'T KNOW? DEATH SURE HASN'T CURED YOU OF STUPIDITY.
SAYAKA'S JUST FOUND A BIG BROTHER – THAT'S YOU – AND SUDDENLY HE'S ABOUT TO BE TAKEN BY A STRANGE GIRL.
NATURALLY SHE WANTS A SAY IN THAT.
"SUDDENLY" ...?
SAYAKA DOESN'T KNOW HOW LONG YOU AND KEIKO HAVE BEEN FRIENDS.
IF YOU HAD JUST TOLD HER "I'M IN LOVE WITH KEIKO"... BUT NO, YOU HAD TO ACT ALL GOOFY AND MACHO.
I CAN'T SAY THAT TO A KID! NOT SOBER, ANYWAY!
JE DIS AU MOINE: "Y CROYEZ-VOUS?" IL MURMURA: "JE NE SAIS PAS." JE REPRIS: "S'IL EXISTAIT SUR LA TERRE D'AUTRES ÊTRES QUE NOUS, COMMENT NE LES CONNAÎTRIONS-NOUS POINT DEPUIS LONGTEMPS; COMMENT NE LES AURIEZ-VOUS PAS VUS, VOUS? COMMENT NE LES AURAIS-JE PAS VUS, MOI?"
2-B
TRÉS BON! MAGNIFIQUE, MADEMOISELLE YUKIMURA!
KEIKO, CAN I SEE YOUR MATH HOMEWORK?
NO WAY. NO CHEATING.
KEIKO, COULD YOU SHOW ME HOW TO SOLVE THIS?

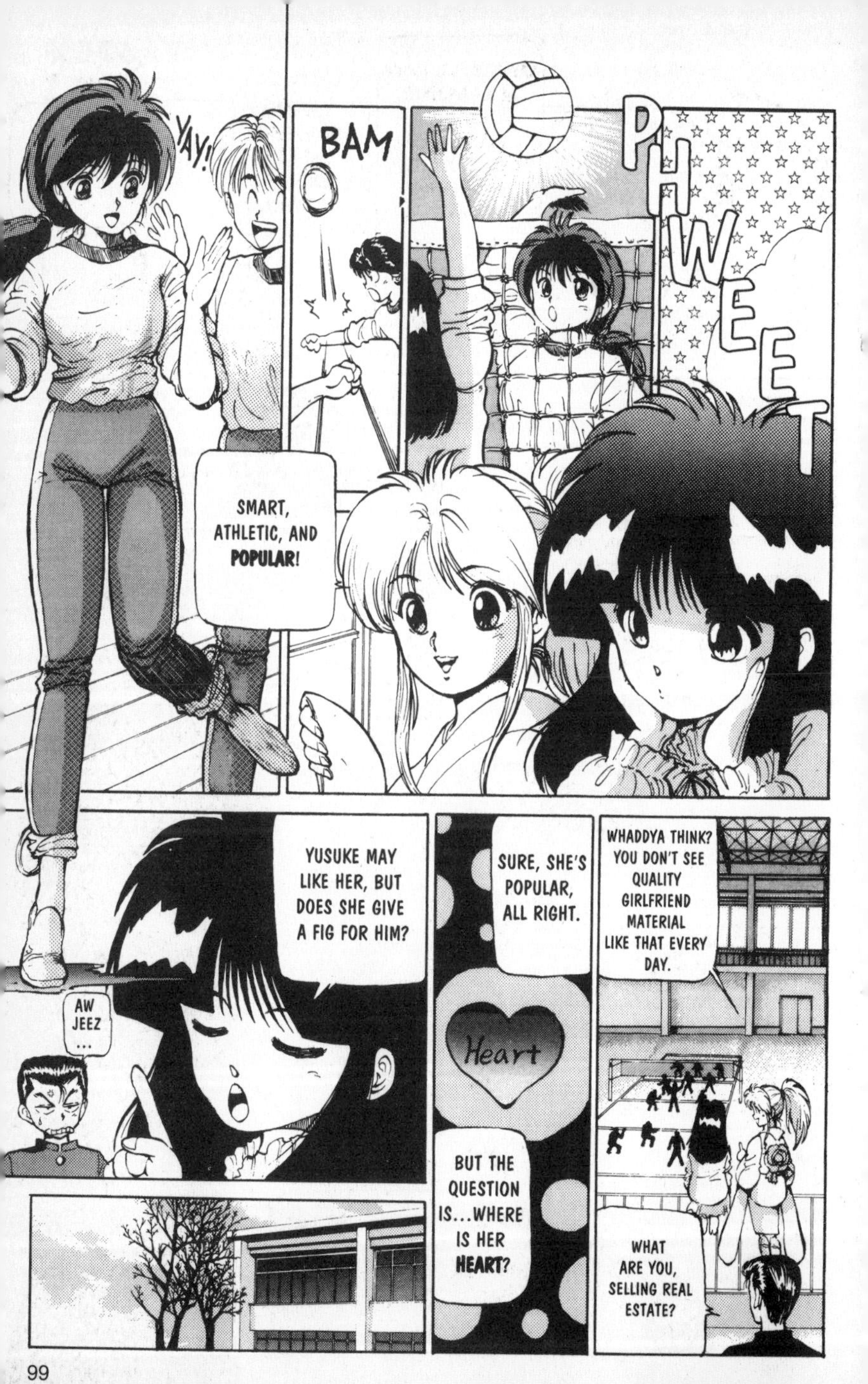
PHWEET
BAM
YAY!
SMART, ATHLETIC, AND **POPULAR**!
WHADDYA THINK? YOU DON'T SEE QUALITY GIRLFRIEND MATERIAL LIKE THAT EVERY DAY.
WHAT ARE YOU, SELLING REAL ESTATE?
SURE, SHE'S POPULAR, ALL RIGHT.
Heart
BUT THE QUESTION IS...WHERE IS HER **HEART**?
YUSUKE MAY LIKE HER, BUT DOES SHE GIVE A FIG FOR HIM?
AW JEEZ ...

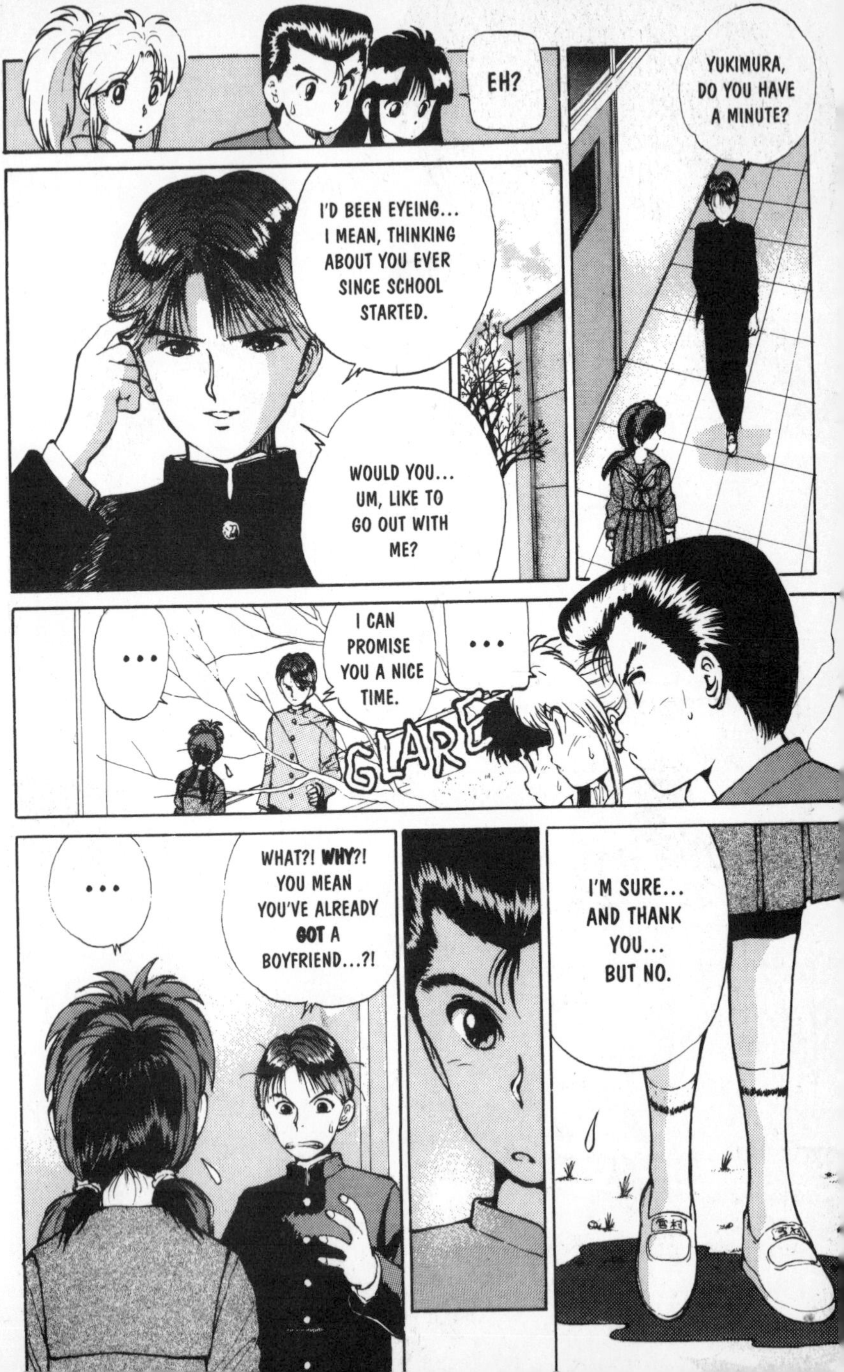
YUKIMURA, DO YOU HAVE A MINUTE?
EH?
I'D BEEN EYEING... I MEAN, THINKING ABOUT YOU EVER SINCE SCHOOL STARTED.
WOULD YOU... UM, LIKE TO GO OUT WITH ME?
...
GLARE
I CAN PROMISE YOU A NICE TIME.
...
I'M SURE... AND THANK YOU... BUT NO.
WHAT?! **WHY**?! YOU MEAN YOU'VE ALREADY **GOT** A BOYFRIEND...?!
...

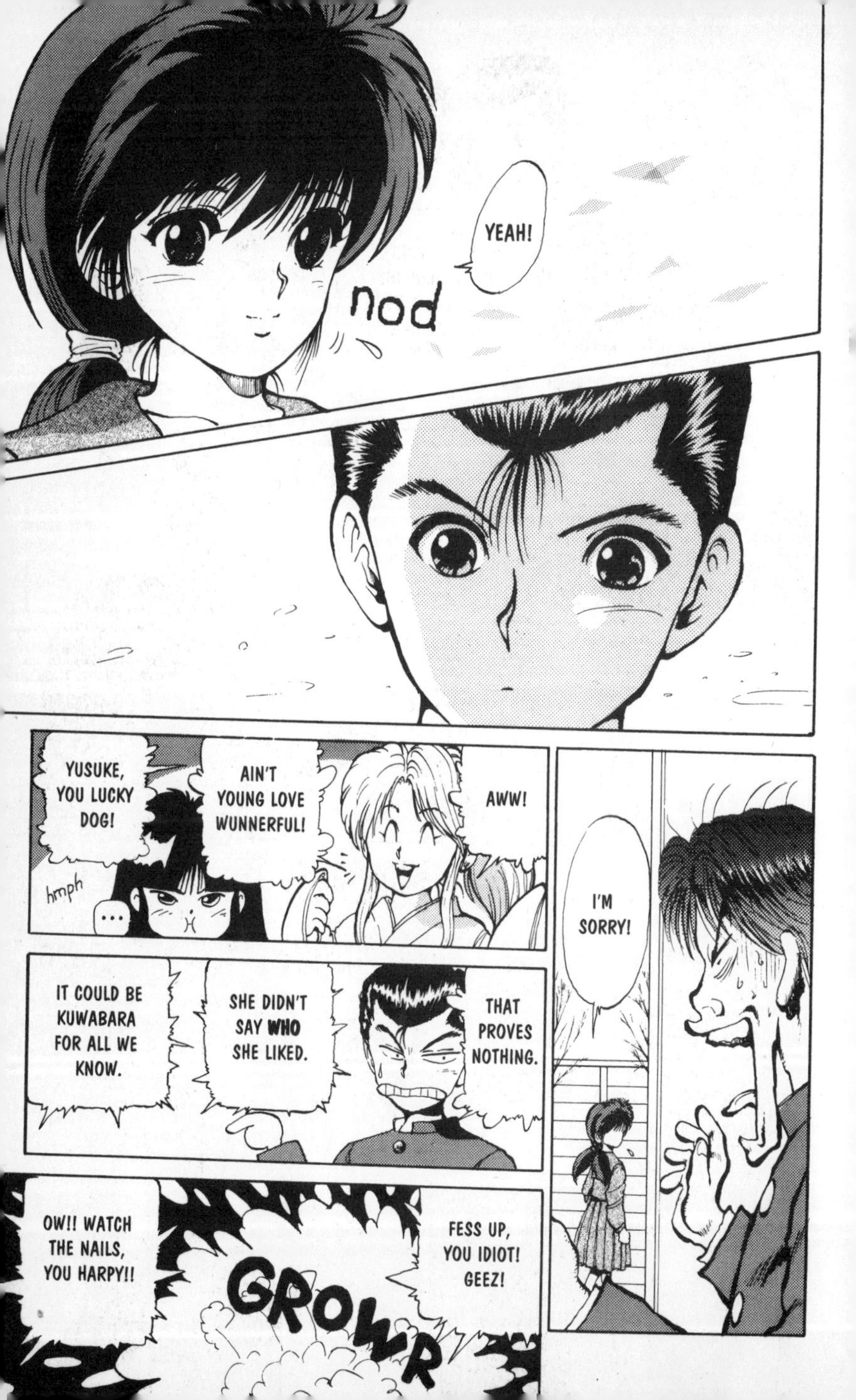
YEAH!
nod
I'M SORRY!
AWW!
AIN'T YOUNG LOVE WUNNERFUL!
YUSUKE, YOU LUCKY DOG!
hmph
...
THAT PROVES NOTHING.
SHE DIDN'T SAY **WHO** SHE LIKED.
IT COULD BE KUWABARA FOR ALL WE KNOW.
FESS UP, YOU IDIOT! GEEZ!
OW!! WATCH THE NAILS, YOU HARPY!!
GROWR

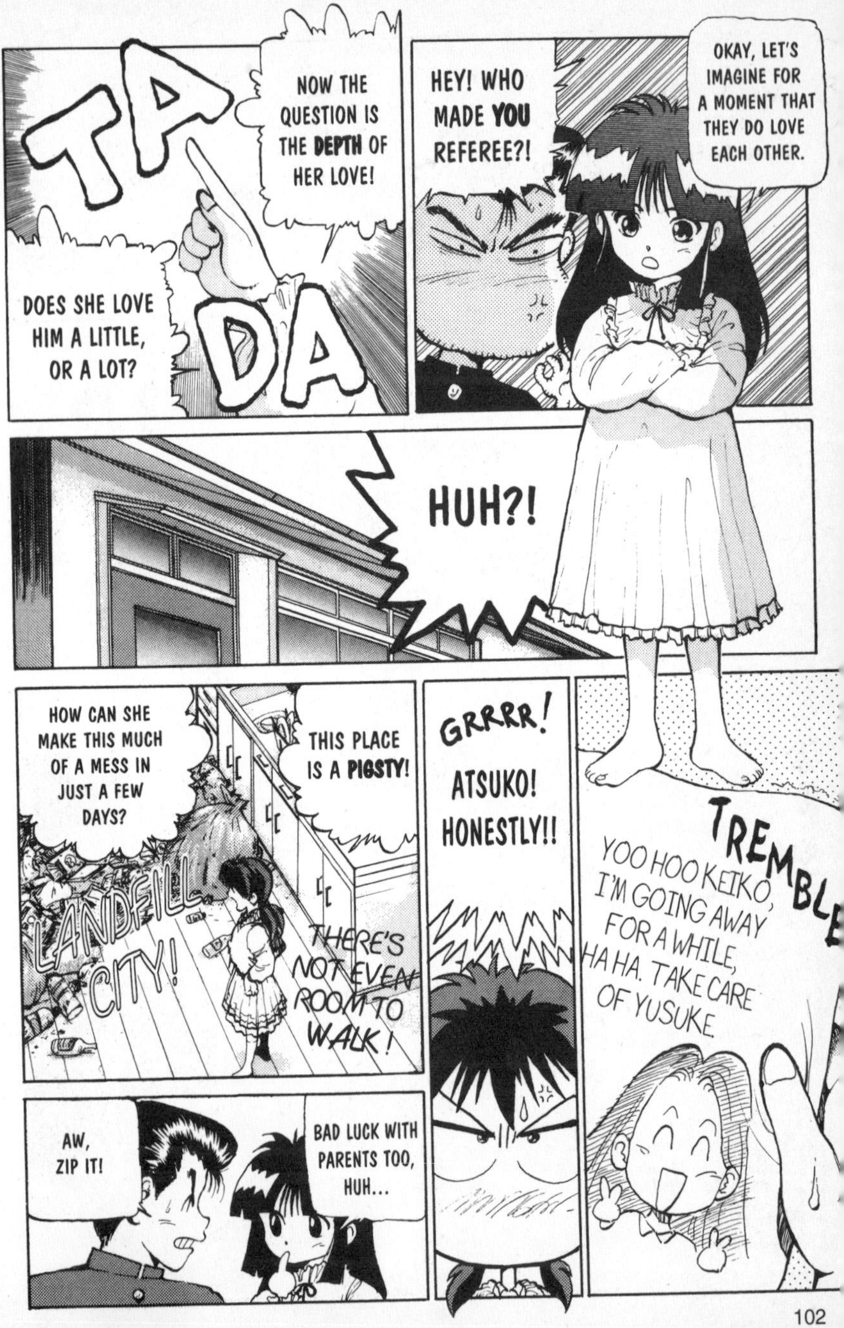

OKAY, LET'S IMAGINE FOR A MOMENT THAT THEY DO LOVE EACH OTHER.
HEY! WHO MADE **YOU** REFEREE?!
TA
NOW THE QUESTION IS THE **DEPTH** OF HER LOVE!
DA
DOES SHE LOVE HIM A LITTLE, OR A LOT?
HUH?!
TREMBLE
YOO HOO KEIKO, I'M GOING AWAY FOR A WHILE, HA HA. TAKE CARE OF YUSUKE.
GRRRR!
ATSUKO! HONESTLY!!
THIS PLACE IS A **PIGSTY**!
HOW CAN SHE MAKE THIS MUCH OF A MESS IN JUST A FEW DAYS?
LANDFILL CITY!
THERE'S NOT EVEN ROOM TO WALK!
BAD LUCK WITH PARENTS TOO, HUH...
AW, ZIP IT!

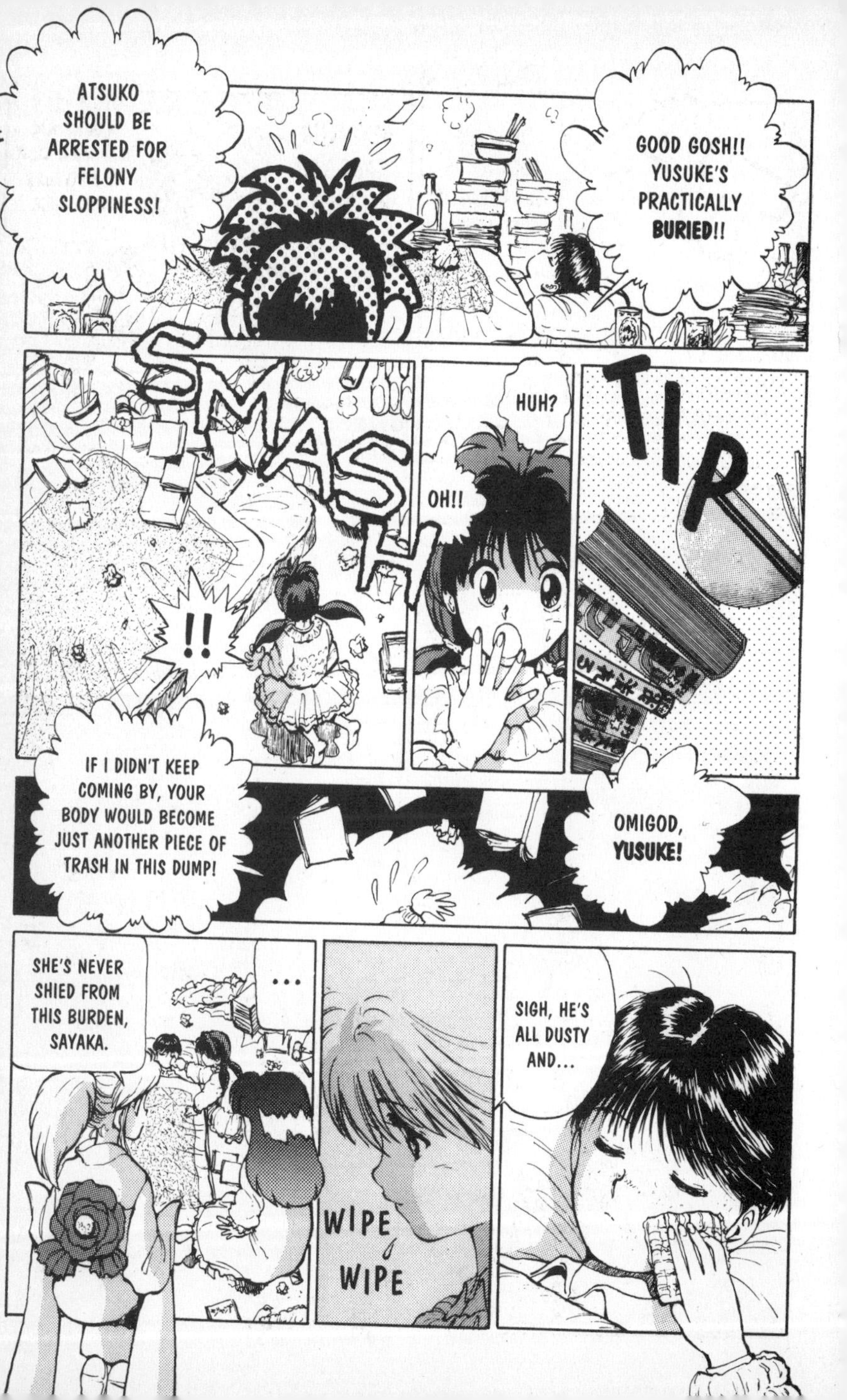
GOOD GOSH!! YUSUKE'S PRACTICALLY **BURIED**!!
ATSUKO SHOULD BE ARRESTED FOR FELONY SLOPPINESS!
TIP
HUH?
OH!!
SMASH
!!
OMIGOD, **YUSUKE!**
IF I DIDN'T KEEP COMING BY, YOUR BODY WOULD BECOME JUST ANOTHER PIECE OF TRASH IN THIS DUMP!
SIGH, HE'S ALL DUSTY AND...
WIPE WIPE
...
SHE'S NEVER SHIED FROM THIS BURDEN, SAYAKA.

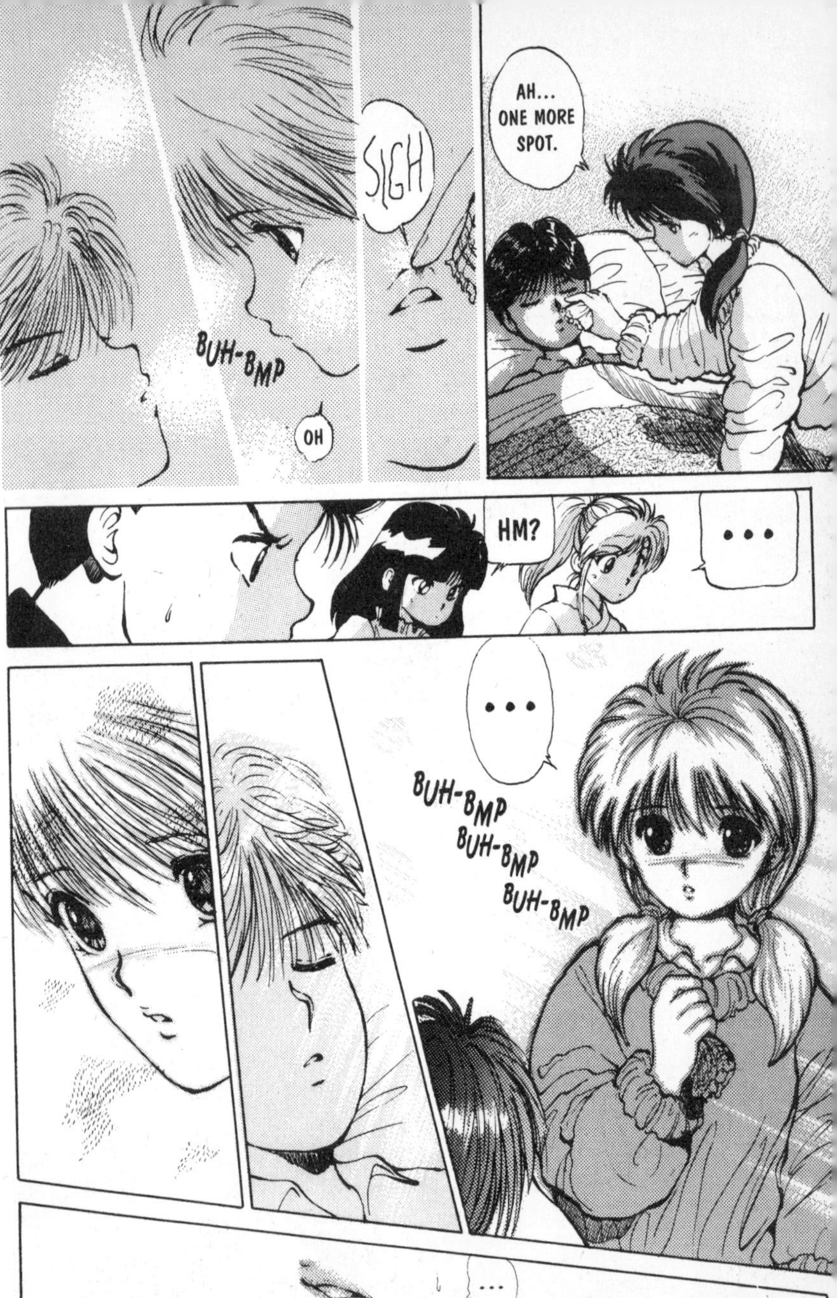
AH... ONE MORE SPOT.
SIGH
OH
BUH-BMP
...
HM?
...
BUH-BMP
BUH-BMP
BUH-BMP
...

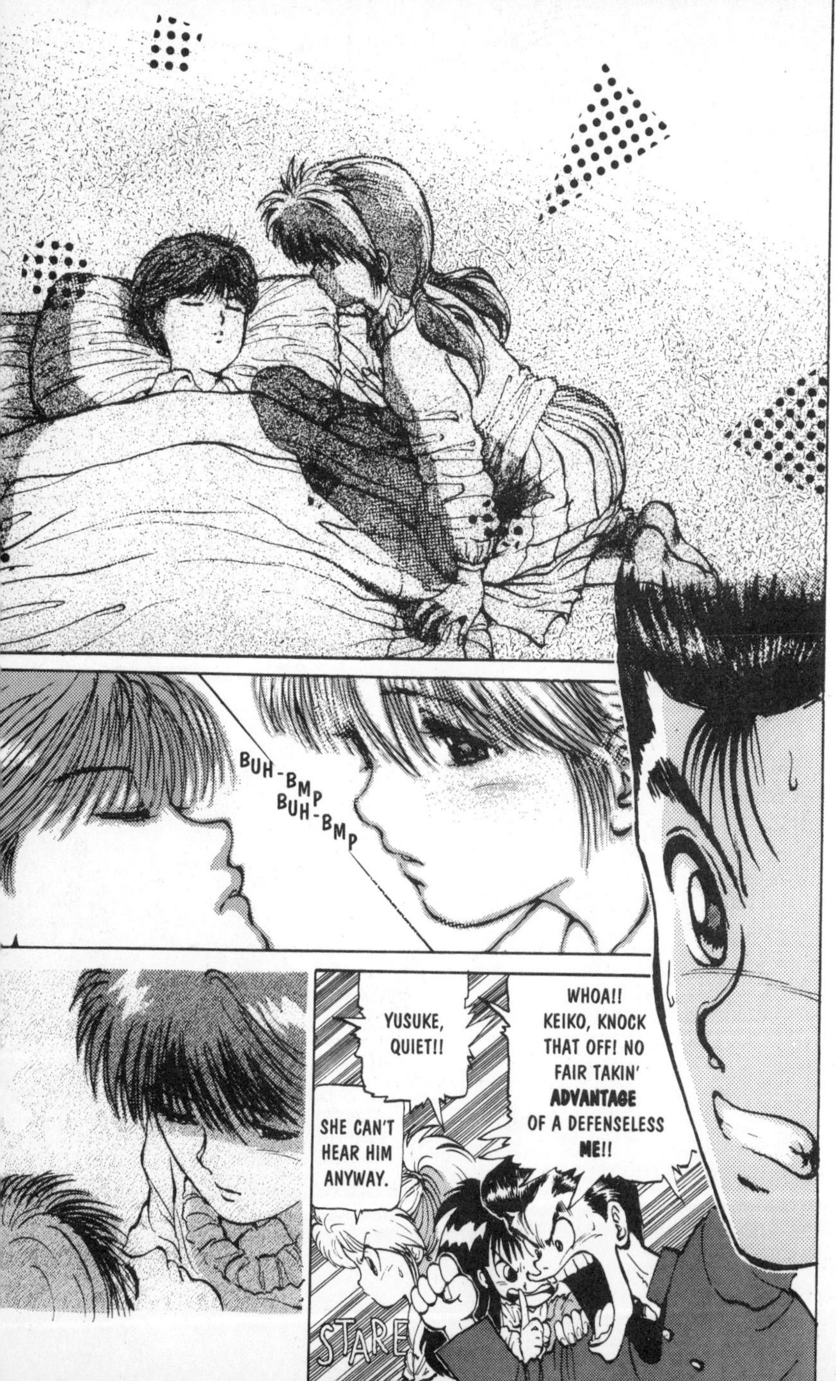
BUH-BMP
BUH-BMP
WHOA!! KEIKO, KNOCK THAT OFF! NO FAIR TAKIN' ADVANTAGE OF A DEFENSELESS ME!!
YUSUKE, QUIET!!
SHE CAN'T HEAR HIM ANYWAY.
STARE

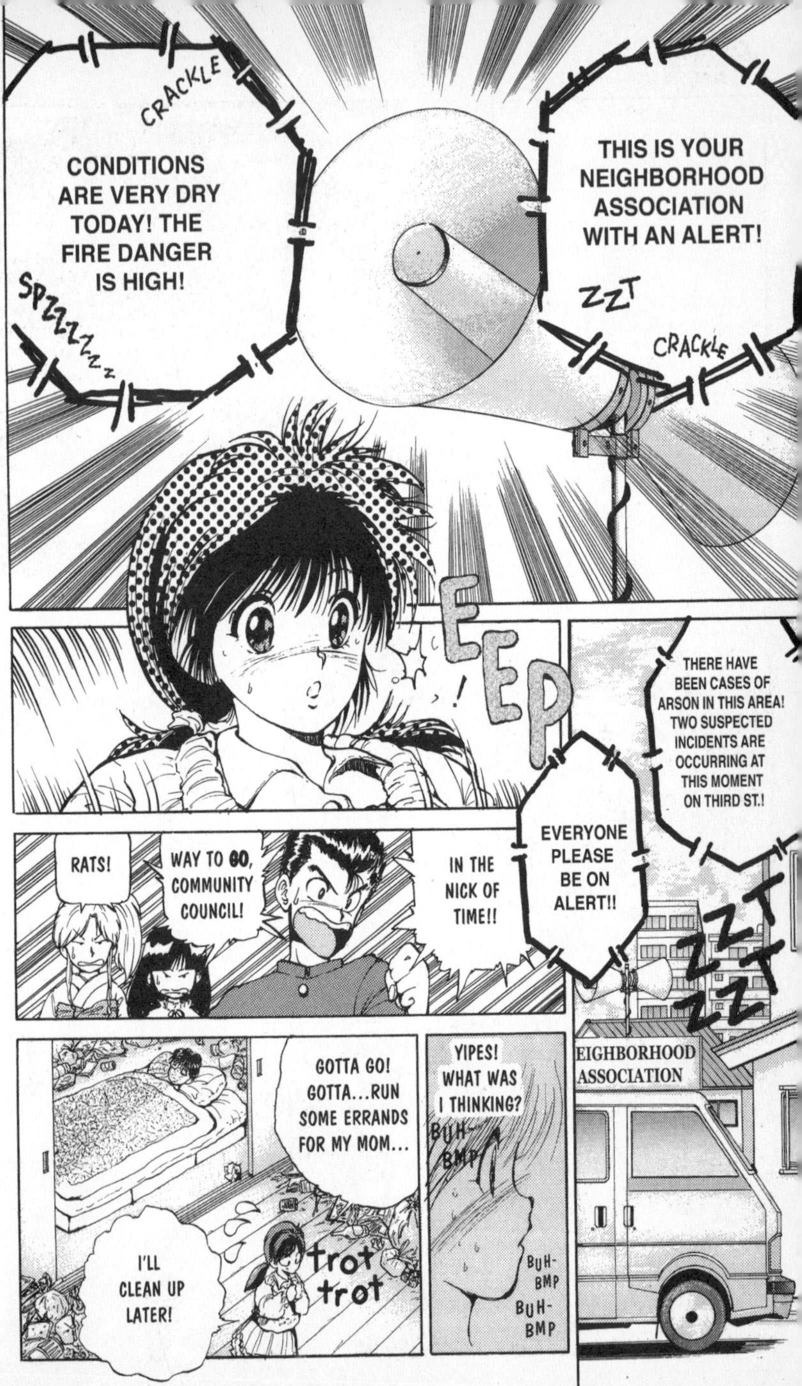
THIS IS YOUR NEIGHBORHOOD ASSOCIATION WITH AN ALERT!
ZZT
CRACKLE
CRACKLE
CONDITIONS ARE VERY DRY TODAY! THE FIRE DANGER IS HIGH!
SPZZZZZZ
THERE HAVE BEEN CASES OF ARSON IN THIS AREA! TWO SUSPECTED INCIDENTS ARE OCCURRING AT THIS MOMENT ON THIRD ST.!
EVERYONE PLEASE BE ON ALERT!!
ZZT ZZT
EIGHBORHOOD ASSOCIATION
EEP
!
IN THE NICK OF TIME!!
WAY TO GO, COMMUNITY COUNCIL!
RATS!
YIPES! WHAT WAS I THINKING?
BUH-BMP
BUH-BMP BUH-BMP
GOTTA GO! GOTTA...RUN SOME ERRANDS FOR MY MOM...
trot trot
I'LL CLEAN UP LATER!

READ THIS WAY

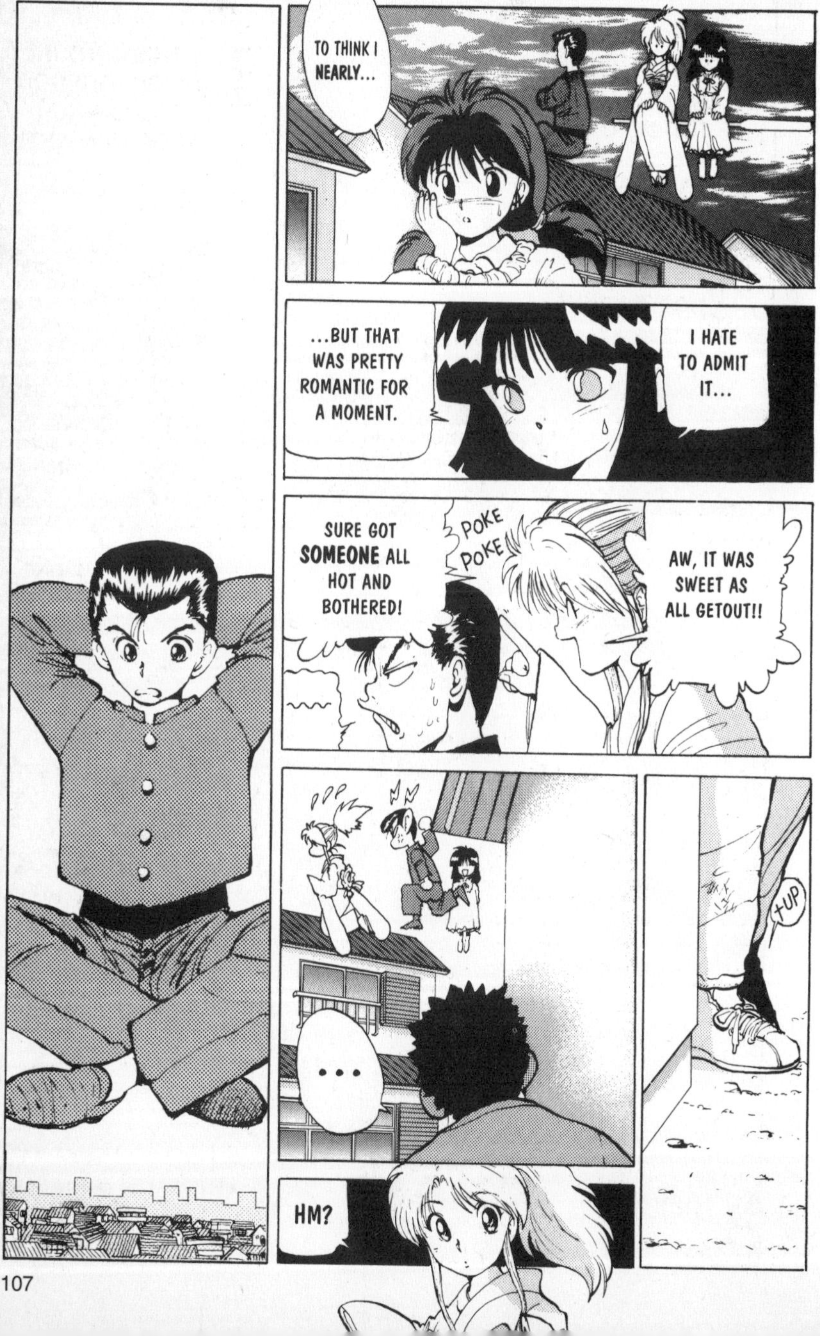

TO THINK I NEARLY...
I HATE TO ADMIT IT...
...BUT THAT WAS PRETTY ROMANTIC FOR A MOMENT.
AW, IT WAS SWEET AS ALL GETOUT!!
POKE POKE
SURE GOT SOMEONE ALL HOT AND BOTHERED!
TUP
• • •
HM?

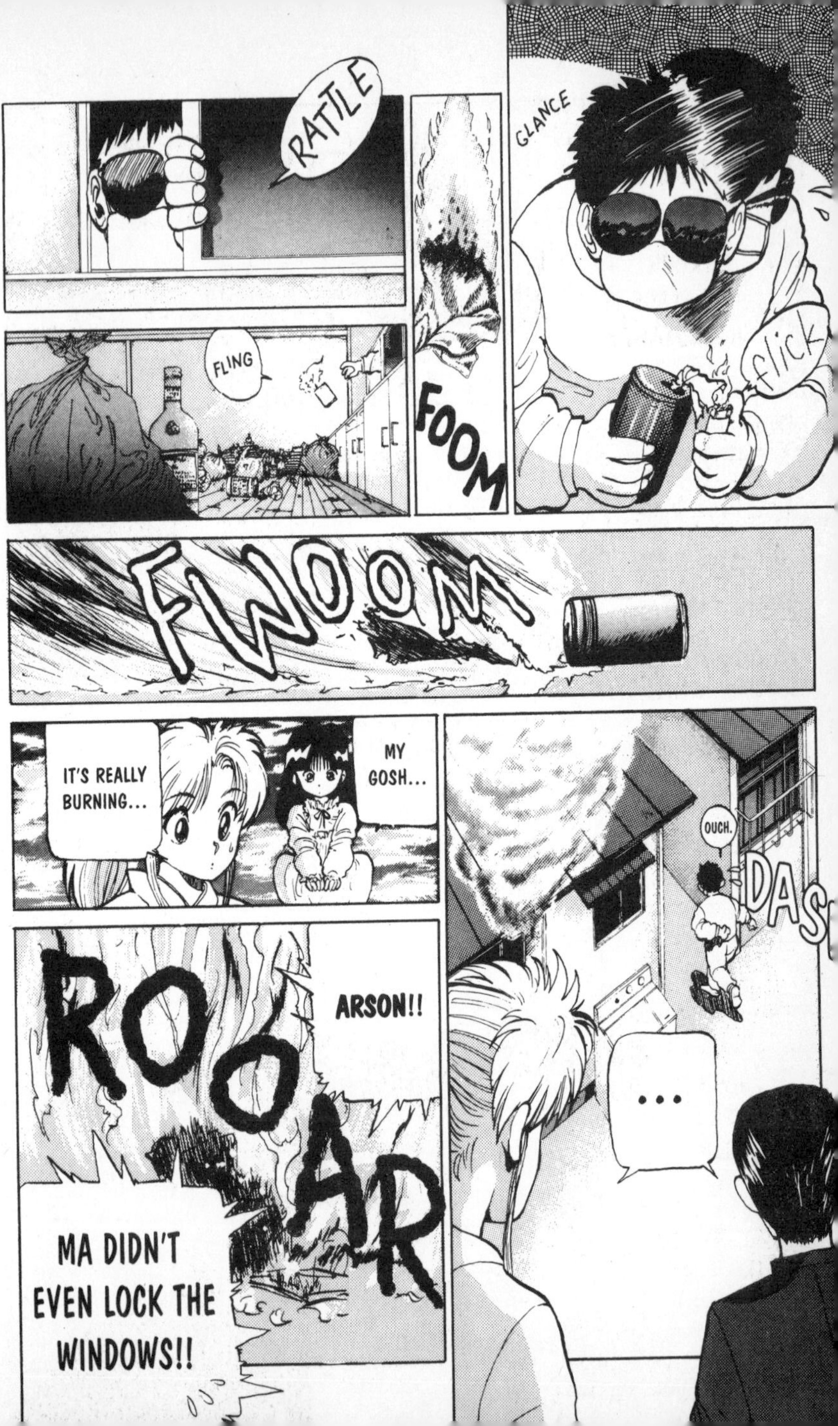
GLANCE
flick
FOOM
RATTLE
FLING
FWOOM
OUCH.
DAS
...
MY GOSH...
IT'S REALLY BURNING...
ARSON!!
ROOAR
MA DIDN'T EVEN LOCK THE WINDOWS!!

READ THIS WAY

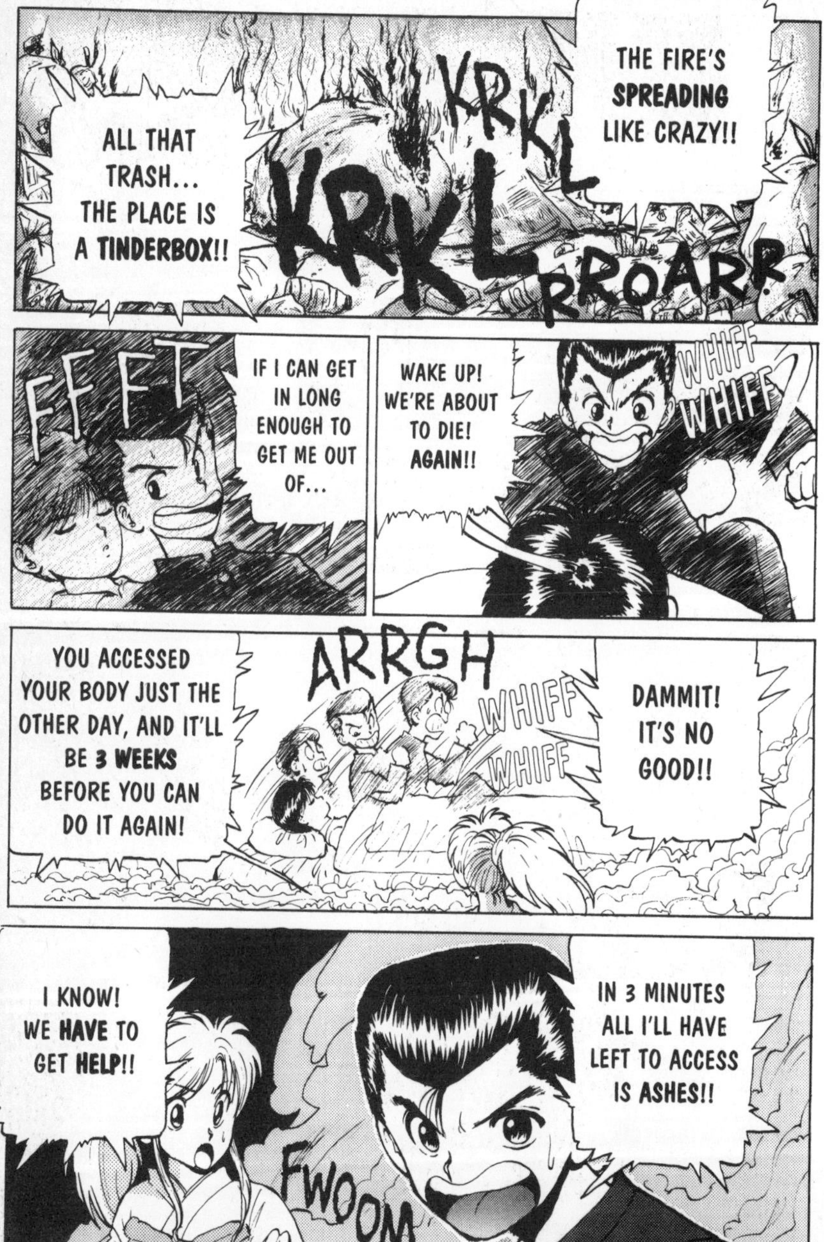
THE FIRE'S SPREADING LIKE CRAZY!!
KRKL
KRKL
ALL THAT TRASH... THE PLACE IS A TINDERBOX!!
RROARR
WHIFF
WHIFF
WAKE UP! WE'RE ABOUT TO DIE! AGAIN!!
IF I CAN GET IN LONG ENOUGH TO GET ME OUT OF...
FFFT
DAMMIT! IT'S NO GOOD!!
ARRGH
WHIFF
WHIFF
YOU ACCESSED YOUR BODY JUST THE OTHER DAY, AND IT'LL BE 3 WEEKS BEFORE YOU CAN DO IT AGAIN!
IN 3 MINUTES ALL I'LL HAVE LEFT TO ACCESS IS ASHES!!
I KNOW! WE HAVE TO GET HELP!!
FWOOM

READ THIS WAY

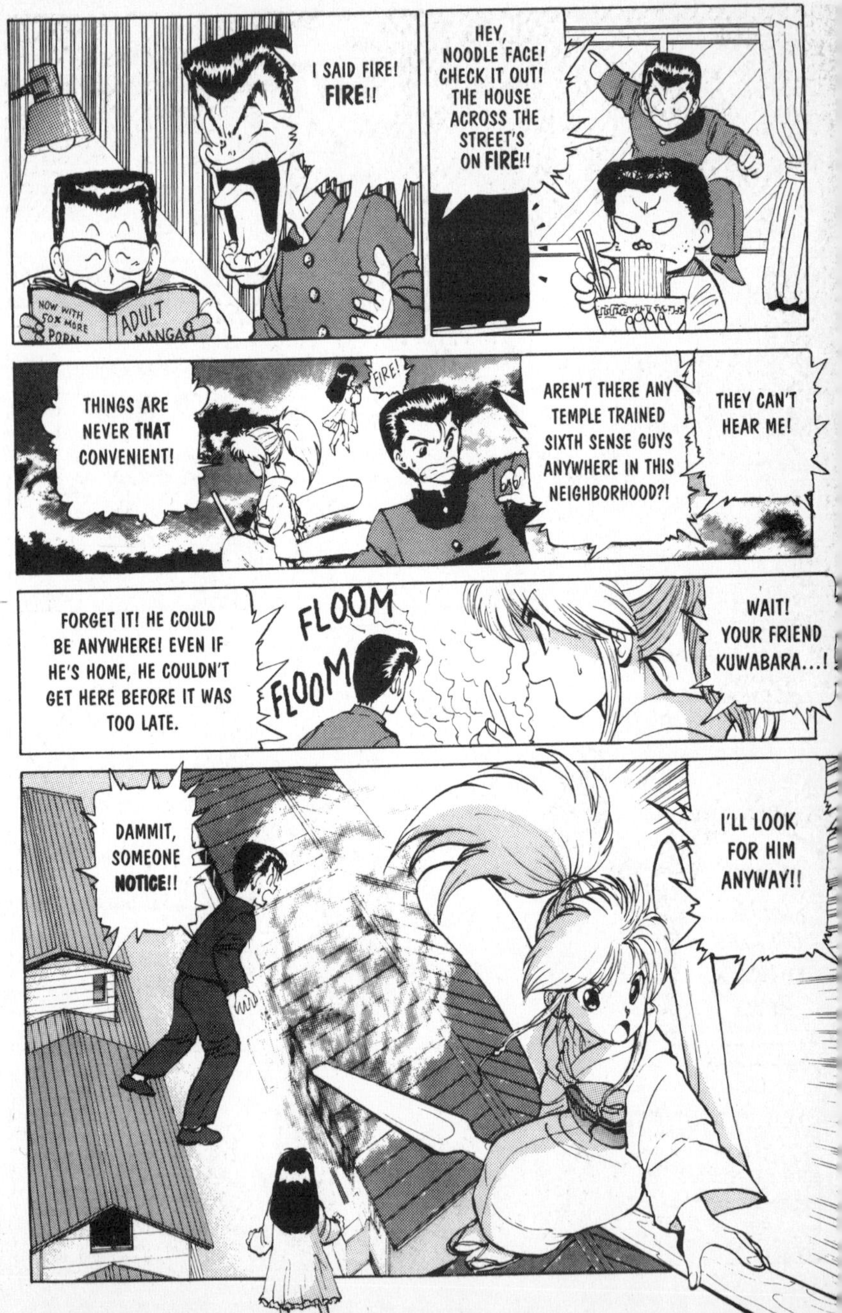
HEY, NOODLE FACE! CHECK IT OUT! THE HOUSE ACROSS THE STREET'S ON FIRE!!
I SAID FIRE! FIRE!!
NOW WITH 50% MORE PORN
ADULT MANGA
THEY CAN'T HEAR ME!
AREN'T THERE ANY TEMPLE TRAINED SIXTH SENSE GUYS ANYWHERE IN THIS NEIGHBORHOOD?!
FIRE!
THINGS ARE NEVER THAT CONVENIENT!
WAIT! YOUR FRIEND KUWABARA...!
FLOOM
FLOOM
FORGET IT! HE COULD BE ANYWHERE! EVEN IF HE'S HOME, HE COULDN'T GET HERE BEFORE IT WAS TOO LATE.
I'LL LOOK FOR HIM ANYWAY!!
DAMMIT, SOMEONE NOTICE!!

READ THIS WAY

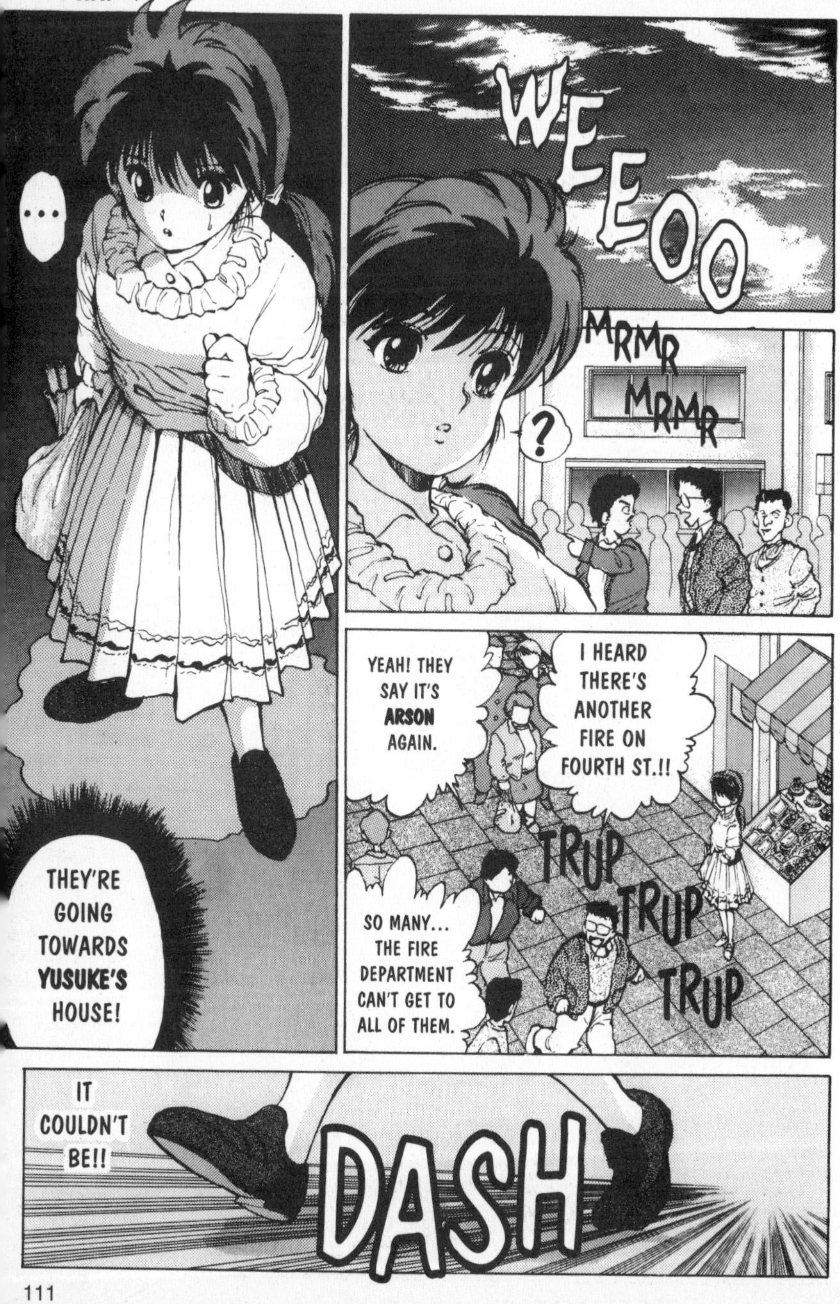
WEEOO
MRMR MRMR
?
I HEARD THERE'S ANOTHER FIRE ON FOURTH ST.!!
YEAH! THEY SAY IT'S **ARSON** AGAIN.
TRUP TRUP TRUP
SO MANY... THE FIRE DEPARTMENT CAN'T GET TO ALL OF THEM.
...
THEY'RE GOING TOWARDS **YUSUKE'S** HOUSE!
DASH
IT COULDN'T BE!!

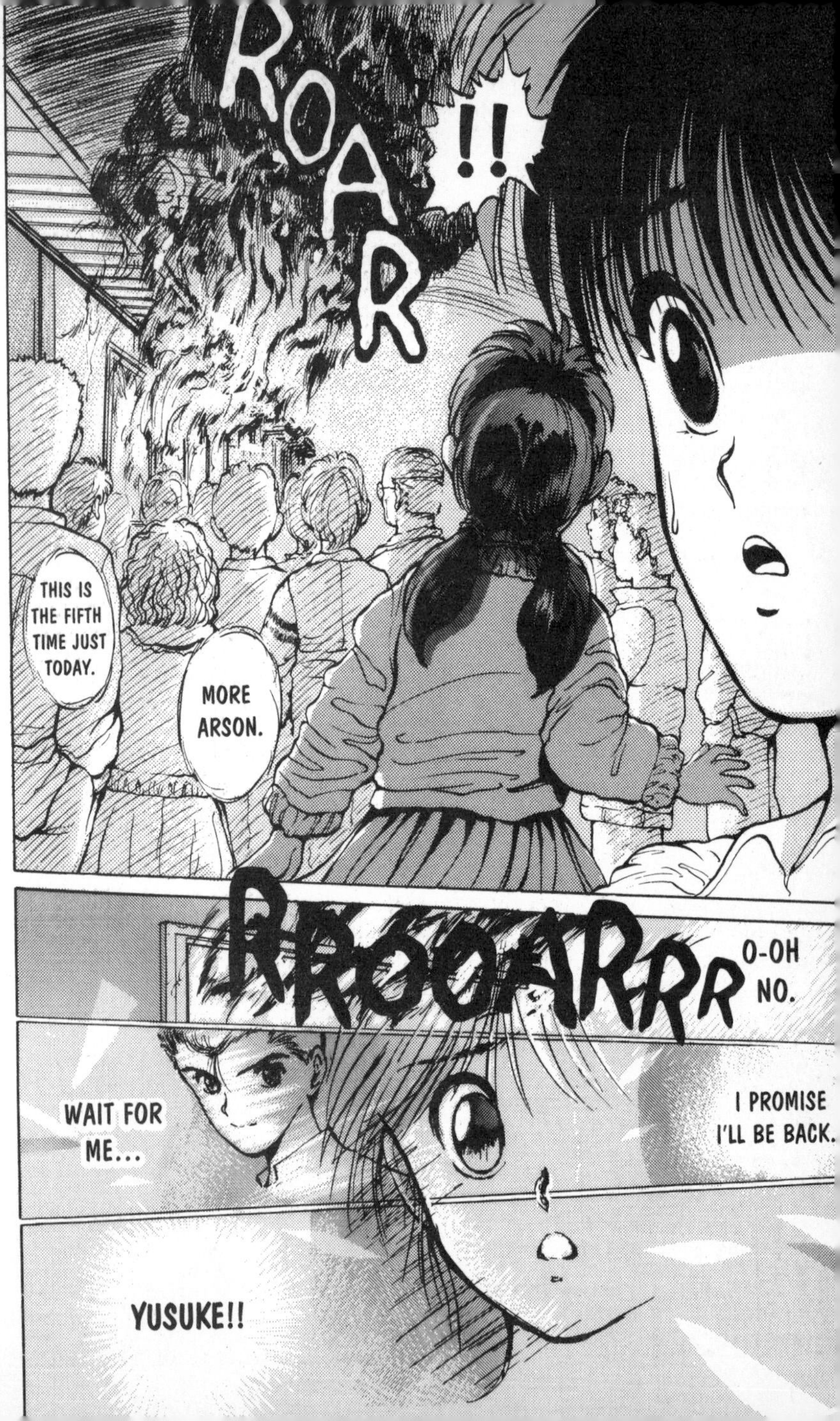
ROAR!!
MORE ARSON.
THIS IS THE FIFTH TIME JUST TODAY.
O-OH NO.
RROOARRR
I PROMISE I'LL BE BACK.
WAIT FOR ME...
YUSUKE!!

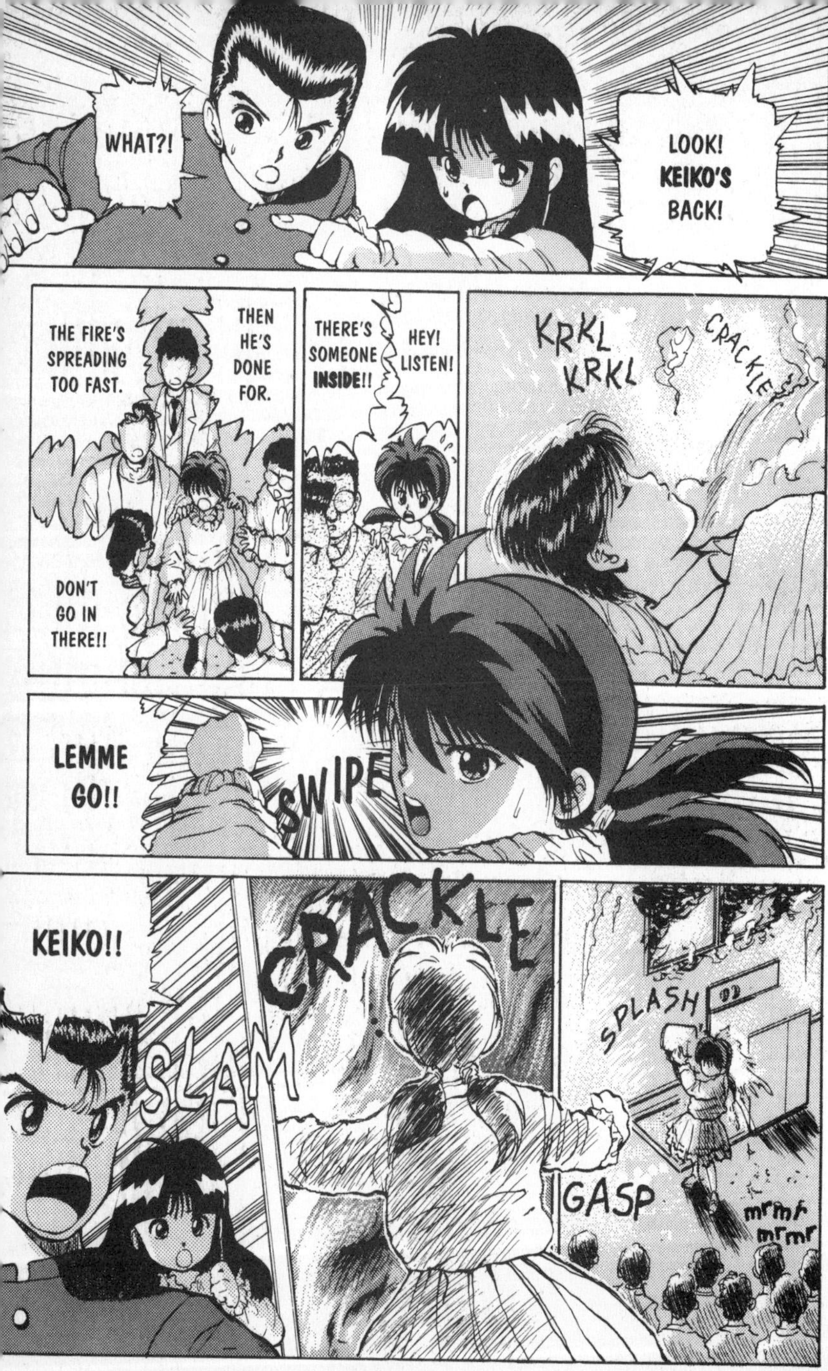
LOOK! KEIKO'S BACK!
WHAT?!
KRKL KRKL
CRACKLE
HEY! LISTEN!
THERE'S SOMEONE INSIDE!!
THEN HE'S DONE FOR.
THE FIRE'S SPREADING TOO FAST.
DON'T GO IN THERE!!
SWIPE
LEMME GO!!
SPLASH
GASP
mrmr mrmr
CRACKLE
KEIKO!!
SLAM

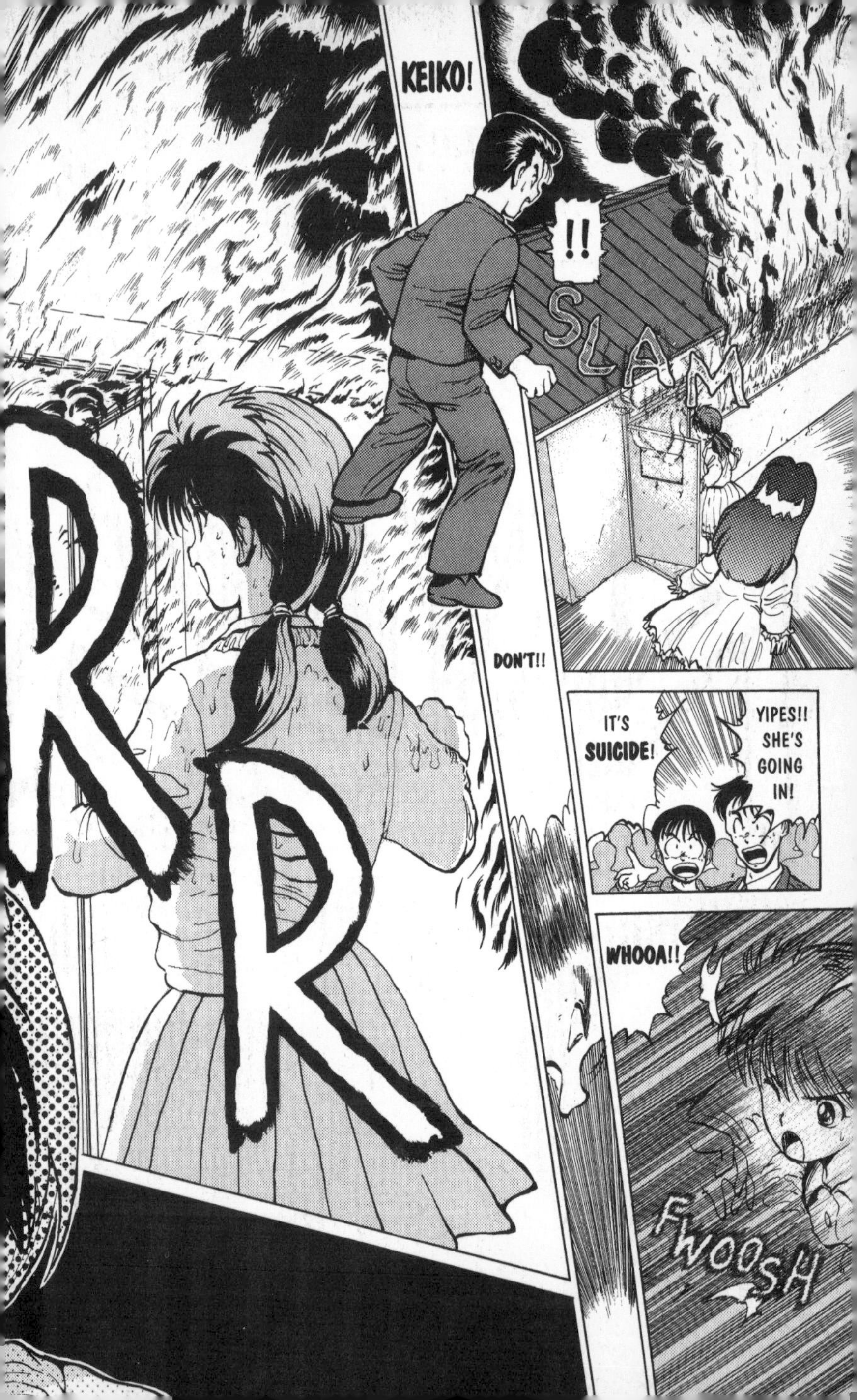
KEIKO!
!!
SLAM
DON'T!!
YIPES!! SHE'S GOING IN!
IT'S SUICIDE!
WHOOA!!
FWOOSH
RR

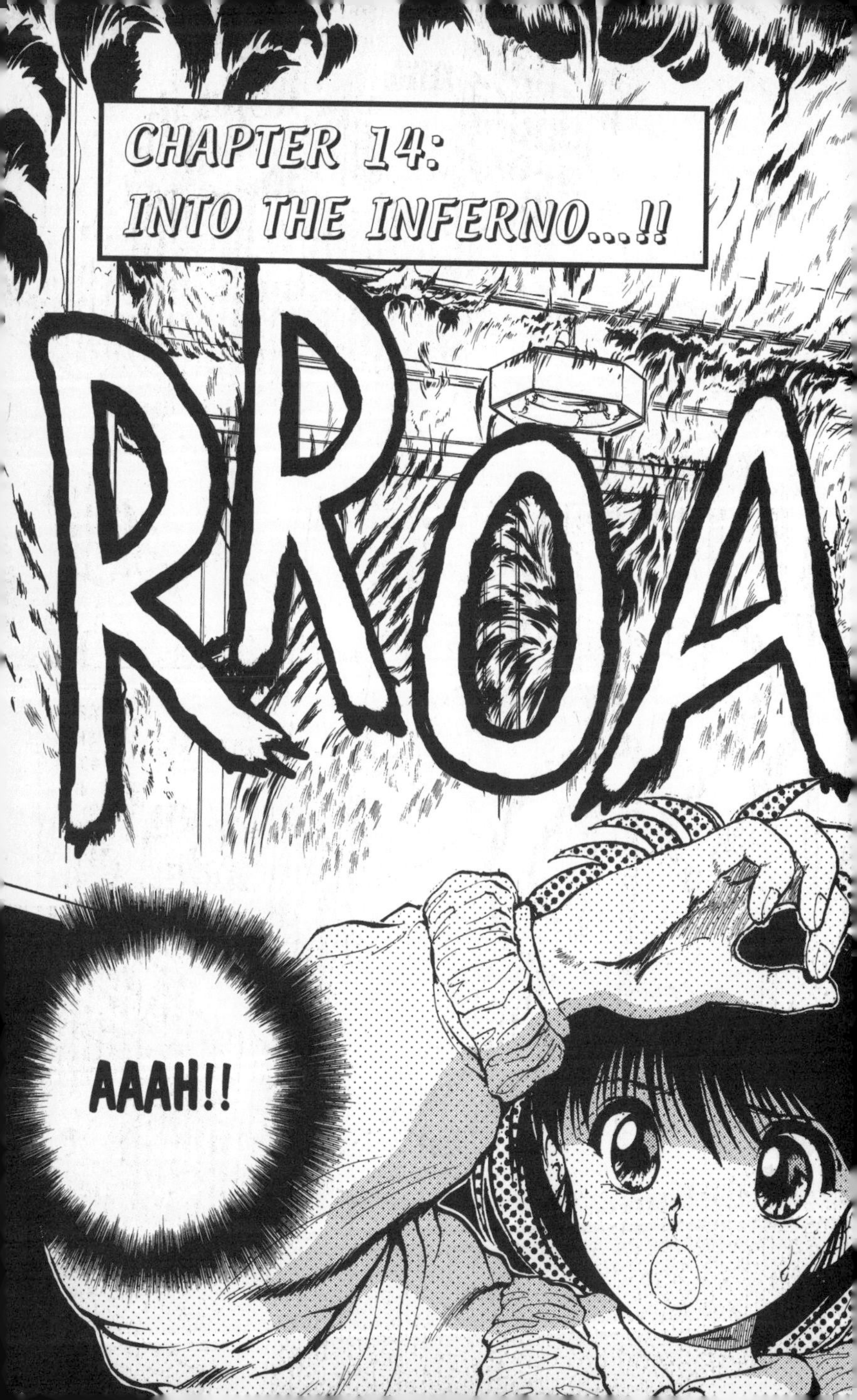
CHAPTER 14:
INTO THE INFERNO...!!
RROA
AAAH!!

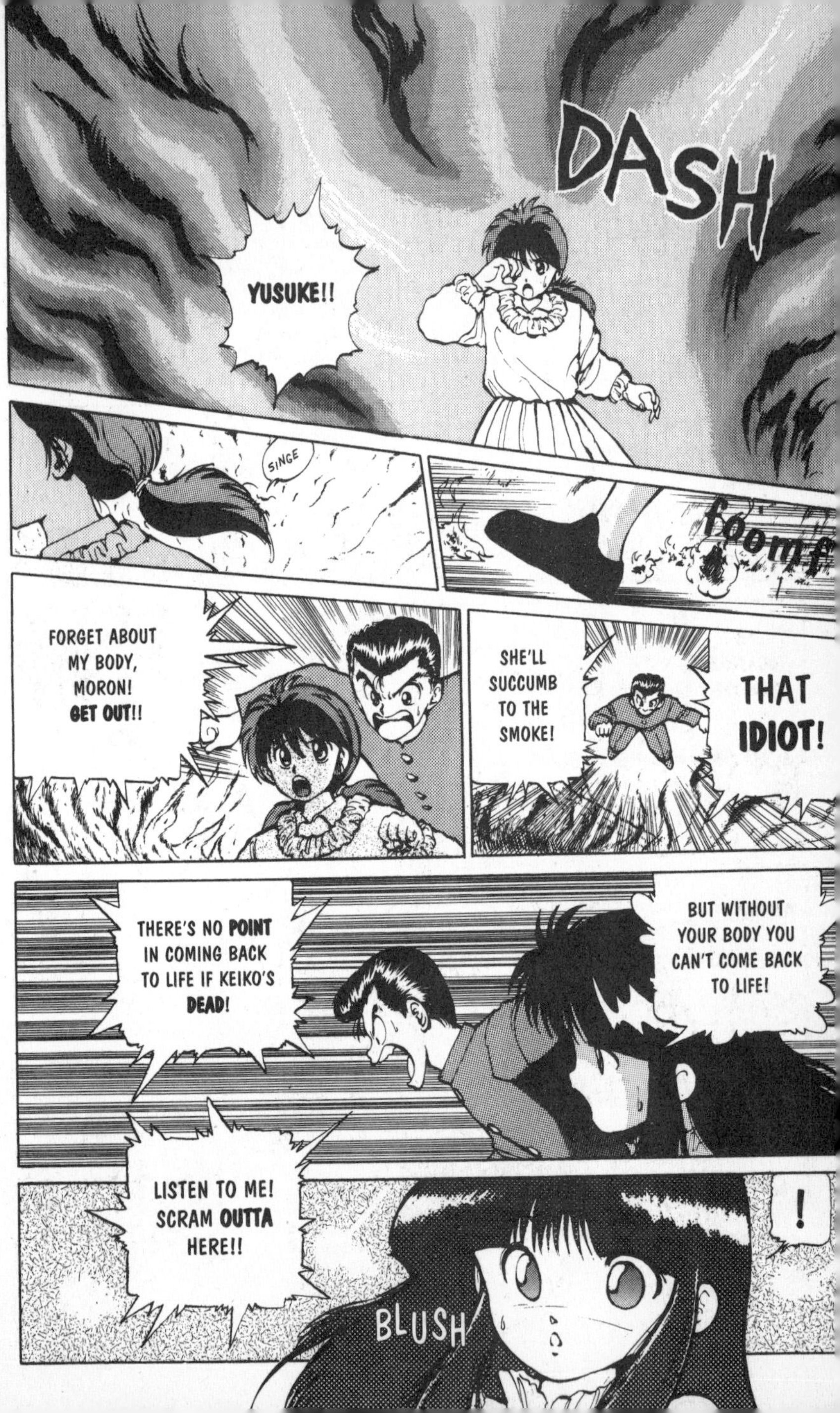
DASH
YUSUKE!!
foomf
SINGE
THAT IDIOT!
SHE'LL SUCCUMB TO THE SMOKE!
FORGET ABOUT MY BODY, MORON! GET OUT!!
BUT WITHOUT YOUR BODY YOU CAN'T COME BACK TO LIFE!
THERE'S NO POINT IN COMING BACK TO LIFE IF KEIKO'S DEAD!
!
LISTEN TO ME! SCRAM OUTTA HERE!!
BLUSH

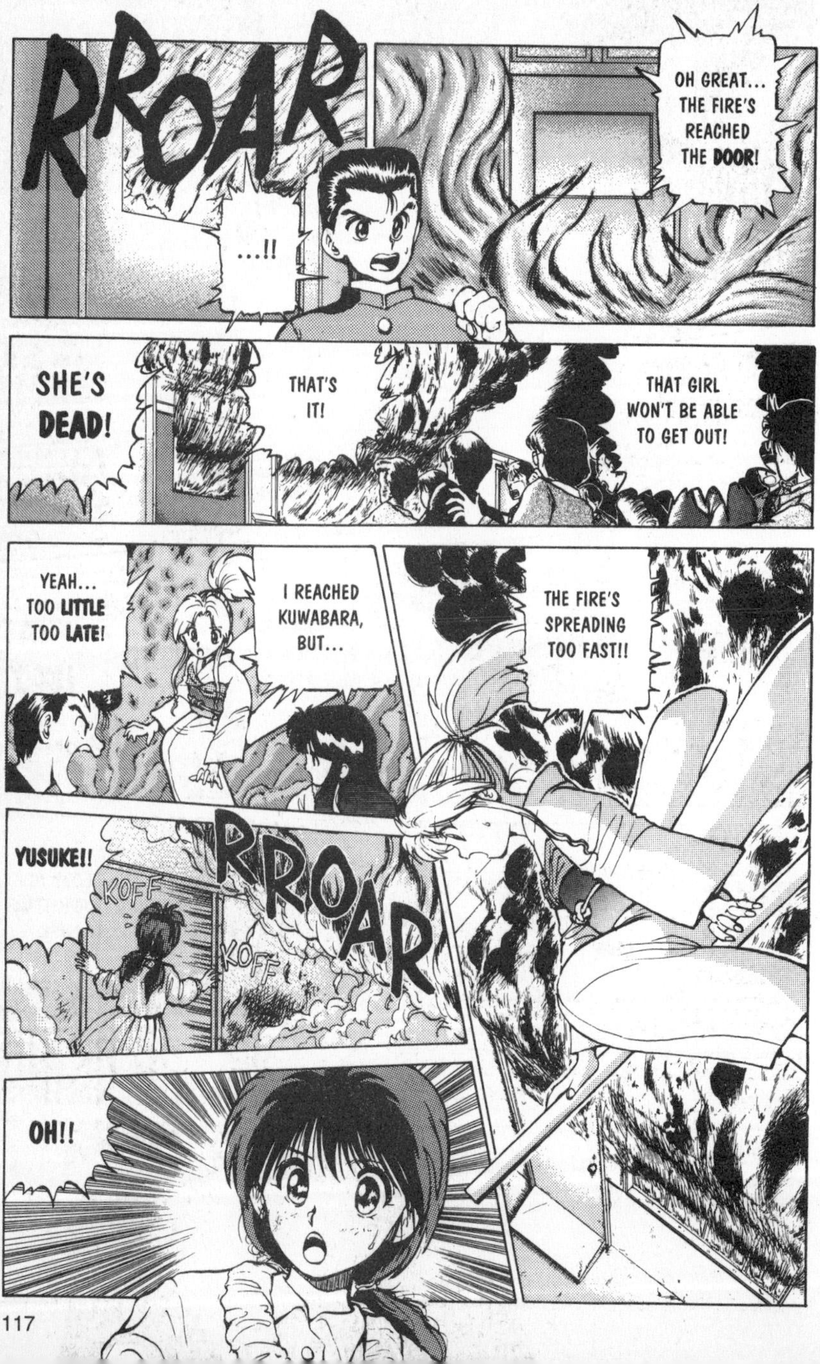

OH GREAT... THE FIRE'S REACHED THE **DOOR**!
...!!
RROAR
THAT GIRL WON'T BE ABLE TO GET OUT!
THAT'S IT!
SHE'S **DEAD**!
THE FIRE'S SPREADING TOO FAST!!
I REACHED KUWABARA, BUT...
YEAH... TOO **LITTLE** TOO **LATE**!
RROAR
YUSUKE!!
KOFF
KOFF
OH!!

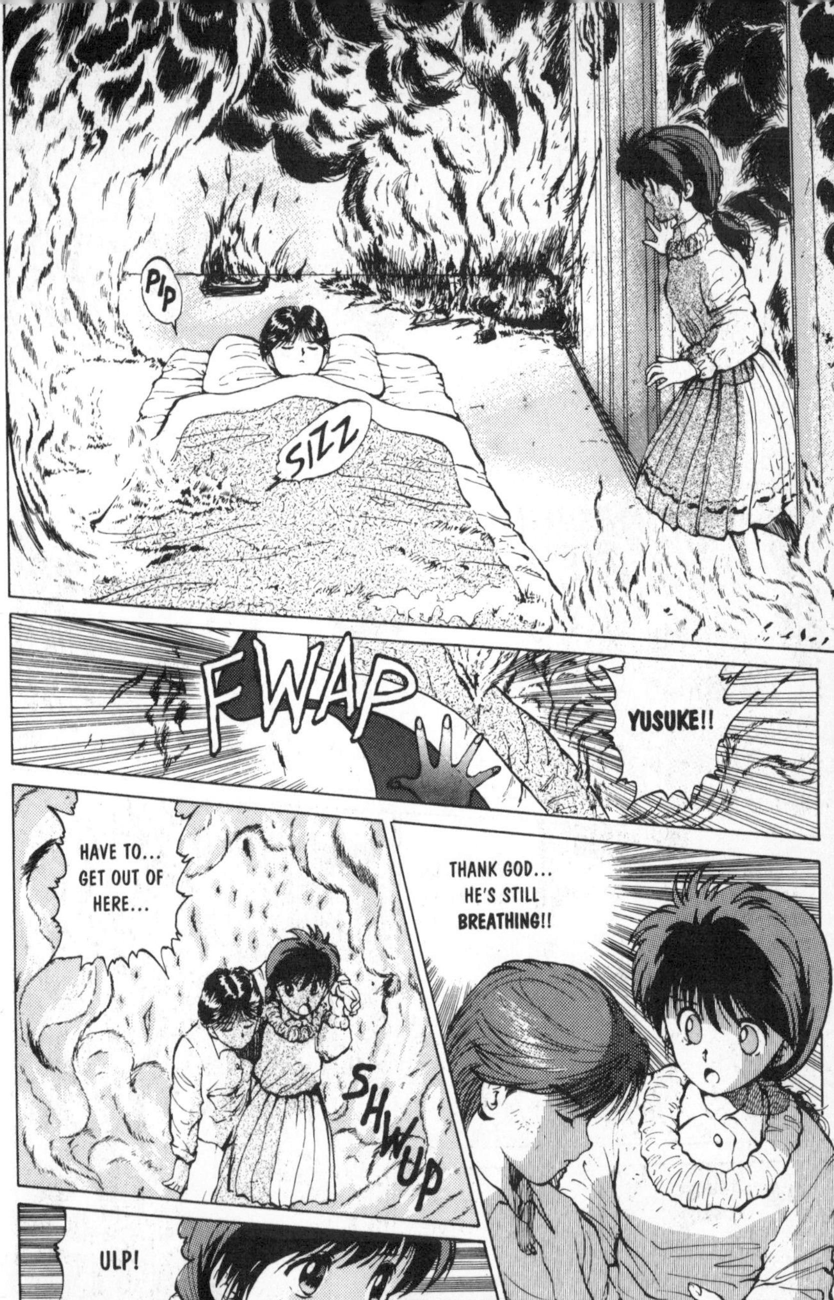
PIP
SIZZ
YUSUKE!!
FWAP
THANK GOD... HE'S STILL BREATHING!!
HAVE TO... GET OUT OF HERE...
SHWUP
ULP!

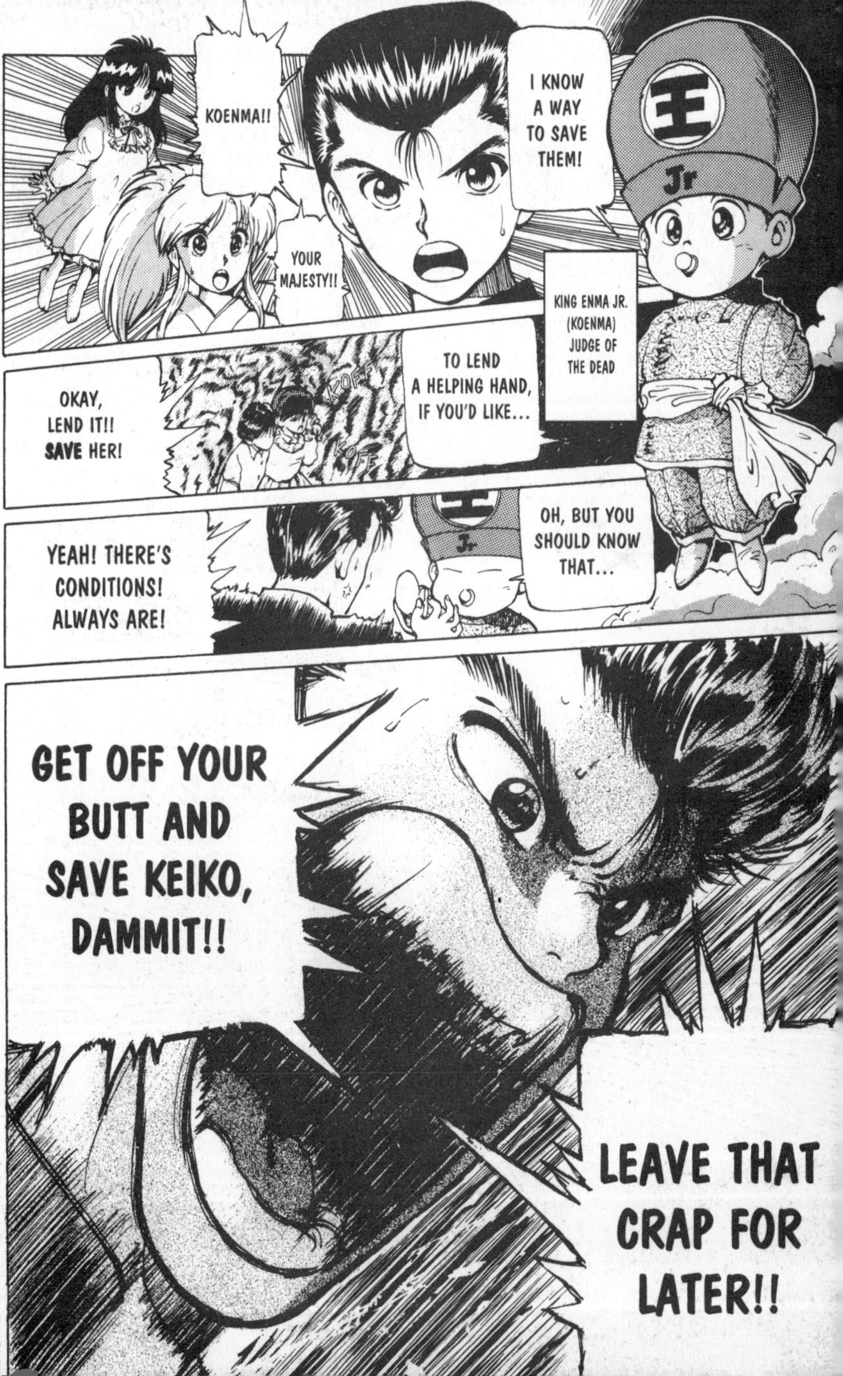
I KNOW A WAY TO SAVE THEM!
KOENMA!!
YOUR MAJESTY!!
KING ENMA JR. (KOENMA) JUDGE OF THE DEAD
TO LEND A HELPING HAND, IF YOU'D LIKE...
KOFF
KOFF
OKAY, LEND IT!! SAVE HER!
OH, BUT YOU SHOULD KNOW THAT...
YEAH! THERE'S CONDITIONS! ALWAYS ARE!
GET OFF YOUR BUTT AND SAVE KEIKO, DAMMIT!!
LEAVE THAT CRAP FOR LATER!!

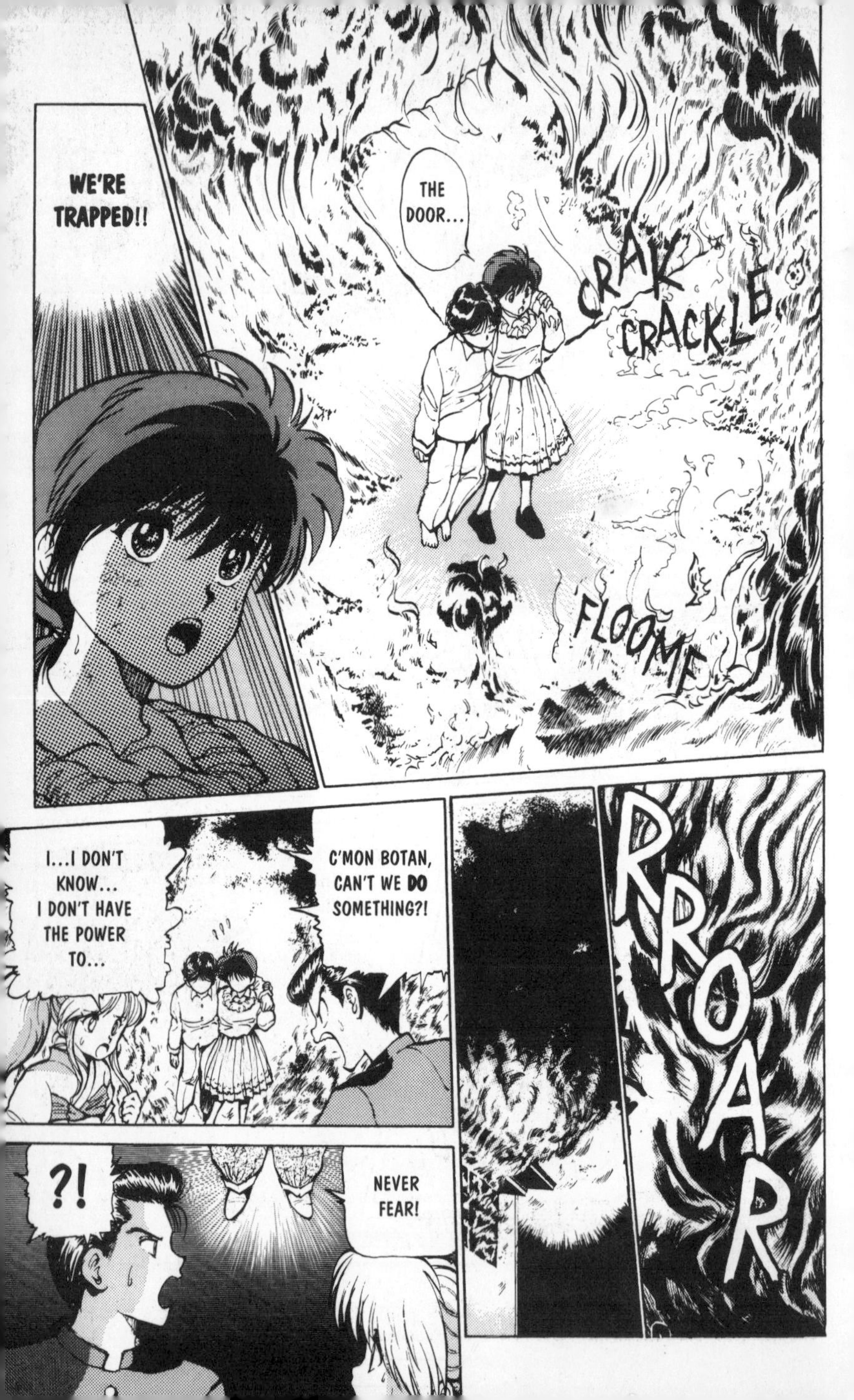
THE DOOR...
CRAK
CRACKLE
FLOOMF
WE'RE TRAPPED!!
RRROAR
C'MON BOTAN, CAN'T WE DO SOMETHING?!
I...I DON'T KNOW... I DON'T HAVE THE POWER TO...
NEVER FEAR!
?!

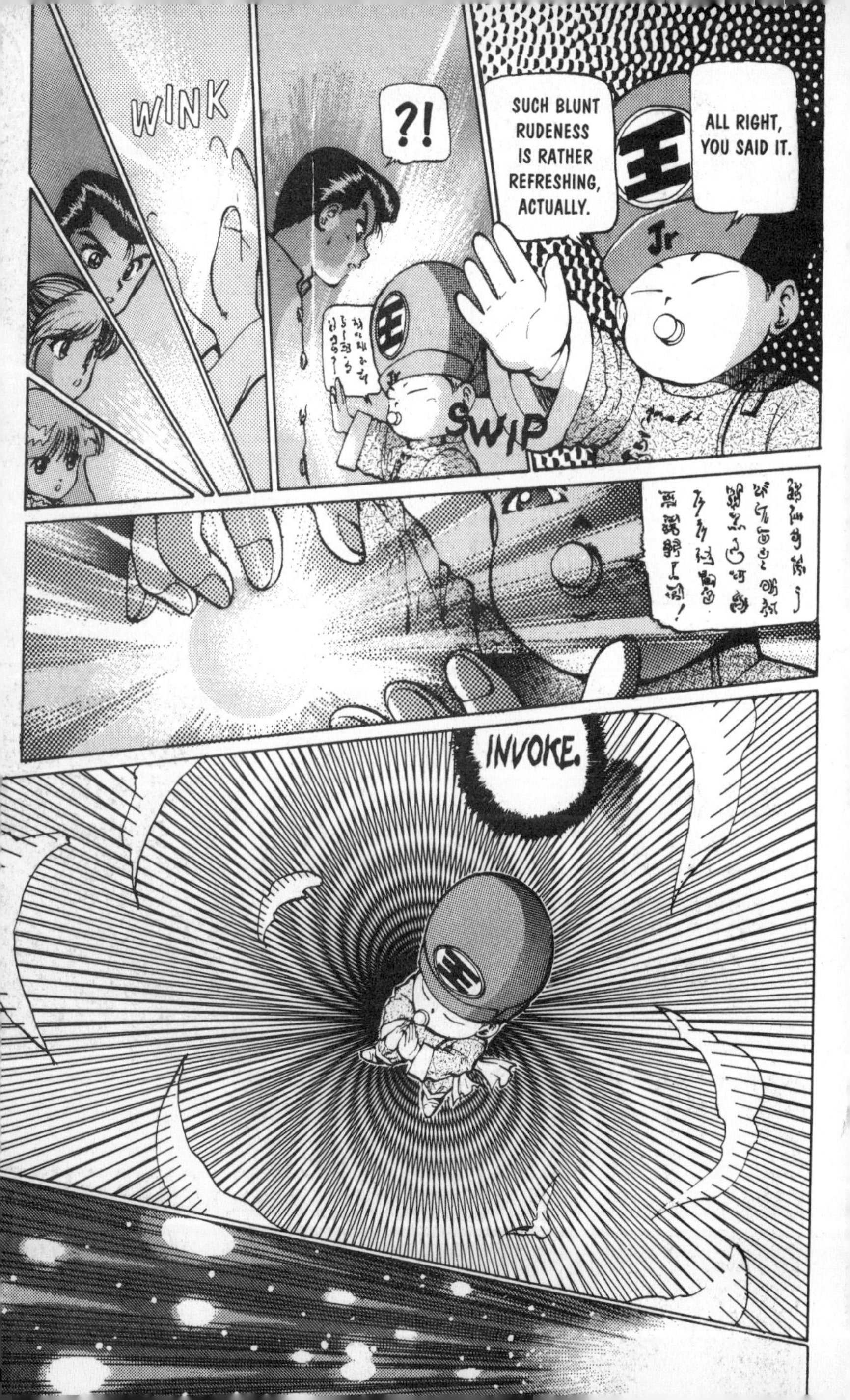
ALL RIGHT, YOU SAID IT.
SUCH BLUNT RUDENESS IS RATHER REFRESHING, ACTUALLY.
SWIP
?!
WINK
INVOKE.

READ THIS WAY

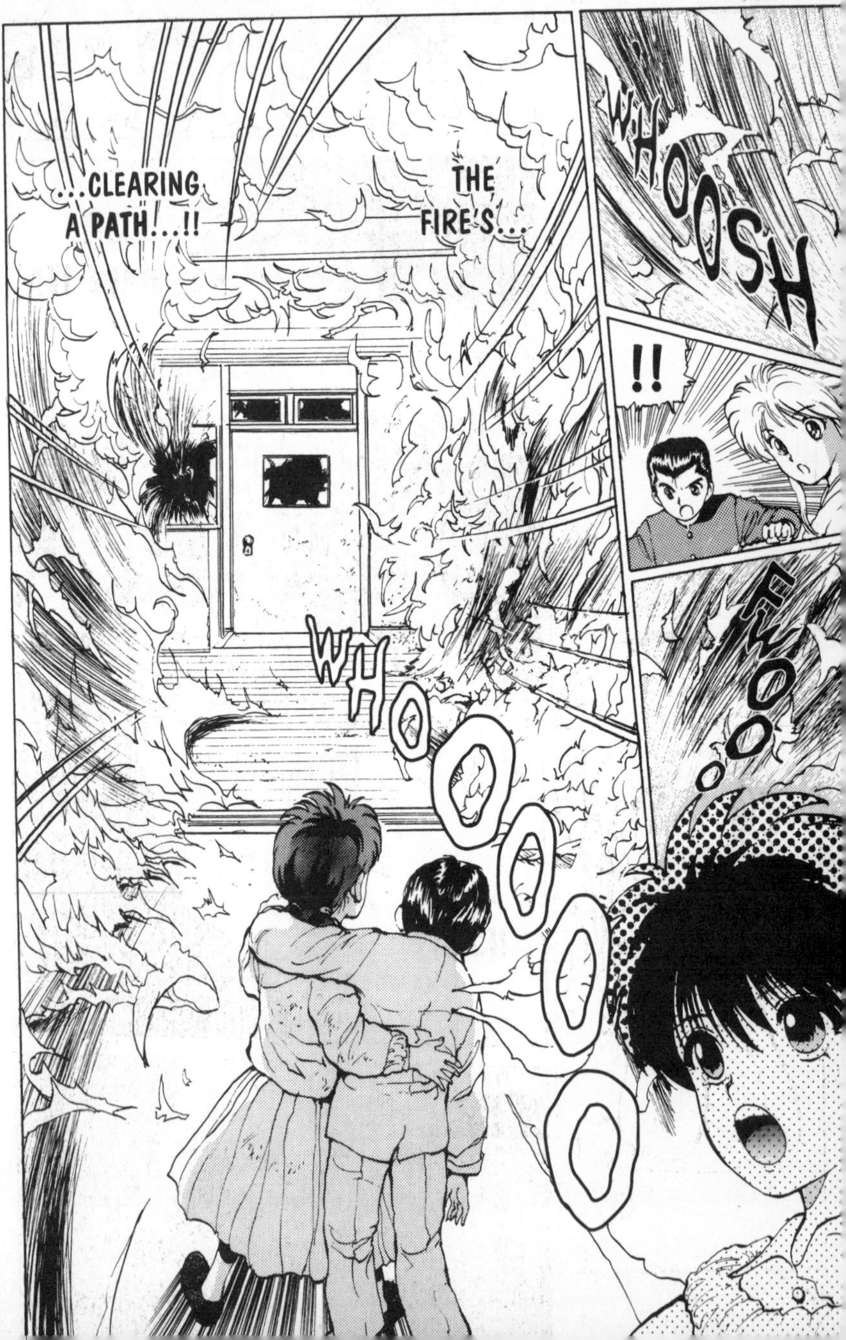
WHOOSH
!!
FWOOOOO
THE FIRE'S...
...CLEARING A PATH...!!
WHOOOOOOO

READ THIS WAY

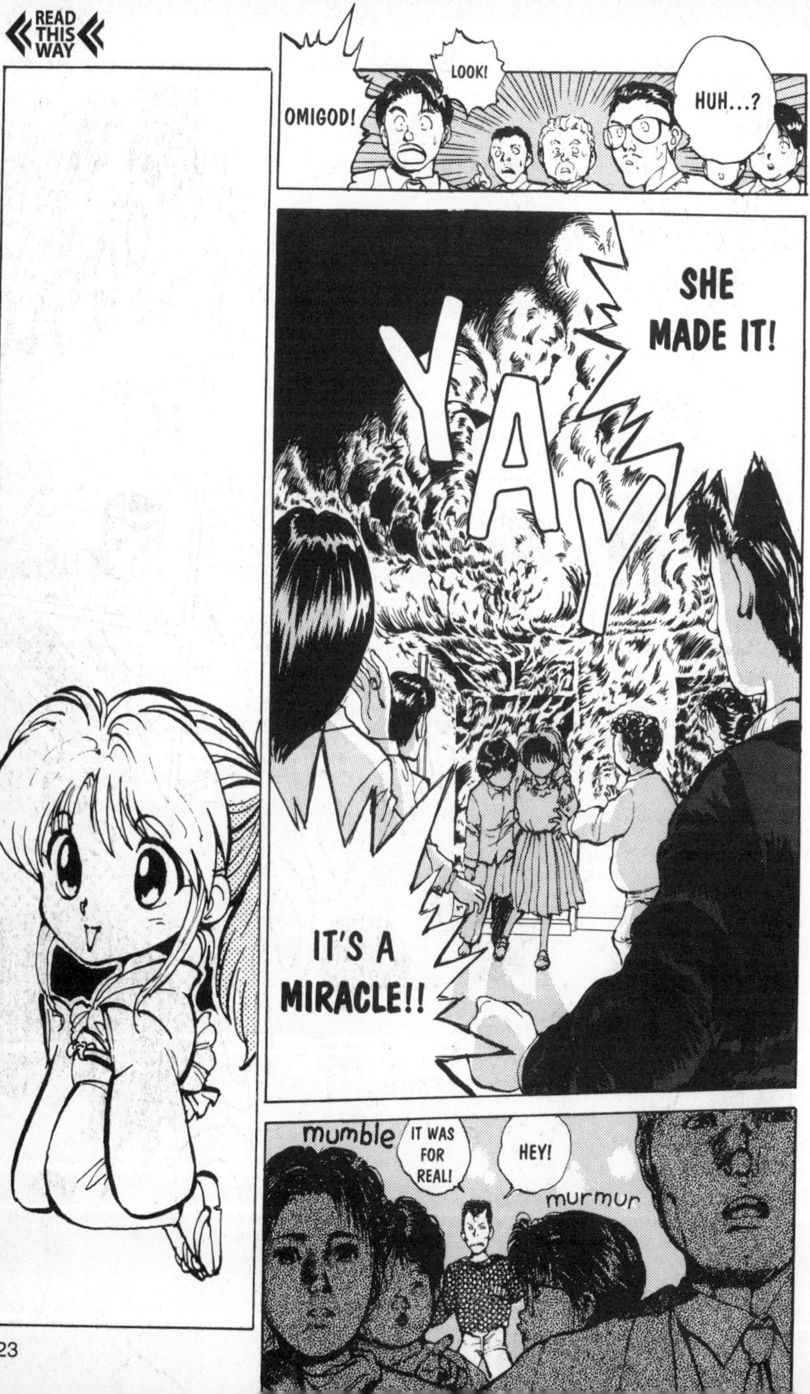

HUH...?
LOOK!
OMIGOD!
SHE MADE IT!
YAY
IT'S A MIRACLE!!
HEY!
murmur
IT WAS FOR REAL!
mumble

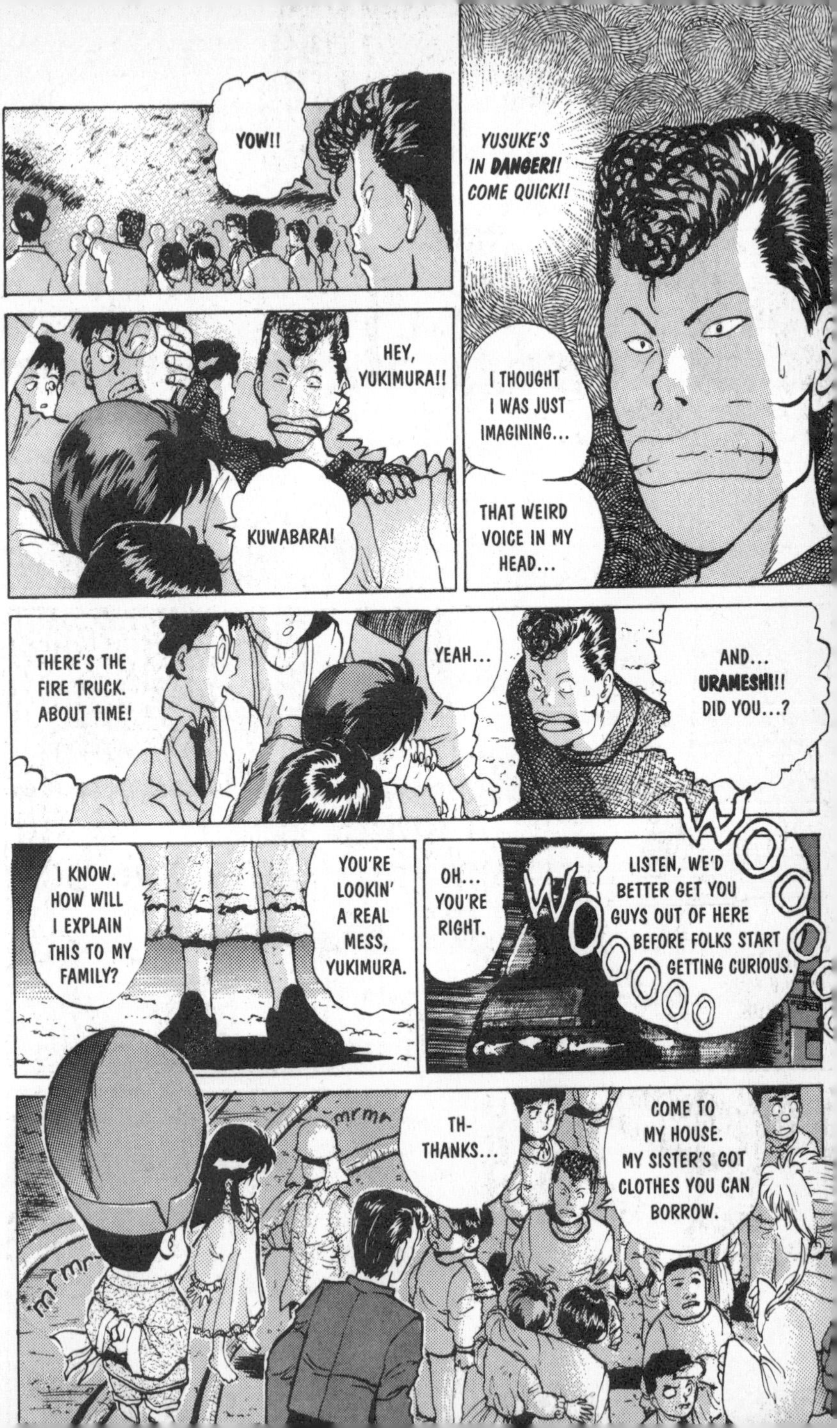
YUSUKE'S IN DANGER!! COME QUICK!!
I THOUGHT I WAS JUST IMAGINING...
THAT WEIRD VOICE IN MY HEAD...
YOW!!
HEY, YUKIMURA!!
KUWABARA!
AND... URAMESHI!! DID YOU...?
YEAH...
THERE'S THE FIRE TRUCK. ABOUT TIME!
WOOOOOOOOO
LISTEN, WE'D BETTER GET YOU GUYS OUT OF HERE BEFORE FOLKS START GETTING CURIOUS.
OH... YOU'RE RIGHT.
YOU'RE LOOKIN' A REAL MESS, YUKIMURA.
I KNOW. HOW WILL I EXPLAIN THIS TO MY FAMILY?
COME TO MY HOUSE. MY SISTER'S GOT CLOTHES YOU CAN BORROW.
TH- THANKS...
mrmr
mrmr

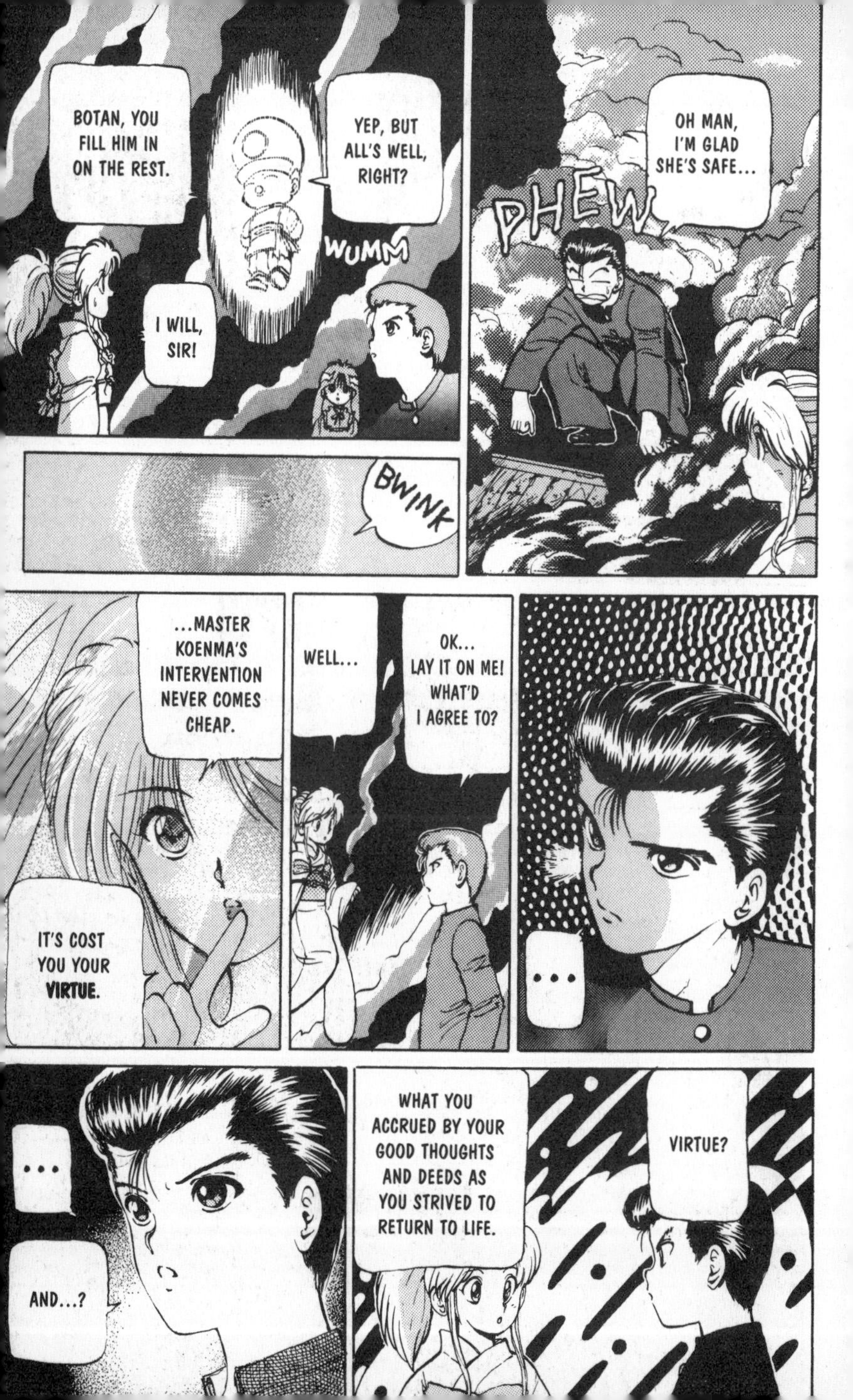

OH MAN, I'M GLAD SHE'S SAFE...
PHEW
YEP, BUT ALL'S WELL, RIGHT?
BOTAN, YOU FILL HIM IN ON THE REST.
WUMM
I WILL, SIR!
BWINK
...
OK... LAY IT ON ME! WHAT'D I AGREE TO?
WELL...
...MASTER KOENMA'S INTERVENTION NEVER COMES CHEAP.
IT'S COST YOU YOUR **VIRTUE.**
VIRTUE?
WHAT YOU ACCRUED BY YOUR GOOD THOUGHTS AND DEEDS AS YOU STRIVED TO RETURN TO LIFE.
...
AND...?

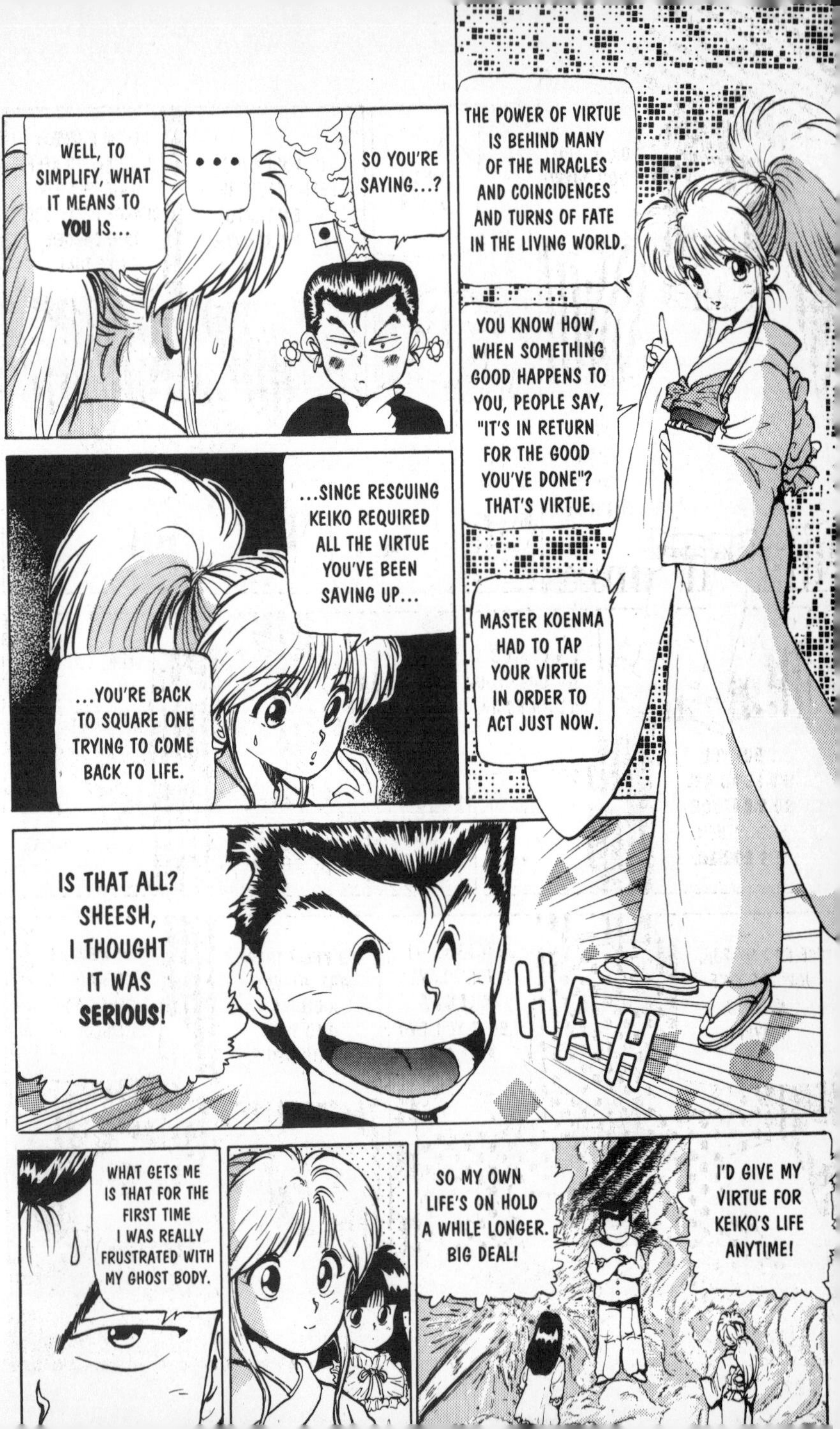
THE POWER OF VIRTUE IS BEHIND MANY OF THE MIRACLES AND COINCIDENCES AND TURNS OF FATE IN THE LIVING WORLD.
YOU KNOW HOW, WHEN SOMETHING GOOD HAPPENS TO YOU, PEOPLE SAY, "IT'S IN RETURN FOR THE GOOD YOU'VE DONE"? THAT'S VIRTUE.
MASTER KOENMA HAD TO TAP YOUR VIRTUE IN ORDER TO ACT JUST NOW.
SO YOU'RE SAYING...?
...
WELL, TO SIMPLIFY, WHAT IT MEANS TO **YOU** IS...
...SINCE RESCUING KEIKO REQUIRED ALL THE VIRTUE YOU'VE BEEN SAVING UP...
...YOU'RE BACK TO SQUARE ONE TRYING TO COME BACK TO LIFE.
IS THAT ALL? SHEESH, I THOUGHT IT WAS **SERIOUS!**
HAH
HAH
I'D GIVE MY VIRTUE FOR KEIKO'S LIFE ANYTIME!
SO MY OWN LIFE'S ON HOLD A WHILE LONGER. BIG DEAL!
WHAT GETS ME IS THAT FOR THE FIRST TIME I WAS REALLY FRUSTRATED WITH MY GHOST BODY.

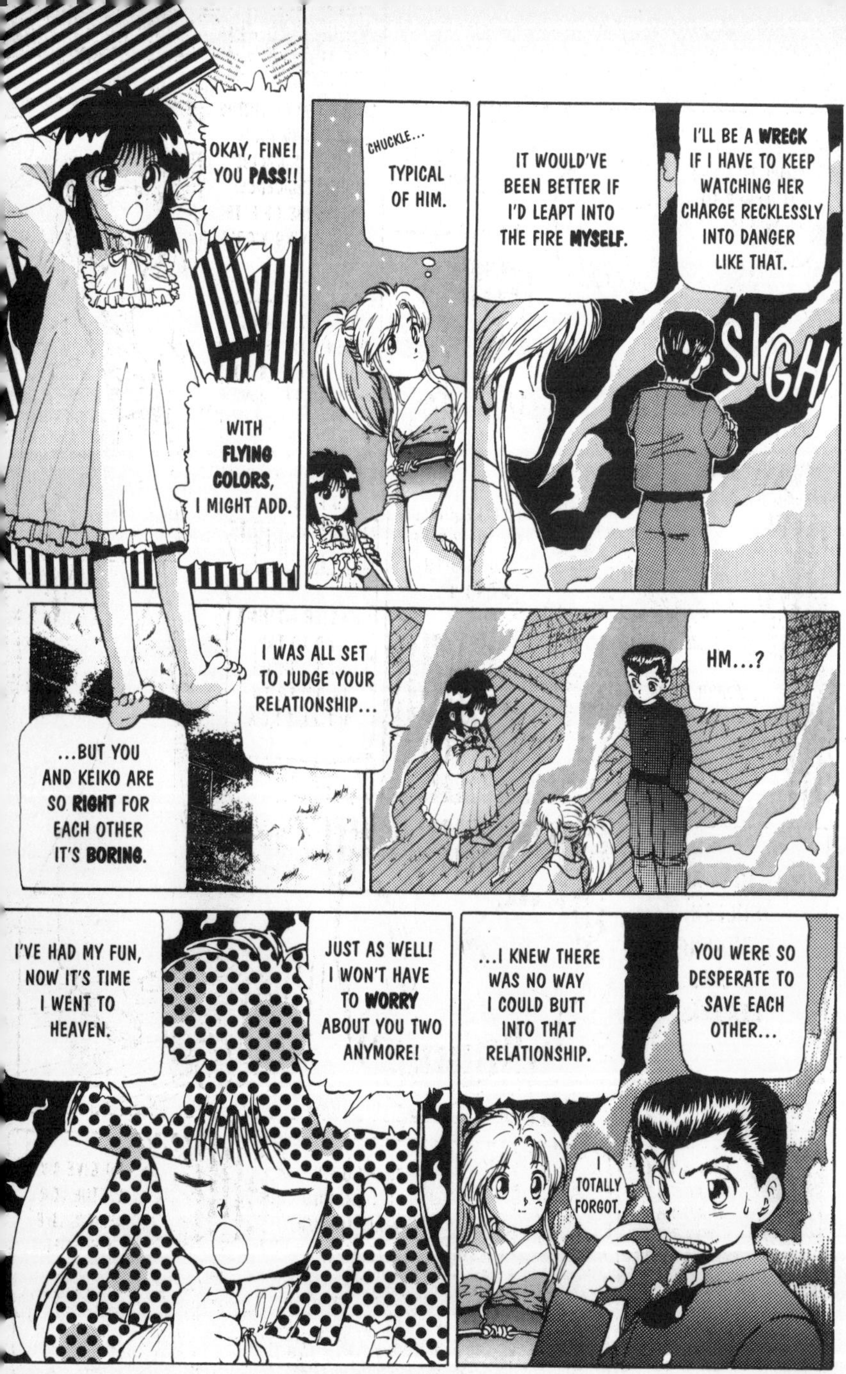
I'LL BE A WRECK IF I HAVE TO KEEP WATCHING HER CHARGE RECKLESSLY INTO DANGER LIKE THAT.
IT WOULD'VE BEEN BETTER IF I'D LEAPT INTO THE FIRE MYSELF.
SIGH
CHUCKLE...
TYPICAL OF HIM.
OKAY, FINE! YOU PASS!!
WITH FLYING COLORS, I MIGHT ADD.
HM...?
I WAS ALL SET TO JUDGE YOUR RELATIONSHIP...
...BUT YOU AND KEIKO ARE SO RIGHT FOR EACH OTHER IT'S BORING.
YOU WERE SO DESPERATE TO SAVE EACH OTHER...
...I KNEW THERE WAS NO WAY I COULD BUTT INTO THAT RELATIONSHIP.
I TOTALLY FORGOT.
JUST AS WELL! I WON'T HAVE TO WORRY ABOUT YOU TWO ANYMORE!
I'VE HAD MY FUN, NOW IT'S TIME I WENT TO HEAVEN.

READ THIS WAY

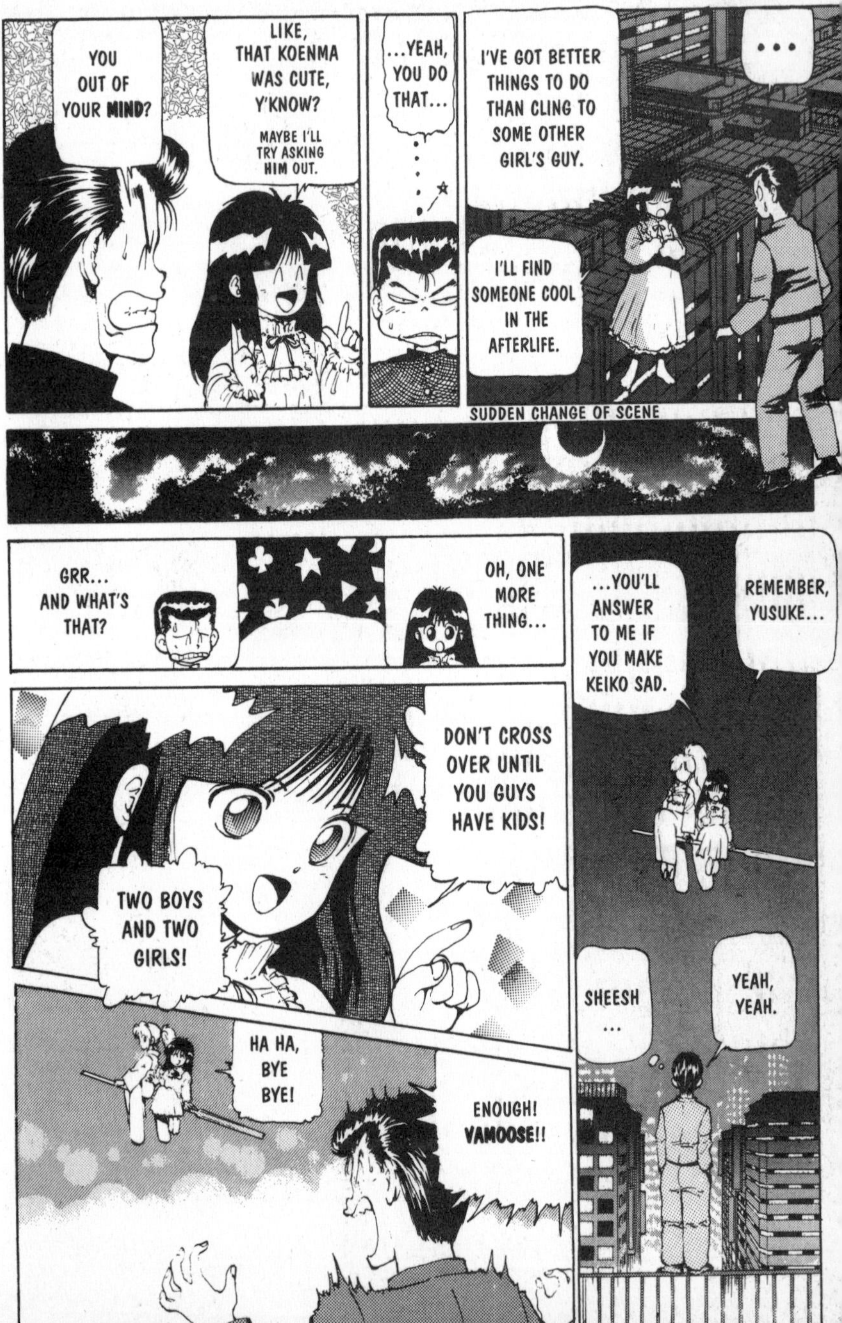

...
I'VE GOT BETTER THINGS TO DO THAN CLING TO SOME OTHER GIRL'S GUY.
I'LL FIND SOMEONE COOL IN THE AFTERLIFE.
...YEAH, YOU DO THAT...
LIKE, THAT KOENMA WAS CUTE, Y'KNOW?
MAYBE I'LL TRY ASKING HIM OUT.
YOU OUT OF YOUR MIND?
SUDDEN CHANGE OF SCENE
REMEMBER, YUSUKE...
...YOU'LL ANSWER TO ME IF YOU MAKE KEIKO SAD.
OH, ONE MORE THING...
GRR... AND WHAT'S THAT?
DON'T CROSS OVER UNTIL YOU GUYS HAVE KIDS!
TWO BOYS AND TWO GIRLS!
HA HA, BYE BYE!
ENOUGH! VAMOOSE!!
YEAH, YEAH.
SHEESH...

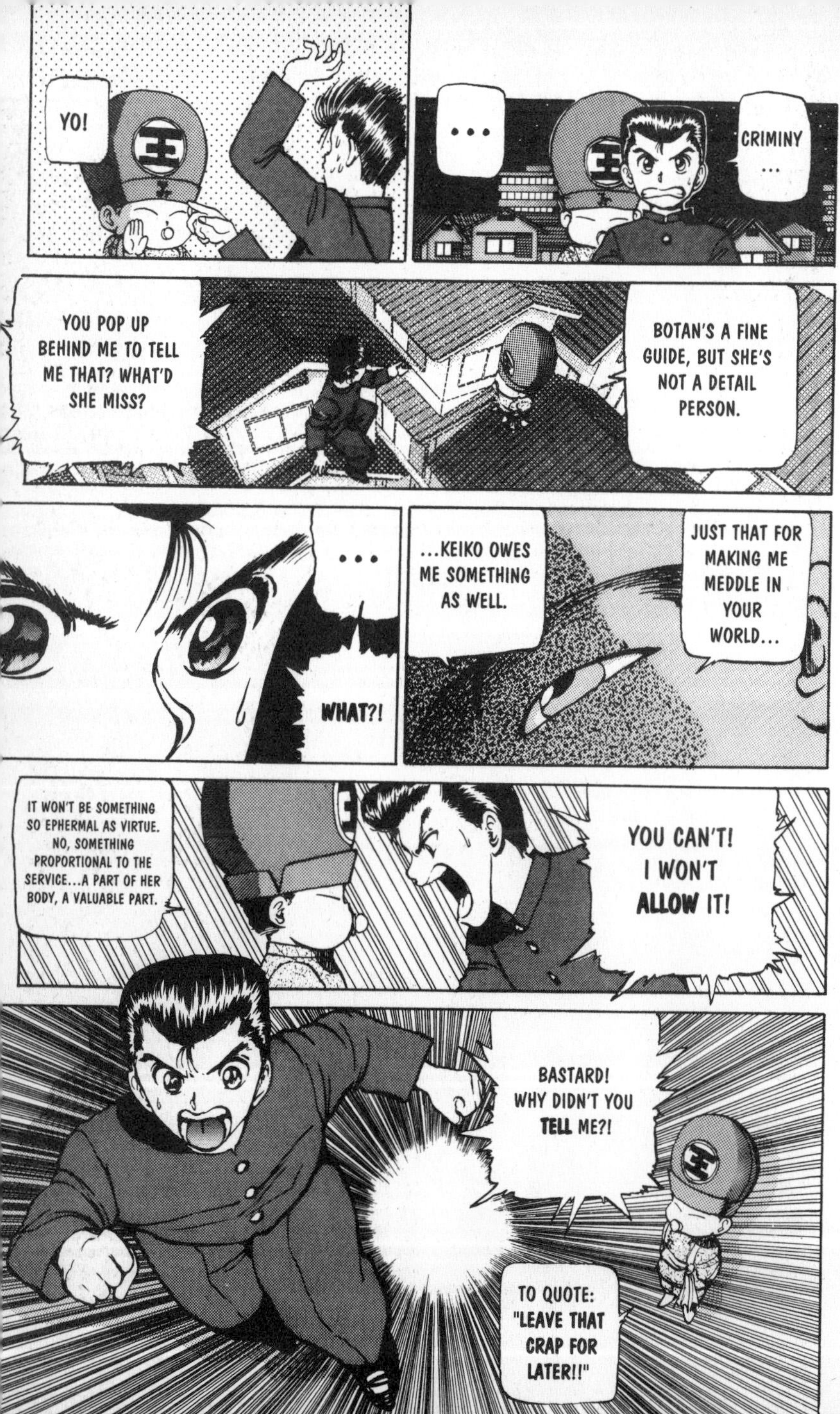

CRIMINY ...
...
YO!
BOTAN'S A FINE GUIDE, BUT SHE'S NOT A DETAIL PERSON.
YOU POP UP BEHIND ME TO TELL ME THAT? WHAT'D SHE MISS?
JUST THAT FOR MAKING ME MEDDLE IN YOUR WORLD...
...KEIKO OWES ME SOMETHING AS WELL.
...
WHAT?!
YOU CAN'T! I WON'T ALLOW IT!
IT WON'T BE SOMETHING SO EPHERMAL AS VIRTUE. NO, SOMETHING PROPORTIONAL TO THE SERVICE...A PART OF HER BODY, A VALUABLE PART.
BASTARD! WHY DIDN'T YOU TELL ME?!
TO QUOTE: "LEAVE THAT CRAP FOR LATER!!"

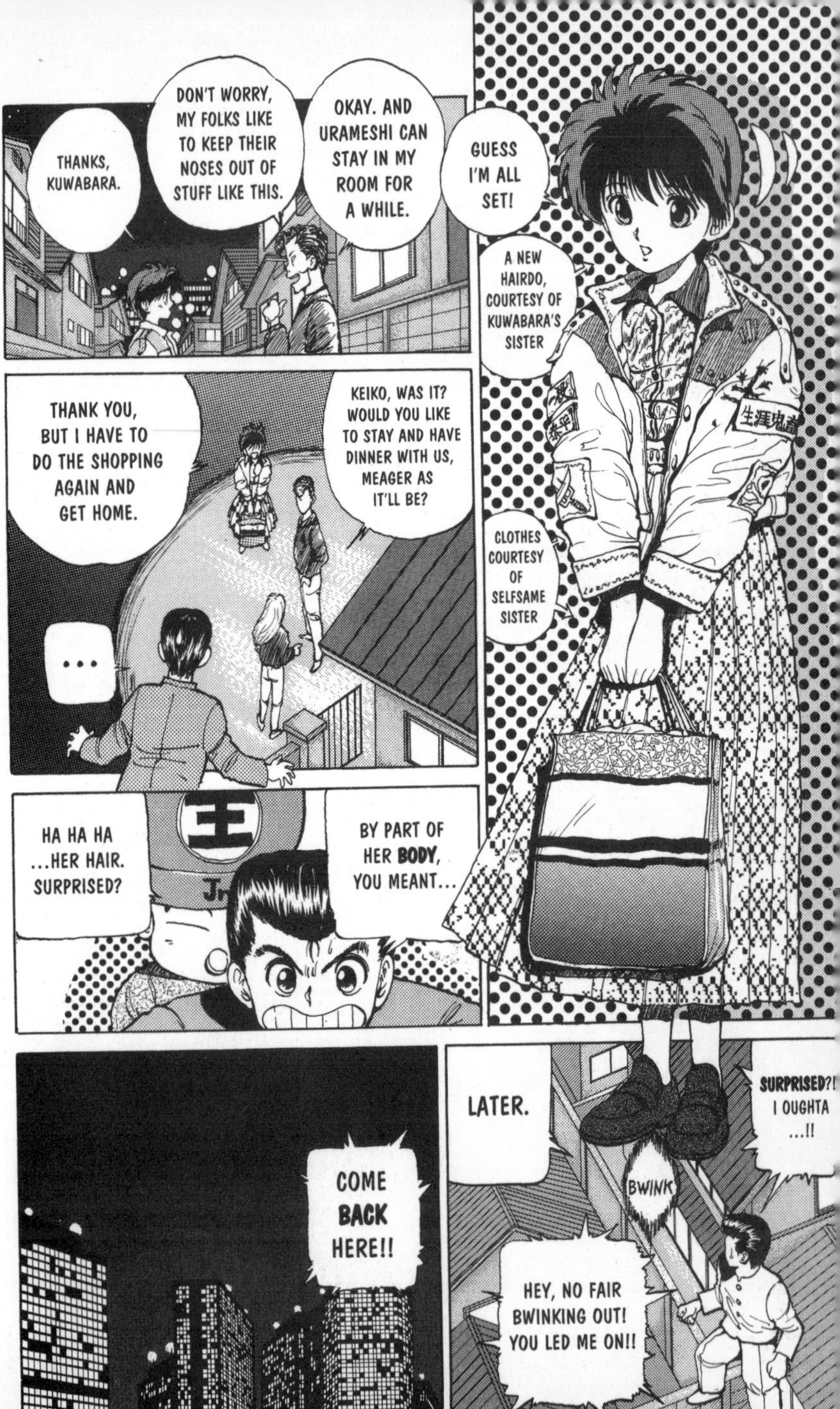
GUESS I'M ALL SET!
A NEW HAIRDO, COURTESY OF KUWABARA'S SISTER
CLOTHES COURTESY OF SELFSAME SISTER
OKAY. AND URAMESHI CAN STAY IN MY ROOM FOR A WHILE.
DON'T WORRY, MY FOLKS LIKE TO KEEP THEIR NOSES OUT OF STUFF LIKE THIS.
THANKS, KUWABARA.
KEIKO, WAS IT? WOULD YOU LIKE TO STAY AND HAVE DINNER WITH US, MEAGER AS IT'LL BE?
THANK YOU, BUT I HAVE TO DO THE SHOPPING AGAIN AND GET HOME.
...
BY PART OF HER BODY, YOU MEANT...
HA HA HA ...HER HAIR. SURPRISED?
SURPRISED?! I OUGHTA ...!!
LATER.
BWINK
HEY, NO FAIR BWINKING OUT! YOU LED ME ON!!
COME BACK HERE!!

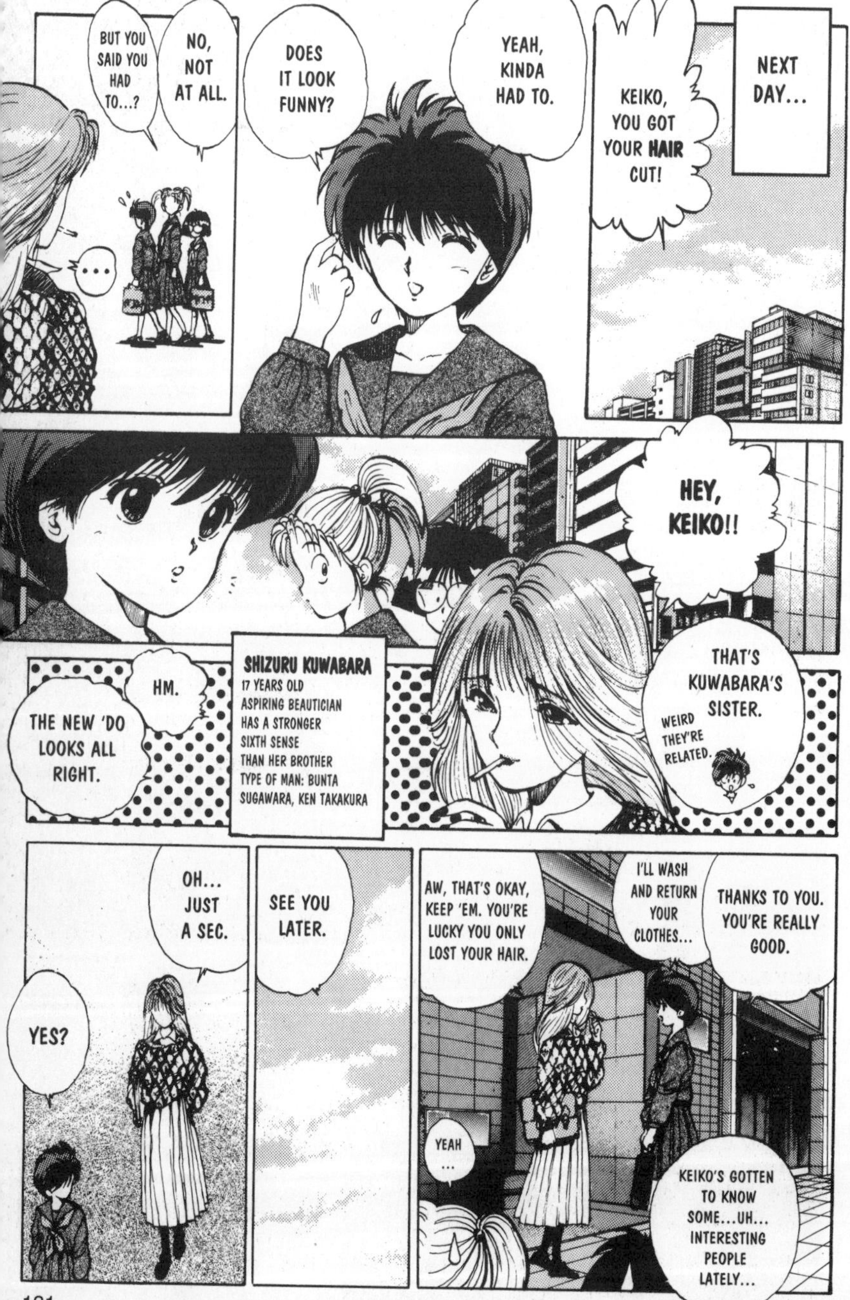
NEXT DAY...
KEIKO, YOU GOT YOUR HAIR CUT!
YEAH, KINDA HAD TO.
DOES IT LOOK FUNNY?
NO, NOT AT ALL.
BUT YOU SAID YOU HAD TO...?
...
HEY, KEIKO!!
THAT'S KUWABARA'S SISTER.
WEIRD THEY'RE RELATED.
SHIZURU KUWABARA
17 YEARS OLD
ASPIRING BEAUTICIAN
HAS A STRONGER SIXTH SENSE THAN HER BROTHER
TYPE OF MAN: BUNTA SUGAWARA, KEN TAKAKURA
HM.
THE NEW 'DO LOOKS ALL RIGHT.
THANKS TO YOU. YOU'RE REALLY GOOD.
I'LL WASH AND RETURN YOUR CLOTHES...
AW, THAT'S OKAY, KEEP 'EM. YOU'RE LUCKY YOU ONLY LOST YOUR HAIR.
YEAH...
KEIKO'S GOTTEN TO KNOW SOME...UH... INTERESTING PEOPLE LATELY...
SEE YOU LATER.
OH... JUST A SEC.
YES?

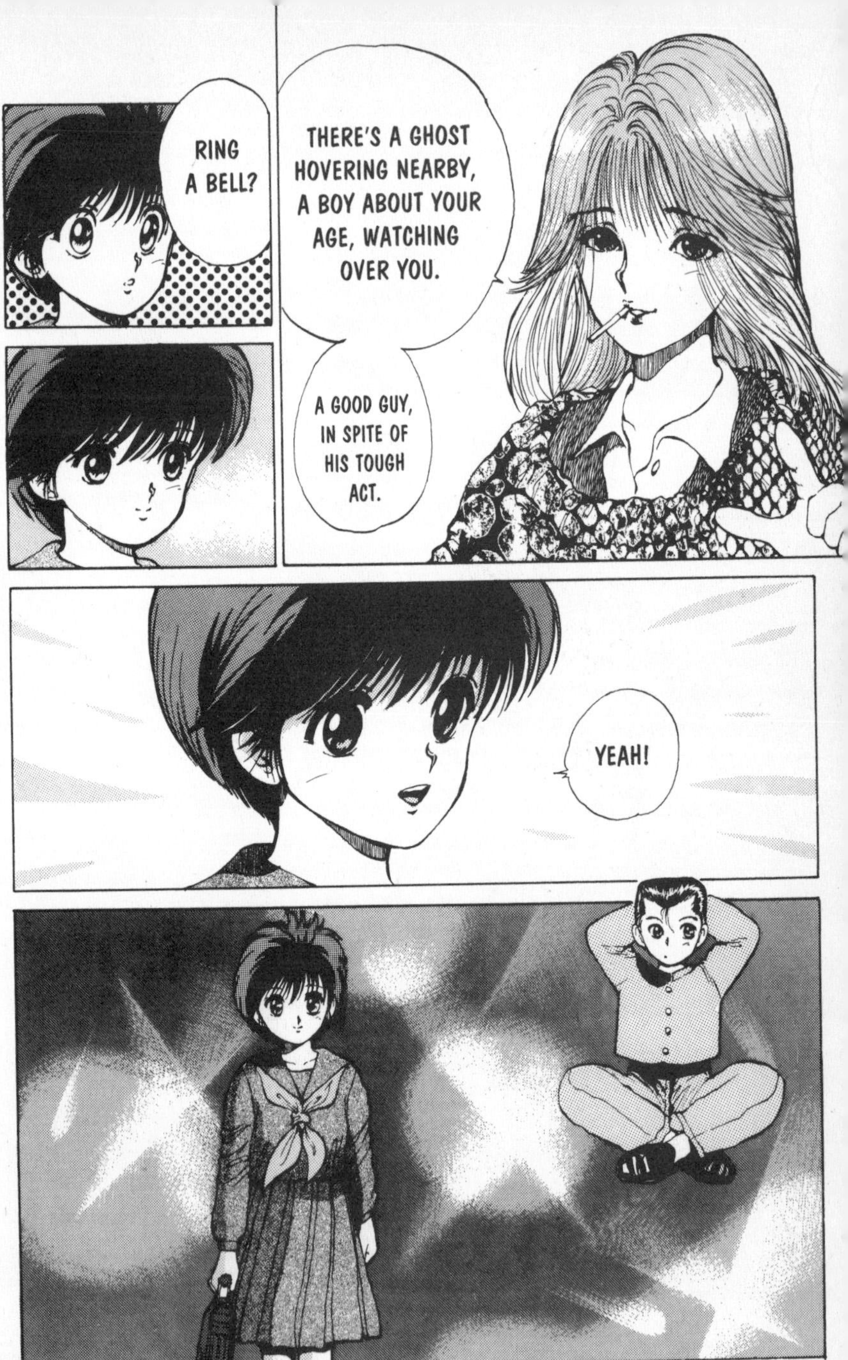
THERE'S A GHOST HOVERING NEARBY, A BOY ABOUT YOUR AGE, WATCHING OVER YOU.
A GOOD GUY, IN SPITE OF HIS TOUGH ACT.
RING A BELL?
YEAH!

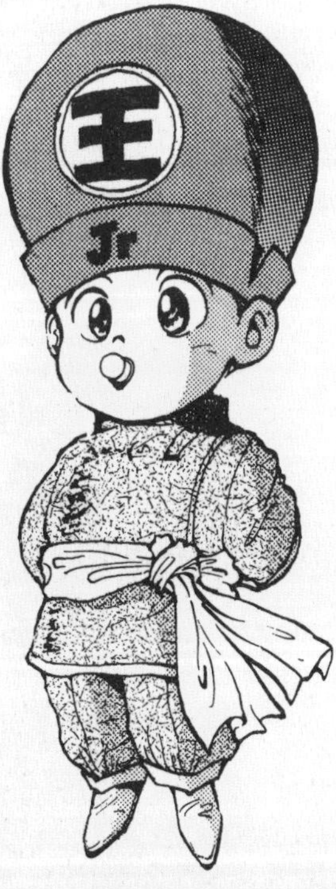
Jr

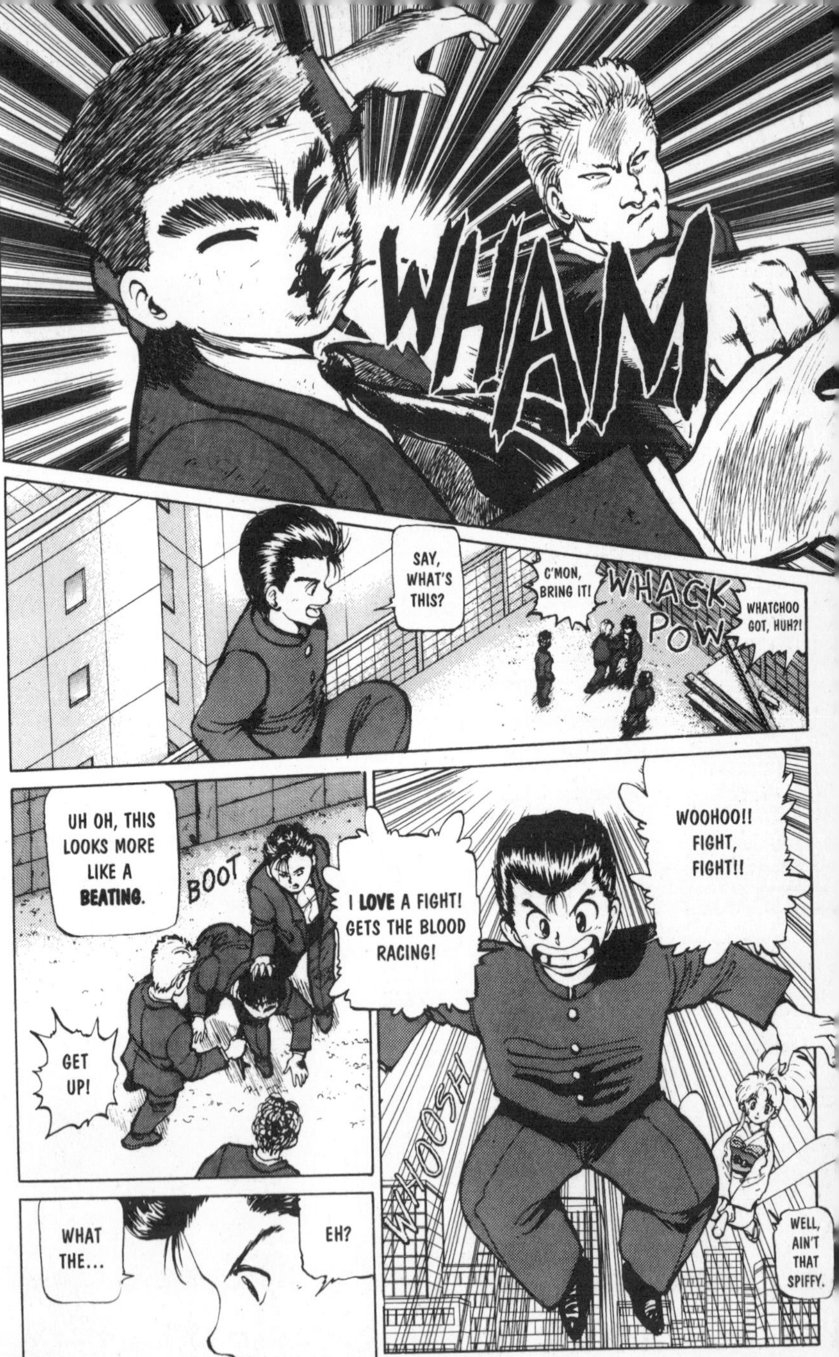
WHAM
WHATCHOO GOT, HUH?!
WHACK
POW
C'MON, BRING IT!
SAY, WHAT'S THIS?
WOOHOO!! FIGHT, FIGHT!!
I LOVE A FIGHT! GETS THE BLOOD RACING!
WHOOSH
WELL, AIN'T THAT SPIFFY.
UH OH, THIS LOOKS MORE LIKE A BEATING.
BOOT
GET UP!
EH?
WHAT THE...

CHAPTER 15: JUST ONE WIN!!

READ THIS WAY

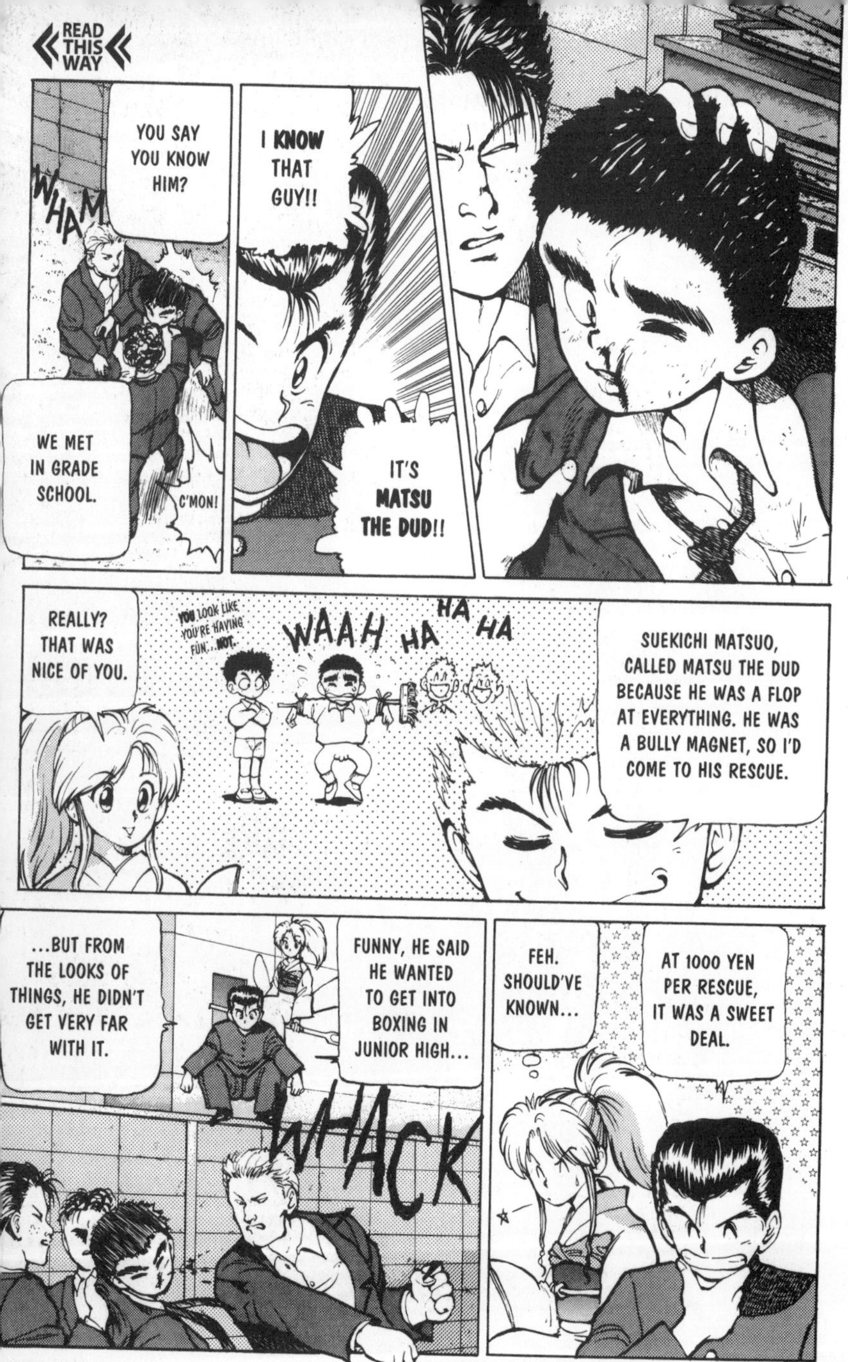

I KNOW THAT GUY!!
IT'S MATSU THE DUD!!
YOU SAY YOU KNOW HIM?
WHAM
WE MET IN GRADE SCHOOL.
C'MON!
SUEKICHI MATSUO, CALLED MATSU THE DUD BECAUSE HE WAS A FLOP AT EVERYTHING. HE WAS A BULLY MAGNET, SO I'D COME TO HIS RESCUE.
WAAH HA HA HA
YOU LOOK LIKE YOU'RE HAVING FUN... NOT.
REALLY? THAT WAS NICE OF YOU.
AT 1000 YEN PER RESCUE, IT WAS A SWEET DEAL.
FEH. SHOULD'VE KNOWN...
FUNNY, HE SAID HE WANTED TO GET INTO BOXING IN JUNIOR HIGH...
...BUT FROM THE LOOKS OF THINGS, HE DIDN'T GET VERY FAR WITH IT.
WHACK

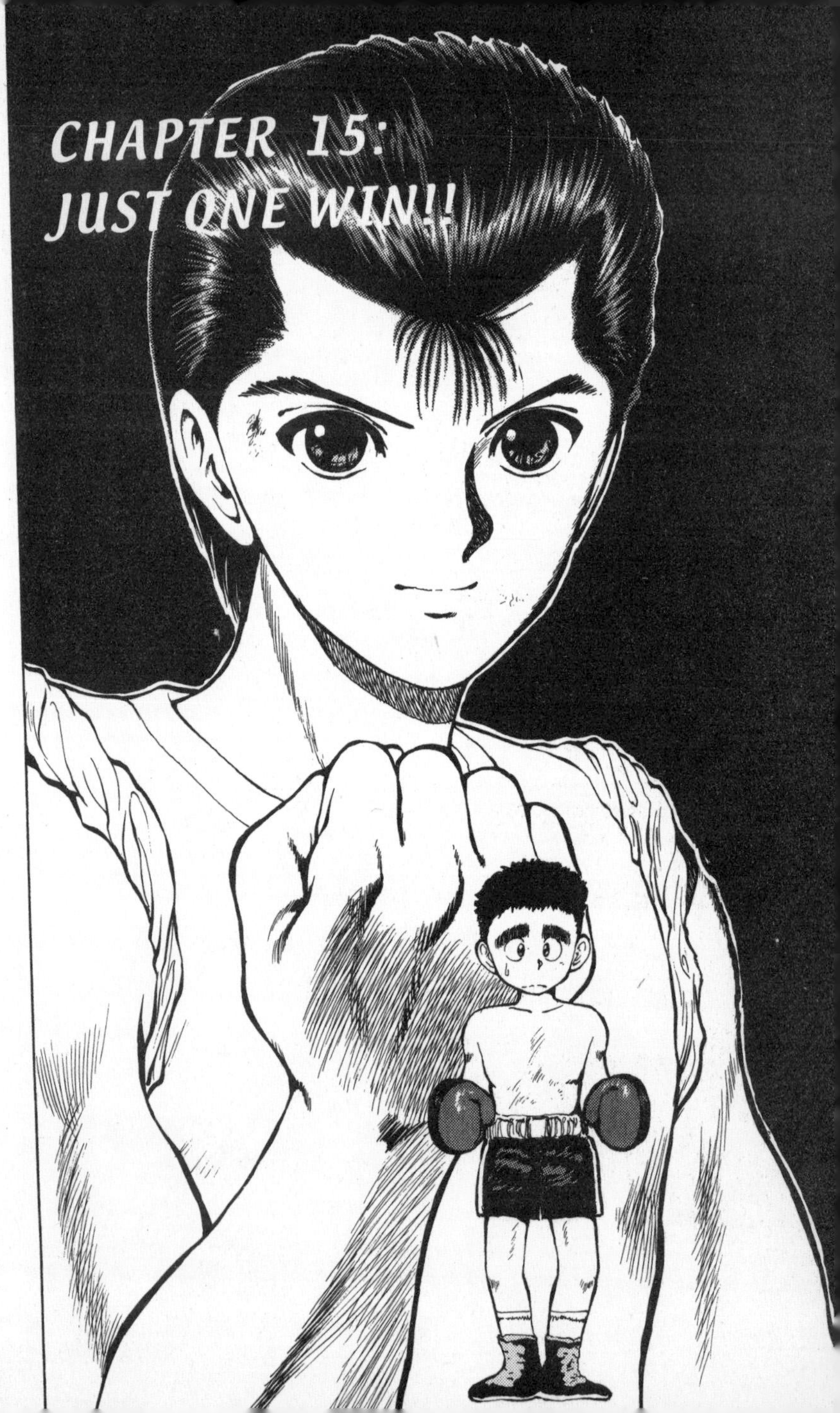
CHAPTER 15:
JUST ONE WIN!!

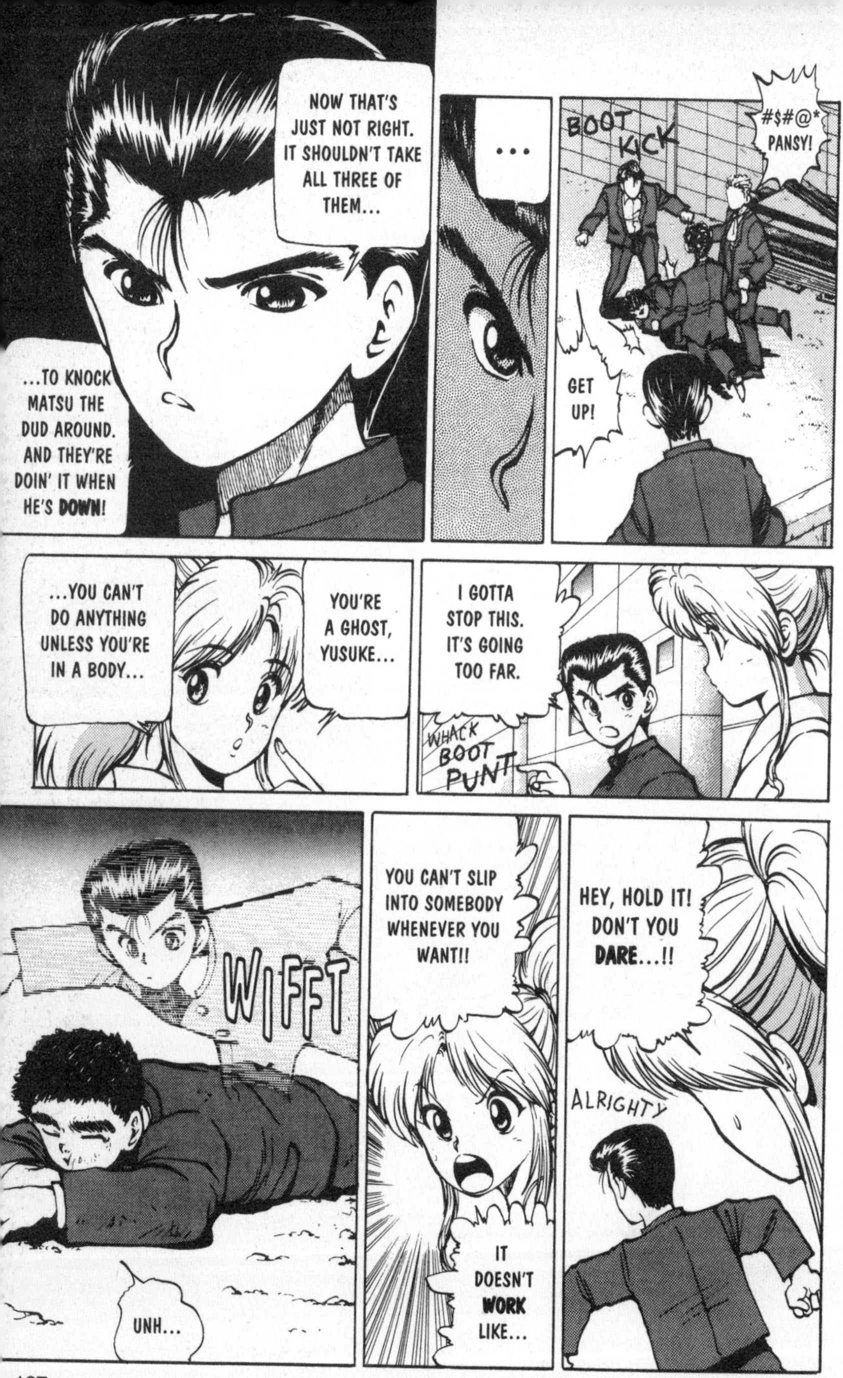
#$#@* PANSY!
BOOT
KICK
GET UP!
...
NOW THAT'S JUST NOT RIGHT. IT SHOULDN'T TAKE ALL THREE OF THEM...
...TO KNOCK MATSU THE DUD AROUND. AND THEY'RE DOIN' IT WHEN HE'S **DOWN**!
I GOTTA STOP THIS. IT'S GOING TOO FAR.
WHACK
BOOT
PUNT
YOU'RE A GHOST, YUSUKE...
...YOU CAN'T DO ANYTHING UNLESS YOU'RE IN A BODY...
HEY, HOLD IT! DON'T YOU **DARE**...!!
ALRIGHTY
YOU CAN'T SLIP INTO SOMEBODY WHENEVER YOU WANT!!
IT DOESN'T **WORK** LIKE...
WIFFT
UNH...

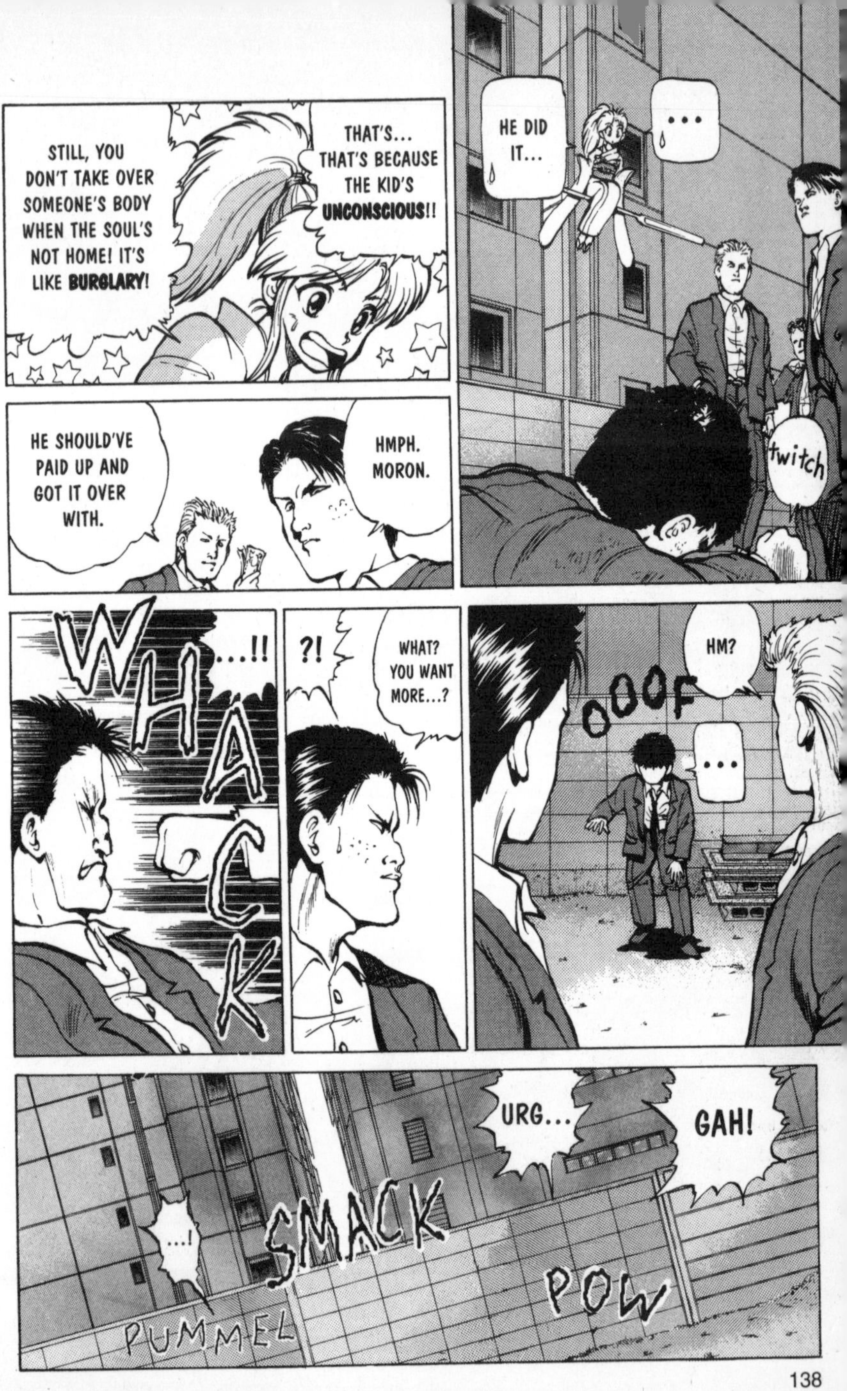
...
HE DID IT...
twitch
THAT'S... THAT'S BECAUSE THE KID'S **UNCONSCIOUS**!!
STILL, YOU DON'T TAKE OVER SOMEONE'S BODY WHEN THE SOUL'S NOT HOME! IT'S LIKE **BURGLARY**!
HMPH. MORON.
HE SHOULD'VE PAID UP AND GOT IT OVER WITH.
HM?
OOOF
...
WHAT? YOU WANT MORE...?
?!
...!!
WHACK
GAH!
URG...
SMACK
...!
POW
PUMMEL

READ THIS WAY

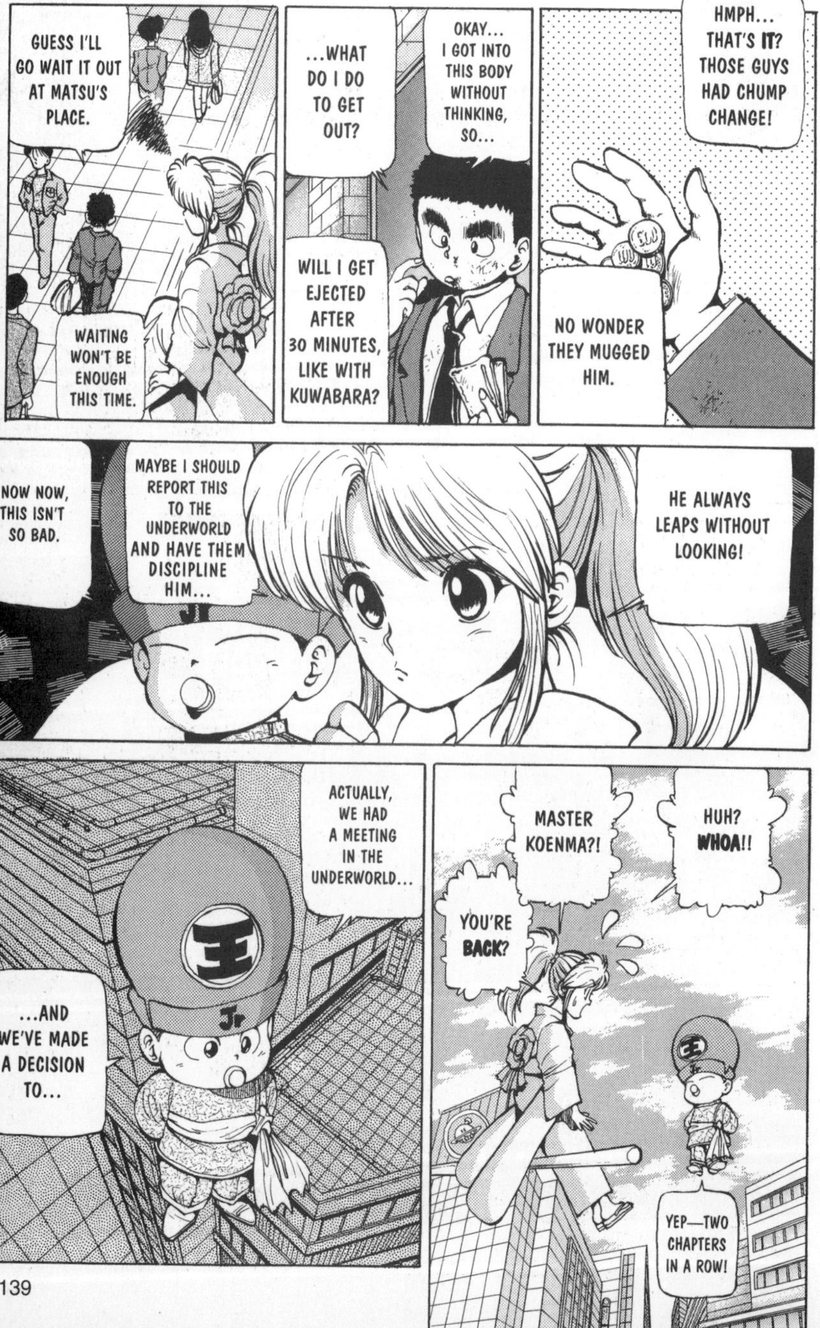

HMPH... THAT'S IT? THOSE GUYS HAD CHUMP CHANGE!
NO WONDER THEY MUGGED HIM.
OKAY... I GOT INTO THIS BODY WITHOUT THINKING, SO...
...WHAT DO I DO TO GET OUT?
WILL I GET EJECTED AFTER 30 MINUTES, LIKE WITH KUWABARA?
GUESS I'LL GO WAIT IT OUT AT MATSU'S PLACE.
WAITING WON'T BE ENOUGH THIS TIME.
HE ALWAYS LEAPS WITHOUT LOOKING!
MAYBE I SHOULD REPORT THIS TO THE UNDERWORLD AND HAVE THEM DISCIPLINE HIM...
NOW NOW, THIS ISN'T SO BAD.
HUH? WHOA!!
MASTER KOENMA?!
YOU'RE BACK?
YEP—TWO CHAPTERS IN A ROW!
ACTUALLY, WE HAD A MEETING IN THE UNDERWORLD...
...AND WE'VE MADE A DECISION TO...

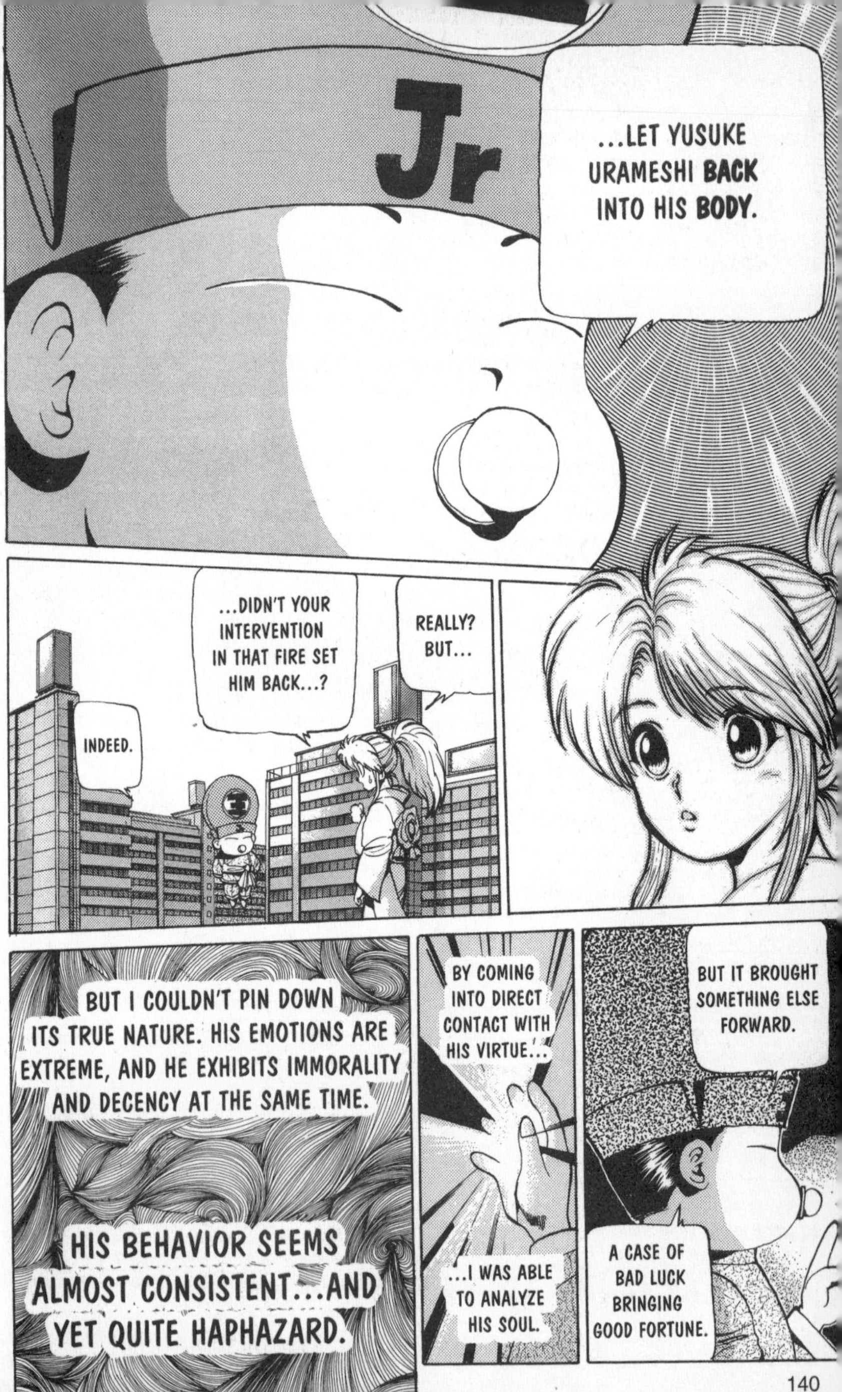
...LET YUSUKE URAMESHI BACK INTO HIS BODY.
REALLY? BUT...
...DIDN'T YOUR INTERVENTION IN THAT FIRE SET HIM BACK...?
INDEED.
BUT IT BROUGHT SOMETHING ELSE FORWARD.
A CASE OF BAD LUCK BRINGING GOOD FORTUNE.
BY COMING INTO DIRECT CONTACT WITH HIS VIRTUE...
...I WAS ABLE TO ANALYZE HIS SOUL.
BUT I COULDN'T PIN DOWN ITS TRUE NATURE. HIS EMOTIONS ARE EXTREME, AND HE EXHIBITS IMMORALITY AND DECENCY AT THE SAME TIME.
HIS BEHAVIOR SEEMS ALMOST CONSISTENT...AND YET QUITE HAPHAZARD.

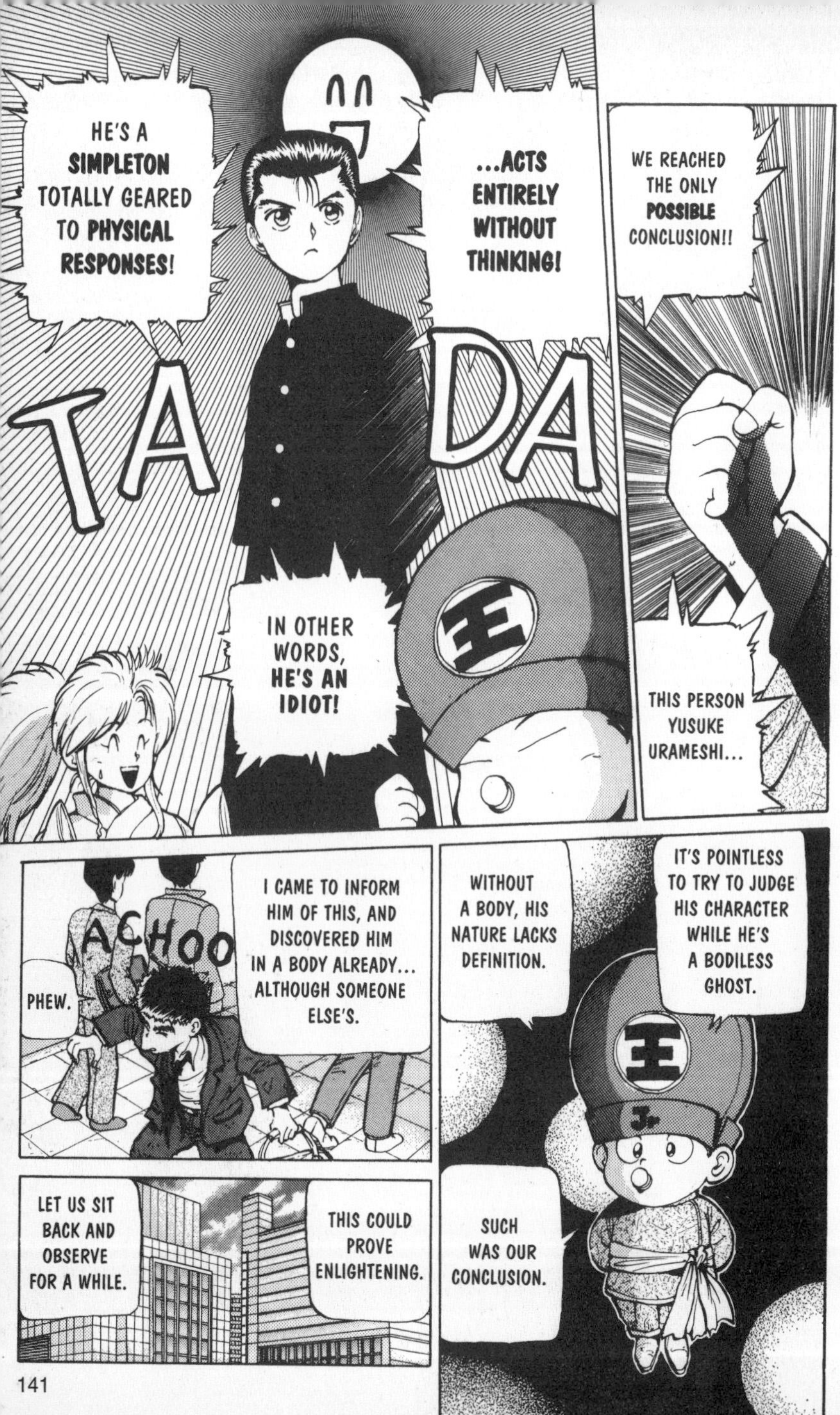
WE REACHED THE ONLY POSSIBLE CONCLUSION!!
THIS PERSON YUSUKE URAMESHI...
...ACTS ENTIRELY WITHOUT THINKING!
HE'S A SIMPLETON TOTALLY GEARED TO PHYSICAL RESPONSES!
TA DA
IN OTHER WORDS, HE'S AN IDIOT!
IT'S POINTLESS TO TRY TO JUDGE HIS CHARACTER WHILE HE'S A BODILESS GHOST.
WITHOUT A BODY, HIS NATURE LACKS DEFINITION.
SUCH WAS OUR CONCLUSION.
I CAME TO INFORM HIM OF THIS, AND DISCOVERED HIM IN A BODY ALREADY... ALTHOUGH SOMEONE ELSE'S.
ACHOO
PHEW.
THIS COULD PROVE ENLIGHTENING.
LET US SIT BACK AND OBSERVE FOR A WHILE.

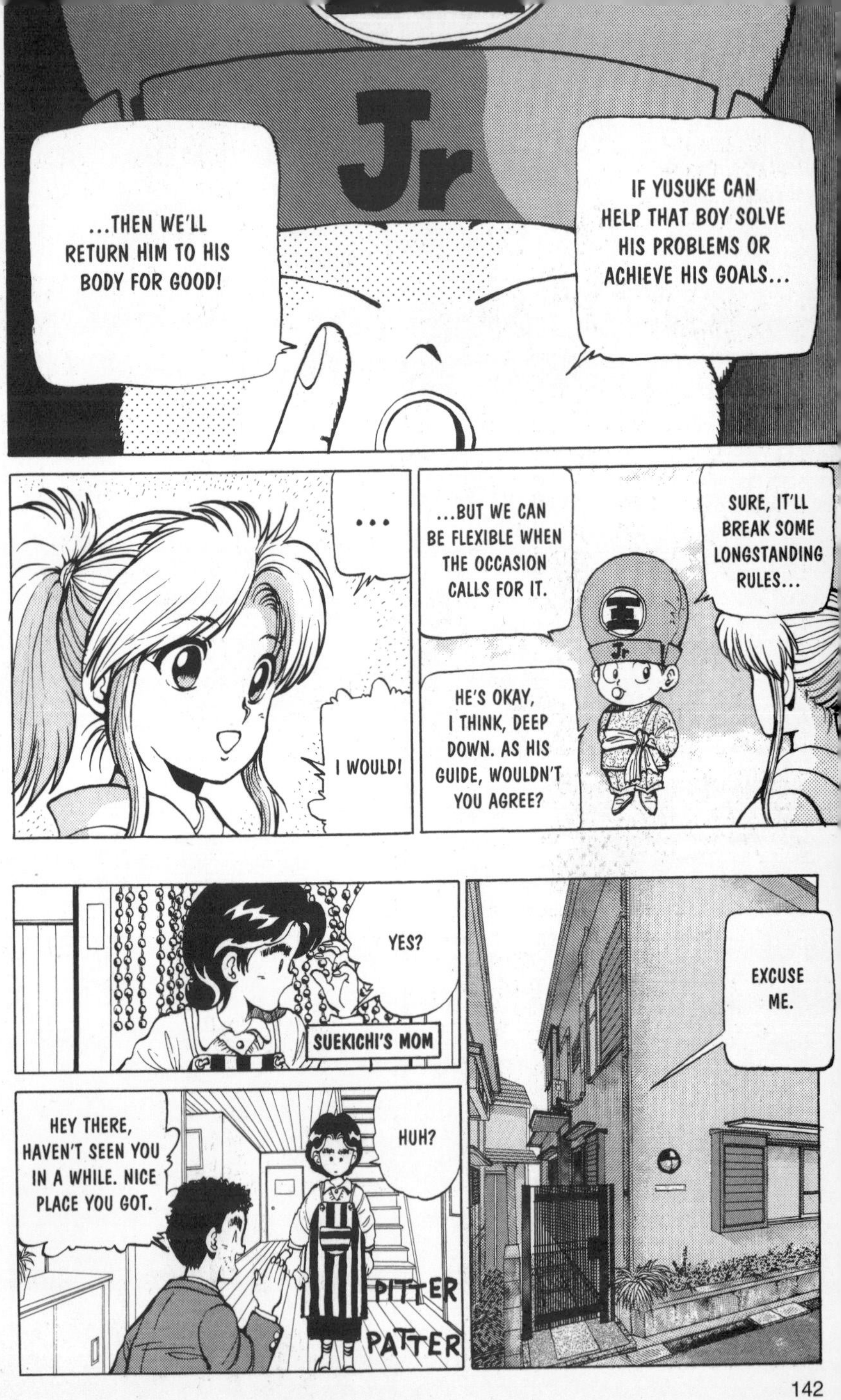
IF YUSUKE CAN HELP THAT BOY SOLVE HIS PROBLEMS OR ACHIEVE HIS GOALS...
...THEN WE'LL RETURN HIM TO HIS BODY FOR GOOD!
SURE, IT'LL BREAK SOME LONGSTANDING RULES...
...BUT WE CAN BE FLEXIBLE WHEN THE OCCASION CALLS FOR IT.
HE'S OKAY, I THINK, DEEP DOWN. AS HIS GUIDE, WOULDN'T YOU AGREE?
...
I WOULD!
EXCUSE ME.
YES?
SUEKICHI'S MOM
HUH?
HEY THERE, HAVEN'T SEEN YOU IN A WHILE. NICE PLACE YOU GOT.
PITTER
PATTER

READ THIS WAY

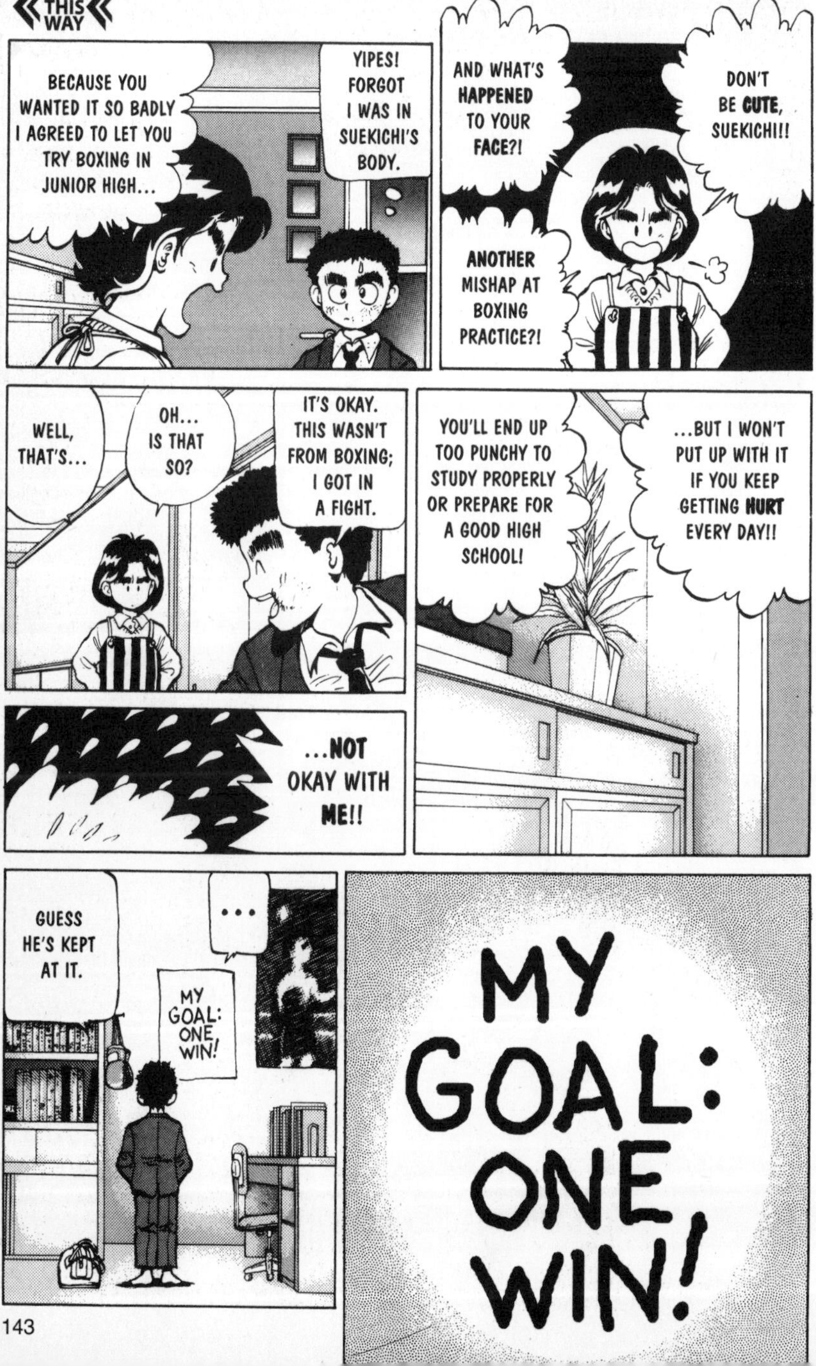
DON'T BE CUTE, SUEKICHI!!
AND WHAT'S HAPPENED TO YOUR FACE?!
ANOTHER MISHAP AT BOXING PRACTICE?!
YIPES! FORGOT I WAS IN SUEKICHI'S BODY.
BECAUSE YOU WANTED IT SO BADLY I AGREED TO LET YOU TRY BOXING IN JUNIOR HIGH...
...BUT I WON'T PUT UP WITH IT IF YOU KEEP GETTING HURT EVERY DAY!!
YOU'LL END UP TOO PUNCHY TO STUDY PROPERLY OR PREPARE FOR A GOOD HIGH SCHOOL!
IT'S OKAY. THIS WASN'T FROM BOXING; I GOT IN A FIGHT.
OH... IS THAT SO?
WELL, THAT'S...
...NOT OKAY WITH ME!!
MY GOAL: ONE WIN!
...
GUESS HE'S KEPT AT IT.
MY GOAL: ONE WIN!

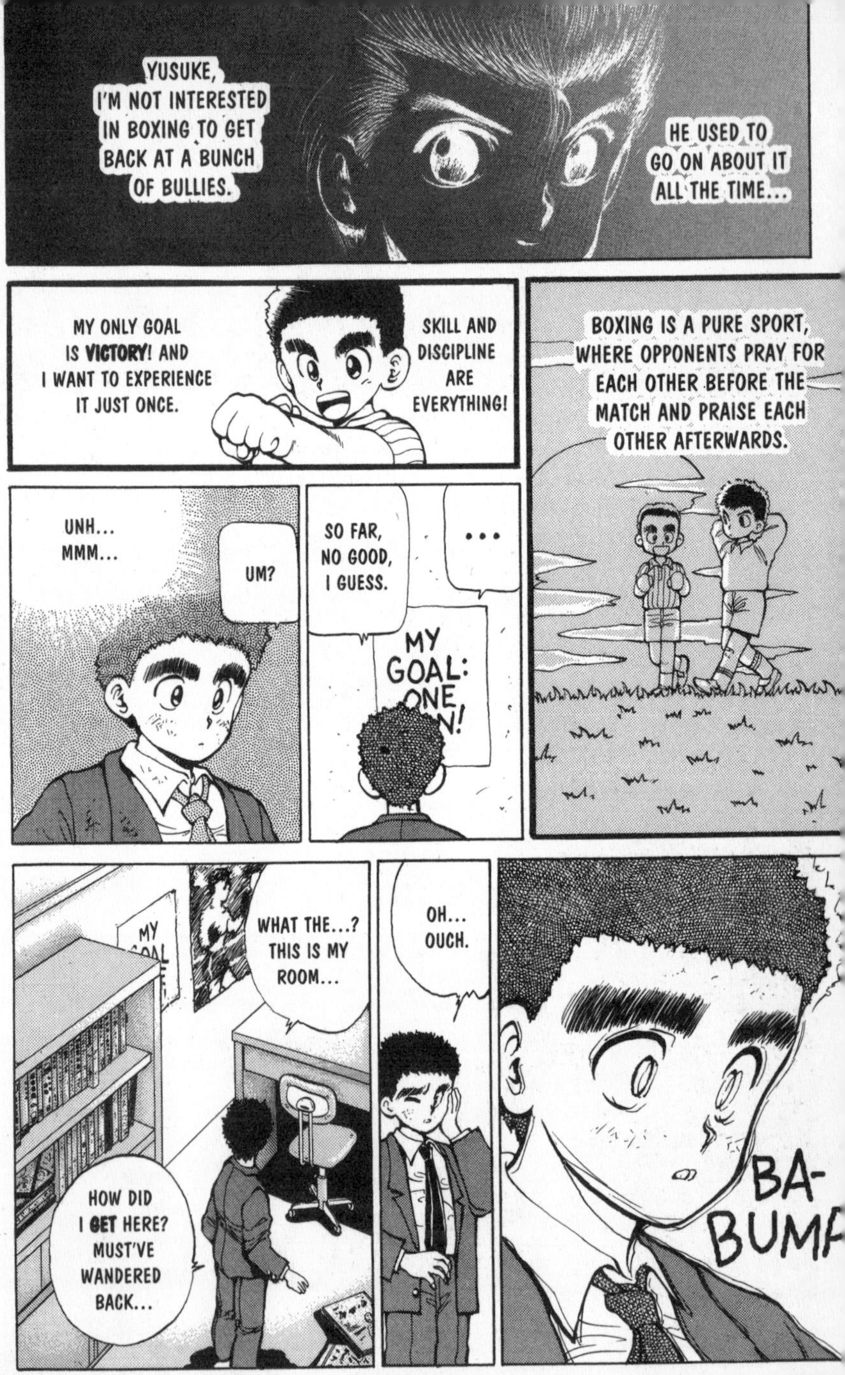
HE USED TO GO ON ABOUT IT ALL THE TIME...
YUSUKE, I'M NOT INTERESTED IN BOXING TO GET BACK AT A BUNCH OF BULLIES.
BOXING IS A PURE SPORT, WHERE OPPONENTS PRAY FOR EACH OTHER BEFORE THE MATCH AND PRAISE EACH OTHER AFTERWARDS.
SKILL AND DISCIPLINE ARE EVERYTHING!
MY ONLY GOAL IS **VICTORY**! AND I WANT TO EXPERIENCE IT JUST ONCE.
...
SO FAR, NO GOOD, I GUESS.
MY GOAL: ONE
UM?
UNH... MMM...
BA-
BUM
OH... OUCH.
WHAT THE...? THIS IS MY ROOM...
HOW DID I **GET** HERE? MUST'VE WANDERED BACK...

READ THIS WAY

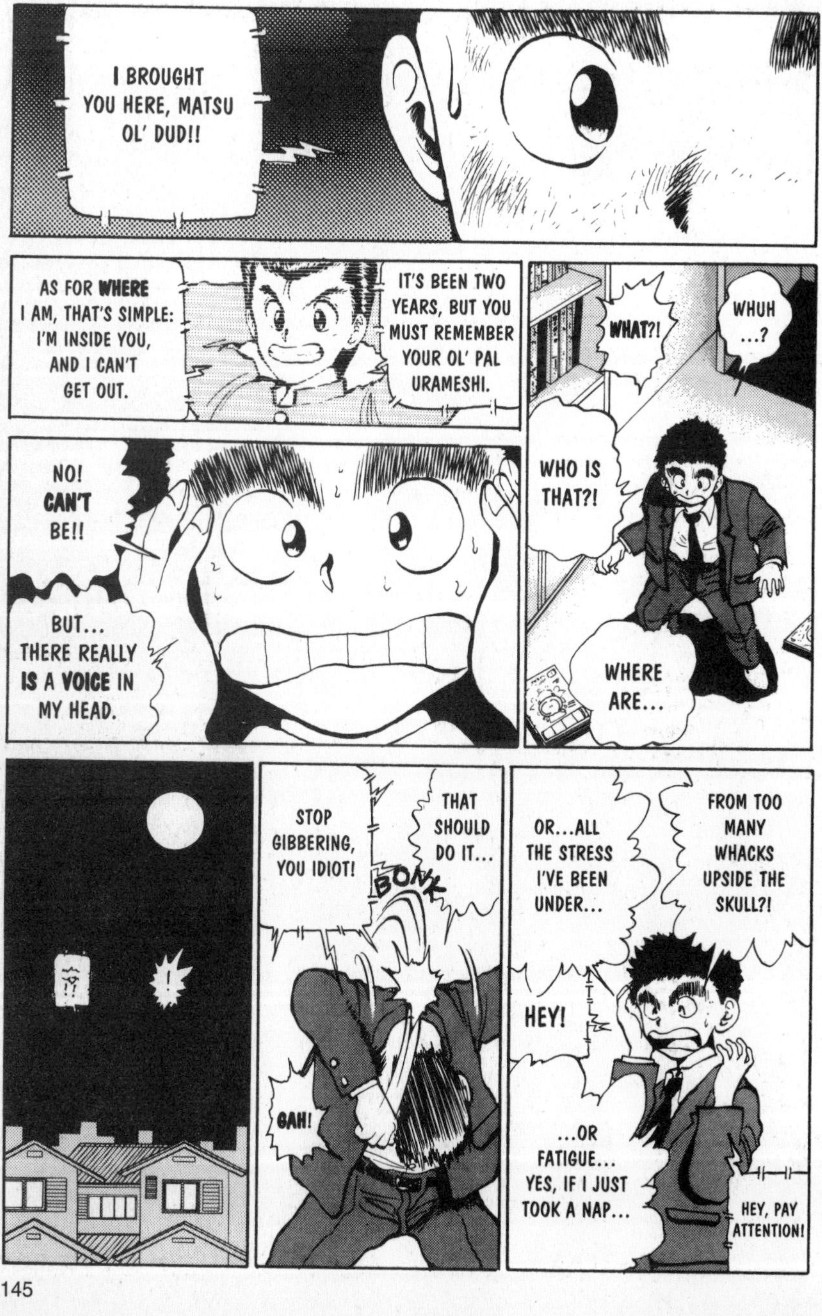
I BROUGHT YOU HERE, MATSU OL' DUD!!
WHUH ...?
WHAT?!
WHO IS THAT?!
WHERE ARE...
IT'S BEEN TWO YEARS, BUT YOU MUST REMEMBER YOUR OL' PAL URAMESHI.
AS FOR WHERE I AM, THAT'S SIMPLE: I'M INSIDE YOU, AND I CAN'T GET OUT.
NO! CAN'T BE!!
BUT... THERE REALLY IS A VOICE IN MY HEAD.
FROM TOO MANY WHACKS UPSIDE THE SKULL?!
OR...ALL THE STRESS I'VE BEEN UNDER...
HEY!
...OR FATIGUE... YES, IF I JUST TOOK A NAP...
HEY, PAY ATTENTION!
THAT SHOULD DO IT...
STOP GIBBERING, YOU IDIOT!
BONK
GAH!
!
!?

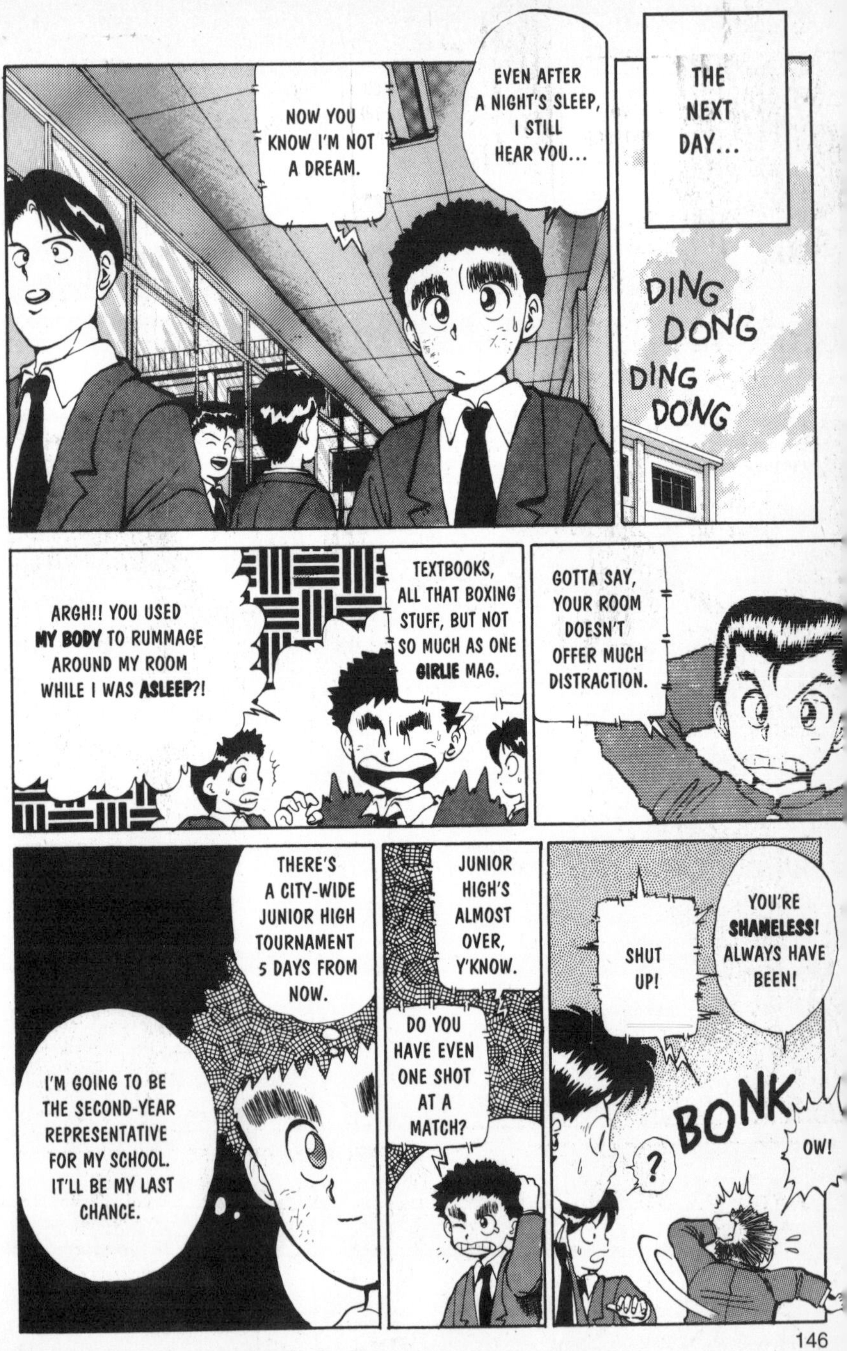
THE NEXT DAY...
DING DONG DING DONG
EVEN AFTER A NIGHT'S SLEEP, I STILL HEAR YOU...
NOW YOU KNOW I'M NOT A DREAM.
GOTTA SAY, YOUR ROOM DOESN'T OFFER MUCH DISTRACTION.
TEXTBOOKS, ALL THAT BOXING STUFF, BUT NOT SO MUCH AS ONE GIRLIE MAG.
ARGH!! YOU USED MY BODY TO RUMMAGE AROUND MY ROOM WHILE I WAS ASLEEP?!
YOU'RE SHAMELESS! ALWAYS HAVE BEEN!
SHUT UP!
BONK
?
OW!
JUNIOR HIGH'S ALMOST OVER, Y'KNOW.
DO YOU HAVE EVEN ONE SHOT AT A MATCH?
THERE'S A CITY-WIDE JUNIOR HIGH TOURNAMENT 5 DAYS FROM NOW.
I'M GOING TO BE THE SECOND-YEAR REPRESENTATIVE FOR MY SCHOOL. IT'LL BE MY LAST CHANCE.

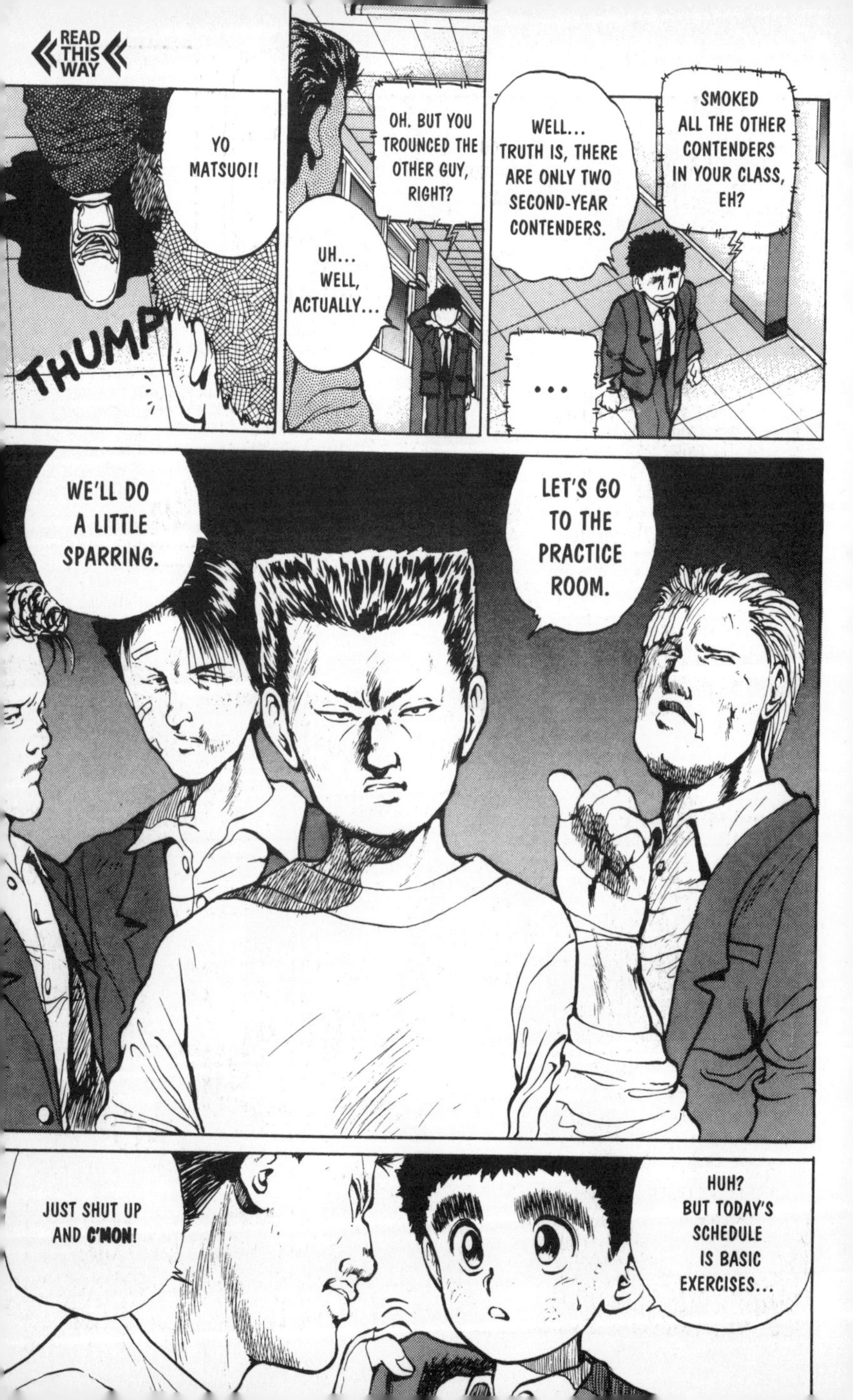
READ THIS WAY
SMOKED ALL THE OTHER CONTENDERS IN YOUR CLASS, EH?
WELL... TRUTH IS, THERE ARE ONLY TWO SECOND-YEAR CONTENDERS.
...
OH. BUT YOU TROUNCED THE OTHER GUY, RIGHT?
UH... WELL, ACTUALLY...
YO MATSUO!!
THUMP
LET'S GO TO THE PRACTICE ROOM.
WE'LL DO A LITTLE SPARRING.
HUH? BUT TODAY'S SCHEDULE IS BASIC EXERCISES...
JUST SHUT UP AND C'MON!

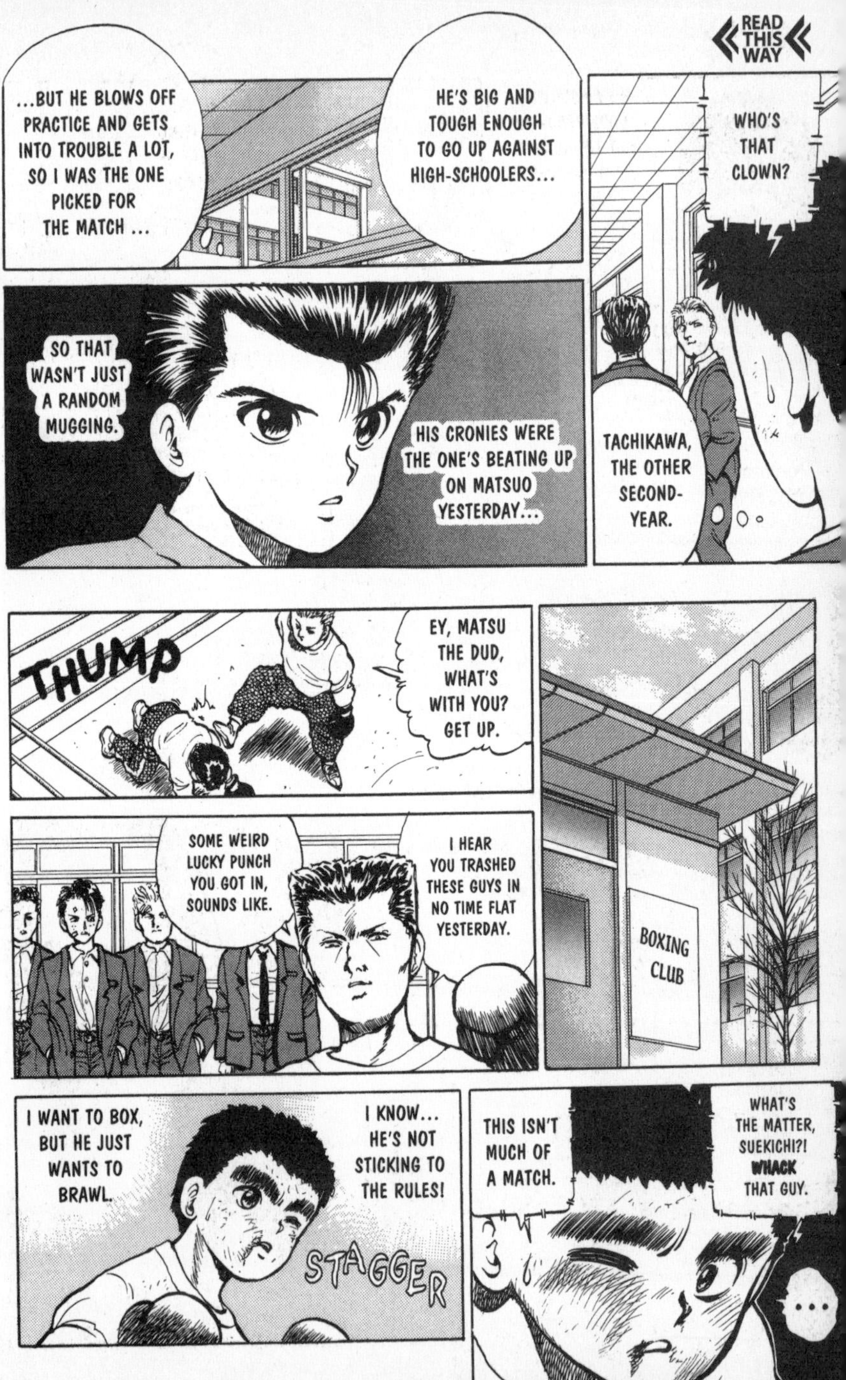
READ THIS WAY
WHO'S THAT CLOWN?
TACHIKAWA, THE OTHER SECOND-YEAR.
HE'S BIG AND TOUGH ENOUGH TO GO UP AGAINST HIGH-SCHOOLERS...
...BUT HE BLOWS OFF PRACTICE AND GETS INTO TROUBLE A LOT, SO I WAS THE ONE PICKED FOR THE MATCH ...
HIS CRONIES WERE THE ONE'S BEATING UP ON MATSUO YESTERDAY...
SO THAT WASN'T JUST A RANDOM MUGGING.
BOXING CLUB
EY, MATSU THE DUD, WHAT'S WITH YOU? GET UP.
THUMP
I HEAR YOU TRASHED THESE GUYS IN NO TIME FLAT YESTERDAY.
SOME WEIRD LUCKY PUNCH YOU GOT IN, SOUNDS LIKE.
WHAT'S THE MATTER, SUEKICHI?! WHACK THAT GUY.
THIS ISN'T MUCH OF A MATCH.
...
I KNOW... HE'S NOT STICKING TO THE RULES!
I WANT TO BOX, BUT HE JUST WANTS TO BRAWL.
STAGGER

READ THIS WAY

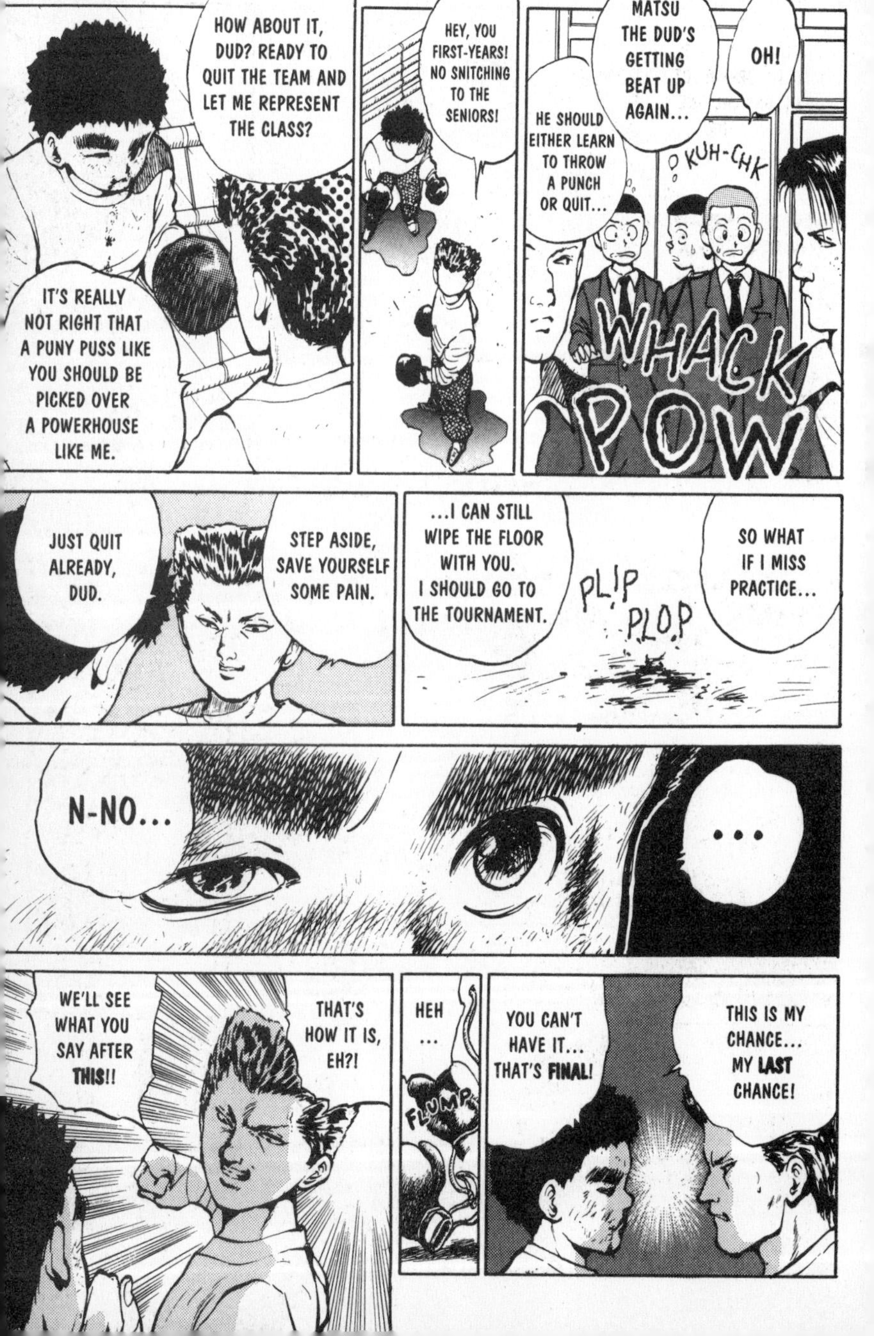
OH!
MATSU THE DUD'S GETTING BEAT UP AGAIN...
HE SHOULD EITHER LEARN TO THROW A PUNCH OR QUIT...
KUH-CHK
WHACK
POW
HEY, YOU FIRST-YEARS! NO SNITCHING TO THE SENIORS!
HOW ABOUT IT, DUD? READY TO QUIT THE TEAM AND LET ME REPRESENT THE CLASS?
IT'S REALLY NOT RIGHT THAT A PUNY PUSS LIKE YOU SHOULD BE PICKED OVER A POWERHOUSE LIKE ME.
SO WHAT IF I MISS PRACTICE...
...I CAN STILL WIPE THE FLOOR WITH YOU. I SHOULD GO TO THE TOURNAMENT.
PLIP
PLOP
STEP ASIDE, SAVE YOURSELF SOME PAIN.
JUST QUIT ALREADY, DUD.
...
N-NO...
THIS IS MY CHANCE... MY **LAST** CHANCE!
YOU CAN'T HAVE IT... THAT'S **FINAL**!
HEH ...
FLUMP
THAT'S HOW IT IS, EH?!
WE'LL SEE WHAT YOU SAY AFTER **THIS**!!

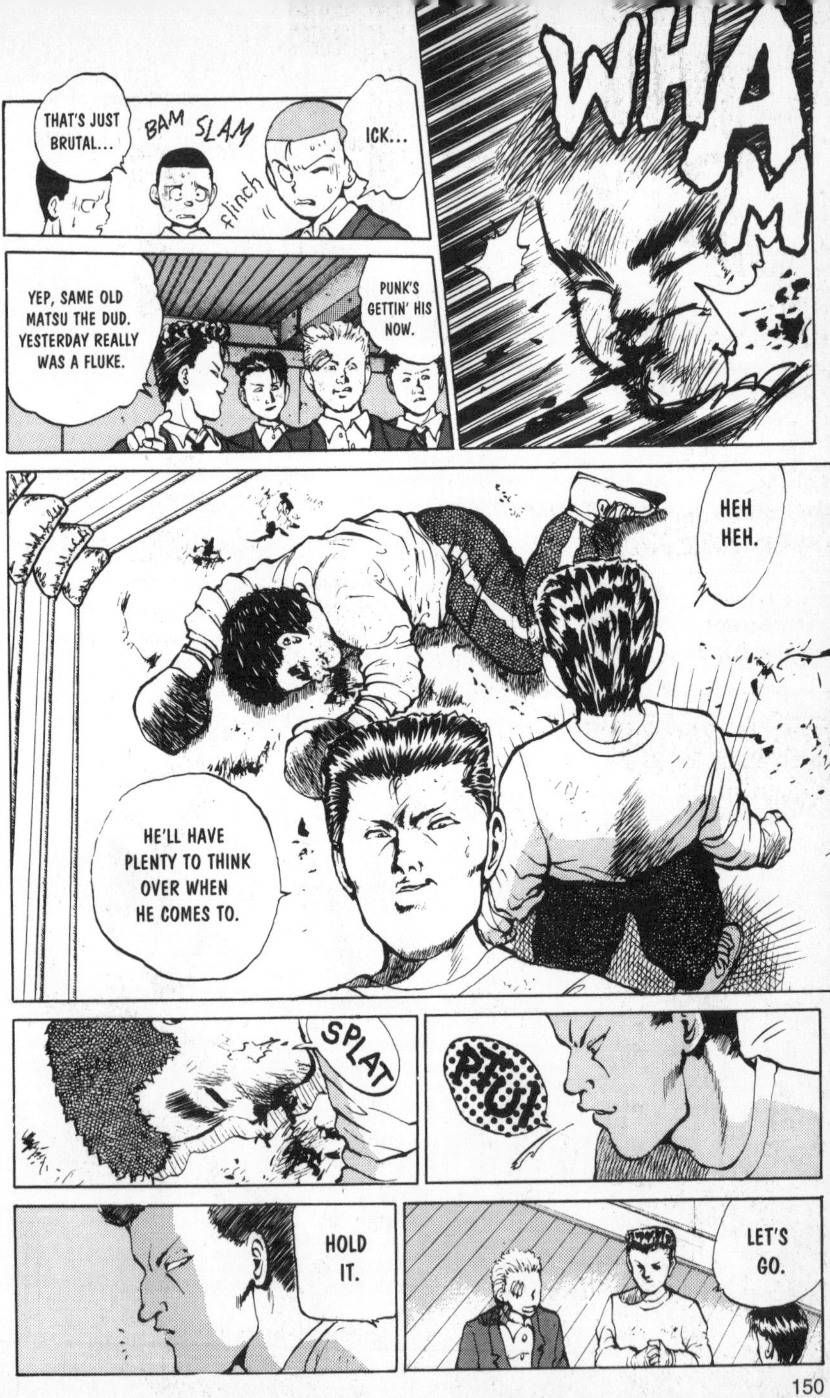
WHAM
ICK...
BAM
SLAM
flinch
THAT'S JUST BRUTAL...
PUNK'S GETTIN' HIS NOW.
YEP, SAME OLD MATSU THE DUD. YESTERDAY REALLY WAS A FLUKE.
HEH HEH.
HE'LL HAVE PLENTY TO THINK OVER WHEN HE COMES TO.
PTUI
SPLAT
LET'S GO.
HOLD IT.

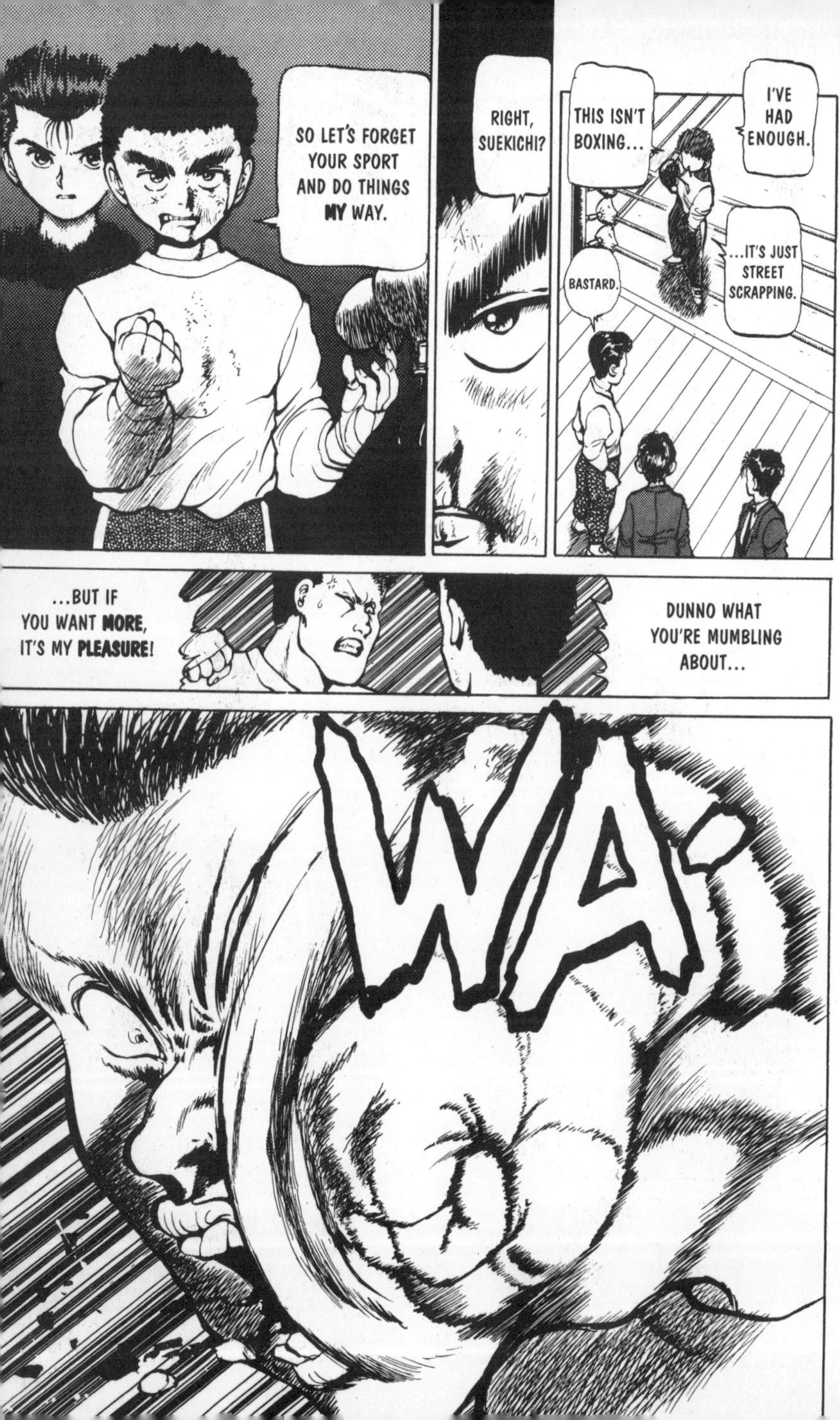
I'VE HAD ENOUGH.
THIS ISN'T BOXING...
...IT'S JUST STREET SCRAPPING.
BASTARD.
RIGHT, SUEKICHI?
SO LET'S FORGET YOUR SPORT AND DO THINGS MY WAY.
DUNNO WHAT YOU'RE MUMBLING ABOUT...
...BUT IF YOU WANT MORE, IT'S MY PLEASURE!
WA

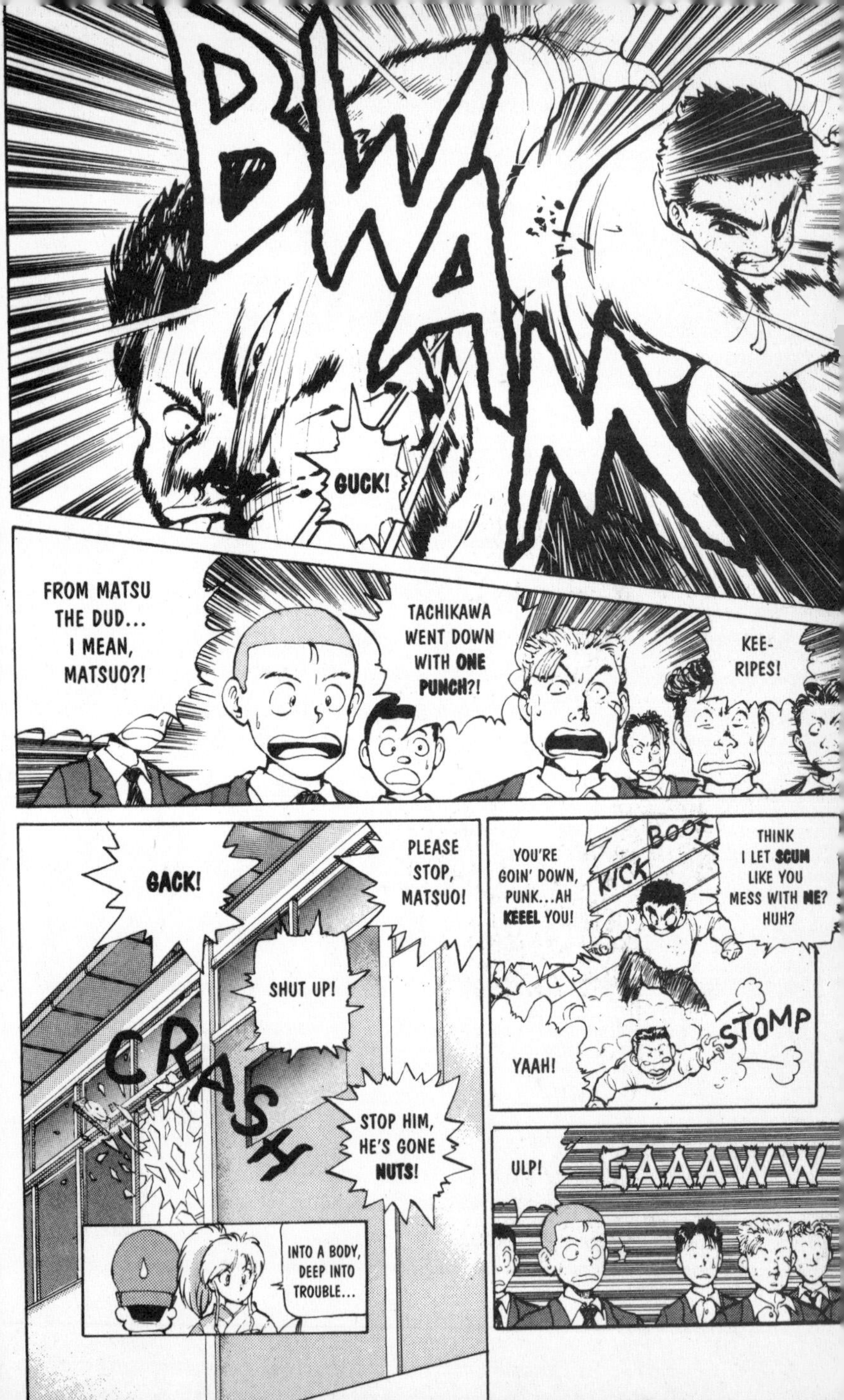
BWAM
GUCK!
KEE-RIPES!
TACHIKAWA WENT DOWN WITH ONE PUNCH?!
FROM MATSU THE DUD... I MEAN, MATSUO?!
THINK I LET SCUM LIKE YOU MESS WITH ME? HUH?
BOOT
KICK
YOU'RE GOIN' DOWN, PUNK...AH KEEEL YOU!
STOMP
YAAH!
GAAAWW
ULP!
PLEASE STOP, MATSUO!
GACK!
SHUT UP!
CRASH
STOP HIM, HE'S GONE NUTS!
INTO A BODY, DEEP INTO TROUBLE...

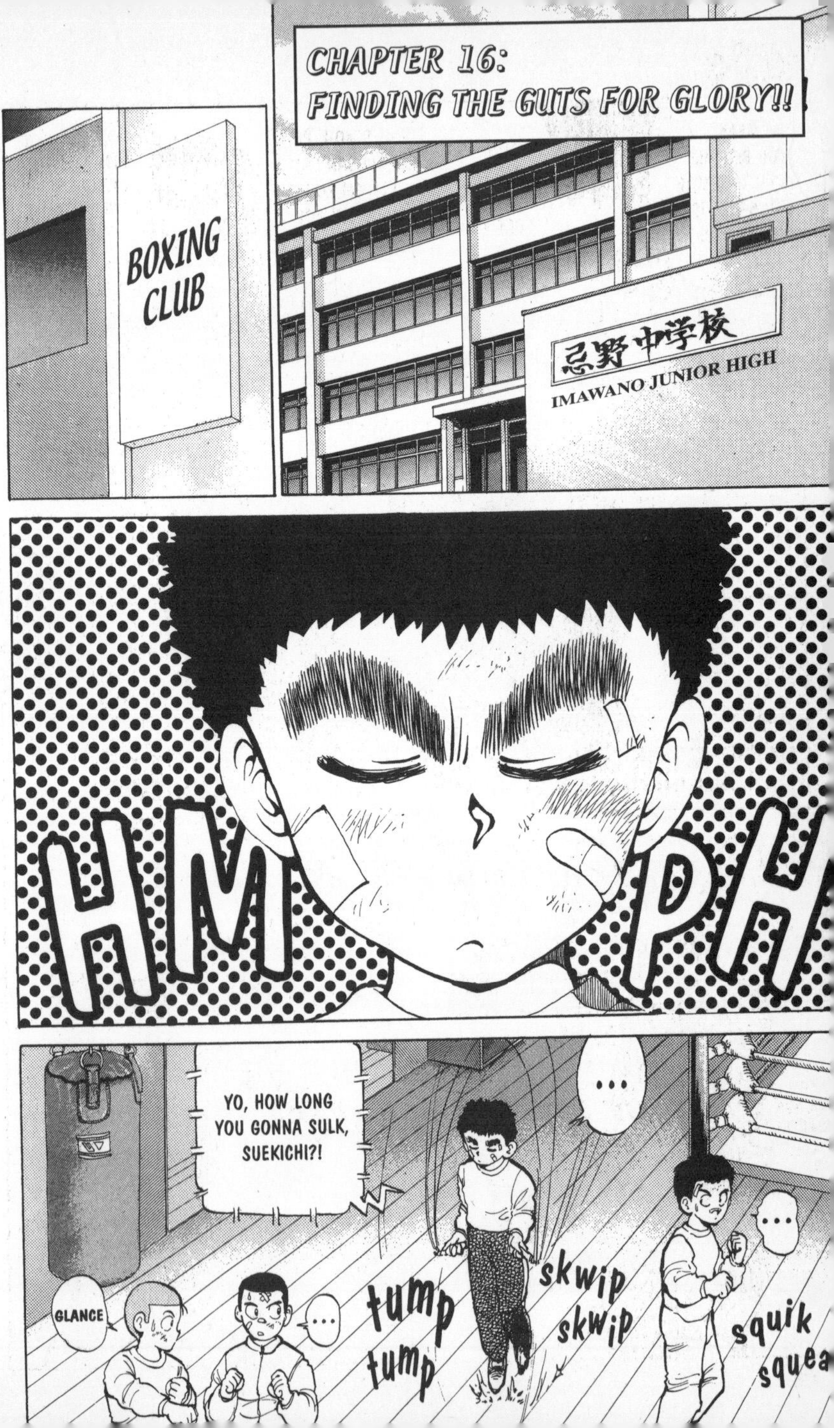
CHAPTER 16: FINDING THE GUTS FOR GLORY!!
忌野中学校
IMAWANO JUNIOR HIGH
BOXING CLUB
HMPH
...
squik squea
...
skwip skwip
tump tump
YO, HOW LONG YOU GONNA SULK, SUEKICHI?!
...
GLANCE

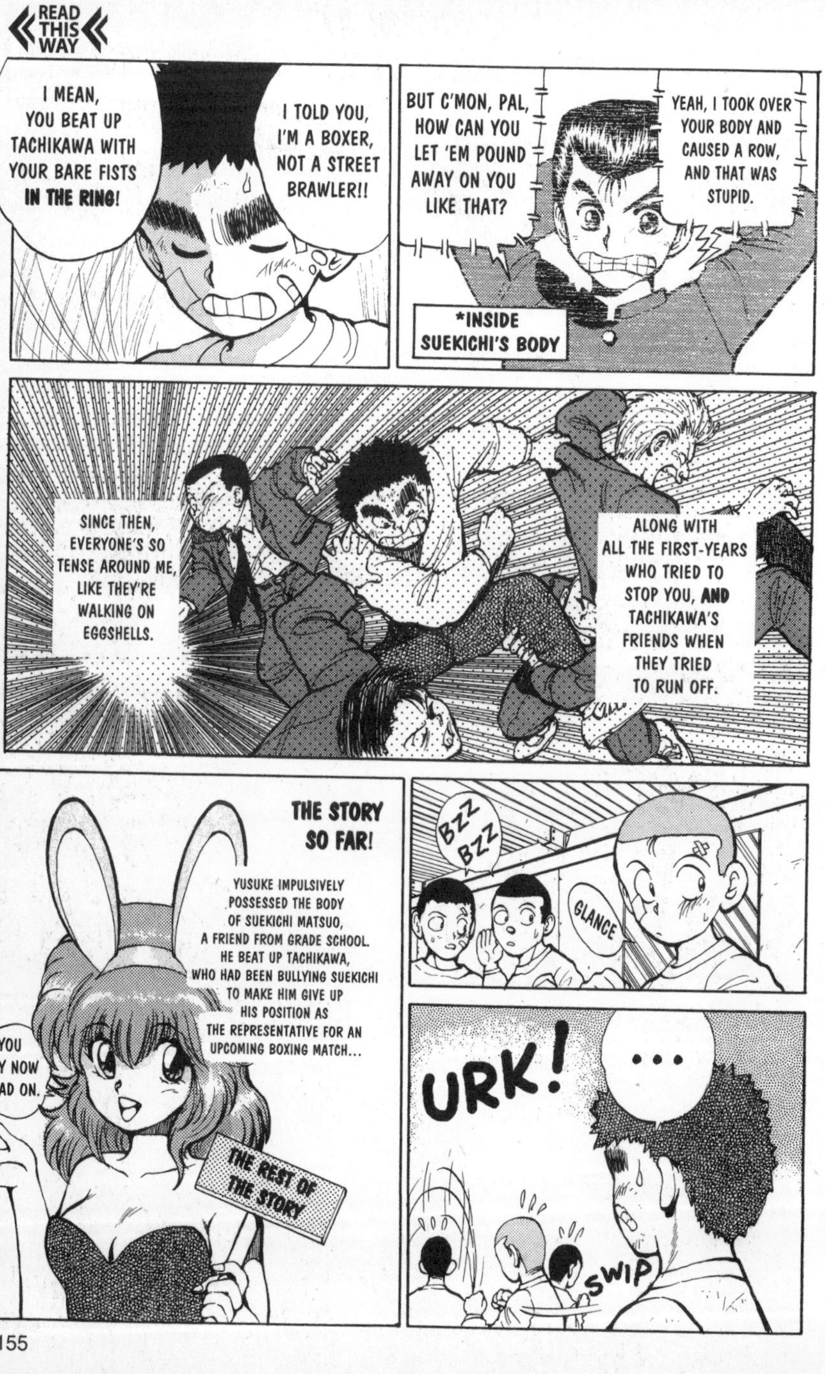
READ THIS WAY
YEAH, I TOOK OVER YOUR BODY AND CAUSED A ROW, AND THAT WAS STUPID.
BUT C'MON, PAL, HOW CAN YOU LET 'EM POUND AWAY ON YOU LIKE THAT?
*INSIDE SUEKICHI'S BODY
I TOLD YOU, I'M A BOXER, NOT A STREET BRAWLER!!
I MEAN, YOU BEAT UP TACHIKAWA WITH YOUR BARE FISTS IN THE RING!
ALONG WITH ALL THE FIRST-YEARS WHO TRIED TO STOP YOU, AND TACHIKAWA'S FRIENDS WHEN THEY TRIED TO RUN OFF.
SINCE THEN, EVERYONE'S SO TENSE AROUND ME, LIKE THEY'RE WALKING ON EGGSHELLS.
BZZ BZZ
GLANCE
...
URK!
SWIP
THE STORY SO FAR!
YUSUKE IMPULSIVELY POSSESSED THE BODY OF SUEKICHI MATSUO, A FRIEND FROM GRADE SCHOOL. HE BEAT UP TACHIKAWA, WHO HAD BEEN BULLYING SUEKICHI TO MAKE HIM GIVE UP HIS POSITION AS THE REPRESENTATIVE FOR AN UPCOMING BOXING MATCH...
YOU MAY NOW READ ON.
THE REST OF THE STORY

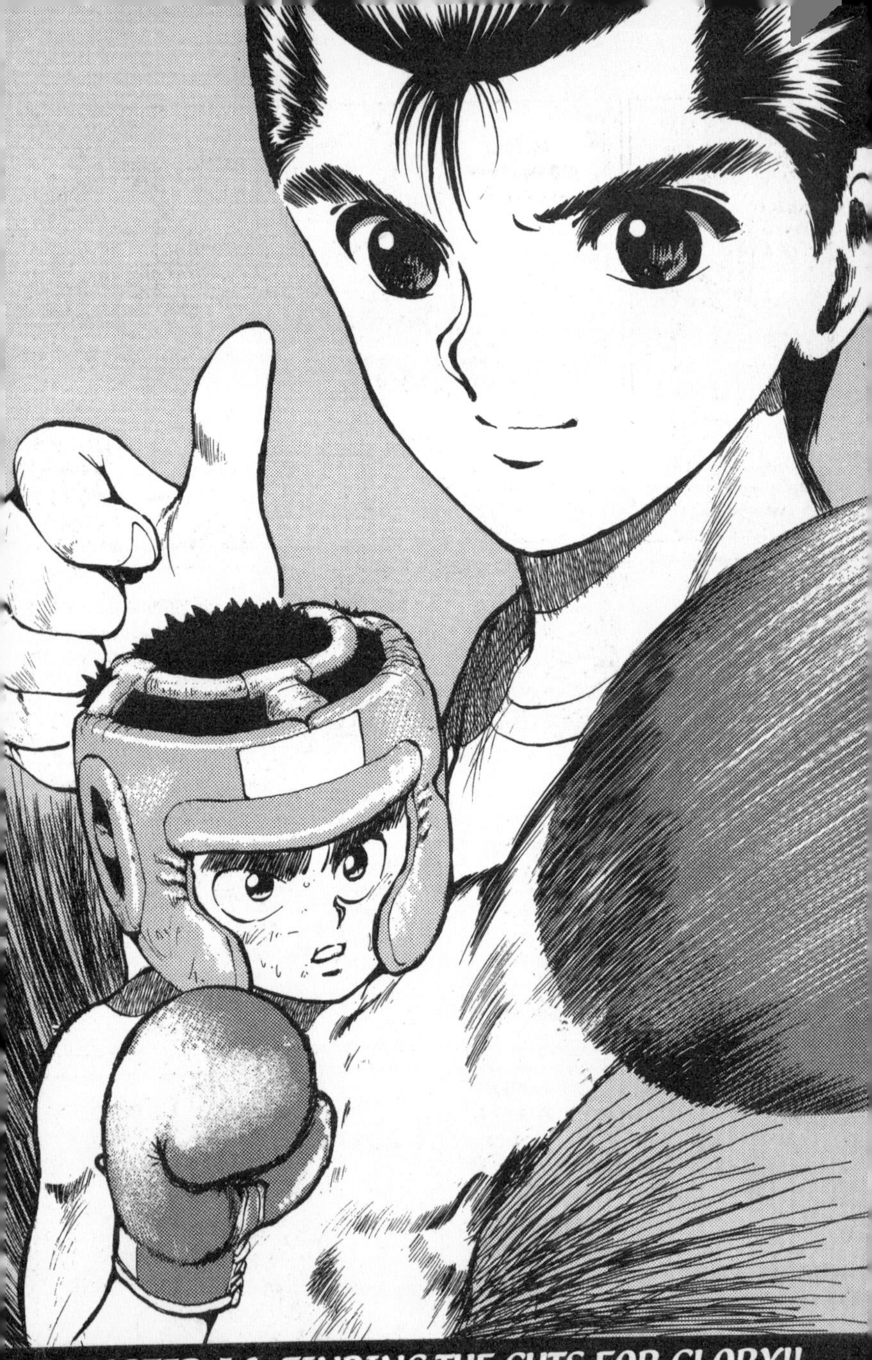

CHAPTER 16: FINDING THE GUTS FOR GLORY!!

READ THIS WAY

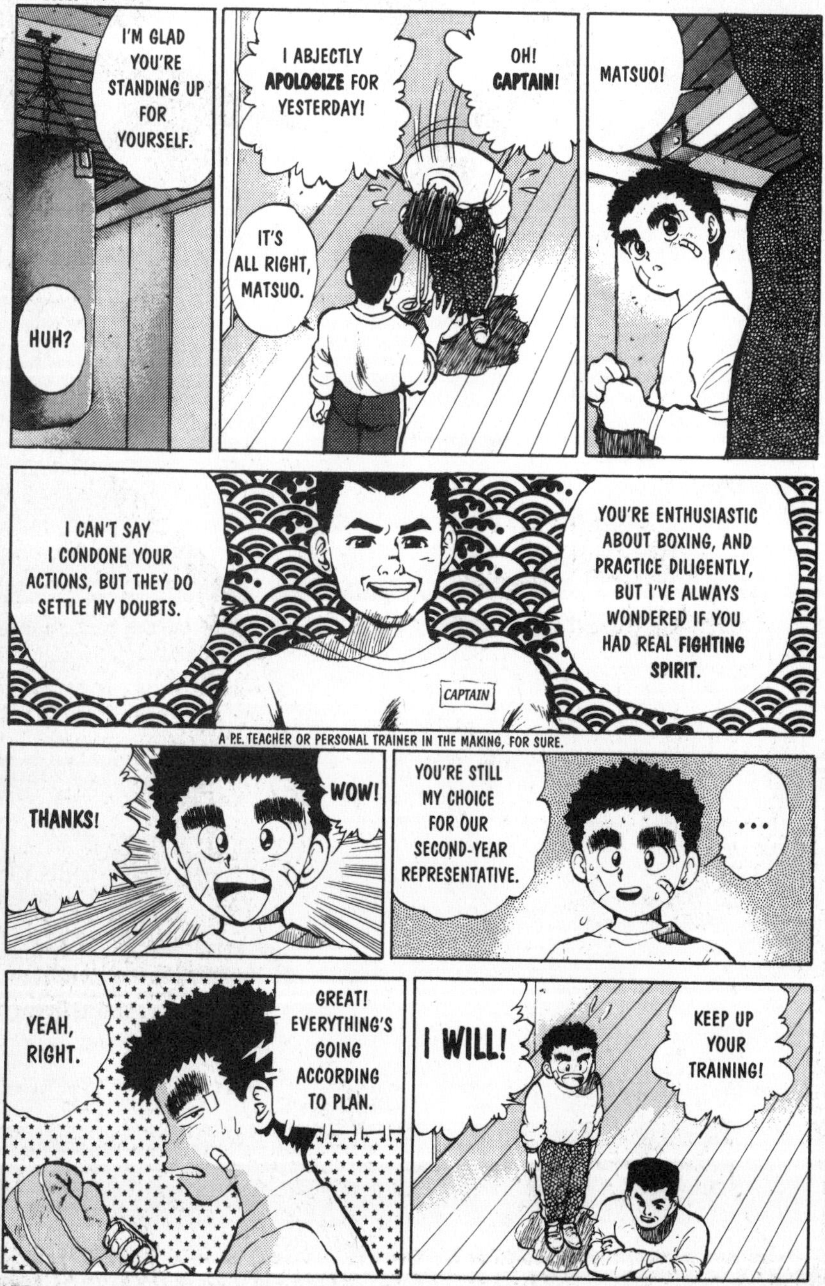
MATSUO!
OH! CAPTAIN!
I ABJECTLY APOLOGIZE FOR YESTERDAY!
IT'S ALL RIGHT, MATSUO.
I'M GLAD YOU'RE STANDING UP FOR YOURSELF.
HUH?
YOU'RE ENTHUSIASTIC ABOUT BOXING, AND PRACTICE DILIGENTLY, BUT I'VE ALWAYS WONDERED IF YOU HAD REAL FIGHTING SPIRIT.
I CAN'T SAY I CONDONE YOUR ACTIONS, BUT THEY DO SETTLE MY DOUBTS.
CAPTAIN
A P.E. TEACHER OR PERSONAL TRAINER IN THE MAKING, FOR SURE.
...
YOU'RE STILL MY CHOICE FOR OUR SECOND-YEAR REPRESENTATIVE.
WOW!
THANKS!
KEEP UP YOUR TRAINING!
I WILL!
GREAT! EVERYTHING'S GOING ACCORDING TO PLAN.
YEAH, RIGHT.

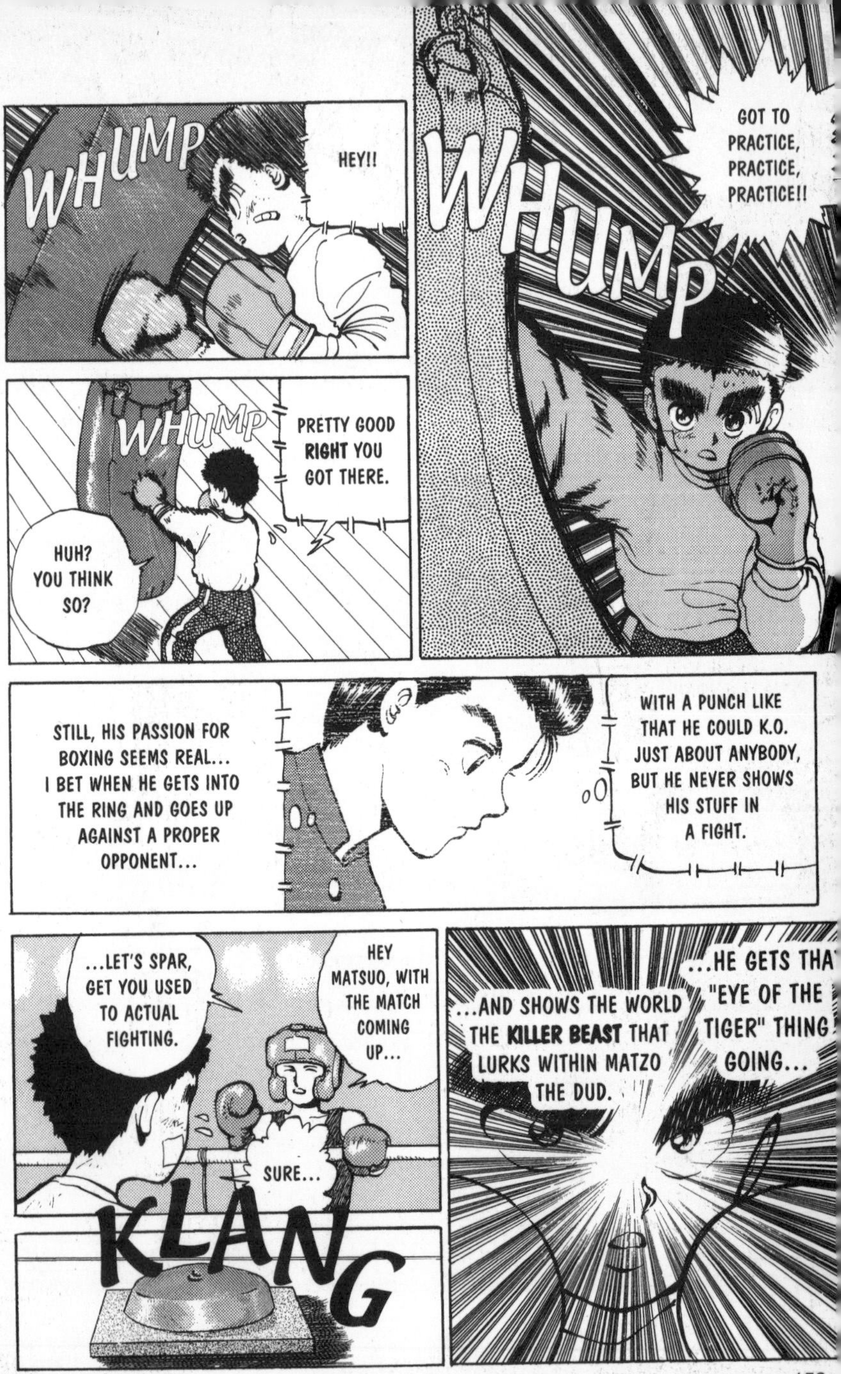
GOT TO PRACTICE, PRACTICE, PRACTICE!!
WHUMP
HEY!!
WHUMP
PRETTY GOOD **RIGHT** YOU GOT THERE.
WHUMP
HUH? YOU THINK SO?
WITH A PUNCH LIKE THAT HE COULD K.O. JUST ABOUT ANYBODY, BUT HE NEVER SHOWS HIS STUFF IN A FIGHT.
STILL, HIS PASSION FOR BOXING SEEMS REAL... I BET WHEN HE GETS INTO THE RING AND GOES UP AGAINST A PROPER OPPONENT...
...HE GETS THA "EYE OF THE TIGER" THING GOING...
...AND SHOWS THE WORLD THE **KILLER BEAST** THAT LURKS WITHIN MATZO THE DUD.
HEY MATSUO, WITH THE MATCH COMING UP...
...LET'S SPAR, GET YOU USED TO ACTUAL FIGHTING.
SURE...
KLANG

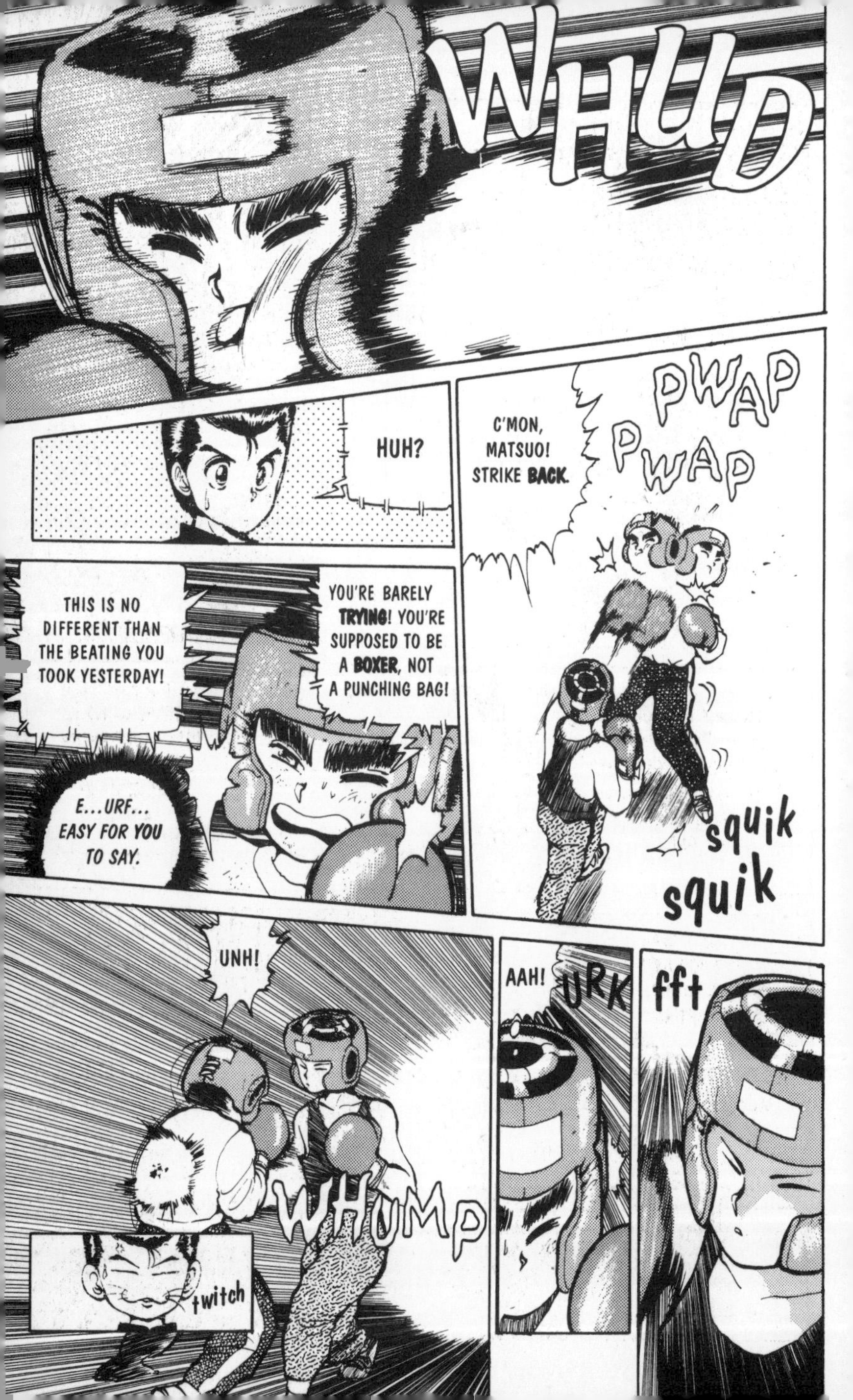
WHUD
C'MON, MATSUO! STRIKE BACK.
PWAP
PWAP
squik
squik
HUH?
YOU'RE BARELY TRYING! YOU'RE SUPPOSED TO BE A BOXER, NOT A PUNCHING BAG!
THIS IS NO DIFFERENT THAN THE BEATING YOU TOOK YESTERDAY!
E...URF... EASY FOR YOU TO SAY.
fft
AAH!
URK
UNH!
WHUMP
twitch

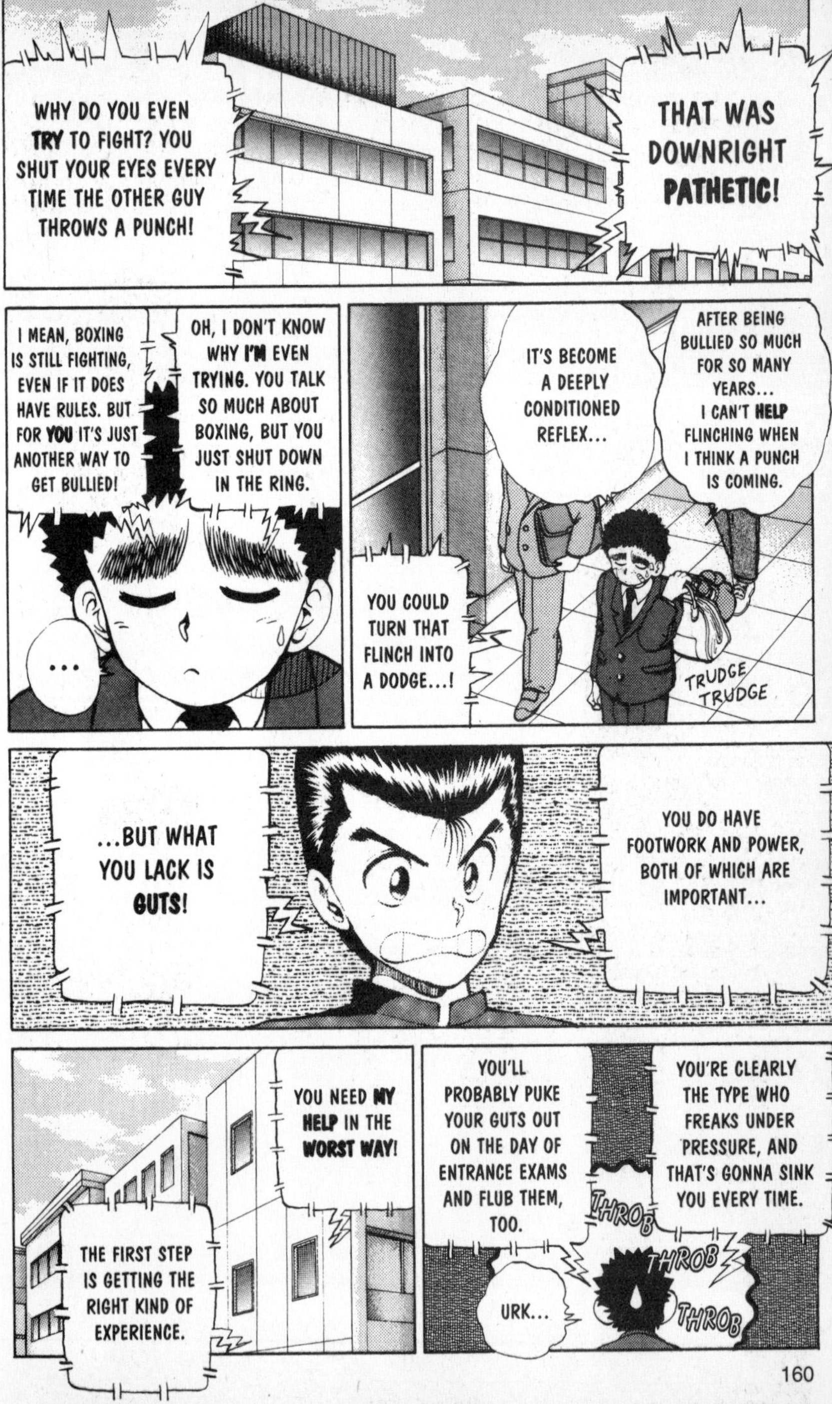
THAT WAS DOWNRIGHT PATHETIC!
WHY DO YOU EVEN TRY TO FIGHT? YOU SHUT YOUR EYES EVERY TIME THE OTHER GUY THROWS A PUNCH!
AFTER BEING BULLIED SO MUCH FOR SO MANY YEARS... I CAN'T HELP FLINCHING WHEN I THINK A PUNCH IS COMING.
IT'S BECOME A DEEPLY CONDITIONED REFLEX...
YOU COULD TURN THAT FLINCH INTO A DODGE...!
TRUDGE TRUDGE
OH, I DON'T KNOW WHY I'M EVEN TRYING. YOU TALK SO MUCH ABOUT BOXING, BUT YOU JUST SHUT DOWN IN THE RING.
I MEAN, BOXING IS STILL FIGHTING, EVEN IF IT DOES HAVE RULES. BUT FOR YOU IT'S JUST ANOTHER WAY TO GET BULLIED!
...
YOU DO HAVE FOOTWORK AND POWER, BOTH OF WHICH ARE IMPORTANT...
...BUT WHAT YOU LACK IS GUTS!
YOU'RE CLEARLY THE TYPE WHO FREAKS UNDER PRESSURE, AND THAT'S GONNA SINK YOU EVERY TIME.
YOU'LL PROBABLY PUKE YOUR GUTS OUT ON THE DAY OF ENTRANCE EXAMS AND FLUB THEM, TOO.
THROB
THROB
THROB
URK...
YOU NEED MY HELP IN THE WORST WAY!
THE FIRST STEP IS GETTING THE RIGHT KIND OF EXPERIENCE.

READ THIS WAY

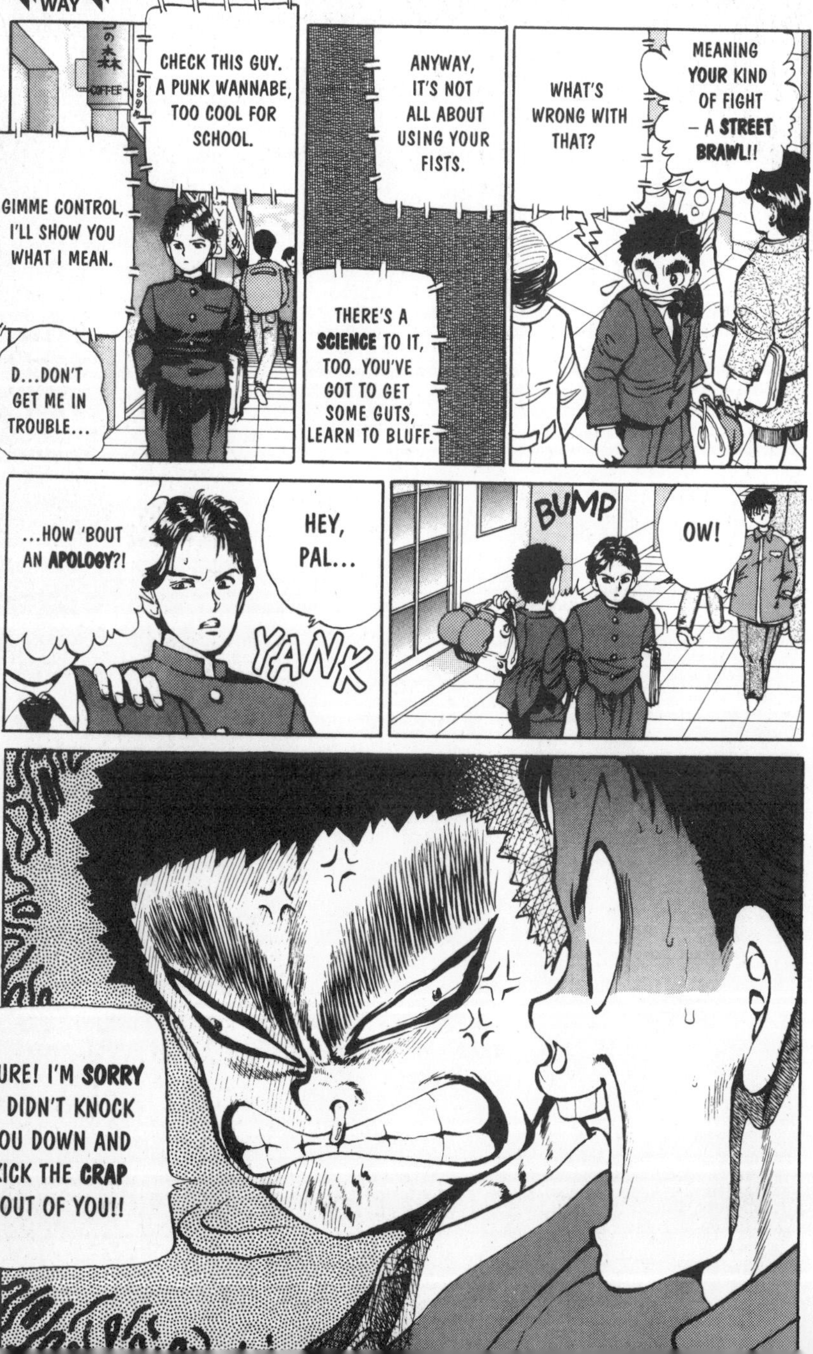
MEANING YOUR KIND OF FIGHT – A STREET BRAWL!!
WHAT'S WRONG WITH THAT?
ANYWAY, IT'S NOT ALL ABOUT USING YOUR FISTS.
THERE'S A SCIENCE TO IT, TOO. YOU'VE GOT TO GET SOME GUTS, LEARN TO BLUFF.
CHECK THIS GUY. A PUNK WANNABE, TOO COOL FOR SCHOOL.
GIMME CONTROL, I'LL SHOW YOU WHAT I MEAN.
D...DON'T GET ME IN TROUBLE...
BUMP
OW!
HEY, PAL...
YANK
...HOW 'BOUT AN APOLOGY?!
SURE! I'M SORRY I DIDN'T KNOCK YOU DOWN AND KICK THE CRAP OUT OF YOU!!

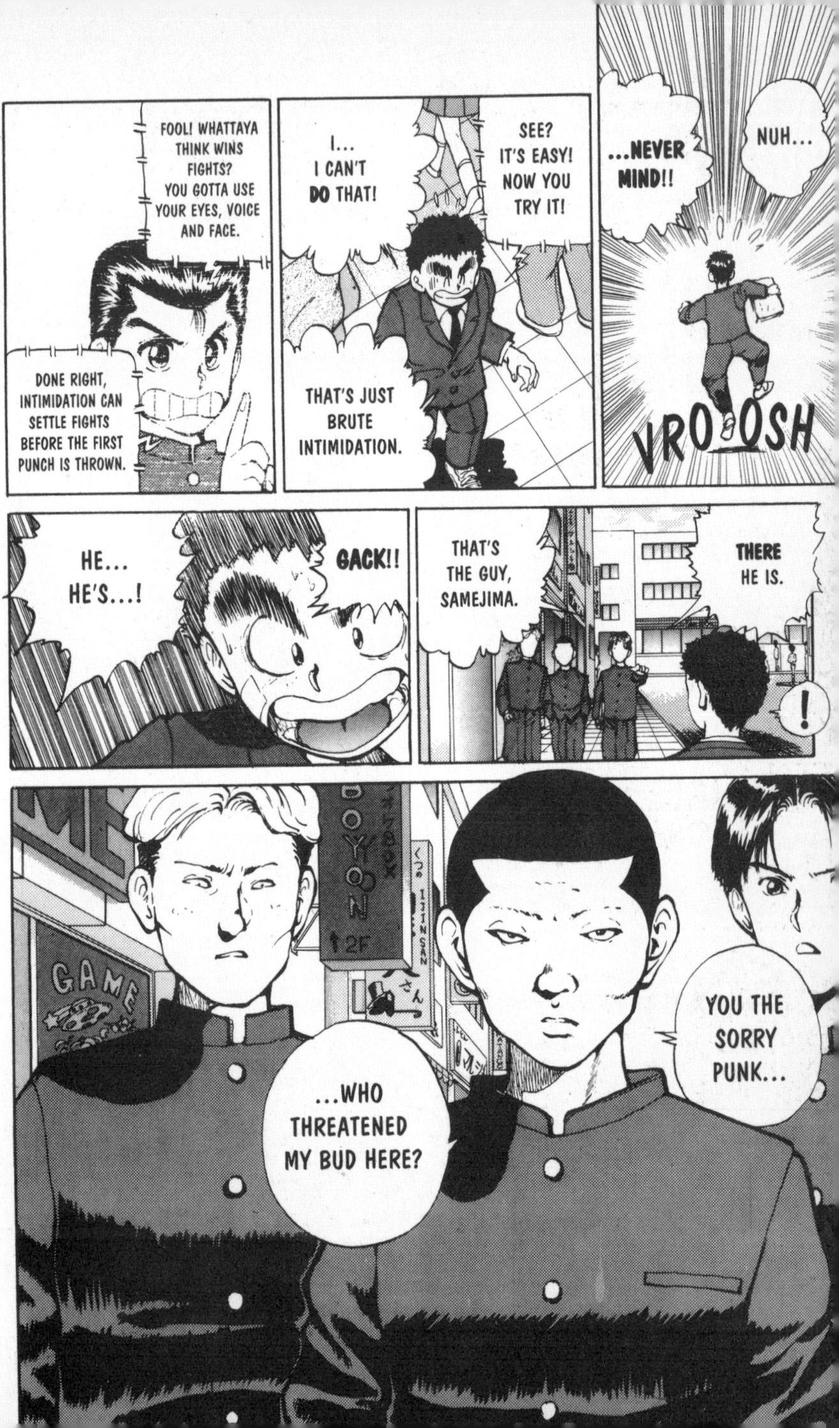
NUH...
...NEVER MIND!!
VROOSH
SEE? IT'S EASY! NOW YOU TRY IT!
I... I CAN'T DO THAT!
THAT'S JUST BRUTE INTIMIDATION.
FOOL! WHATTAYA THINK WINS FIGHTS? YOU GOTTA USE YOUR EYES, VOICE AND FACE.
DONE RIGHT, INTIMIDATION CAN SETTLE FIGHTS BEFORE THE FIRST PUNCH IS THROWN.
THERE HE IS.
!
THAT'S THE GUY, SAMEJIMA.
GACK!!
HE... HE'S...!
YOU THE SORRY PUNK...
...WHO THREATENED MY BUD HERE?
DOYON
2F
GAME

READ THIS WAY

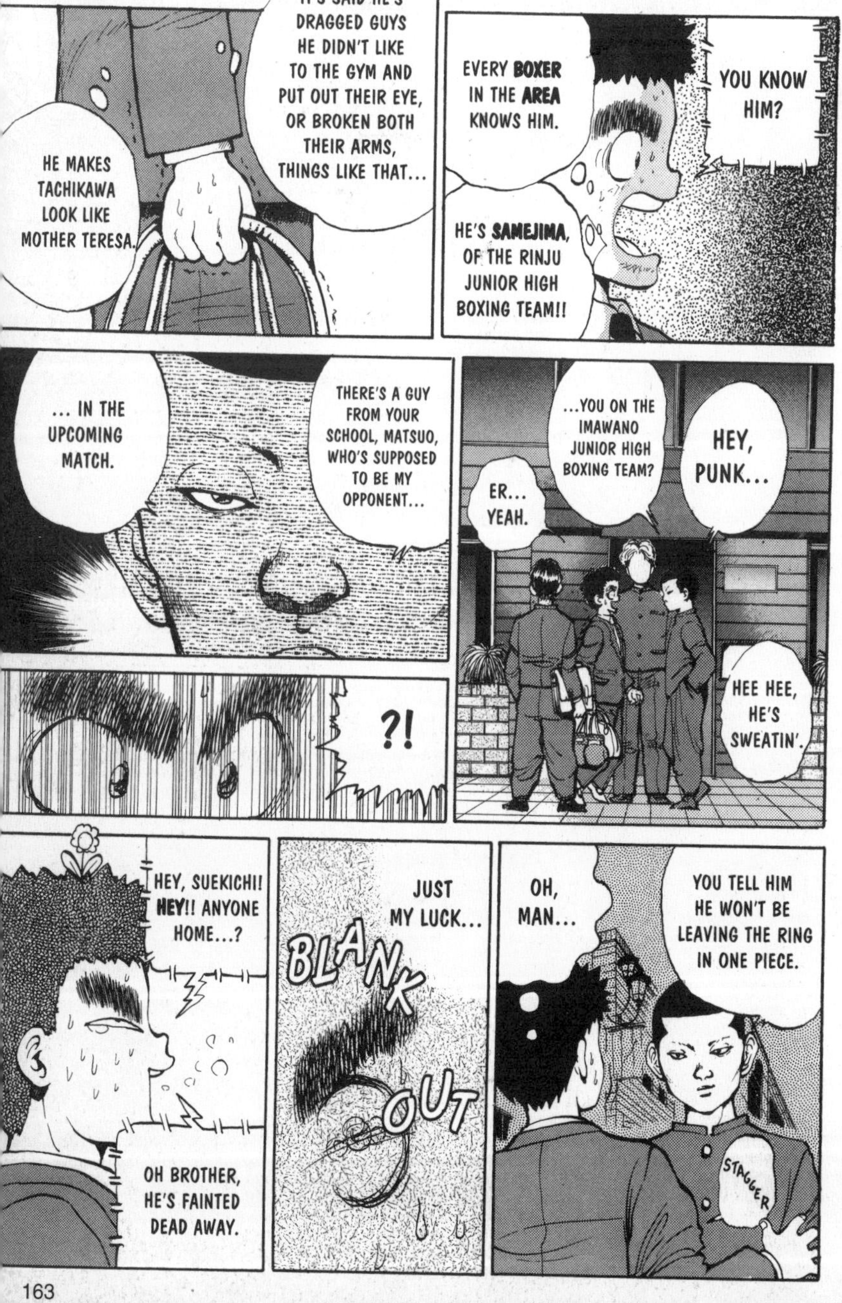
YOU KNOW HIM?
EVERY BOXER IN THE AREA KNOWS HIM.
HE'S SAMEJIMA, OF THE RINJU JUNIOR HIGH BOXING TEAM!!
IT'S SAID HE'S DRAGGED GUYS HE DIDN'T LIKE TO THE GYM AND PUT OUT THEIR EYE, OR BROKEN BOTH THEIR ARMS, THINGS LIKE THAT...
HE MAKES TACHIKAWA LOOK LIKE MOTHER TERESA.
HEY, PUNK...
...YOU ON THE IMAWANO JUNIOR HIGH BOXING TEAM?
ER... YEAH.
HEE HEE, HE'S SWEATIN'.
THERE'S A GUY FROM YOUR SCHOOL, MATSUO, WHO'S SUPPOSED TO BE MY OPPONENT...
... IN THE UPCOMING MATCH.
?!
YOU TELL HIM HE WON'T BE LEAVING THE RING IN ONE PIECE.
OH, MAN...
STAGGER
JUST MY LUCK...
BLANK OUT
HEY, SUEKICHI! HEY!! ANYONE HOME...?
OH BROTHER, HE'S FAINTED DEAD AWAY.

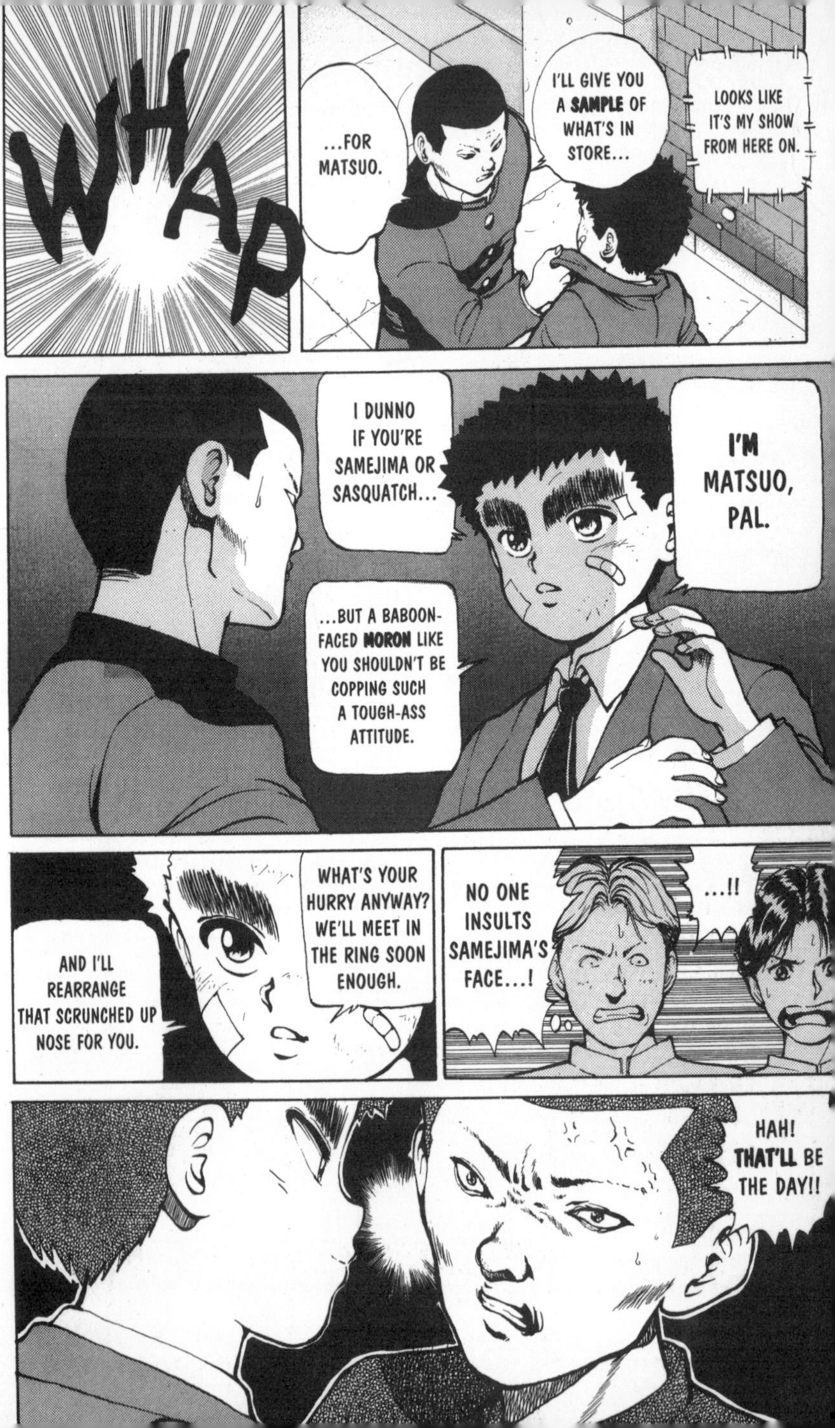
LOOKS LIKE IT'S MY SHOW FROM HERE ON.
I'LL GIVE YOU A SAMPLE OF WHAT'S IN STORE...
...FOR MATSUO.
WHAP
I'M MATSUO, PAL.
I DUNNO IF YOU'RE SAMEJIMA OR SASQUATCH...
...BUT A BABOON-FACED MORON LIKE YOU SHOULDN'T BE COPPING SUCH A TOUGH-ASS ATTITUDE.
...!!
NO ONE INSULTS SAMEJIMA'S FACE...!
WHAT'S YOUR HURRY ANYWAY? WE'LL MEET IN THE RING SOON ENOUGH.
AND I'LL REARRANGE THAT SCRUNCHED UP NOSE FOR YOU.
HAH! THAT'LL BE THE DAY!!

READ THIS WAY

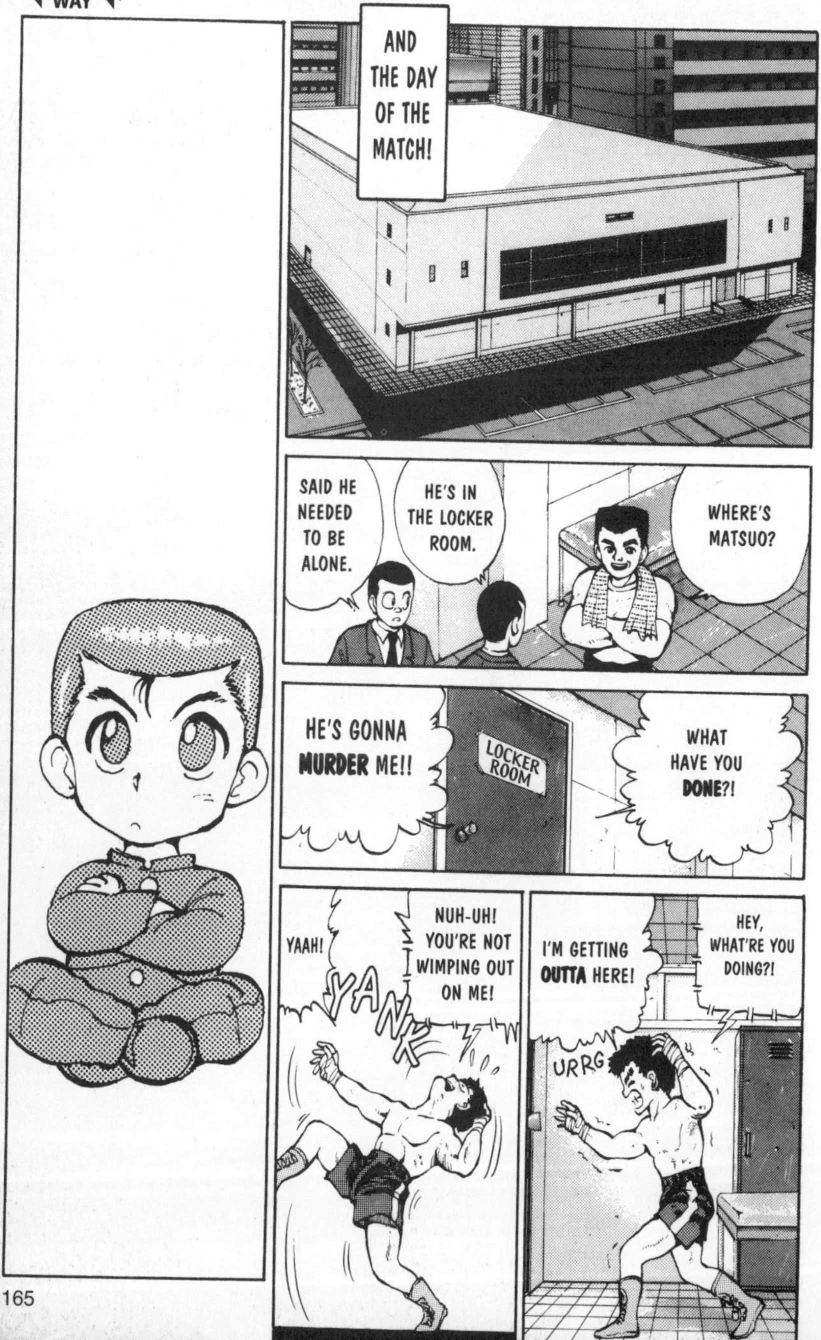

AND THE DAY OF THE MATCH!
WHERE'S MATSUO?
HE'S IN THE LOCKER ROOM.
SAID HE NEEDED TO BE ALONE.
WHAT HAVE YOU DONE?!
LOCKER ROOM
HE'S GONNA MURDER ME!!
HEY, WHAT'RE YOU DOING?!
I'M GETTING OUTTA HERE!
URRG
NUH-UH! YOU'RE NOT WIMPING OUT ON ME!
YAAH!
YANK

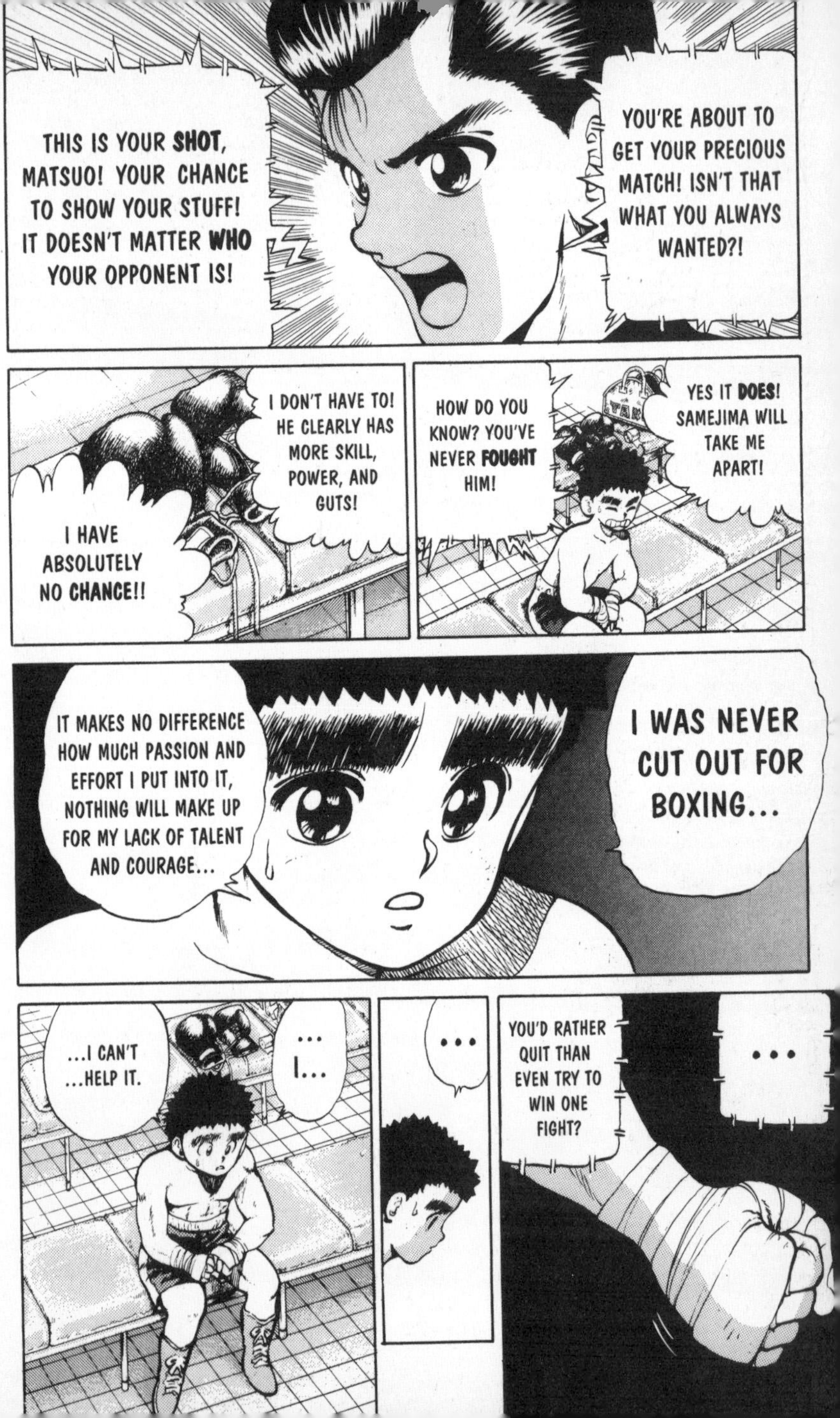
YOU'RE ABOUT TO GET YOUR PRECIOUS MATCH! ISN'T THAT WHAT YOU ALWAYS WANTED?!
THIS IS YOUR SHOT, MATSUO! YOUR CHANCE TO SHOW YOUR STUFF! IT DOESN'T MATTER WHO YOUR OPPONENT IS!
YES IT DOES! SAMEJIMA WILL TAKE ME APART!
HOW DO YOU KNOW? YOU'VE NEVER FOUGHT HIM!
I DON'T HAVE TO! HE CLEARLY HAS MORE SKILL, POWER, AND GUTS!
I HAVE ABSOLUTELY NO CHANCE!!
I WAS NEVER CUT OUT FOR BOXING...
IT MAKES NO DIFFERENCE HOW MUCH PASSION AND EFFORT I PUT INTO IT, NOTHING WILL MAKE UP FOR MY LACK OF TALENT AND COURAGE...
...
YOU'D RATHER QUIT THAN EVEN TRY TO WIN ONE FIGHT?
...
... I...
...I CAN'T ...HELP IT.

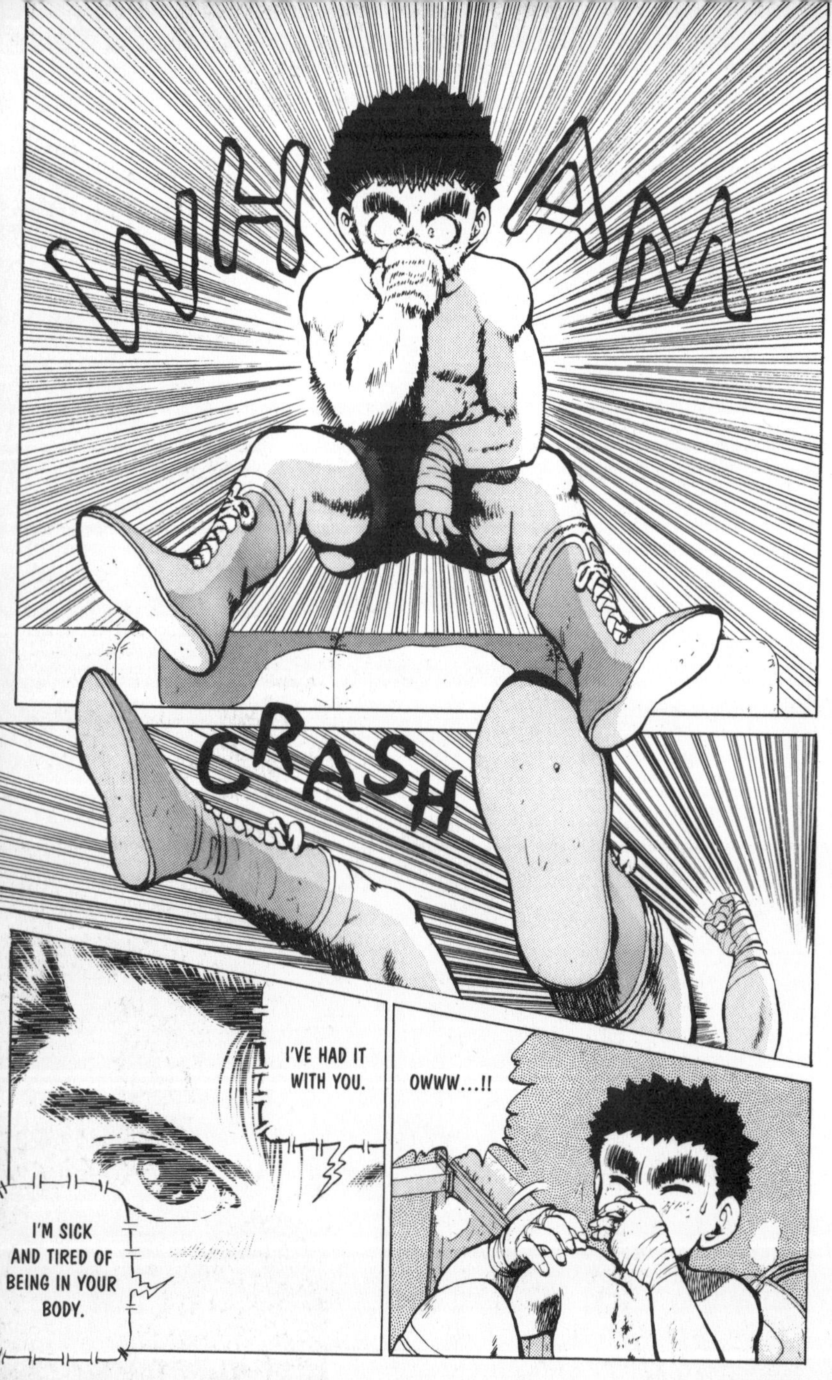
WHAM
CRASH
OWWW...!!
I'VE HAD IT WITH YOU.
I'M SICK AND TIRED OF BEING IN YOUR BODY.

READ THIS WAY

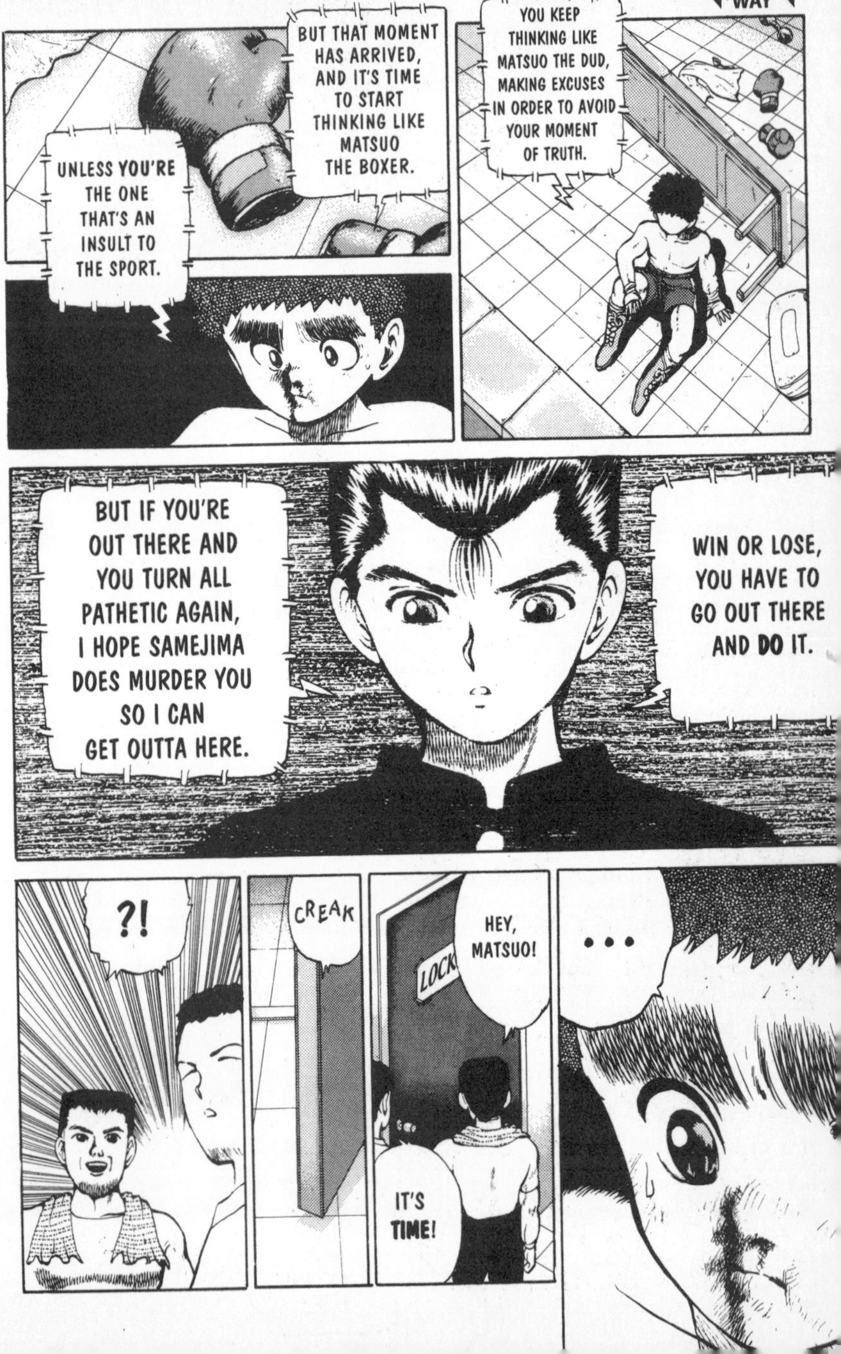
YOU KEEP THINKING LIKE MATSUO THE DUD, MAKING EXCUSES IN ORDER TO AVOID YOUR MOMENT OF TRUTH.
BUT THAT MOMENT HAS ARRIVED, AND IT'S TIME TO START THINKING LIKE MATSUO THE BOXER.
UNLESS YOU'RE THE ONE THAT'S AN INSULT TO THE SPORT.
WIN OR LOSE, YOU HAVE TO GO OUT THERE AND DO IT.
BUT IF YOU'RE OUT THERE AND YOU TURN ALL PATHETIC AGAIN, I HOPE SAMEJIMA DOES MURDER YOU SO I CAN GET OUTTA HERE.
...
HEY, MATSUO!
LOCK
IT'S TIME!
CREAK
?!

READ THIS WAY

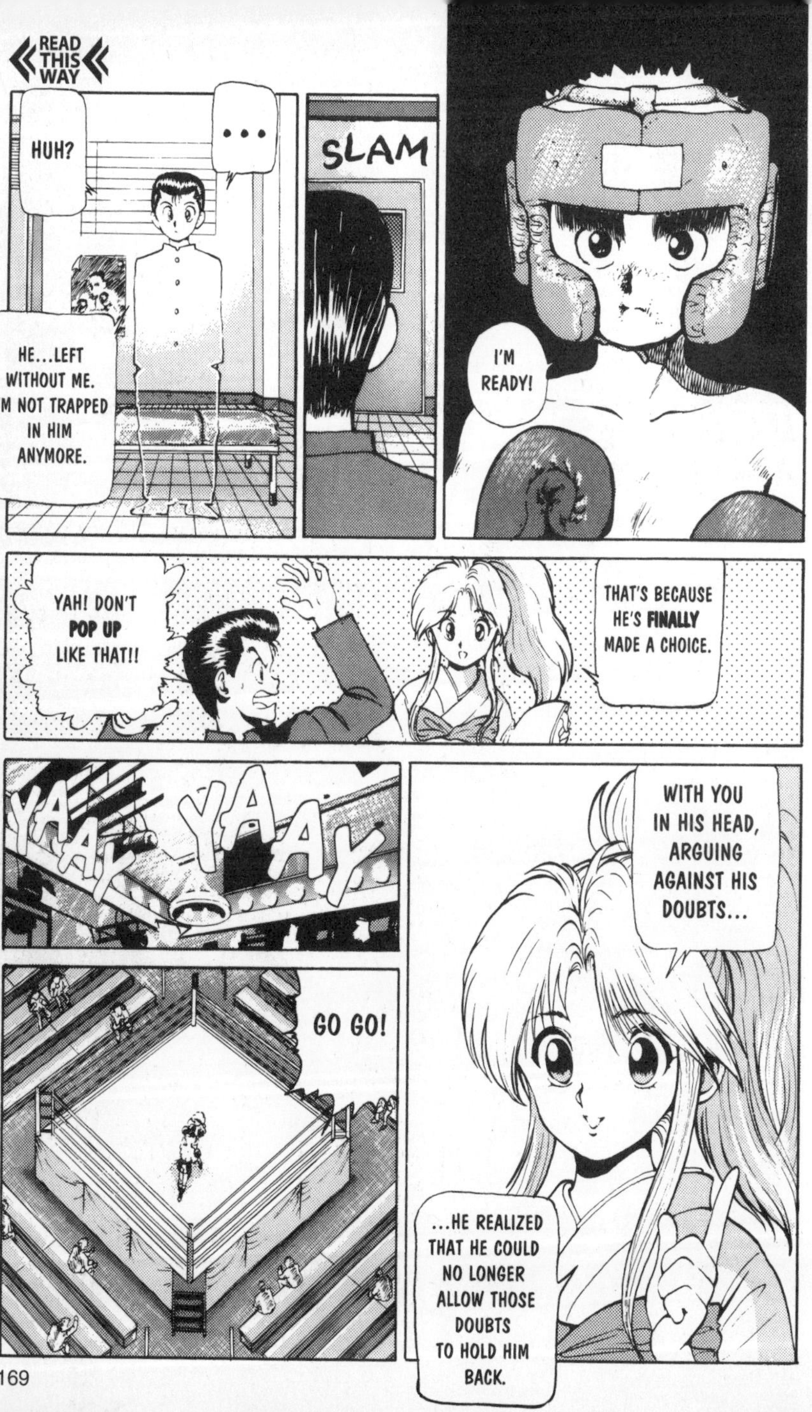
I'M READY!
SLAM
...
HUH?
HE...LEFT WITHOUT ME. I'M NOT TRAPPED IN HIM ANYMORE.
THAT'S BECAUSE HE'S FINALLY MADE A CHOICE.
YAH! DON'T POP UP LIKE THAT!!
WITH YOU IN HIS HEAD, ARGUING AGAINST HIS DOUBTS...
...HE REALIZED THAT HE COULD NO LONGER ALLOW THOSE DOUBTS TO HOLD HIM BACK.
YAAY YAAY
GO GO!

READ THIS WAY

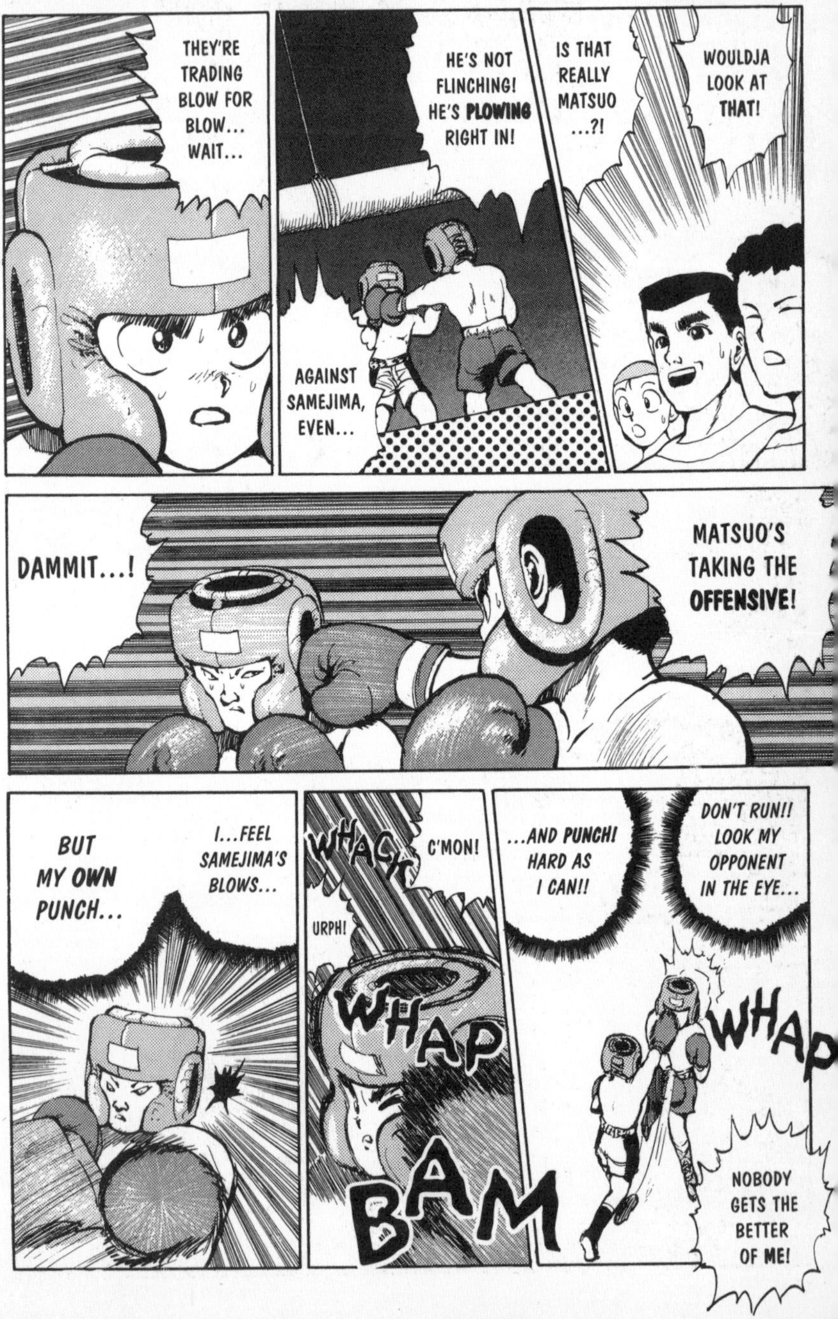
WOULDJA LOOK AT THAT!
IS THAT REALLY MATSUO ...?!
HE'S NOT FLINCHING! HE'S PLOWING RIGHT IN!
AGAINST SAMEJIMA, EVEN...
THEY'RE TRADING BLOW FOR BLOW... WAIT...
MATSUO'S TAKING THE OFFENSIVE!
DAMMIT...!
DON'T RUN!! LOOK MY OPPONENT IN THE EYE...
...AND PUNCH! HARD AS I CAN!!
WHAP
NOBODY GETS THE BETTER OF ME!
C'MON!
WHACK
URPH!
WHAP
BAM
I...FEEL SAMEJIMA'S BLOWS...
BUT MY OWN PUNCH...

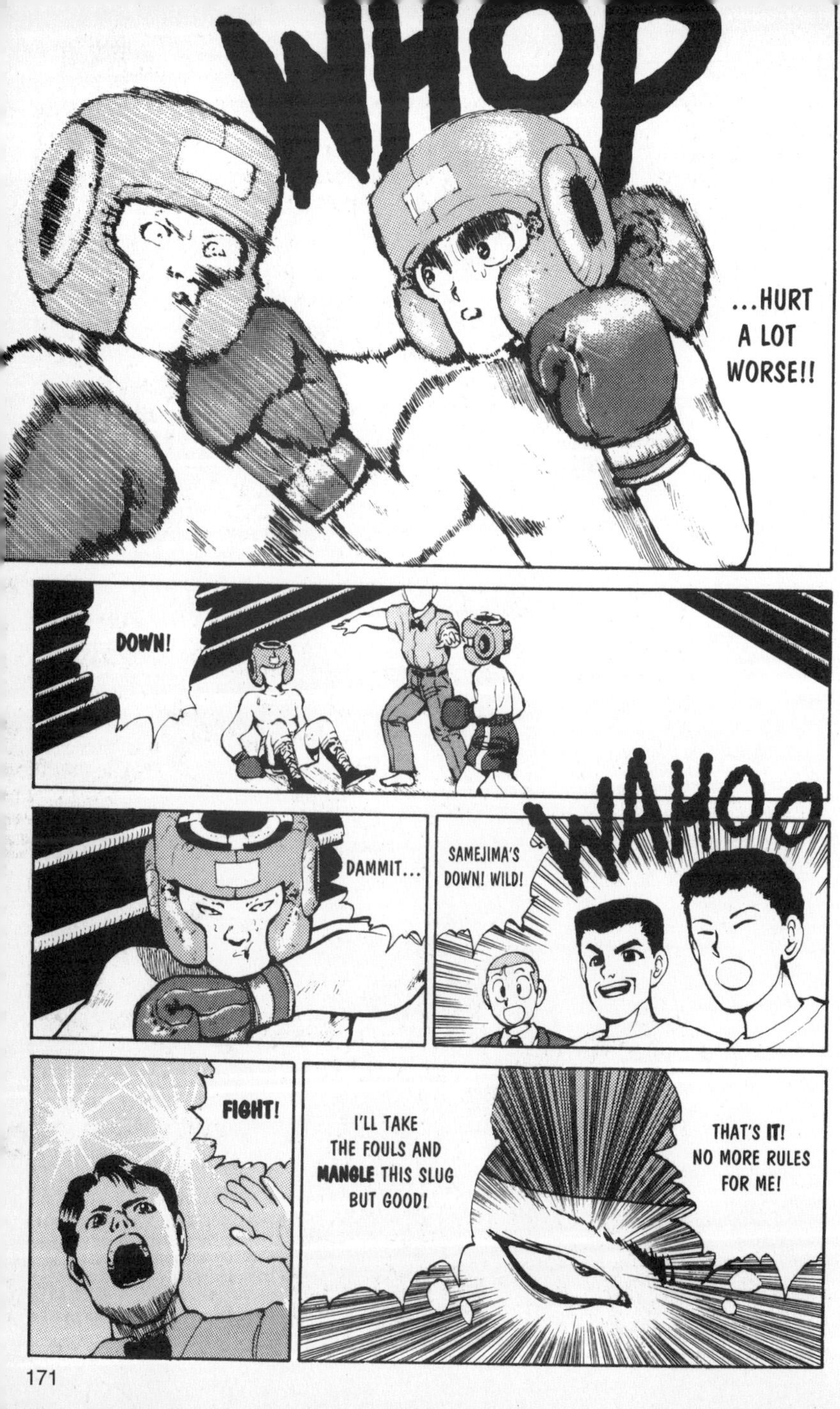
WHOP
...HURT A LOT WORSE!!
DOWN!
WAHOO
SAMEJIMA'S DOWN! WILD!
DAMMIT...
THAT'S IT! NO MORE RULES FOR ME!
I'LL TAKE THE FOULS AND MANGLE THIS SLUG BUT GOOD!
FIGHT!

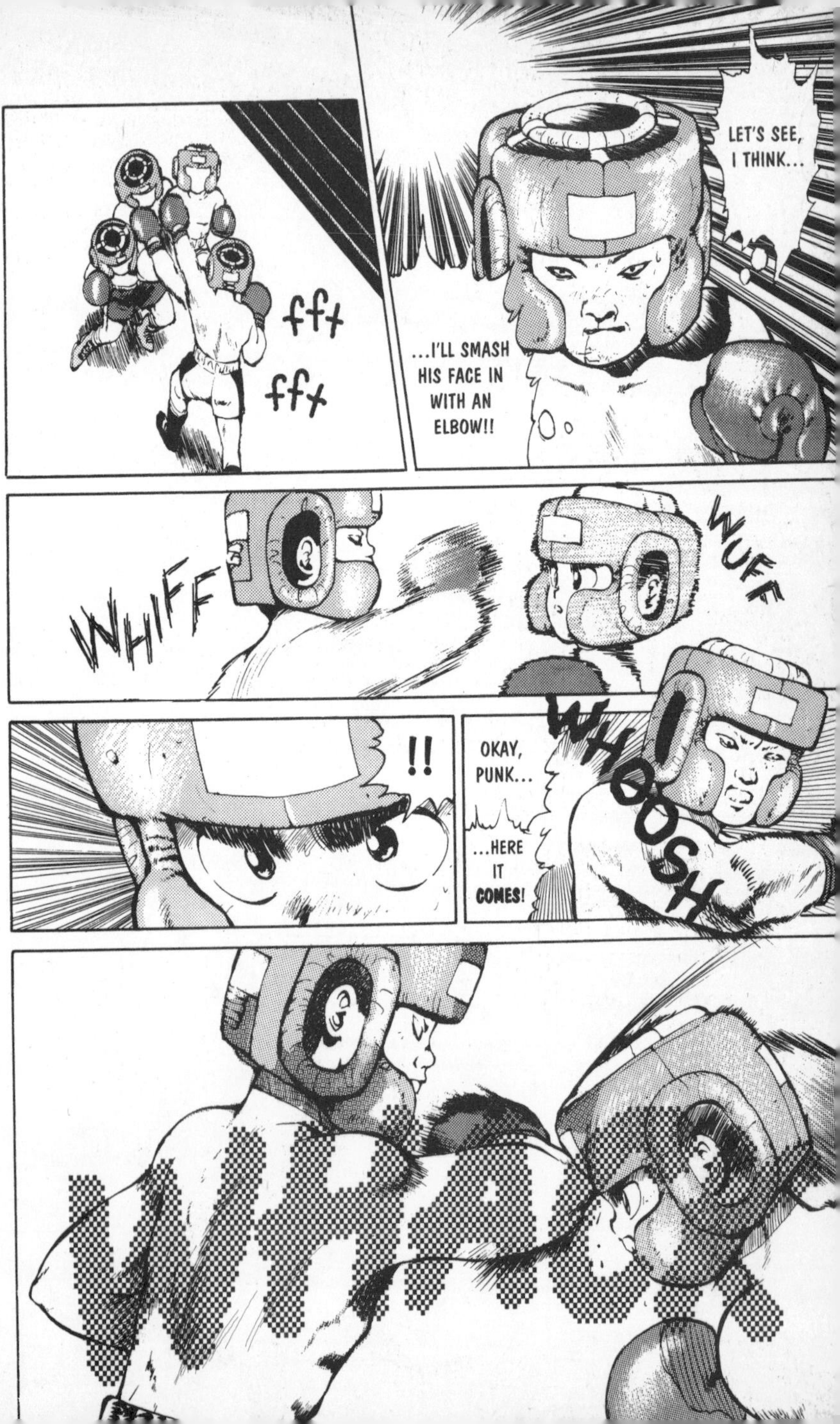
LET'S SEE, I THINK...
...I'LL SMASH HIS FACE IN WITH AN ELBOW!!
fft
fft
WUFF
WHIFF
OKAY, PUNK...
WHOOSH
...HERE IT **COMES!**
!!
WHACK

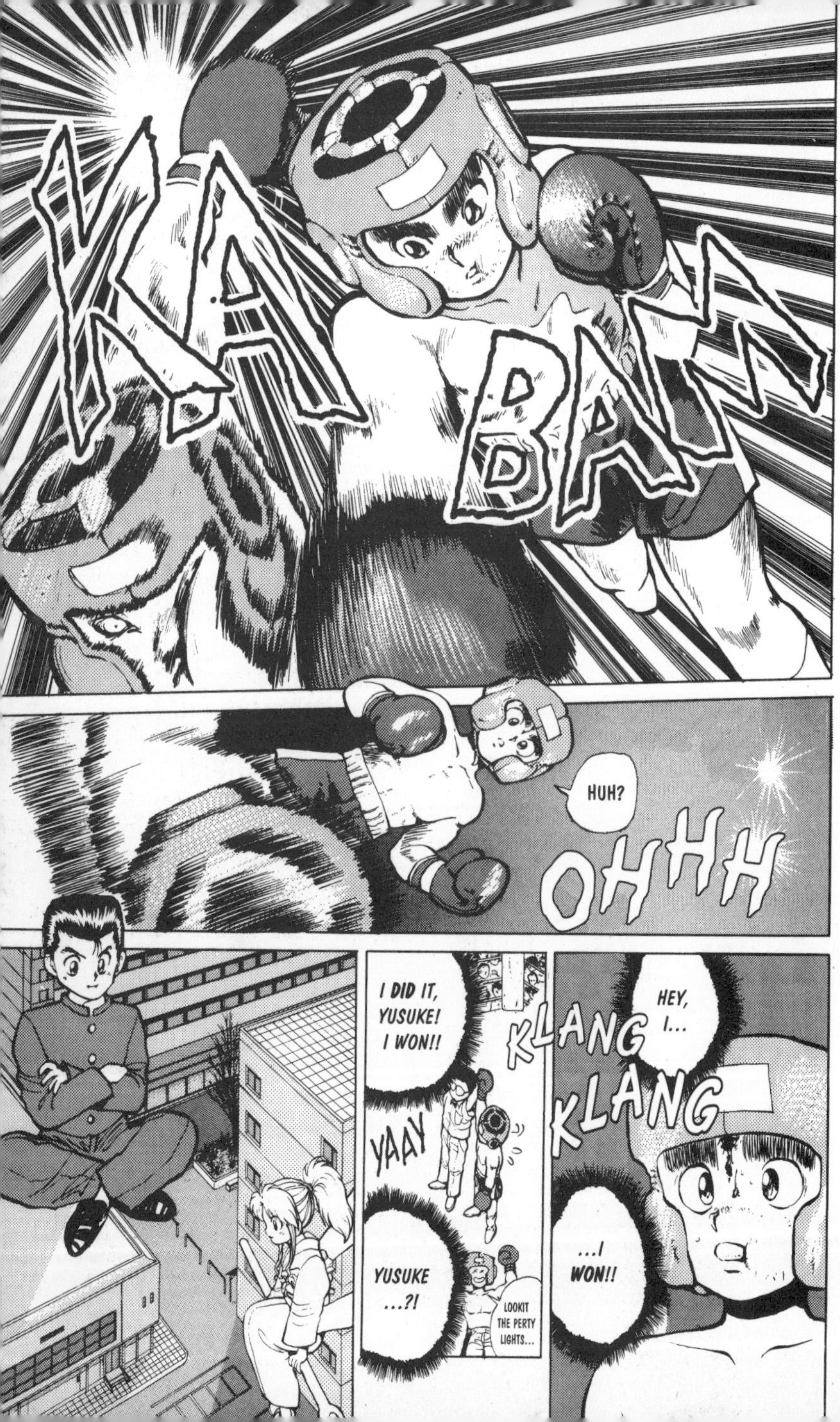
KA-BAM
HUH?
OHHH
HEY, I...
KLANG
KLANG
...I WON!!
I DID IT, YUSUKE! I WON!!
YAAY
YUSUKE ...?!
LOOKIT THE PERTY LIGHTS...

CHAPTER 17: THE GOLDEN AWAKENING!!

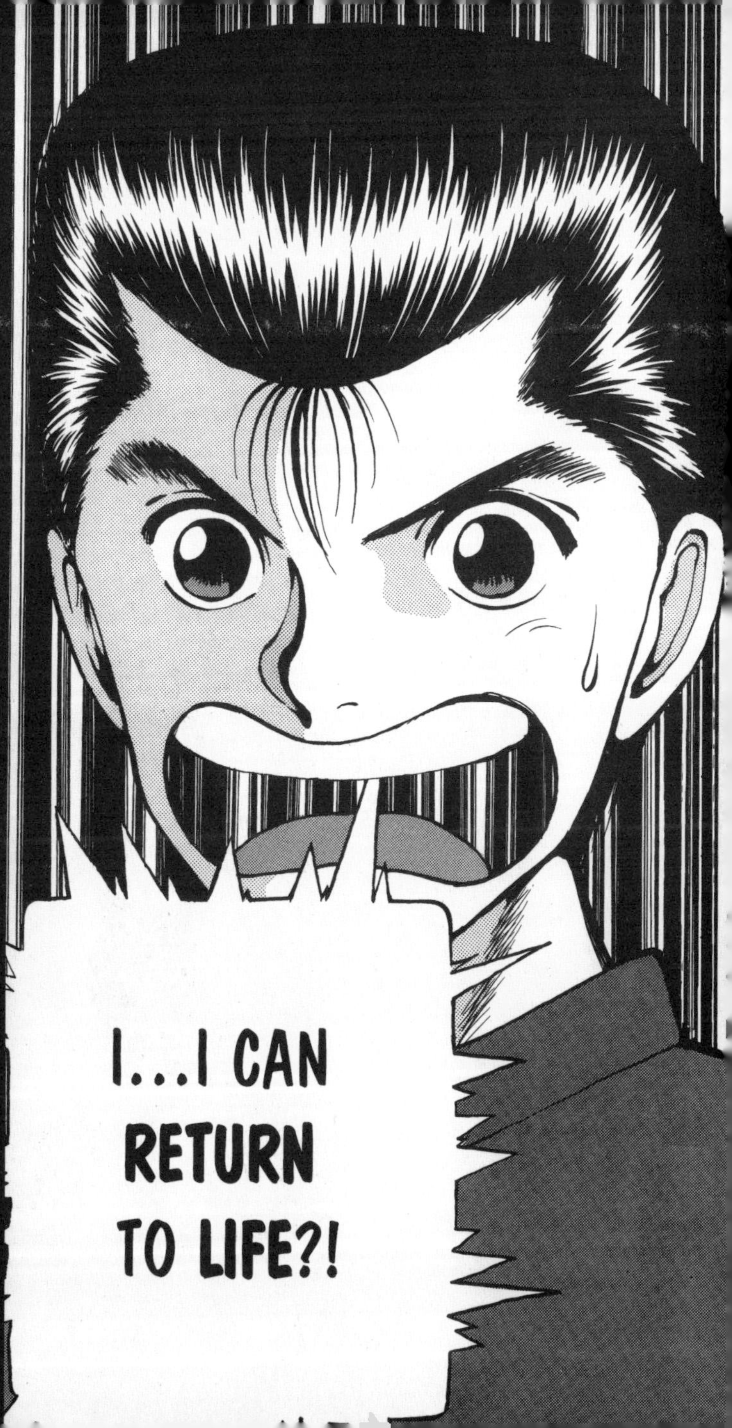
I...I CAN RETURN TO LIFE?!

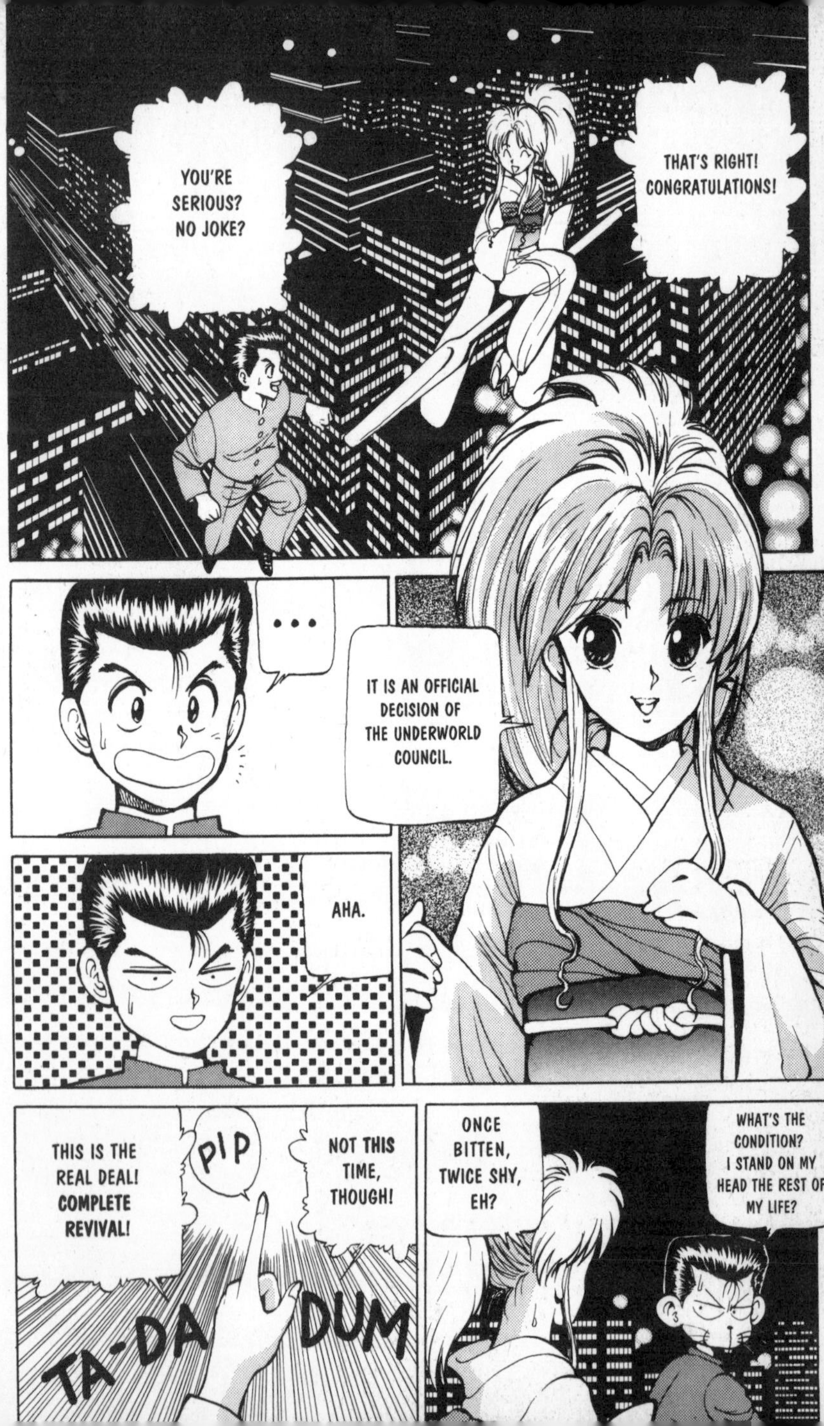
THAT'S RIGHT! CONGRATULATIONS!
YOU'RE SERIOUS? NO JOKE?
. . .
IT IS AN OFFICIAL DECISION OF THE UNDERWORLD COUNCIL.
AHA.
WHAT'S THE CONDITION? I STAND ON MY HEAD THE REST OF MY LIFE?
ONCE BITTEN, TWICE SHY, EH?
NOT THIS TIME, THOUGH!
PIP
THIS IS THE REAL DEAL! COMPLETE REVIVAL!
TA-DA DUM

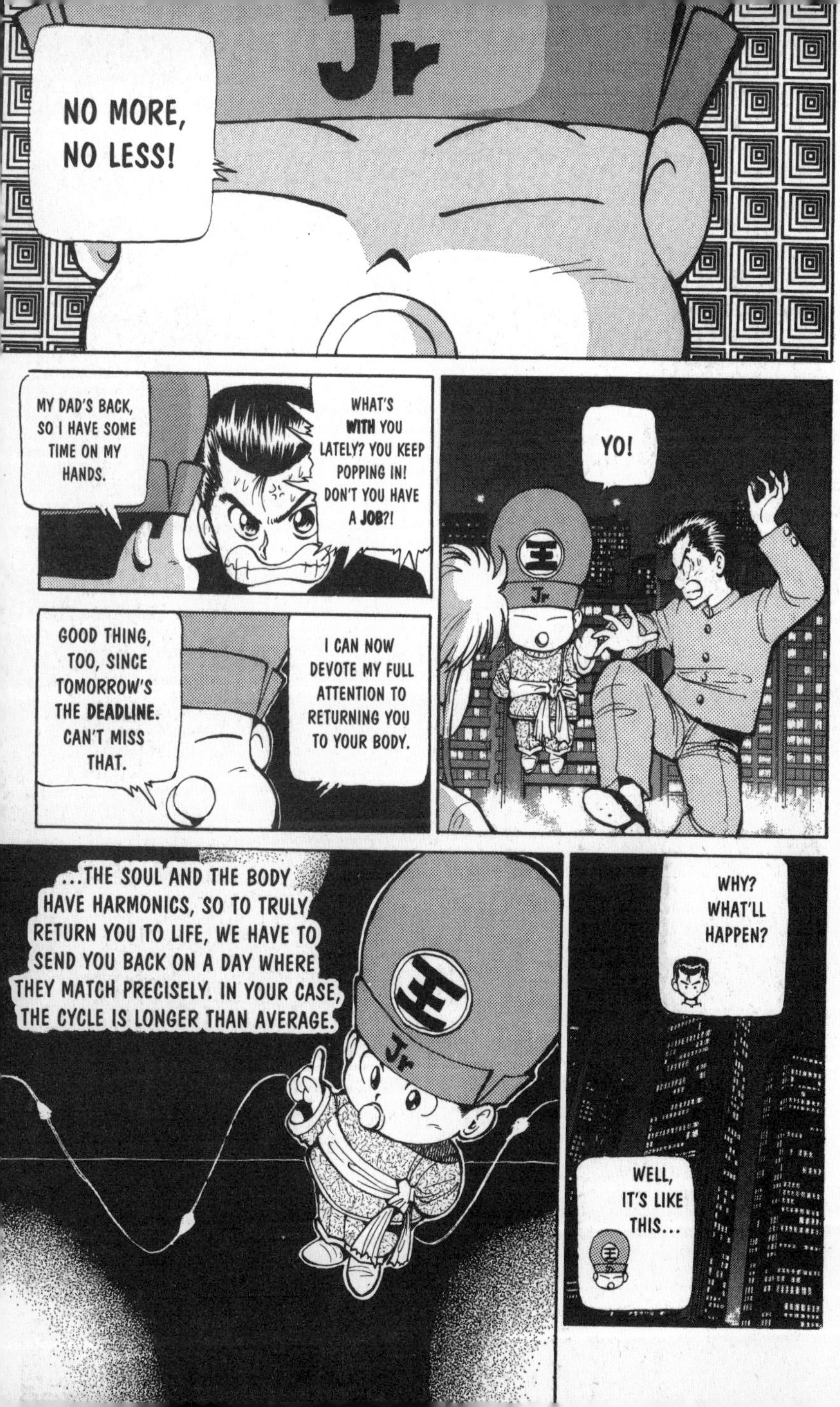
NO MORE, NO LESS!
YO!
WHAT'S WITH YOU LATELY? YOU KEEP POPPING IN! DON'T YOU HAVE A JOB?!
MY DAD'S BACK, SO I HAVE SOME TIME ON MY HANDS.
I CAN NOW DEVOTE MY FULL ATTENTION TO RETURNING YOU TO YOUR BODY.
GOOD THING, TOO, SINCE TOMORROW'S THE DEADLINE. CAN'T MISS THAT.
WHY? WHAT'LL HAPPEN?
WELL, IT'S LIKE THIS...
...THE SOUL AND THE BODY HAVE HARMONICS, SO TO TRULY RETURN YOU TO LIFE, WE HAVE TO SEND YOU BACK ON A DAY WHERE THEY MATCH PRECISELY. IN YOUR CASE, THE CYCLE IS LONGER THAN AVERAGE.

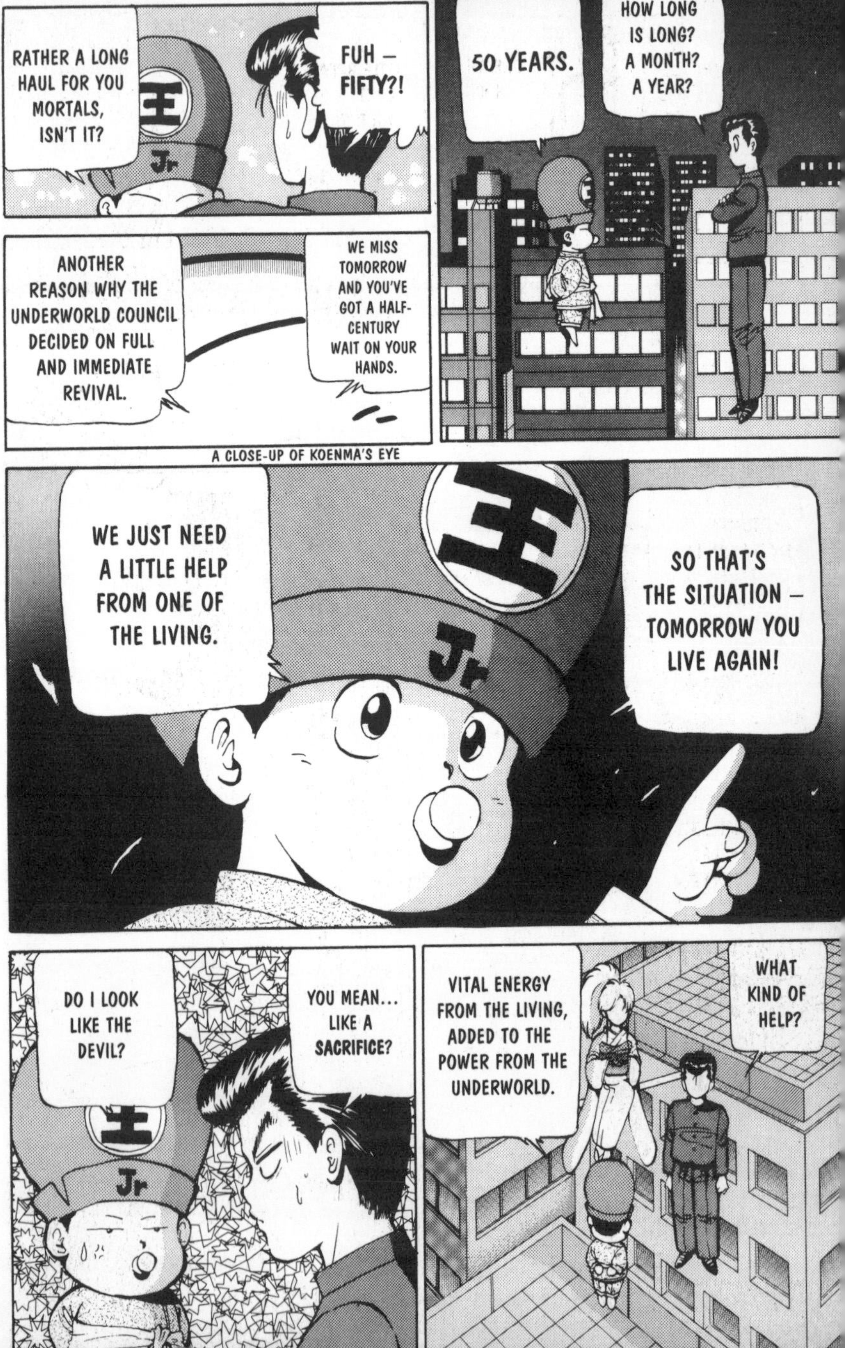
HOW LONG IS LONG? A MONTH? A YEAR?
50 YEARS.
FUH – FIFTY?!
RATHER A LONG HAUL FOR YOU MORTALS, ISN'T IT?
WE MISS TOMORROW AND YOU'VE GOT A HALF-CENTURY WAIT ON YOUR HANDS.
ANOTHER REASON WHY THE UNDERWORLD COUNCIL DECIDED ON FULL AND IMMEDIATE REVIVAL.
A CLOSE-UP OF KOENMA'S EYE
SO THAT'S THE SITUATION – TOMORROW YOU LIVE AGAIN!
WE JUST NEED A LITTLE HELP FROM ONE OF THE LIVING.
WHAT KIND OF HELP?
VITAL ENERGY FROM THE LIVING, ADDED TO THE POWER FROM THE UNDERWORLD.
YOU MEAN... LIKE A SACRIFICE?
DO I LOOK LIKE THE DEVIL?

READ THIS WAY

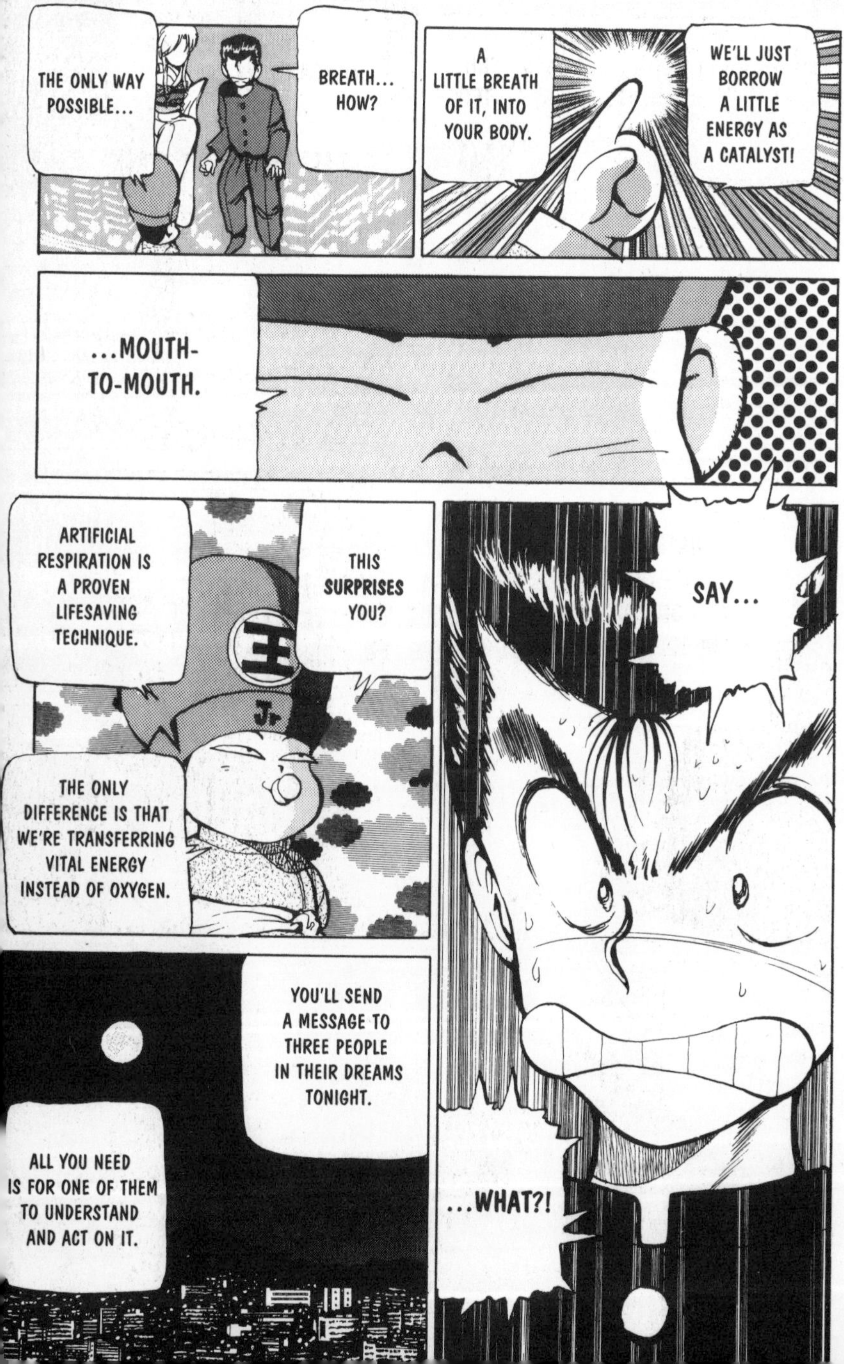

WE'LL JUST BORROW A LITTLE ENERGY AS A CATALYST!
A LITTLE BREATH OF IT, INTO YOUR BODY.
BREATH... HOW?
THE ONLY WAY POSSIBLE...
...MOUTH-TO-MOUTH.
SAY...
...WHAT?!
THIS SURPRISES YOU?
ARTIFICIAL RESPIRATION IS A PROVEN LIFESAVING TECHNIQUE.
THE ONLY DIFFERENCE IS THAT WE'RE TRANSFERRING VITAL ENERGY INSTEAD OF OXYGEN.
YOU'LL SEND A MESSAGE TO THREE PEOPLE IN THEIR DREAMS TONIGHT.
ALL YOU NEED IS FOR ONE OF THEM TO UNDERSTAND AND ACT ON IT.

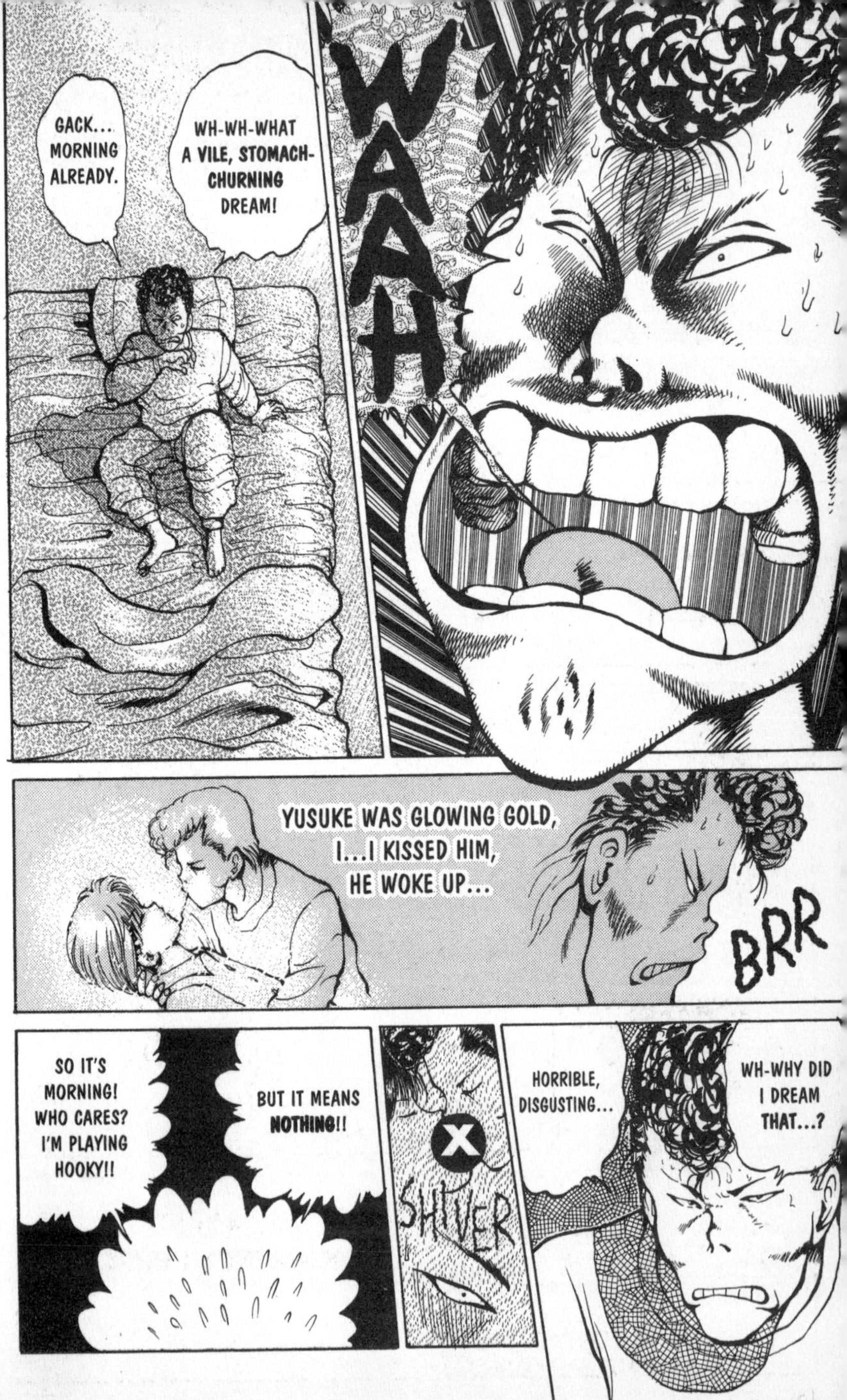
WAAH
WH-WH-WHAT A VILE, STOMACH-CHURNING DREAM!
GACK... MORNING ALREADY.
YUSUKE WAS GLOWING GOLD, I...I KISSED HIM, HE WOKE UP...
BRR
WH-WHY DID I DREAM THAT...?
HORRIBLE, DISGUSTING...
SHIVER
BUT IT MEANS **NOTHING**!!
SO IT'S MORNING! WHO CARES? I'M PLAYING HOOKY!!

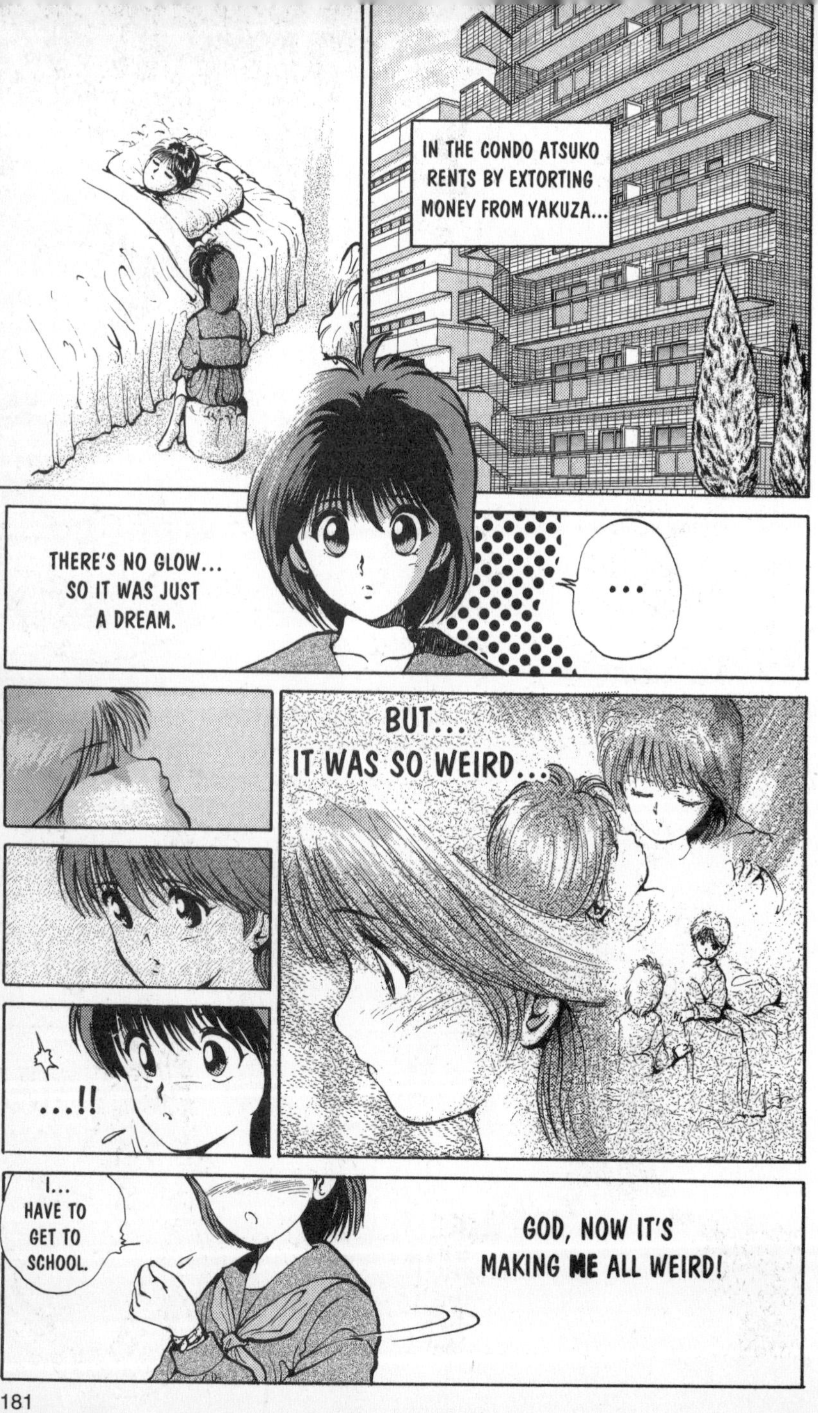
IN THE CONDO ATSUKO RENTS BY EXTORTING MONEY FROM YAKUZA...
...
THERE'S NO GLOW... SO IT WAS JUST A DREAM.
BUT... IT WAS SO WEIRD...
...!!
GOD, NOW IT'S MAKING **ME** ALL WEIRD!
I... HAVE TO GET TO SCHOOL.

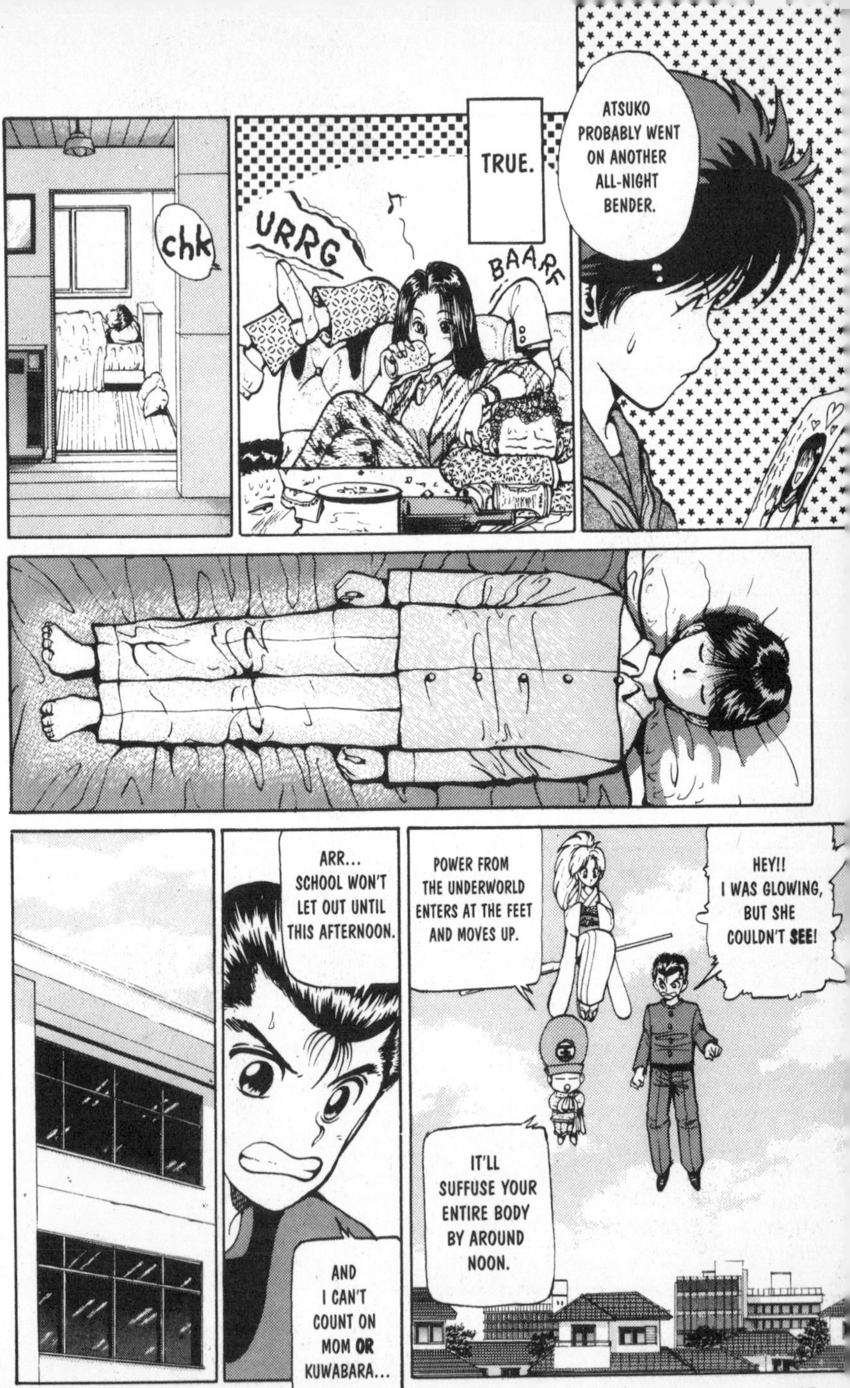
ATSUKO PROBABLY WENT ON ANOTHER ALL-NIGHT BENDER.
TRUE.
URRG
BAARF
chk
HEY!! I WAS GLOWING, BUT SHE COULDN'T **SEE**!
POWER FROM THE UNDERWORLD ENTERS AT THE FEET AND MOVES UP.
IT'LL SUFFUSE YOUR ENTIRE BODY BY AROUND NOON.
ARR... SCHOOL WON'T LET OUT UNTIL THIS AFTERNOON.
AND I CAN'T COUNT ON MOM **OR** KUWABARA...

READ THIS WAY

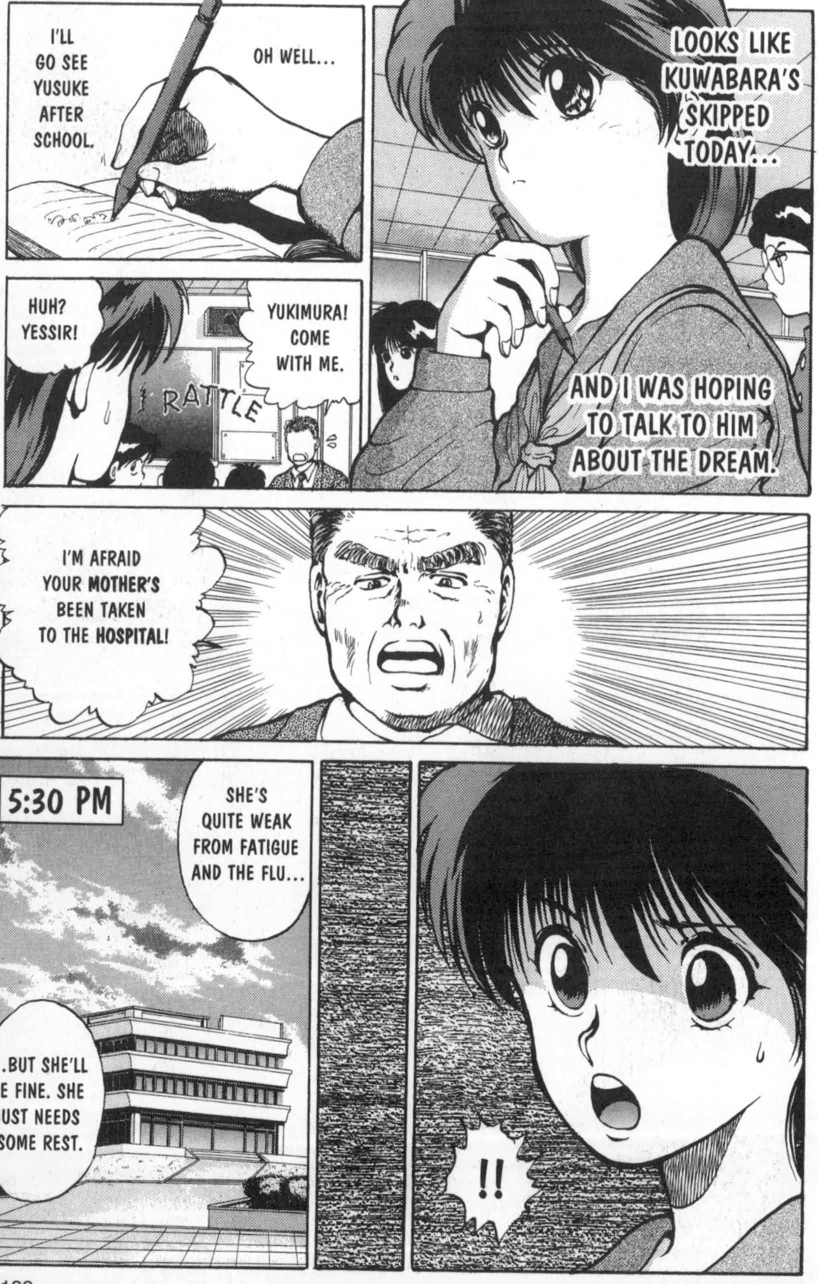
LOOKS LIKE KUWABARA'S SKIPPED TODAY...
AND I WAS HOPING TO TALK TO HIM ABOUT THE DREAM.
OH WELL...
I'LL GO SEE YUSUKE AFTER SCHOOL.
YUKIMURA! COME WITH ME.
RATTLE
HUH? YESSIR!
I'M AFRAID YOUR MOTHER'S BEEN TAKEN TO THE HOSPITAL!
!!
5:30 PM
SHE'S QUITE WEAK FROM FATIGUE AND THE FLU...
...BUT SHE'LL BE FINE. SHE JUST NEEDS SOME REST.

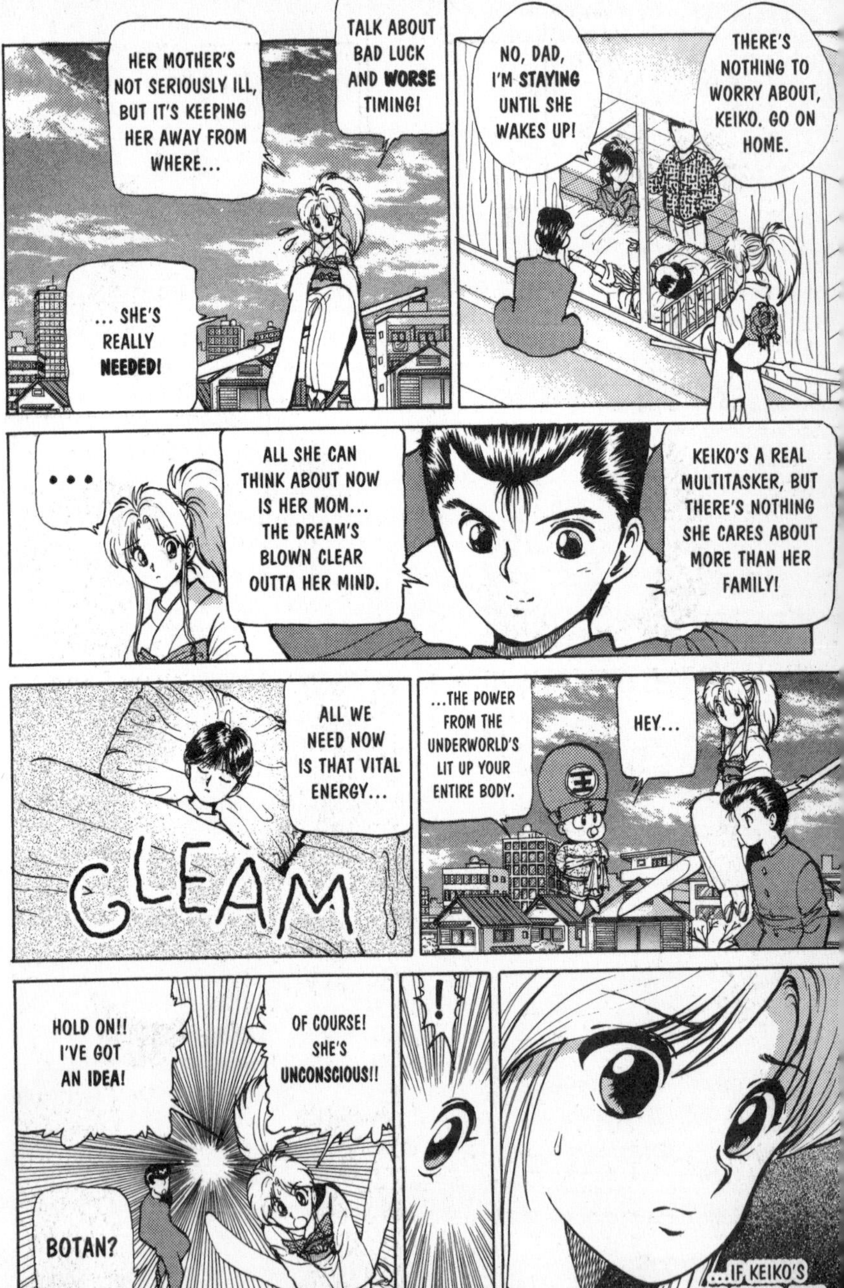
THERE'S NOTHING TO WORRY ABOUT, KEIKO. GO ON HOME.
NO, DAD, I'M **STAYING** UNTIL SHE WAKES UP!
TALK ABOUT BAD LUCK AND **WORSE** TIMING!
HER MOTHER'S NOT SERIOUSLY ILL, BUT IT'S KEEPING HER AWAY FROM WHERE...
... SHE'S REALLY **NEEDED!**
KEIKO'S A REAL MULTITASKER, BUT THERE'S NOTHING SHE CARES ABOUT MORE THAN HER FAMILY!
ALL SHE CAN THINK ABOUT NOW IS HER MOM... THE DREAM'S BLOWN CLEAR OUTTA HER MIND.
...
HEY...
...THE POWER FROM THE UNDERWORLD'S LIT UP YOUR ENTIRE BODY.
ALL WE NEED NOW IS THAT VITAL ENERGY...
GLEAM
...IF KEIKO'S MOM WOULD JUST WAKE UP...
!
OF COURSE! SHE'S **UNCONSCIOUS!!**
HOLD ON!! I'VE GOT AN **IDEA!**
BOTAN?

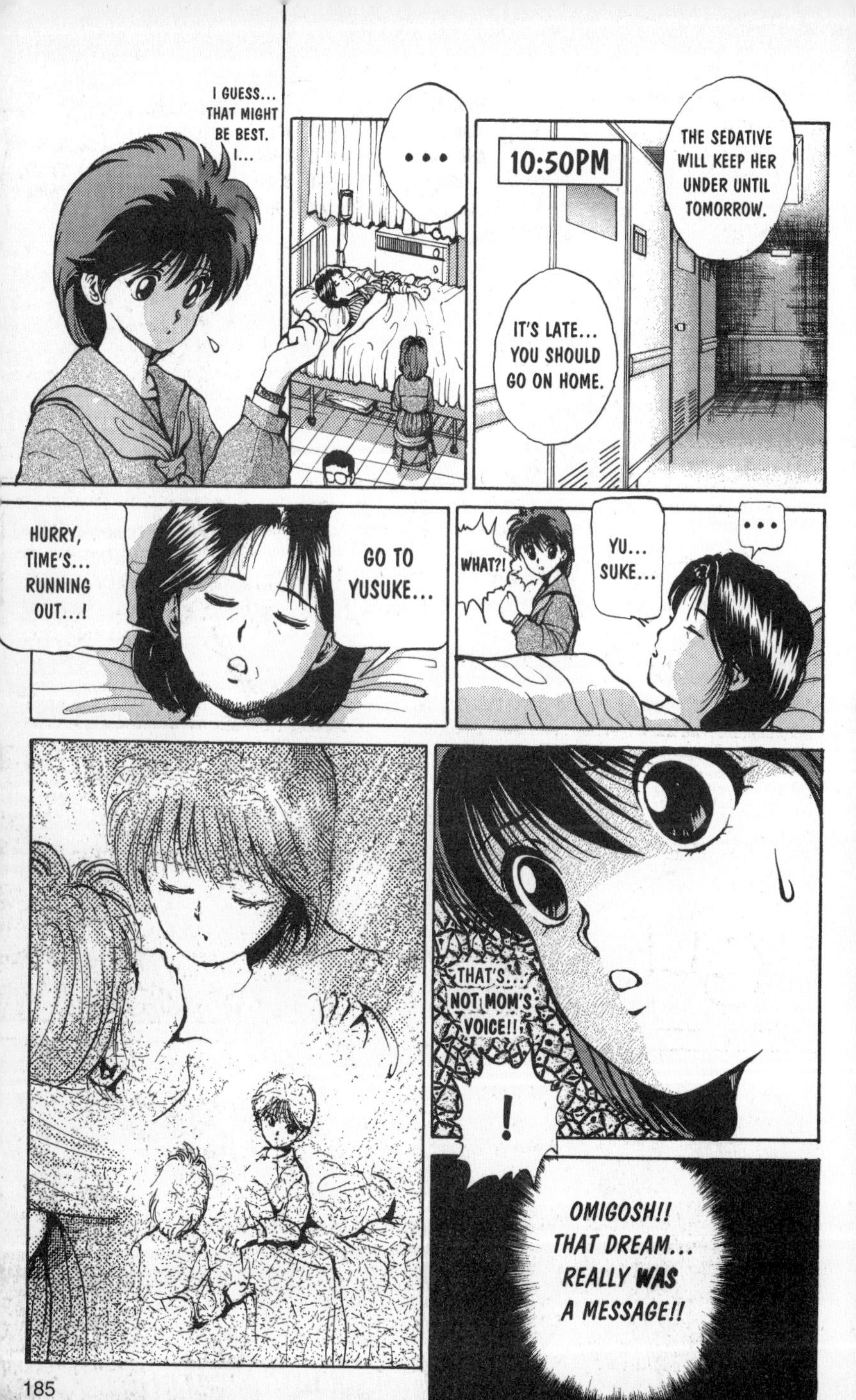
10:50PM
THE SEDATIVE WILL KEEP HER UNDER UNTIL TOMORROW.
IT'S LATE... YOU SHOULD GO ON HOME.
...
I GUESS... THAT MIGHT BE BEST. I...
...
YU... SUKE...
WHAT?!
GO TO YUSUKE...
HURRY, TIME'S... RUNNING OUT...!
THAT'S... NOT MOM'S VOICE!!
!
OMIGOSH!! THAT DREAM... REALLY WAS A MESSAGE!!

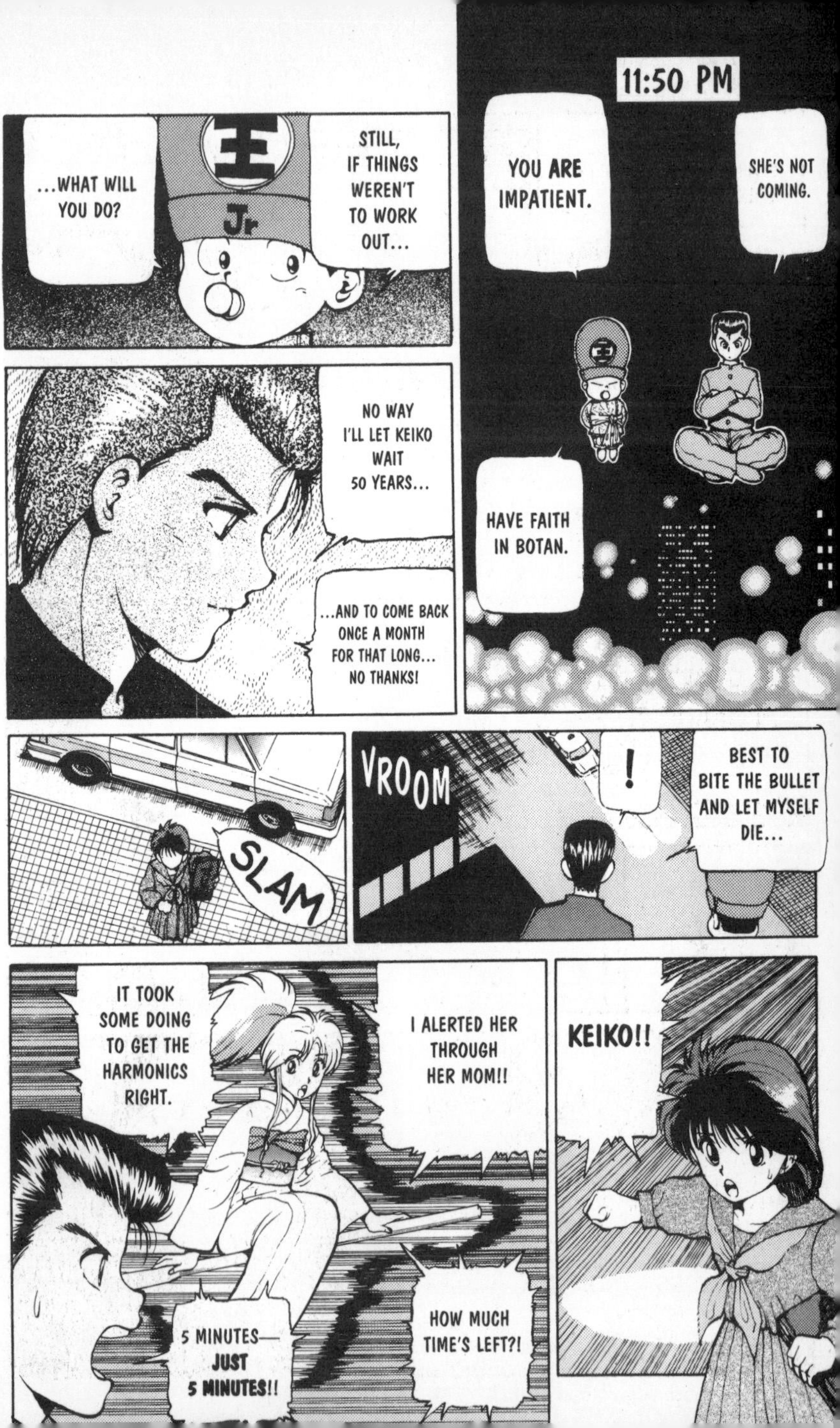
11:50 PM
SHE'S NOT COMING.
YOU ARE IMPATIENT.
HAVE FAITH IN BOTAN.
STILL, IF THINGS WEREN'T TO WORK OUT...
...WHAT WILL YOU DO?
NO WAY I'LL LET KEIKO WAIT 50 YEARS...
...AND TO COME BACK ONCE A MONTH FOR THAT LONG... NO THANKS!
BEST TO BITE THE BULLET AND LET MYSELF DIE...
!
VROOM
SLAM
KEIKO!!
I ALERTED HER THROUGH HER MOM!!
IT TOOK SOME DOING TO GET THE HARMONICS RIGHT.
HOW MUCH TIME'S LEFT?!
5 MINUTES— JUST 5 MINUTES!!

READ THIS WAY

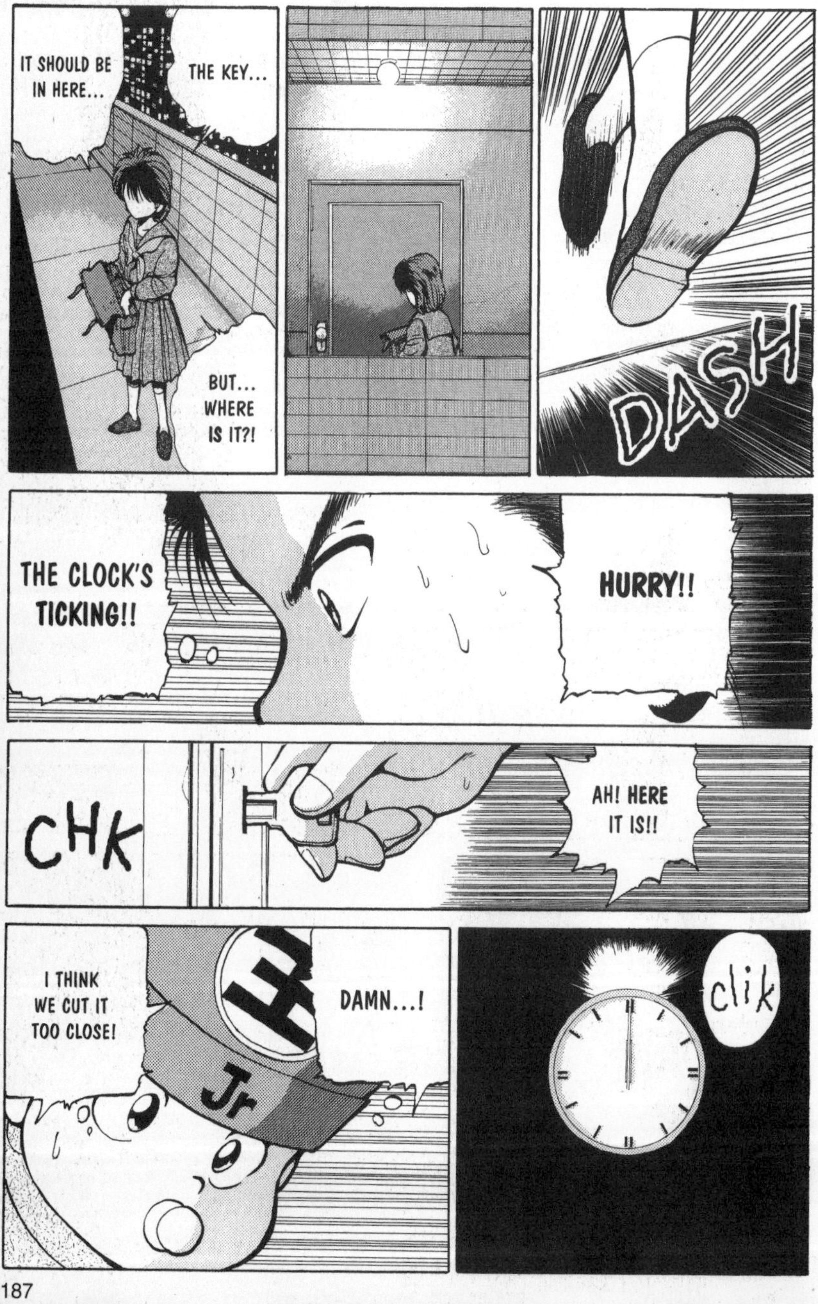

DASH
THE KEY...
IT SHOULD BE IN HERE...
BUT... WHERE IS IT?!
HURRY!!
THE CLOCK'S TICKING!!
AH! HERE IT IS!!
CHK
clik
DAMN...!
I THINK WE CUT IT TOO CLOSE!

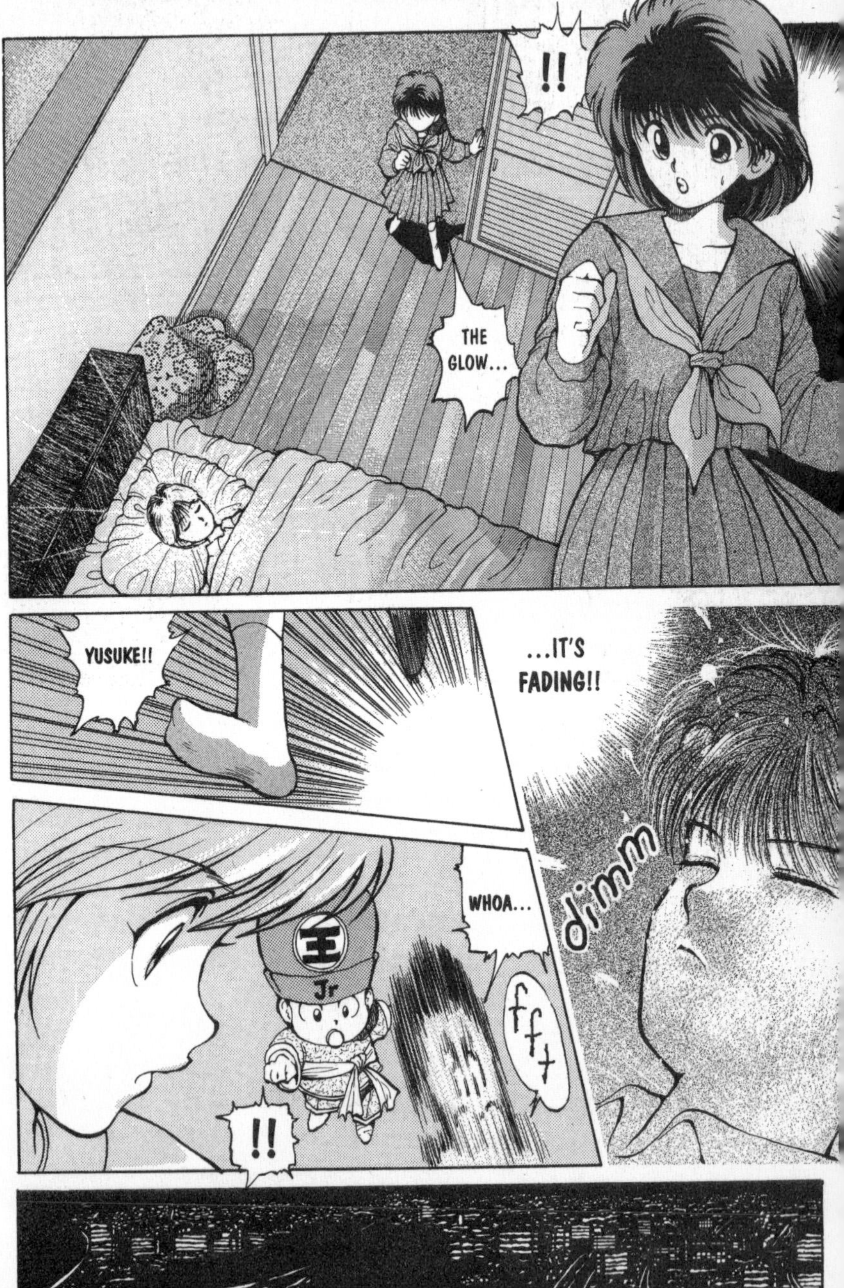
!!
THE GLOW...
...IT'S FADING!!
dimm
YUSUKE!!
WHOA...
fft
!!

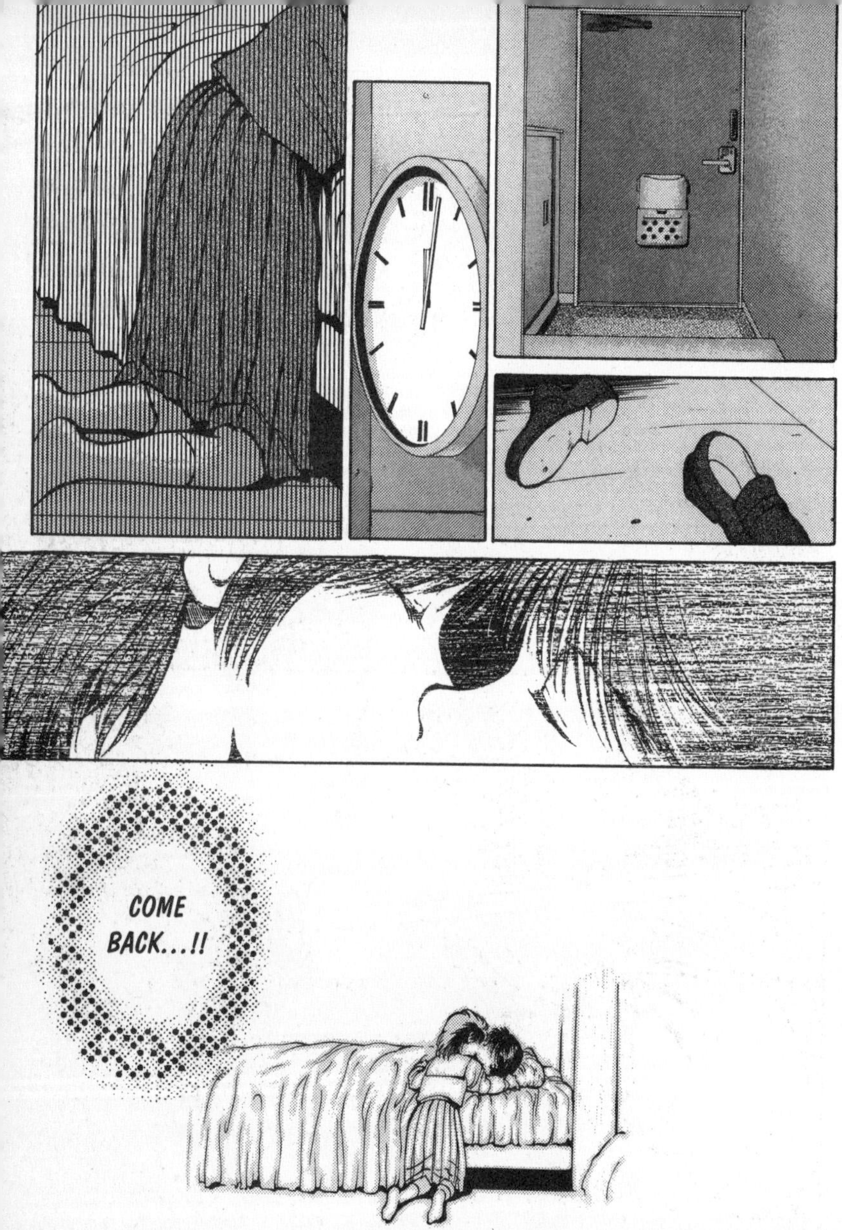
COME BACK...!!

COME BACK...
PLEASE...
PLEASE...
TOO LATE... I DIDN'T MAKE IT...
NO...
SLUMP

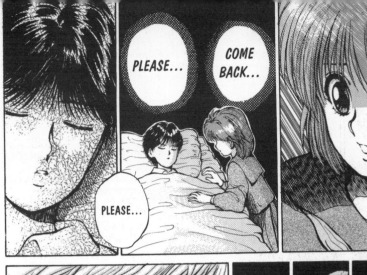

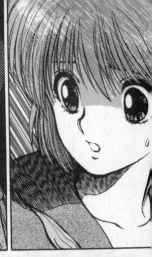

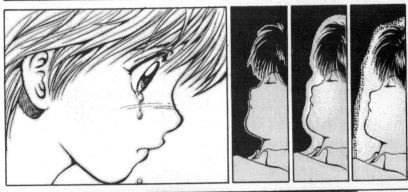

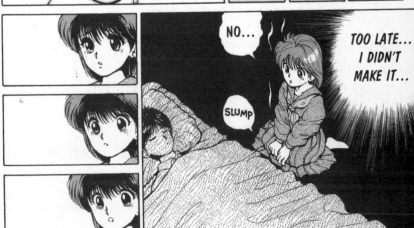

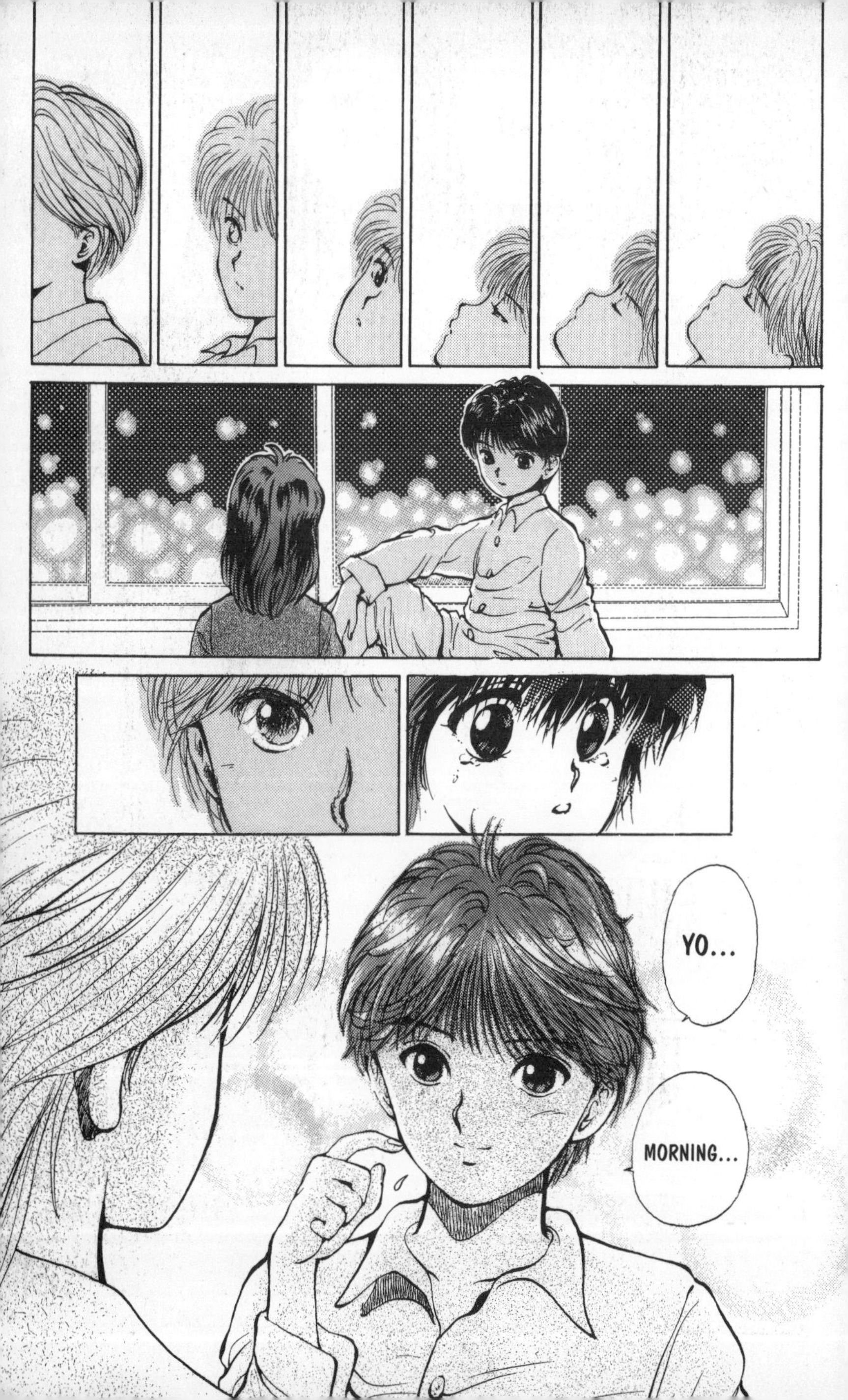
YO...
MORNING...

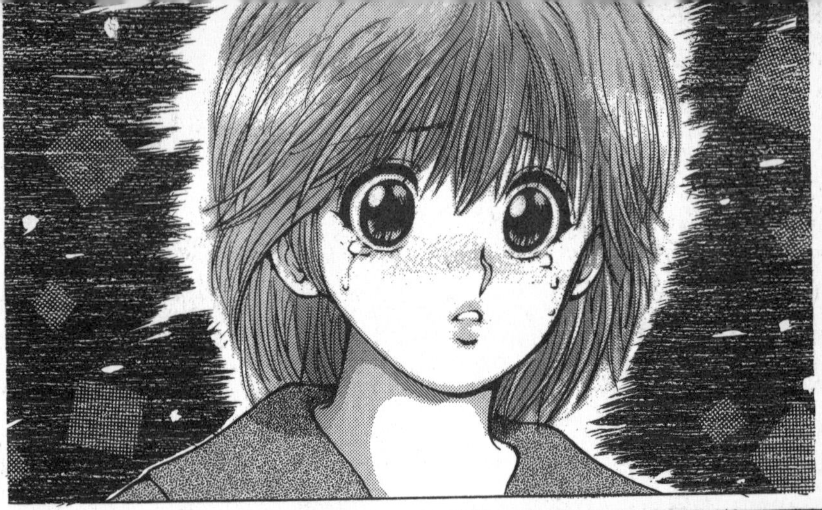
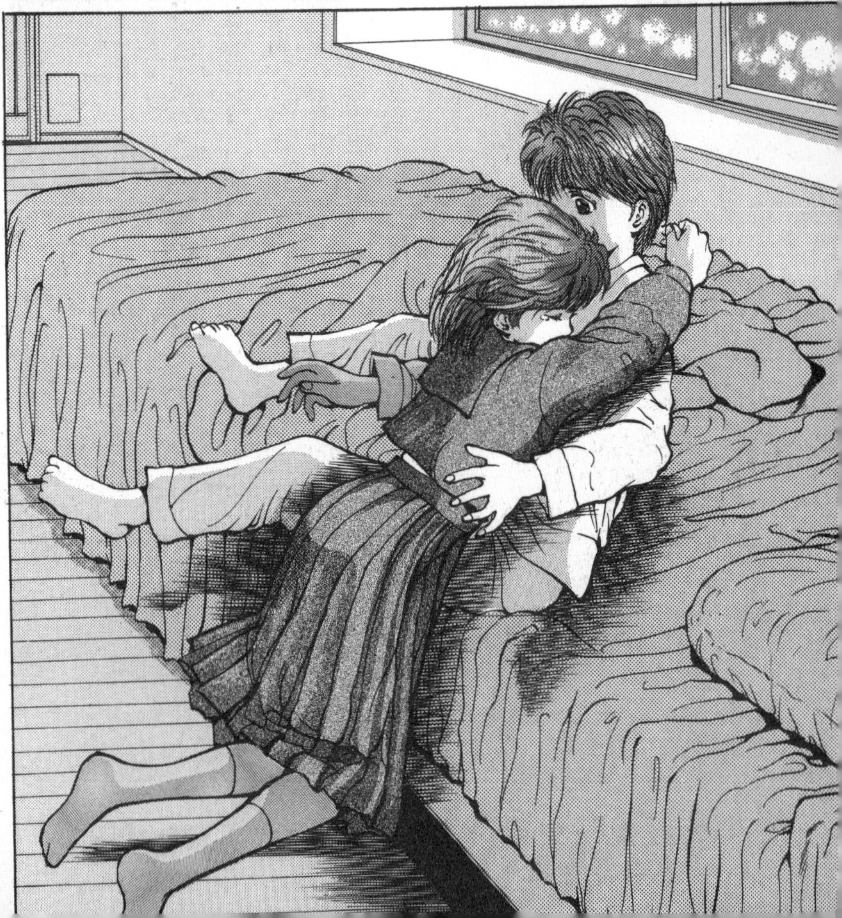

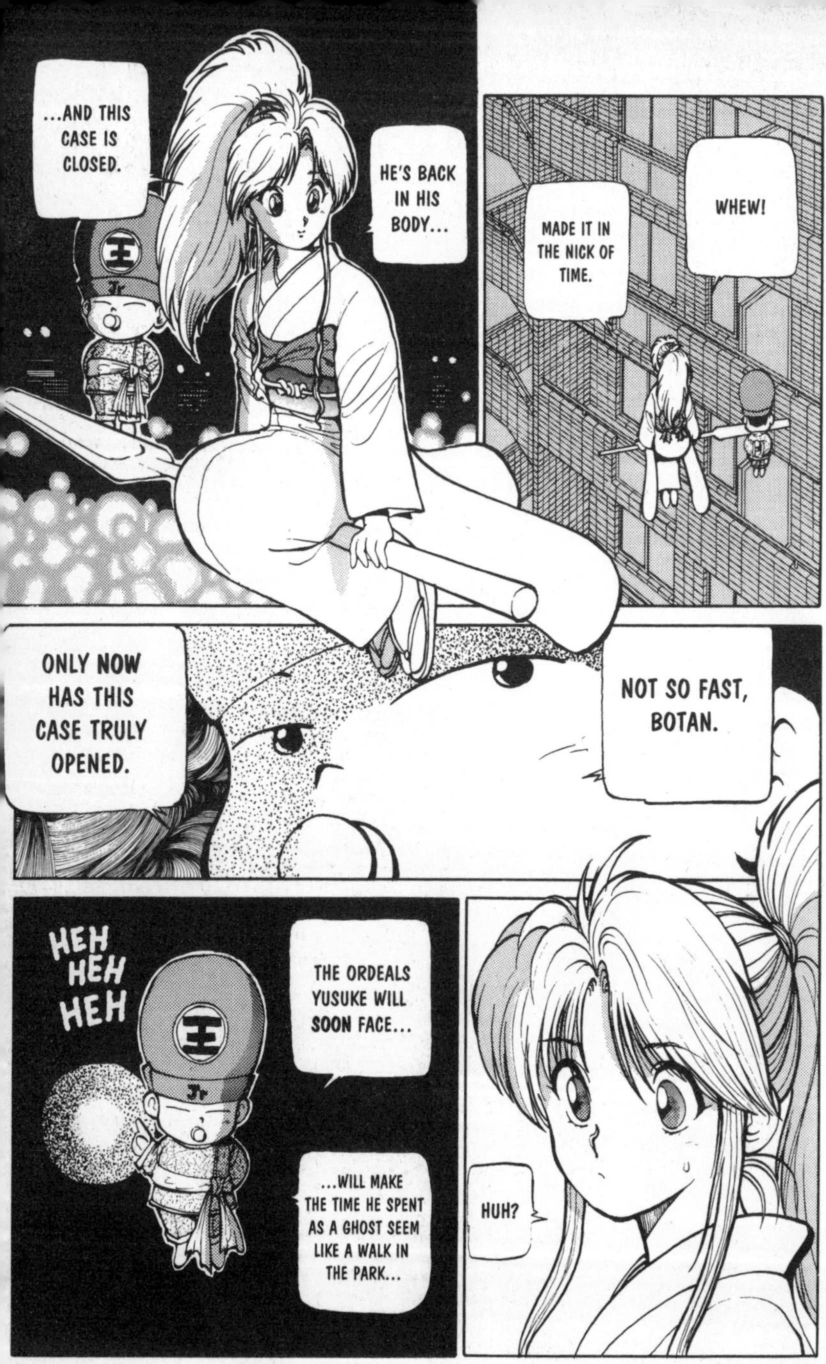
WHEW!
MADE IT IN THE NICK OF TIME.
HE'S BACK IN HIS BODY...
...AND THIS CASE IS CLOSED.
NOT SO FAST, BOTAN.
ONLY NOW HAS THIS CASE TRULY OPENED.
HUH?
THE ORDEALS YUSUKE WILL SOON FACE...
...WILL MAKE THE TIME HE SPENT AS A GHOST SEEM LIKE A WALK IN THE PARK...
HEH HEH HEH

TO BE CONTINUED IN YUYU HAKUSHO VOL. 3!

IN THE NEXT VOLUME...

Get out of your deathbed, Yusuke—there's work to be done! As an Underworld Detective working for Botan and Koenma, Yusuke must bring in renegade demons and solve mysteries that only an ex-ghost can figure out! But when three fiends escape to the human world, Yusuke's new job turns into a trial by fire. Now, armed only with his wits, his guts, and the mystic power of the "Rei Gun", he must face Goki, Kurama, and the deadliest demon of all, Hiei of the Evil Eye...

COMING FEBRUARY 2004!

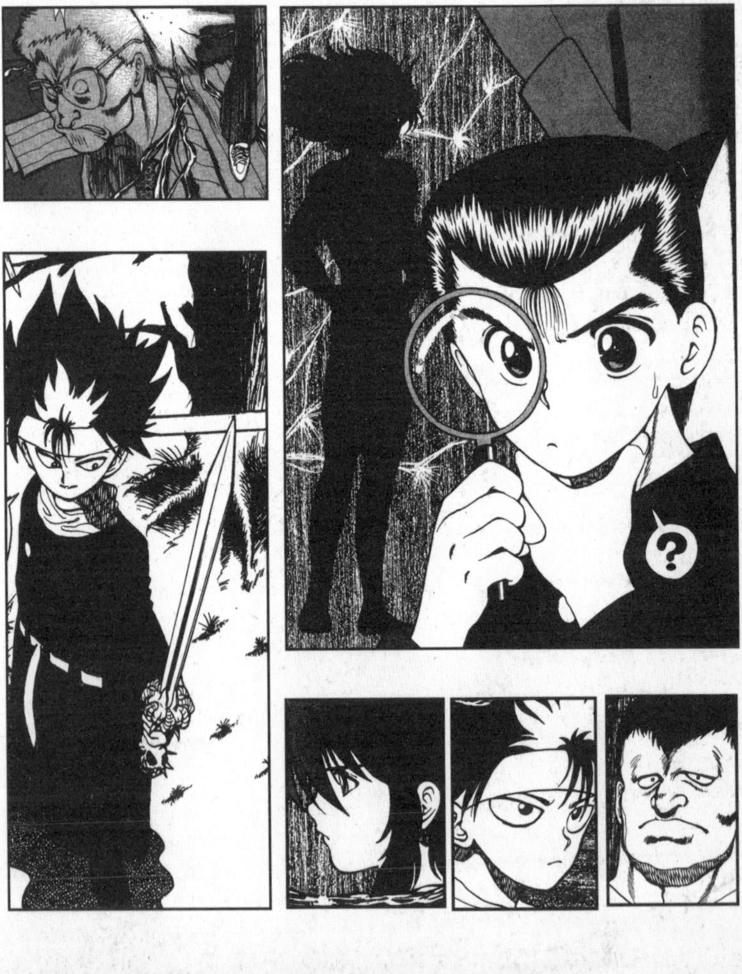
?

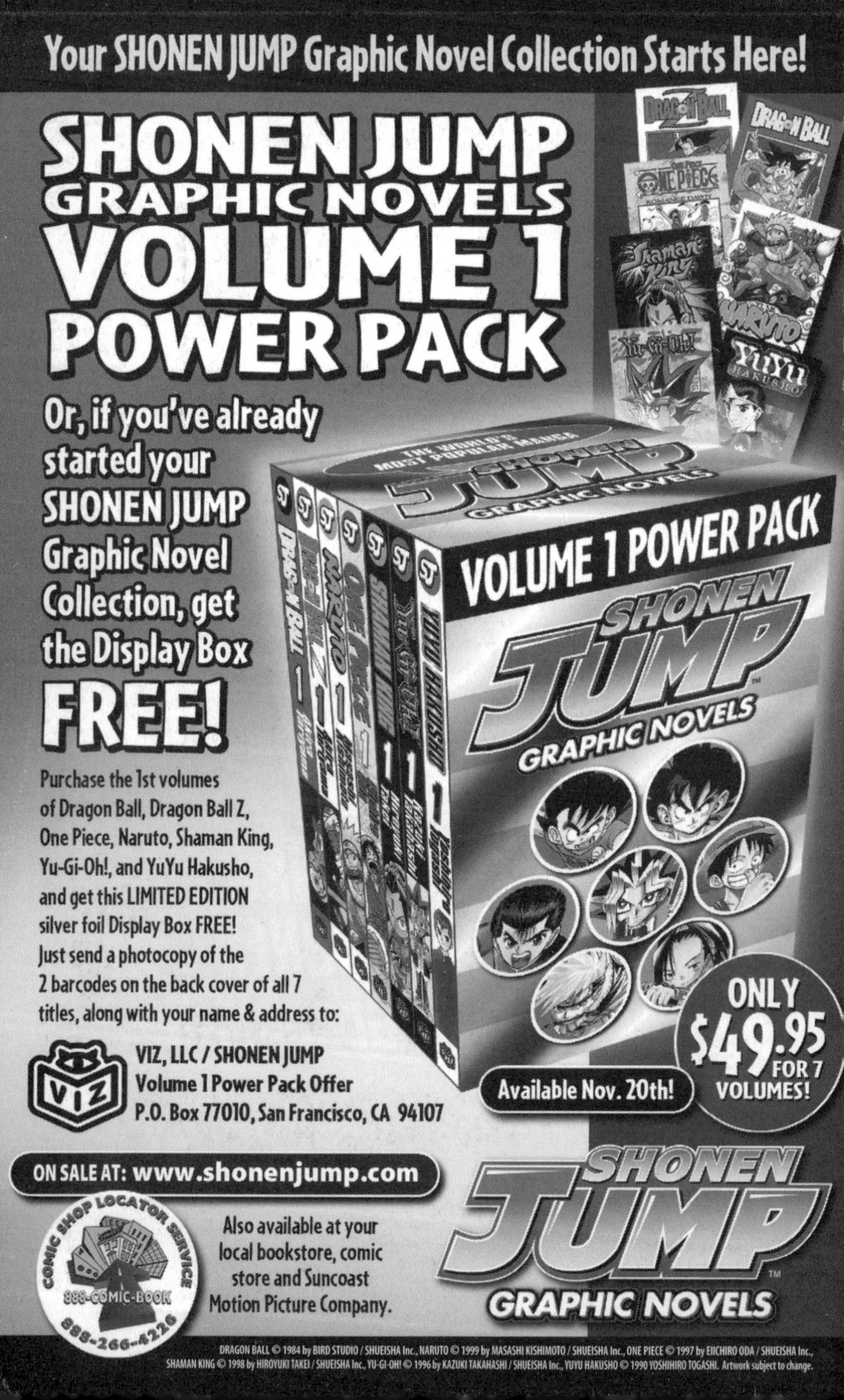
Your SHONEN JUMP Graphic Novel Collection Starts Here!
SHONEN JUMP GRAPHIC NOVELS VOLUME 1 POWER PACK
Or, if you've already started your SHONEN JUMP Graphic Novel Collection, get the Display Box FREE!
Purchase the 1st volumes of Dragon Ball, Dragon Ball Z, One Piece, Naruto, Shaman King, Yu-Gi-Oh!, and YuYu Hakusho, and get this LIMITED EDITION silver foil Display Box FREE! Just send a photocopy of the 2 barcodes on the back cover of all 7 titles, along with your name & address to:
VIZ, LLC / SHONEN JUMP
Volume 1 Power Pack Offer
P.O. Box 77010, San Francisco, CA 94107
VOLUME 1 POWER PACK
SHONEN JUMP GRAPHIC NOVELS
ONLY $49.95 FOR 7 VOLUMES!
Available Nov. 20th!
ON SALE AT: www.shonenjump.com
COMIC SHOP LOCATOR SERVICE
888-COMIC-BOOK
888-266-4226
Also available at your local bookstore, comic store and Suncoast Motion Picture Company.
SHONEN JUMP GRAPHIC NOVELS
DRAGON BALL © 1984 by BIRD STUDIO / SHUEISHA Inc., NARUTO © 1999 by MASASHI KISHIMOTO / SHUEISHA Inc., ONE PIECE © 1997 by EIICHIRO ODA / SHUEISHA Inc., SHAMAN KING © 1998 by HIROYUKI TAKEI / SHUEISHA Inc., YU-GI-OH! © 1996 by KAZUKI TAKAHASHI / SHUEISHA Inc., YUYU HAKUSHO © 1990 YOSHIHIRO TOGASHI. Artwork subject to change.

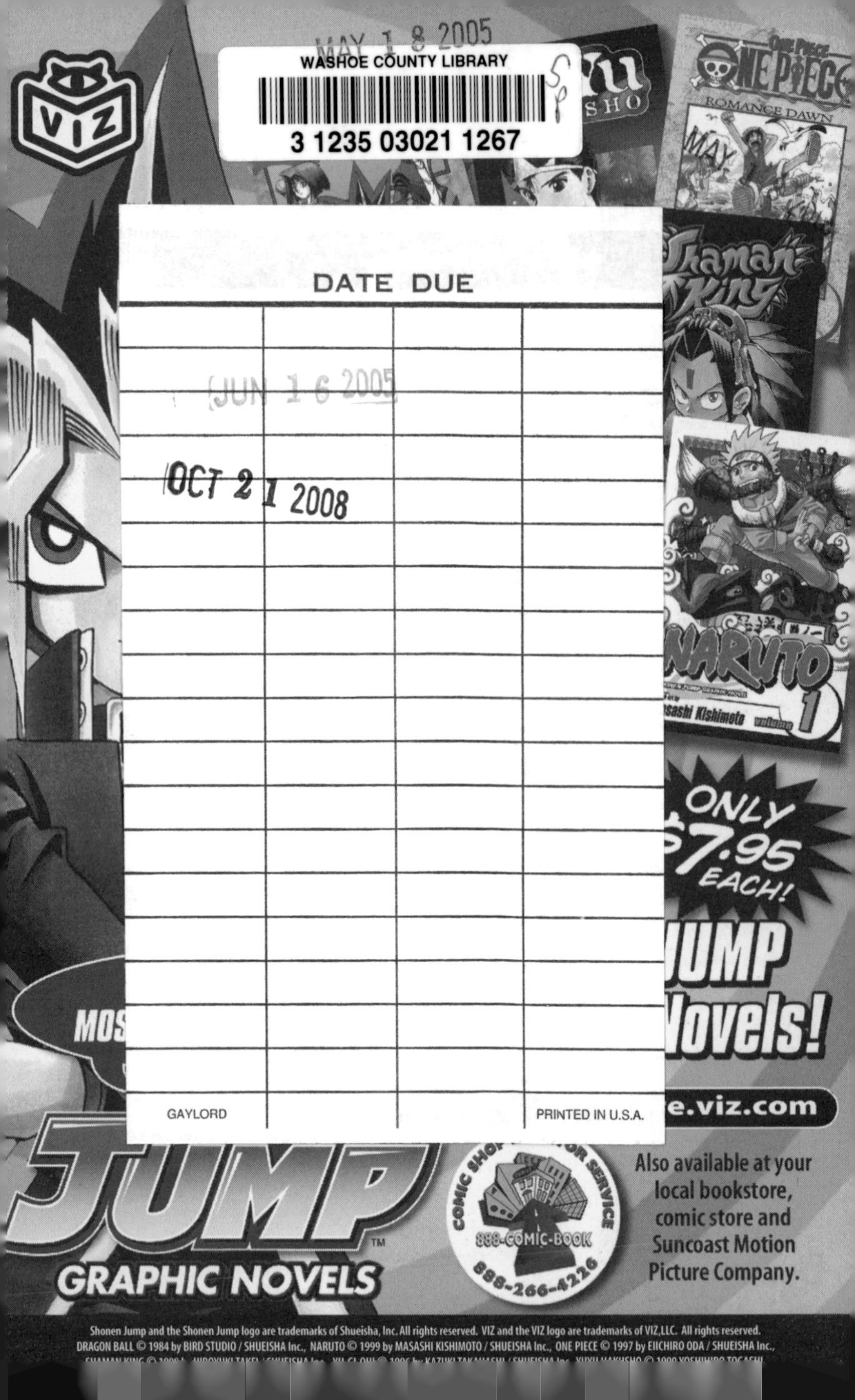
VIZ
ONE PIECE
ROMANCE DAWN
Shaman King
NARUTO
Masashi Kishimoto
volume 1
ONLY $7.95 EACH!
JUMP
Novels!
e.viz.com
JUMP
GRAPHIC NOVELS
COMIC SHOP ... OR SERVICE
888-COMIC-BOOK
888-266-4226
Also available at your local bookstore, comic store and Suncoast Motion Picture Company.
Shonen Jump and the Shonen Jump logo are trademarks of Shueisha, Inc. All rights reserved. VIZ and the VIZ logo are trademarks of VIZ,LLC. All rights reserved.
DRAGON BALL © 1984 by BIRD STUDIO / SHUEISHA Inc., NARUTO © 1999 by MASASHI KISHIMOTO / SHUEISHA Inc., ONE PIECE © 1997 by EIICHIRO ODA / SHUEISHA Inc.,

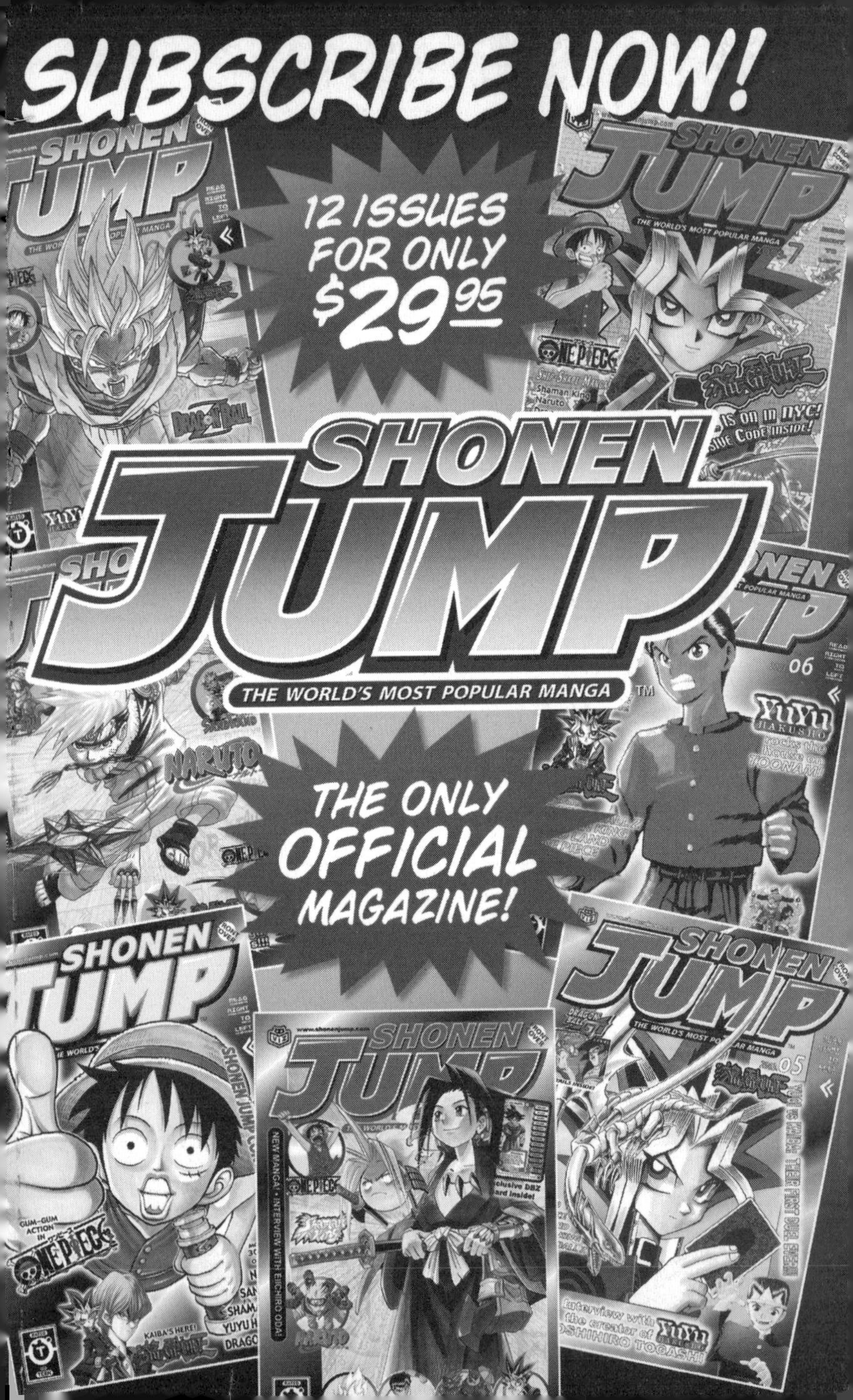
SUBSCRIBE NOW!
12 ISSUES FOR ONLY $29.95
SHONEN JUMP
THE WORLD'S MOST POPULAR MANGA ™
THE ONLY OFFICIAL MAGAZINE!

How many anime and/or manga titles have you purchased in the last year? How many were VIZ titles? **(please check one from each column)**

ANIME	MANGA	VIZ
☐ None	☐ None	☐ None
☐ 1-4	☐ 1-4	☐ 1-4
☐ 5-10	☐ 5-10	☐ 5-10
☐ 11+	☐ 11+	☐ 11+

find the pricing of VIZ products to be: **(please check one)**

☐ Cheap ☐ Reasonable ☐ Expensive

What genre of manga and anime would you like to see from VIZ? **(please check two)**

☐ Adventure ☐ Comic Strip ☐ Detective ☐ Fighting
☐ Horror ☐ Romance ☐ Sci-Fi/Fantasy ☐ Sports

What do you think of VIZ's new look?

☐ Love It ☐ It's OK ☐ Hate It ☐ Didn't Notice ☐ No Opinion

THANK YOU! Please send the completed form to:

NJW Research
42 Catharine St.
Poughkeepsie, NY 12601

All information provided will be used for internal purposes only. We promise not to sell or otherwise divulge your information.

COMPLETE OUR SURVEY AND LET US KNOW WHAT YOU THINK!

☐ Please check here if you DO NOT wish to receive information or future offers from VIZ

Name: _____

Address: _____

City: _____ State: _____ Zip: _____

E-mail: _____

☐ Male ☐ Female   Date of Birth (mm/dd/yyyy): ___/___/___   (Under 13? Parental consent required)

What race/ethnicity do you consider yourself? (please check one)

☐ Asian/Pacific Islander   ☐ Black/African American   ☐ Hispanic/Latino

☐ Native American/Alaskan Native   ☐ White/Caucasian   ☐ Other: _____

What VIZ product did you purchase? (check all that apply and indicate title purchased)

☐ DVD/VHS _____

☐ Graphic Novel _____

☐ Magazines _____

☐ Merchandise _____

Reason for purchase: (check all that apply)

☐ Special offer   ☐ Favorite title   ☐ Gift

☐ Recommendation   ☐ Other _____

Where did you make your purchase? (please check one)

☐ Comic store   ☐ Bookstore   ☐ Mass/Grocery Store

☐ Newsstand   ☐ Video/Video Game Store   ☐ Other: _____

☐ Online (site: _____)

What other VIZ properties have you purchased/own? _____

_____